NAHMANIDES
in Medieval Catalonia

NAHMANIDES
in Medieval Catalonia

History, Community, & Messianism

NINA CAPUTO

University of Notre Dame Press
Notre Dame, Indiana

Copyright © 2007 by University of Notre Dame
Notre Dame, Indiana 46556
www.undpress.nd.edu
All Rights Reserved

Designed by Wendy McMillen
Set in 10.3/13.2 Minion by EM Studio
Printed on 55# Natures Recycle paper in the U.S.A. by Versa Press, Inc.

Library of Congress Cataloging-in-Publication Data

Caputo, Nina, 1966–
Nahmanides in medieval Catalonia : history, community,
and messianism / Nina Caputo.
    p.   cm.
Includes bibliographical references and index.
ISBN-13: 978-0-268-02293-8 (pbk. : alk. paper)
ISBN-10: 0-268-02293-3 (pbk. : alk. paper)
1. Nahmanides, ca. 1195–ca. 1270. 2. Maimonides, Moses, 1135–1204.
3. Bible. O.T. Genesis—Commentaries. 4. Nahmanides, ca. 1195–ca. 1270.
Vikuah ha-Ramban. 5. Barcelona Disputation, Barcelona, Spain, 1263.
6. Christianity—Controversial literature—History and criticism.
7. Judaism—Apologetic works—History and criticism. 8. Christianity
and other religions—Judaism. 9. Judaism—Relations—Christianity.
10. Messianic era (Judaism) 11. Messiah—Judaism. 12. Nahmanides,
ca. 1195–ca. 1270—Language. 13. Catalan language. I. Title.
BM755.M62C35 2007
296.3'96092—dc22
2007033427

♻ *This book printed on recycled paper.*

Contents

Acknowledgments vii

Introduction 1

ONE   The Maimonidean Controversy: In Defense of
Reasonable Faith   19

TWO   Timely Matters: Nahmanides' Historical Reading
of Genesis   53

THREE   The Barcelona Disputation: Text, Rhetoric,
and Cultural Politics   91

FOUR   At the Threshold of Redemption: Daniel and
Messianic Discourse in Thirteenth-Century Catalonia   129

FIVE   Language and Literature: Nahmanides' Disputation
Account and Narrative in the Catalonian Vernacular   159

Notes 181

Bibliography 259

Index 313

Acknowledgments

I HAVE HAD THE GOOD FORTUNE TO BE SURROUNDED BY MANY VERY creative and inspiring people in California (in the departments of history at UCLA and UC Berkeley), Florida (Florida International University and the University of Florida), and Pennsylvania (under the auspices of a Mellon Foundation Fellowship at the Penn Humanities Forum at the University of Pennsylvania). Eleanor Yadin in the Dorot Collection at the New York Public Library and Arthur Kiron and Seth Jerchower at the Center for Advanced Judaic Studies Library at the University of Pennsylvania were generous with their time and knowledge. I would also like to thank my editor at the University of Notre Dame Press for her patience and kind advice.

It was my great privilege to study with Amos Funkenstein and I continue learning from him still, a decade after his death. Many friends and teachers have been in various ways sources of both motivation and support: Gil Anidjar, Daniel Boyarin, Bonnie Effros, Susanna Elm, Peter Gordon, Jessica Harland-Jacobs, Todd Hasak-Lowy, Taal Hasak-Lowy, Wulf Kansteiner, Gwynn Kessler, Deeana Klepper, Geoffrey Koziol, Howard Louthan, Tony Michels, Leah Rosenberg, Andrea Sterk, Lori Weintraub, Rebecca Winer, Michael Wintroub, and Steven Zipperstein. My family—Angelo, Kara and Adam, Ivon and Deborah—have been patient and supportive of me as I immerse myself in obscure and distant places. My mother, Helen, who did not live to see this project in a completed state, cultivated a life of the imagination; it was through her gift of *The Book of the City of Ladies* that I became interested in the middle ages. Finally, Mitch Hart has for twenty years been a source of laughter, emotional strength, and encouragement.

Earlier drafts of portions of this book have been published elsewhere. An earlier version of chapter 1 appeared as "'To kill the thorns in the vineyard': A Medieval Rabbi's Argument for Diversity within Unity," in *Orthodoxie, Christianisme, Histoire*, ed. Susanna Elm, Éric Rebillard, and Anotella Romano, 35–55 (Rome: École Française de Rome, 2000). Sections of chapter 2 appeared as "'*In the beginning*': Typology, History, and the Unfolding Meaning of Creation in Nahmanides' Exegesis," *Jewish Social Studies* 6, no. 1 (Fall 1999): 54–82, in an earlier draft. Parts of chapter 4 appeared in a much earlier formulation in "Prophecy and Redemption: Messianic Expectation in Nahmanides' *Sefer ha-Geulah*," in *Time and Eternity in the Middle Ages*, ed. Gerson Moreno-Riaño and Axel Müller, 171–189 (Turnhout [Belgium]: Brepols, 2003).

Introduction

THIS BOOK EXAMINES MEDIEVAL JEWISH CONCEPTIONS OF HISTORY and messianic redemption in the writings of the Catalonian rabbi, Nahmanides (Rabbi Moses ben Nahman, or Ramban, ca. 1195–1270). A brilliant talmudic and biblical commentator and an early exponent of Kabbalah, Nahmanides was also a shrewd and well-regarded intermediary between the Jewish communities and the royal administration. He has long been the subject of intellectual histories set against the context of medieval Jewish inter- and intra-communal relations, and specifically the encounter between philosophy and mysticism. However, intensive focus on the fairly insular context of Jewish community dynamics and interpretive disputes allows for only a limited view of thirteenth-century Aragonese Jewish intellectual and cultural life.[1] Jews played a significant role in the expansion of the Crown of Aragon during the thirteenth century. It comes as no surprise, then, that as members of this society, Jews actively contributed to, reacted to, and participated in broader Aragonese culture. There is a fairly sizable body of social history based on materials held in the royal archives examining Jewish-Christian relations in the medieval Crown of Aragon, especially in the increasingly important urban centers.[2] The encounter between Jewish and Christian interpretations of history and redemption in the setting of late medieval Aragon, however, remains largely unexamined.

This study reads Nahmanides' reflections on the contours of Judaism and conceptions of redemption as a negotiation with Catalonian and, more generally, Aragonese culture and society. The broader cultural context adds a crucial dimension to an understanding of the forces that shaped his compositions and the expectations his audience may have held when reading them. Nahmanides' writings, from his biblical exegesis to his poems, letters, and specifically polemical works, presented a self-conscious interpretation of the shape and meaning of historical time and change. In large measure, this discourse actively confronted Christian views of history and scripture, sometimes embracing Christian forms, but at other times directly refuting them. This complex engagement with Christian understandings of the significance of continuity and community is also reflected in the interpretive or exegetical models Nahmanides presented to his reader. A concern with revealing messianic redemption as imminent is a recurring theme throughout his writings. His careful articulation of this argument in various works, cast as an exegesis of biblical texts and historical events, illustrates an effort to preserve a cohesive and commonly held understanding that Jewish, not Christian, worship and interpretation would ultimately pave the way to redemption. Nevertheless, the structure of his arguments, the literary forms they took, and the way he introduced and grouped prooftexts all reflect Nahmanides' conception of Christian interpretations of Jewish history and scripture as both powerful and deeply problematic.

Nahmanides' ambivalence about Christian interpretations of the common historical origins of Judaism and Christianity as well as the culture and history they shared in the diaspora is mirrored by a similar ambivalence on the part of modern scholars about how to represent and understand the historical context for the roles and treatment of Jews in the medieval Crown of Aragon. Until the middle of the fifteenth century, the Jews of medieval Iberia enjoyed a degree of social, cultural, and intellectual integration that was unparalleled in late medieval European Christendom. Iberian Jewry's cultural and social ascent has been cast in scholarly and popular narratives either as a model of medieval tolerance[3] or as a lesson in the dangers of Jewish comfort and acculturation in the diaspora.[4] Both interpretations can be supported with substantial documentary evidence, but neither provides a thoroughly satisfying interpretation of how Jews in late medieval Iberia negotiated the difficult terrain of interfaith relations in a multi-faith society.

The first of these narrative models presents medieval Iberian Jews as nearly full participants in the public sphere, encountering legal discrimination or persecution primarily in times of political or economic pressure. Scholars who adopt this approach tend to view the history of Jews under Christian and Muslim rule as part of a cultural and social continuum.[5]

Under Iberian Christian rule, Jewish communities enjoyed many benefits of royal protection and privilege, while individuals were entrusted with positions of significant influence and prestige. Christian Spain during the high middle ages was a diverse, multilingual society which contained significant minority populations of Jews and Muslims. As such, the public sphere, especially in urban centers, encouraged some measure of 'secular' culture—a culture in which close business and intellectual relationships could form across confessional lines. This interpretation focuses on the unique conditions of Iberian religious and political history that provided the necessary context for a thriving interfaith symbiosis, a true *convivencia*, to use Americo Castro's evocative language.[6]

The late medieval decline of Jewish communities in Iberia provides evidence for an equally dramatic and compelling if teleological interpretation. A mass uprising in 1391, spurred on by preachers who viewed the cultural and social permissiveness and the close ties between the crown and the Jewish communities as threatening to Iberian Christianity, resulted in the murder or forced conversion of nearly two-thirds of Spanish Jewry.[7] The imposition of restrictions on Jewish religious and business practices followed, then nearly a century of concentrated persecution of Jewish communities, and finally the wholesale expulsion of Jewish communities from Christian Spain in 1492. This emphasis on the tragedy of late medieval Iberian Jewish history evaluates the thirteenth and fourteenth centuries through the lens of the Inquisition.[8] Modern critics assume that the relative comfort and ease of Jewish-Christian relations during this period blinded Jewish leaders to signs of inevitable decline that should have been obvious at the time. Because it focuses on the final chapter of Iberian Jewish history, this interpretation implicitly negates any positive or creative exchange between Jews and Christians during the high middle ages.[9]

When analyzing the circumstances of medieval Iberian Jewish history and culture over the long term, whether constructed in heroic or tragic terms, scholars must account for a broad and complex assortment of causes and outcomes while using a relatively limited set of explanatory models. Circumscribing the temporal and/or geographic range of study provides one means of complicating and enriching both the terms used to describe the conditions of medieval Jewish life in Christian Spain and the explanatory mechanisms used to account for change. Though he belonged to an international Jewish diaspora, Nahmanides' engagement with Jewish traditions and texts and his negotiation with Christian traditions, culture, and politics were informed by his daily life in the Crown of Aragon.[10]

Jewish communities in the Crown of Aragon remained largely self-governed and autonomous; Jews practiced a wide variety of occupations, ranging from agricultural production to high-stakes commerce. While some members of the intellectual and economic elites attained a measure of acculturation, Jewish forms of cultural expression—including exegesis, polemics, mysticism, as well as institutions of self-government—continued to thrive even into the fifteenth century. Nahmanides' biography offers a compelling illustration of the techniques Catalonian Jewry used in negotiating their role in and alienation from Christian society and culture. Nahmanides' intellectual heritage bears the influence of the Talmud-centered tosaphist interpretations from Northern France, as well as the more philosophically inflected methods of Provençal commentators. This confluence of methods, the instinct toward compromise, is emblematic of Nahmanides' approach to interpretation and leadership. He was a prolific writer on a wide array of topics who employed innovative narrative and exegetical methods and had a great faculty for finding the common ground between diverse opinions and interpretations. His works of biblical exegesis and *halakhah* (interpretation of Jewish law) gained almost immediate recognition and acclaim.[11] Moreover, Nahmanides distinguished himself as a capable leader and representative of his community during two public disputes, each of which was publicized far beyond the confines of his immediate community. Both the controversy over Maimonides' writings in 1232[12] and the Barcelona disputation of 1263[13] are known to historians through texts written by Nahmanides which were copied and continued to circulate long after his death. His wide readership indicates that he mastered a manner of literary presentation that appealed to a diverse audience.

Precisely the qualities and achievements that distinguished Nahmanides as an extraordinary man and scholar make his writings a particularly valuable source for addressing issues of medieval Jewish identity building and historical consciousness. While he was a respected teacher and authority on Talmud and Torah revered throughout the Jewish diaspora, Nahmanides also maintained a relationship with the Catholic clergy of Girona and with such temporal authorities as the king of the Crown of Aragon. One might suggest that cordial relations with Christian authorities during a time of political subjugation indicate solely that as a rabbi of a fairly sizable community, Nahmanides allowed himself to get only as close to Christian culture as was necessary to protect the rights and privileges of his community. Yet, the way he conducted himself as a public figure, the views of history and creation espoused in his biblical exegesis, his strong emphasis on the promise of the messianic redemption suggest that his relationship with Christian culture was deeper and more complex than that. Nahmanides' approach to *halakhah*, exegesis, and community leadership has at times an almost catholic feel to it. I do not suggest that Nahmanides, or for that matter the majority of his contemporaries, accepted Christian dogma, nor that he embodied a modern standard of tolerance for different beliefs and points of view. But to the degree that Nahmanides found some of the fundamental tenets of Christianity unappealing, this distaste was the product of an intimate knowledge and understanding of Christian doctrine and belief that grew out of his deep commitment to the place of Jews in that culture.

Other scholars have noted Nahmanides' familiarity with Christian modes of interpretation. Amos Funkenstein and Gershom Scholem both drew attention to echoes of Christian exegetical methods and theology in Nahmanides' biblical exegesis.[14] Most dramatically, Christian influence in Nahmanides' writing is clearly evident in his use of typological interpretations of the creation story. Moreover, as Funkenstein argues, it is clear that Nahmanides used typologies with a full recognition that typological exegesis was favored by Christian exegetes, who mobilized such readings at times in the service of anti-Jewish polemics.[15] Nahmanides employed typologies only with caution and was careful to limit his typological interpretations to verses for which Christian readings in that vein were not common. It seems likely, therefore, that he was aware that his engagement with Christian thought and culture ran quite deep. Moreover, the technical terminology Nahmanides used to explain his typological interpretations appears to be a direct translation of Christian exegetical terminology into Hebrew.[16] But while the echo of discussions with Christian scholars registered in Nahmanides' biblical exegesis, there has been little scholarly effort devoted to examining how his engagement with Christian interpretive methods corresponded with the way he presented himself as a leader within the Jewish community and in exchanges with Christians. Indeed, there has been a tendency in recent scholarship to presume an impermeable divide between his public persona, most clearly illustrated by his participation in and account of the Barcelona disputation, and his "true" beliefs, carefully guarded in his exegesis.[17] By focusing on the attention Nahmanides paid to the dynamics of history, community, and the place of Jews and Judaism in the diaspora, this study will bring Nahmanides' leadership, his exegetical works, and his engagement with Christian society into a single line of focus.

One of the features of Nahmanides' exegesis is a consistent effort to examine and analyze how historical change transformed Jewish culture and ritual. He demonstrated a similar interest in the tension between continuity and change and its impact on Jewish ritual and interpretation throughout his writings from his exegesis to his account of the Barcelona disputation. This study traces Nahmanides' conceptualization of the time in which he lived as a singular historical period in the unfolding story of human history. I use an analysis of his interpretations and perceptions of change in time to illustrate his understanding of Jewish cultural uniqueness and exclusiveness. Nahmanides' attempt to wrestle with the meaning and significance of historical change and the linear and limited structure of time provided a common thread linking his interpretations of scripture and *halakhah*, exile and redemption, the uniqueness of Jewish history, and the way Jews were expected to conduct themselves vis-à-vis both Jews and non-Jews. His interpretation of local and historical changes was shaped, in part, by his understanding of the relationship between God and the Jewish people. This conception of historical and cosmic time provides the interpretive framework he used to reconcile contemporary events with his broad view of history as a process which, in his view, started at a definite and identifiable point in time (i.e., creation), and was wending its way to a conclusion (messianic redemption). In this sense, the political and cultural setting in which he lived helped shape his formulation of an interpretive method and model of leadership.

Jewish Life and Culture in the Crown of Aragon

The region of Catalonia was both prosperous and cosmopolitan during the middle ages. This was due, in part, to the proximity of such cities as Barcelona (the capital of Catalonia) and Girona to the Pyrenees in the north and the Mediterranean on the east. Geographically, politically, and culturally, Catalonia was a medieval crossroads: between Christianity and Islam, between France and Spain, and between the unified Crown of Aragon and the independent principalities and counties that were joined under the Crown. As a result of the conquest of Majorca under James I, trade in such items as silks, spices, grain, cotton, weapons, and dyes increased substantially by the middle of the thirteenth century, laying the foundation for a complex credit economy.[18] The Jewish population of Aragon was integral to this economic boom, first as interested merchants and financiers of the military conquest of Majorca, and later joining the ranks of creditors and moneychangers and communities integral to the 'repopulation' of formerly Muslim territories.[19]

In addition to the native Jewish population in the Crown of Aragon, visiting Jewish traders and immigrants from northern Europe, southern Spain, and North Africa also made a mark on the dynamics of the local culture, economy, and politics.[20] Taking advantage of the linguistic and mercantile skills for which the Jews of North Africa were known, King James I circulated a letter in 1247 inviting Jews to settle in Catalonia, Valencia, and Majorca.[21] The Crown of Aragon nearly doubled in size by 1250 with the successful conquest of Majorca and Valencia, incorporating a considerable Muslim minority into the Crown's population. The influx of diverse linguistic and religious populations into the Crown is indicative of the conditions in Aragon and Catalonia which fostered creative and vibrant minority cultures during the middle ages throughout the region. The Crown of Aragon was a confederation of independent counties united under a single kingdom. Due to the diverse nature of this union, as well as a strong local nobility, it was in the best interest of the kings to facilitate a significant measure of local distinctiveness and autonomy in the various districts.[22] In the case of Barcelona, for example, King James established a policy that preserved a balance between royal domination and local self-rule.[23] In effect, this meant that the king appointed (or permitted the community to elect) native representatives who served as intermediaries between the urban population and the Crown. The degree to which the Crown controlled or interfered in local administration varied from king to king and county to county. Local traditions of government, education, methods of trade and taxation were permitted to continue and flourish under this system, provided that all obligations to the royal *fisc* and to the Crown in general were met in a satisfactory manner.

A similar system of local autonomy had also been in effect among the Jews of the region at least since the twelfth century.[24] Jewish communities in the Crown of Aragon were independent and self-governed.[25] Corporate status was granted either by the king or by the local ruling nobility under local charters which spelled out the conditions of Jewish autonomy. Each community, or *aljama*,[26] was governed by a local body of elected officials, referred to in the Hebrew documents as *berurim*. The political and demographic character of each community was locally determined, thus election processes, the number of officials elected,[27] the roles allotted to them, and the titles of elected officials varied from one *aljama* to the next.[28] Those who participated in an election, whether as candidates or as voters, were frequently required to pay a minimum tax.[29] It is clear, however, that the process of election was seldom egalitarian in a strict sense, at least not before the late thirteenth century.[30] Practical administrative power—specifically, control of revenue and institutions fundamental to Jewish ritual, such as the slaughterhouse or burial grounds, and decisions permitting individuals to travel, engage in certain businesses, or enter as a new member of the community—rested in the hands of the wealthiest local families. In most cases only the most affluent families participated in community elections.

Since each *aljama* ran according to its own guidelines, it is very difficult to arrive at a general reconstruction of the methods and mechanisms of *aljama* government. The effort is further complicated by the fact that Hebrew documents dealing with the structure of *aljamas* before the second half of the thirteenth century are few and far between. However, it is possible to discern the extent to which *aljamas* were truly self-governing by examining the royal documents that discuss Jews and Judaism. During the time of King James I *aljamas* were permitted significant freedom. The only practical matters of Jewish community administration with which King James was officially concerned were the collection of taxes to the royal *fisc* and overseeing elections of judges (*dayyanim*) and *berurim*.[31] Leadership positions on local *aljamas* remained under the control of a small number of elite families—such as the Alconstantini family of Saragossa—until the turn of the fourteenth century.[32]

It was virtually impossible for Jewish leaders to prevent temporal rulers from interfering in the administration of Jewish communities. However, like their social and scholarly equivalents throughout the Jewish diaspora, leaders of the *aljamas* vigorously protected their local autonomy against challenges or incursions from leaders of distant Jewish communities. The freedom of local Jewish leaders to define the parameters of proper social conduct, ritual practice, and protocols for education and interpretation to meet the immediate needs of their distinct communities was tremendously important for the preservation of tradition and stable leadership. The rabbinic tradition represented in the Talmud also endorsed political and cultural independence. Talmudic support for the validation of local difference can be found in the form of legal precedent and example in addition to talmudic discussion. As the first chapter in this study illustrates, tradition and practice generally held that the democratic principle of majority rule applied in *betei din* (courts of law). The same principle directed application of ordinances regulating public behavior, such as business practices: if the majority of the population could not comply with the rule of law without hardship, then that law could not be mandated. According to one frequently cited formula, "it is forbidden to declare a ruling on the population unless the majority of the population is able to abide by it."[33] Hence, no rabbi or group of rabbis could hold members of another community to a ruling without the consent of the leadership of the community receiving the instruction.

Local Jewish cultures developed in conjunction with the economic, political, and cultural climate in which they settled. Jewish community governments expected that Jews would automatically turn to the *aljama* for administration of legal claims and disputes, yet municipal and royal archives in the Crown of Aragon hold substantial evidence that Aragonese Jewry also sought protection in royal courts. Business agreements and wills, for example, composed in Latin and copied in Hebrew point to a fairly intricate set of links between Jewish and Christian political cultures at the ground level.[34] The rising notarial class in the Crown of Aragon provided an alternative to the Jewish community scribe (*sofer*). By the thirteenth century, institutions of the *aljama* required that all business and legal transactions cohere to rabbinic law. In the case of wills, this meant that the conditions under which one might record a last will and testament were clearly delineated by talmudic tradition: rabbinic law demands that all testators be in good heath and standing when dividing property and that the bequeathal follow a line of succession in keeping with biblical traditions of inheritance.[35] While all legal documents held sway in royal courts regardless of which authorities composed them or in which language they were written, royal notaries placed none of the limitations of rabbinic law on the distribution of property. The fact that a significant number of Jews chose notaries employed in the royal courts to record their final testaments indicates that neither the taboo on appealing to gentile courts,[36] nor the Christian affiliation of the notaries marked the public sphere as foreign or dangerous for many Catalonian Jews.

The conditions necessary for maintaining active Jewish life in the diaspora varied widely from one settlement to the next. Jewish leaders were challenged to reconcile *halakhah* with diverse cultural and social demands while also attending to the integrity of rabbinic practice. One benchmark of valid legal precedent was the degree to which it was culturally, socially, or economically practicable. For example, Gershom ben Judah Meor ha-Golah, the great tenth- and eleventh-century halakhist and teacher, forbade the practice of polygyny among the Jews under his jurisdiction. While other rabbis in the western European diaspora adopted the same restriction, the ruling, which conformed to a principle of Christian mores, was not intended to be binding on communities in Islamic lands, where polygyny remained an accepted, even common practice.[37] Negotiations between local cultural specificity and notions of universal Jewish norms were not always resolved without aftershocks of contention. The dispute that erupted in 1232 over Maimonides' hermeneutics, for example, also represented a move towards conventional reform; however, this encounter between two distinct norms of behavior and practice escalated into a clash over the jurisdictional boundaries of a *herem*, or ban of excommunication. The conflict was resolved after a *herem* that was intended as a universal prohibition on some of Maimonides' writing was revoked in part because several communities refused to recognize the universal ban as authoritative outside of the issuing community.[38]

Within the Jewish communities (*kehillah*, sing., *kehillot*, pl., meaning a group of Jews who shared the same local custom, law, and place of worship), *halakhah* dictated the order and rhythm of life. In practical terms, many of the responsibilities for maintaining stability and continuity in Jewish society fell to the elected community officials (*berurim, dayyanim,* etc.). However, the authority to interpret *halakhah*, to oversee ritually permissible slaughter of meat, or to adjudicate in legal claims such as capital disputes or divorce proceedings, required a certain expertise in rabbinic law. Leaders or representatives of the *aljama* often arrived at positions of authority after having attained some success in trade or through associations with powerful members of the Christian community. In contrast, great scholars generally rose to prominence by gathering a following of disciples, by demonstrating their mastery of the rabbinic sources, and by showing good judgment when offering counsel in matters of *halakhah* and community politics. During the thirteenth century halakhic proficiency was also the domain of the upper class. Advanced tutelage with a renowned scholar or rabbi was a luxury afforded primarily to those who could pay the tuition or, if the scholar was generous with his time, to those whose families had sufficient enough means that the lack of a laboring body would not prove burdensome.[39]

Until the end of the thirteenth century, the title 'rabbi' was largely an honorific designation, not a vocational one.[40] Though the sources refer to Nahmanides as the rabbi of Girona, this does not mean that his vocation was the performance of Shabbat services, nor did he receive official ordination from an established board of authorities. Like many other prominent scholars in the Crown of Aragon, Nahmanides was a local scholar whose reputation as a talented teacher, a skilled exegete, and a talmudist was known throughout the Jewish communities in the Crown of Aragon, and in much of the Jewish diaspora as well. His role was to teach and propagate a distinct scholarly tradition. Although there were no official duties attached to the title of rabbi,[41] it was not uncommon for the community leadership or temporal authorities to request a great scholar to act in some official capacity. Nahmanides' leadership skills were tested on at least two significant occasions. In the first instance, he asserted himself in the controversy over Maimonides' philosophical writings (1232). His position in this dispute was a strong endorsement of the autonomy of local Jewish government and halakhic interpretation. Three decades later he represented his community in the Barcelona disputation (1263). In this case his actions appear to have been motivated both by obligation to the king and by responsibility to his community.

Nahmanides' practical brand of leadership driven by intensive scholarship was emblematic of the type of Jewish culture that flourished in the northern principality of Catalonia. The political aptitude he exhibited during the controversy over Maimonides' writings and the Barcelona disputation reflects an ability to move with fluidity between very different modes of decorum and to engage in meaningful, courteous, and successful dialogue with diverse authorities. In both instances, he was able to employ a variety of different rhetorical methods, depending upon which was appropriate for the audience addressed.

Community, History, and Messianic Expectation

This book examines the modes of expression, types of arguments, and exchange between innovation and tradition in Nahmanides' writings. It follows Nahmanides' discourse, beginning with works that largely address the dynamics of and issues internal to the Jewish community, and then moves towards works that reflect his engagement with the more diverse culture of Catalonia. Works such as Nahmanides' letters concerning the Maimonidean controversy and his commentary on Genesis reflect an inward focus relative to the Jewish community in which Jewish communities and Jewish practice were figured as fundamentally self-interested and self-sustaining. His account of the Barcelona disputation and *Sefer ha-Geulah* (*The Book of Redemption*) reveal a thinker wrapped up in an ongoing and multilateral exchange concerning the structure and meaning of history and redemption.

Jewish communities functioned as independent, autonomous entities, but they were also linked, whether as subjects of the same king or as communities that practiced the same traditions. Maintaining a balance between these conditions proved challenging at times. Chapter one examines the political and cultural dynamics that contributed to and were played out in the controversy over Maimonides' writings. This chapter presents a set of questions about the methods available first to medieval Jews in general, and then to Nahmanides in particular, to establish interpretive authority beyond the local boundaries of the *kehillah* or a cluster of *kehillot* grouped within a single kingdom or political domain. To what degree was local Jewish government autonomous? What mechanisms were available for resolving interpretive disputes between disparate authorities? I argue that the instigators of this dispute, Rabbi Solomon ben Abraham and his students, took Maimonides' writings as their cause cèlébre partially under the influence of the tense and contentious climate created by efforts to crush the Albigensian heresy during the same period in Languedoc.

A survey of documents extant from both sides of the controversy show that the vast array of opponents to Solomon ben Abraham's campaign—including Nahmanides—matched the vigor, dedication, and desperation of Solomon ben Abraham's call for a universal *herem* in their responses. A close examination of his letter to the French rabbis illustrates how Nahmanides' conception of history informed the role he designated for himself as a leader within the Jewish community. As a distinguished scholar who occupied no official or elected position in the *aljama* or *bet din* (court), it was necessary for him to establish the basis of his authority elsewhere. He turned to prophecy. Biblical prophecy tells the story of politics (or leadership) with beautifully constructed rhetoric and poetry.

Emulating the biblical prophets, frequently mobilizing their very words, Nahmanides addressed the circumstances of the Maimonidean controversy by fitting it into the context of the Jews' ongoing struggle to negotiate with the conflicting historical circumstances of subjugation, on the one hand, and chosenness on the other. He used historical examples, poetry, and a demonstrated mastery of biblical and talmudic literature to sway the French rabbis from their dangerous convictions. A parallel between the course of action Nahmanides suggested to the French rabbis and the form and content of his argument also indicates that the letter was intended to serve as a theoretical and practical model for Jews in the diaspora.

Chapter two examines Nahmanides' reading of creation. Throughout his biblical exegesis, Nahmanides demonstrated and advocated an integrated interpretive method making use of traditional interpretations as well as fresh, innovative approaches. This is most clearly the case in his commentary on Genesis. He understood the story of creation as a blueprint both for human history as a whole (including the covenant between God and the people of Israel) and for interpretive devices that might be applied to divine revelation in all its textual forms. As such, proper understanding of Genesis was, according to Nahmanides, vital to Jewish faith. Throughout his commentary on the book of Genesis, Nahmanides set out exegetical guidelines designed to unveil layers of meaning relevant specifically to the Jews of his time.

Questions of narrative sequence, authorial intent, and the timeliness of biblical interpretation concerned Nahmanides throughout his interpretation of Genesis. This chapter explores the introduction to Nahmanides' biblical commentary, which provided a synthetic guide to some of the methods and concerns that drive his interpretation of the creation story and its relationship to human history, and the history of the people of Israel in particular. According to one layer of meaning Nahmanides identified in his introduction, the narrative of creation represented a plan for human history, which predated and prefigured creation and revelation. Rooting his interpretation in a body of accepted authorities, Nahmanides presented his innovations in understanding the time and sequence of creation as represented in Genesis as simple distillation of the widely accepted interpretations rendered by the most influential exegetes in the Jewish past. Recognition of Moses' authorship and his agency as storyteller are thus of fundamental significance to the interpretive method Nahmanides introduced in his biblical commentary.

Nahmanides complicated the beginning of creation and history by suggesting that both the law of Torah and the narrative of history predated creation. However, his reading of biblical history presented the time of redemption as both immanent and certain. Nahmanides' messianic prediction as presented in his biblical interpretation and elsewhere provided a model for interpretation and behavior which applied to all of the people of Israel. He understood the structure of the creation story—six days of work followed by a day of rest—as a prefiguration of the arrangement of human history: six one thousand year epochs, followed by a thousand year epoch of redemption. This interpretation was built upon a careful consideration of the relationship between God's work and the biblical description of this creative process. He concluded that the description of creation, like prophecy, represented a covenant between God and the people of Israel such that the events, patterns, and consequences have meaning beyond the narrative that contained them. Using this interpretive structure, Nahmanides revealed to his reader a precise time frame for the messianic advent, one that he claimed had simply been concealed in the biblical narrative.

Nahmanides also projected an exact time frame for the arrival of the Jewish messiah in his disputation account, though the continuities between these texts have received little attention. Here I argue that the messianic expectation Nahmanides outlined in the disputation account was more than a mere trope employed for dramatic effect. Instead, he articulated an organized hermeneutic method which viewed prophecy in the Hebrew Bible as timebound and directed exclusively to the Jewish people. The documentary evidence remaining from the disputation agrees that the discussion revolved around the time of messianic redemption. A good part of this debate, according to the Hebrew account, focused on the conversion of biblical prophetic hints concerning the time of redemption into a time frame that fit with historical events. Nahmanides' account of the event draws attention to symbolic renderings of temporal phrases, such as day, week, and hour, in prophecy.

Chapter three turns from Nahmanides' conversation with Jewish authorities and traditions to his involvement in an exchange with and about Christians and apostates. The well-documented Barcelona disputation of 1263 allows an important view of Nahmanides' facility with the traditions and beliefs of Christianity as well as his ability to navigate the complexities of court culture and patronage in the Crown of Aragon. Both the event of the disputation and its textual records have received significant attention in modern scholarship; however, this chapter poses some new questions to Nahmanides' Hebrew disputation account. I make the case for a fresh understanding of the intersection between Jewish and Christian elite culture in Catalonia, including aesthetic values as applied to literary forms and interpretive structures.

King James I of Aragon compelled Nahmanides to participate in a public disputation in which he was expected to defend the Jews' continued messianic expectation in a debate with Friar Paul, a recent convert to Christianity. Accounts of the Barcelona disputation are preserved in two contemporary documents: the first is a Hebrew account written by Nahmanides, and the second an anonymous Latin report. Each offers a highly self-interested representation of the event. Two years following the disputation some of Nahmanides' Dominican adversaries charged him with circulating a false and blasphemous narrative of the disputation. A royal court convicted Nahmanides of these charges, and subsequently expelled him from the Crown of Aragon. A summary of the hearing remains in the royal archives in Barcelona. The first part of chapter three presents the narrative of the disputation and the remaining textual evidence. Because the Barcelona disputation has been so well documented in the secondary literature, this chapter also provides a critical survey of the issues and concerns that have been addressed in this scholarship. Focusing on the rhetorical structure and evidentiary claims employed in the considerable scholarship on this event, I suggest that the majority of the previous treatments of the Barcelona disputation and its significance have preserved, even replicated the adversarial tone of the documentary evidence. This discussion of secondary literature attempts to come to terms with why this particular set of events and texts has been so compelling as to occupy dozens of books and articles, not to mention a popular play and a BBC television production. As such, it lays the foundation for a fresh approach examining the narrative devices Nahmanides employed in recording the disputation and rhetorically linking this text with other works he wrote near the end of his life.

The remainder of this chapter examines the rhetoric Nahmanides employed in his treatment of apostates and Christians. I argue that the introductory paragraph of Nahmanides' Hebrew disputation account provided an interpretive frame intended to guide his Jewish readers' understanding of the events represented. This portion of the text includes a provocative quotation from the Babylonian Talmud depicting the (fictional) trial and execution of several of Jesus' apostles. Nahmanides encouraged his reader to make a clear distinction between apostates from Judaism and native Christians. Through an implicit equation between the apostles—who, according to this talmudic passage, were executed as idolaters—and recent Jewish converts to Christianity, he suggested that it is not contact with Christians per se that threatened the cohesion of Jewish life and culture in the diaspora, but rather the persistent intrusion of apostates into Jewish affairs, both individual and corporate.

Chapter four looks more closely at Nahmanides' interpretive methods, especially in so far as they were directed at making sense of the nature of history and prophecy. I demonstrate here that Nahmanides' understanding of the historical past, the dynamics of society in the present, and the promise of redemption in the future were built upon a methodical consideration of how to extract meaning from the historical and prophetical material contained in the Hebrew Bible. Nahmanides' full-length treatise on redemption, *Sefer ha-Geulah* (*The Book of Redemption*) distinguished between prophecies already fulfilled and prophecies yet to be realized. This work made an important contribution to an apocalyptic discourse that flourished between the late thirteenth and mid-fourteenth centuries in the Crown of Aragon. Nahmanides argued that the time of redemption was in relatively near proximity, and that crucial information about the messianic era—including information about when it would begin—could be gleaned from a careful and disciplined reading of the Hebrew scriptures. His contribution to a rapidly expanding literature contemplating the imminence of the end-time reacted to aggressive Christian polemics, but his manner of response, the methods of interpretation he employed, had a reciprocal influence on his Christian interlocutors. A comparison between *Sefer ha-Geulah* and the works of the physician turned exegete, Arnau of Vilanova, demonstrates a process of cross-fertilization between Nahmanides and millenarian exegetes in the Crown of Aragon. In *Sefer ha-Geulah* Nahmanides used the same methods of analysis and arrived at the same conclusions as he did in his biblical commentary and the disputation account. In each of these works, he addressed the time frame of messianic expectation, the shape and duration of human history, and problems of interpreting divine revelation. Nahmanides' end-time speculations represent just one example within a much larger body of work that belied the notion that the greatest rabbis of this period practiced a "purely Jewish" mode of interpretation.

Developing the argument already presented in previous chapters that Nahmanides' Hebrew disputation account contains numerous interwoven layers of meaning, the final chapter of this book suggests that Nahmanides' disputation account contributes to a body of literature written in the Catalan vernacular. Here I interrogate Nahmanides' production of a narrative account of the disputation to determine the degree to which Jews participated in conventions of court society and literary patronage in the Crown of Aragon. A dramatic turn in Nahmanides' account, in which the author introduced a term in the vernacular to clarify the meaning of a Hebrew phrase, provides the entry point. Nahmanides came under attack by the Dominicans for writing an account of the disputation and showing it to the bishop of Girona.

The scholarship on the Barcelona disputation has gone to great lengths to make sense of the feeling of threat that followed the circulation of Nahmanides' account. There has been no parallel effort to take seriously Nahmanides' defense against charges of blasphemy after the bishop of Girona requested that the rabbi produce a personal account of his debate with Friar Paul. Since no physical evidence of such a text remains, it is impossible to determine whether the extant Hebrew account was related to the text Nahmanides showed to the bishop. However, the existing Hebrew text does bear formal and stylistic similarities to other works that were written during this period in Catalan. This chapter argues that Nahmanides' disputation account contributed to and participated in an important turn in the development of vernacular literary and narrative forms in the Crown of Aragon. The friars' accusation that Nahmanides engaged in a literary dialogue with the bishop of Girona suggests that Jews of a certain position in society participated in an economy of cultural exchange that was both mutual and productive. The imbalance of power between Nahmanides and his patrons not withstanding, the Hebrew record of the Barcelona disputation reflects cultural and aesthetic sensibilities that were shared by Catalonian Jews and Christians.

CHAPTER ONE

The Maimonidean Controversy

In Defense of Reasonable Faith

IN 1230 RABBI SOLOMON BEN ABRAHAM OF MONTPELLIER, A RENOWNED teacher and talmudic scholar, sent a series of circular letters lobbying the rabbis and leaders of Jewish Provence officially to forbid the study of Maimonides' writings in their communities. Already by the beginning of the thirteenth century, Maimonides' innovative methods had attracted a large following in Spain and North Africa. By 1225 Hebrew translations of Maimonides' philosophical works, originally written in Judeo-Arabic, began circulating north of the Pyrenees. Critics like Solomon ben Abraham viewed Maimonides' philosophical interpretation and pedagogy as a threat to the cohesion of Jewish teaching and study. The efforts of Rabbi Solomon ben Abraham and his disciples to mark certain methods of interpretation as dangerous set in motion a dispute involving leaders throughout the Jewish world and solidified the unique cultures of study and leadership that developed in each diaspora community.

The question that quickly came to the fore in this dispute was whether Maimonides' synthesis of rabbinic teachings, shaped as it was by an Aristotelian hierarchy of categories and genre, offered a legitimate method of interpreting Jewish ritual and texts. Maimonides' systematic use of philosophical methods to read and interpret Jewish tradition had a profound influence on the way Jews understood and practiced their traditions. His

Mishneh Torah represents the first attempt to present the fundamental elements of Jewish faith and practice in a systematic digest organized thematically according to Aristotelian principles of argument, evidence, and proof based on observation and philosophical assumptions.[1] The hallmark of this approach, and the very characteristic of Maimonides' philosophical writing that troubled the scholars of Montpellier, was a sustained effort to seek explanations for Jewish practice outside the accepted rabbinic and biblical canon. As many of his critics noted, this methodical presentation limited the necessity of mastering traditional rabbinical methods of argument in which dissenting opinions appear in the flow of talmudic text. It was feared that students would now master the philosophical method instead, then use that method as a key for extracting hidden or secondary meanings from the text. Also troubling for the opponents to philosophical exegesis was Maimonides' success in accommodating the Bible to a philosophically logical or rational paradigm. This methodological innovation shifted pedagogical and interpretive priorities, favoring the assumption that philosophical questioning and argument could lead directly to the correct understanding of the Torah and the reasons behind its form and content. For example, Maimonides sought logical rationales for the laws of the Torah.

> Now if there is a thing for which no reason is known and that does not either procure something useful or ward off something harmful, why should one say of one who believes in it or practices it that he is *wise and understanding* and of great worth? And why should the religious communities think it a wonder? Rather things are indubitably as we have mentioned: every *commandment* from among these *six hundred and thirteen commandments* exists either with a view to communicating a correct opinion, or to putting an end to an unhealthy opinion, or to communicating a rule of justice, or to warding off an injustice, or to endowing men with a noble moral quality, or to warning them against an evil moral quality. Thus all [the commandments] are bound up with three things: opinions, moral qualities, and political civic actions.[2]

Traditional rabbinic readings of Torah and *halakhah* (rabbinic law), in contrast, accepted divine authorship as sufficient explanation for the purpose and meaning of such commandments, asserting that God's purpose is by definition inaccessible to the imperfect human intellect.

Solomon ben Abraham's campaign began in Montpellier, but soon expanded to involve rabbis and leaders throughout the Jewish diaspora. Some of the community leaders Solomon ben Abraham contacted in Provence failed to appreciate the threat he perceived in Maimonidean interpretation. Rather than ban those individuals in their communities who had accepted and continued to teach Maimonides' methods, they instead called for a *herem,* an official ban, on Solomon ben Abraham and his students for impugning the great rabbi and his writings.[3] The communities of Provence split immediately into two contentious factions, one favoring a prohibition of Maimonides' philosophical works, the other defining Maimonides' methods of interpretation as indispensable. Unsuccessful in their drive to attract a following for their cause locally, Solomon ben Abraham and his supporters cast a wider net and implored rabbinic authorities in Aragon, Castile, and France to recognize Maimonides' works as dangerous to the coherence of Jewish faith and practice. In this second set of letters, Solomon ben Abraham apparently called for a universal *herem* carrying the penalty of excommunication for anyone in the Jewish diaspora caught in possession of two of Maimonides' most important works: *Moreh ha-Nevukhim* (*The Guide of the Perplexed*), which reconciles the central tenets of Judaism with the methods and assumptions of Aristotelian philosophy, and *Sefer ha-Madda* (*The Book of Knowledge*), the philosophical introduction to his *Mishneh Torah,* or *The Code of Judaism.*

Though Maimonides' writings were well known throughout the Iberian peninsula, they remained obscure in Northern Europe. Solomon ben Abraham dispatched his disciple Jonah Gerondi to hand-deliver copies of *Sefer ha-Madda* and a translation into Hebrew from the original Judeo-Arabic of the relevant passages of *Moreh ha-Nevukhim.*[4] The French rabbis responded with an unqualified condemnation of Maimonides' philosophical methods. A hasty review of the relevant works convinced the French rabbis that Maimonides' writings posed a clear threat to Judaism. They immediately issued a universal ban on the study of *Moreh ha-Nevukhim* and *Sefer ha-Madda.* Anybody who owned or taught Maimonides' books faced the penalty of excommunication.[5]

The vitriol and factionalism of the controversy escalated following the French *herem.* Ardent supporters of Maimonides' interpretations in Provence responded with an angry counter-ban, excommunicating Solomon ben Abraham, Jonah Gerondi, and another disciple, David ben Saul, from the general community of Jews. Less strident leaders on both sides appealed to other well-reputed rabbis—including Nahmanides—either for support of one or the other *herem* or for its repeal. Rivals exchanged numerous letters between 1230 and 1232, solidifying the factional divide. The controversy apparently ended, though it was not truly resolved, when a representative of Cardinal Romanus, who happened to be in Montpellier investigating the Cathar heresy, confiscated and burned the banned Maimonidean writings.[6] Where the impetus for this action originated is not clear. According to Rabbi David Kimhi, the prominent exegete, polemicist, and philosopher, a member of Solomon ben Abraham's faction appealed to the Christian clergy to fold the campaign against Maimonidean philosophy into the ongoing effort to enforce orthodoxy throughout Latin Christendom.

> When it became apparent to him [Solomon ben Abraham] that the French rabbis abandoned him, believing him to be a fool and recognizing him to be a bearer of false testimony, he turned to the idols and worshippers of false gods [i.e., Christians] and appealed to them to help in his harmful intentions against the Jews and they heeded him. He appealed first to the barefooted youths [i.e., the Franciscans] and said to them: "Look, many of our people are heretics and unbelievers, for they were misled by the words of Rabbi Moses of Egypt [i.e., Maimonides] who wrote heretical books. Since you are destroying the heretics among you, destroy ours as well. Order the burning of those books; they are the *Sefer ha-Madda* and *Sefer Moreh*." And his uncircumcised heart did not rest, so he also spoke to those preachers called the *Predicatores* and to the priests with similar words, until his appeal reached the cardinal, which place the Jews of Montpellier and those dependent upon them in great danger, and subjecting them to mockery and derision from the mouths of gentiles. The evil slander went from city to city and they [the Christians] said "Look, the Torah of the Jews is destroyed, for they formed two factions over it. There is no Torah other than ours."[7]

Though the available sources preclude an accurate reconstruction of how the various bans of excommunication were reconciled, it seems clear that the unexpected and unwelcome intrusion of Christian authorities in an internal Jewish dispute quickly overshadowed the perceived threat of Maimonidean philosophy. There is reason to believe that neither *herem* was actively enforced. Solomon ben Abraham, Jonah Gerondi, and David ben Saul returned to Montpellier and remained prominent figures in the community; Maimonides' teachings continued to draw a devoted following among students in Provence, Languedoc, and Spain.

The way this controversy over Maimonides' philosophical interpretations of Judaism unfolded offers a glimpse at the multiple registers at which power and authority were negotiated among medieval Jewish communities. From the perspective of Solomon ben Abraham and his disciples, what was at stake was the definition of acceptable interpretations of the Jewish canon. Their efforts to limit the scope of Maimonidean teachings imply a shift in the way these leaders viewed both the collective body of Jewish communities and the corpus of texts that comprised Judaism. Responses to this movement among those who supported the *herem* as well as detractors from it also reflect changes in the way that Jewish communities—in particular those in the Crown of Aragon and Languedoc—conceptualized and practiced governance. As Elka Klein has shown, the qualifications for leadership within the Jewish community were increasingly formalized over the course of the thirteenth century in terms of expertise in Jewish law and learning rather than status and heredity.[8] The Maimonidean controversy allowed an ideal context for establishing the local boundaries of legal and political power.

Interpretive Innovation and the Local Boundaries of Authority

Underlying Solomon ben Abraham's attack on Maimonides' writings were pressing questions of legal authority. More precisely, the call for a universal *herem* forced the dispute into the dangerous territory of conflicting notions of orthodoxy. Solomon ben Abraham and his opponents struggled over some weighty questions relating to the definition of Jewish community and identity: What methods and interpretations could be legitimately considered Jewish? If interpretive methods came under question, as they did in the Maimonidean controversy, what defined an impermissible method? And who was in the position to distinguish between valid and invalid methods of reading?[9] Such issues were a natural outgrowth of the effort on the part of Solomon ben Abraham and his disciples to eradicate what they saw as the danger of Maimonidean interpretation.

Representatives of both sides in this dispute distributed circular letters to rabbis and recognized community authorities scattered throughout the diaspora. In these communiqués, they honed and promoted their views of what constituted orthodox hermeneutics or leadership practices vis-à-vis the regulation of Maimonides' writings. Solomon ben Abraham, for example, hoped to gain the support of rabbis and *betei din* (law courts) around Europe for a universal ban on Maimonidean interpretation. Yet his effort to enforce this ban across geographic and jurisdictional boundaries threatened to rend the fabric of Jewish government in the diaspora. Judgments about the exclusion of individuals from the community of Jews due to inappropriate behavior or teachings could be made only by a recognized local *bet din*. Solomon ben Abraham's appeal to the rabbis of France—who followed their own local customs and interpretations of *halakhah*—to ban Maimonidean interpretation introduced the potential for a radical shift in the structure of Jewish community organization.

The call for a general *herem* throughout the Jewish world shifted what was at stake in this conflict. Maintaining legal autonomy within local Jewish communities was fundamental to preserving ritual and behavioral norms on a local basis. Each Jewish community faced unique challenges in the effort to sustain the continuity and integrity of Jewish life within a society governed by the precepts and values of another faith, many of which were self-consciously hostile to Judaism.[10] Unique traditions, laws, and power mechanisms thus developed in each settlement or *kehillah*. This meant that local Jewish leaders were cautious about imposing their will on other communities or declaring universal standards against which Jewish life throughout the diaspora should be measured.

The *herem* was the most effective instrument of legal coercion and social control available to Jewish communities. Essentially a vow or an oath binding either individuals or the corporate group, the *herem* was used to sever from the community individuals who dissociated themselves from the larger society of Jews, to limit who could join an established community, or to establish a norm of behavior or practice as binding throughout that community.[11] The very nature of the *herem* underscores the complexity of Jewish life in the diaspora. A *herem* could only be applied on a local basis, but the circumstances mitigating the imposition of a *herem* had to be recognized as damaging or dangerous by the standards of Judaism as a whole. Because there was no central authority overseeing or universalizing the administration of local law in dispersed Jewish communities, the *herem* was only effective as a method of social control if its implementation remained entirely local. Solomon ben Abraham's attempt to make the question of Maimonidean interpretation a question of universal Jewish orthodoxy broke with accepted conduct and set a precedent for the way future controversies over the same question would be played out.[12]

The first call for action against Maimonidean interpretation involved Jewish community governments under French royal authority—contested as French authority in the region of Languedoc may have been at that time.[13] The city of Montpellier had a politically and fiscally complicated history. At the time that Solomon ben Abraham made his first charges against Maimonidean learning, the Capetians claimed political and military sovereignty over the city; justice and administration were handled by local nobility. Revenue from taxes, on the other hand, was collected by the Crown of Aragon.[14] The problem for Jewish religious government in this case was compounded by the fact that the suggested *herem* would cross boundaries of temporal Christian governments as well as the local boundaries of *kehillot*. The response to Solomon ben Abraham's request among Jewish leaders in Aragon and Castile was by no means unanimous. Community leaders used the opportunity of a public dispute to demonstrate their concern over local disputes between neighboring communities that had historically vied for resources and royal privilege.[15]

The legal issues raised in this exchange were complicated. For the sake of legal autonomy, Jewish courts and rabbinic authorities refrained from imposing legal sanctions outside the limits of their own communities.[16] But more problematic than the audacity of the universal *herem* against Maimonides' writing was the effort to involve gentile leaders in the conflict as a policing agency. Informing gentile authorities about another Jew's transgressions was considered a clear violation of Jewish law and autonomy—all the more so if the informer turned to gentile authorities after failing to achieve the desired result before a Jewish court.[17] An appeal to gentile authorities to police the inner workings of rabbinic authority clearly represented a challenge to that authority; the community was thus obligated to respond.

Power and Authority in Provence and Languedoc

Responsa and other documentary sources openly discuss and define fundamental components of identity primarily at moments of internal community discord. The Maimonidean controversy therefore has been a tantalizing event for historians of the Jewish middle ages. Through the study of inter-community conflict, negotiations over such issues as interpretive methods as well as the relationship between politics and culture and between time and space come to the fore. Under normal circumstances individuals expressed their opinions about the validity of various interpretive methods with less urgency and in less programmatic terms. In the case of the Maimonidean controversy, the extant documents offer a rare view of how internal Jewish politics were negotiated and executed.

For several historians of the Jewish middle ages, this conflict has come to be viewed as indicative of a wide palette of cultural and intellectual shifts in the fabric of medieval Jewry. The translation from Judeo-Arabic into Hebrew of philosophical interpretations of Torah and Talmud and their distribution in Northern Europe was viewed by early twentieth-century historians as an initial threat to the innocence of the previously isolated and insular Jews of Ashkenaz. Since the individual who informed the Christian authorities left no explanation for his actions, we can only speculate about his motivations. It is possible that at least one disciple of Solomon ben Abraham believed that the Church and his own tradition of learning and study shared common goals and assumptions about the proper means of interpreting tradition and nature, even if they did not share rudimentary beliefs about the nature of divine involvement in human history. Alternatively, it is possible that the anonymous informer viewed Maimonides' methods to be so foreign and dangerous to Judaism that his books would naturally fall subject to a foreign or external power. According to a third scenario, the informer may have been so traumatized by the struggle between Jewish leaders that he turned to the Church as a means of restoring harmony among the foremost Jewish teachers and legal experts of his time. But regardless of the fundamental impetus, it is not surprising that the involvement of Christian authorities ultimately had a profound impact on the outcome of this conflict: the leading figures on both sides canceled their bans and questions about the orthodoxy of Maimonides' interpretation faded.[18]

The involvement of Christian clergy in condemning Maimonides' writings has also been viewed as a byproduct of an organized policy of Church intervention in Jewish practice and belief, a dramatic shift away from a policy which protected Jews and their practice of Jewish ritual, provided they occupied a position of humility in relation to their Christian neighbors.[19] There are, of course, other known instances in which Christian authorities mediated in business or personal disputes between

Jews, but this kind of Church involvement in conflicts internal to the organization, administration, and educational practices of Jewish communities was unprecedented.

This heated dispute over the validity of Maimonides' interpretive method occurred at a delicate point of intersection between Jewish and Christian religious and cultural lives. It was no accident, it seems, that Solomon ben Abraham and his students began investigating innovations within Judaism precisely at the beginning of the 1230s. Much of the drama of the Albigensian crusade took place within a sixty-mile radius from their native Montpellier. The Capetian government, at this time only recently established in Provence, collaborated with the papal inquisition (also a newcomer to the power relations in the region) to eradicate the local Catharist interpretation of Christianity known as the Albigensian heresy. Indeed, the heated political and religious struggle between different interpretations of Christian orthodoxy was carried out intermittently during the decade under discussion.[20] In addition, during the 1230s the newly established orders of Dominican and Franciscan friars, who were employed to study and correct the Cathars, also took a heightened interest in the beliefs and practices of Jews living among them.[21]

Local Christian culture in Provence and Languedoc came under the scrutiny of outside authorities who were brought in, according to the contemporary rhetoric, to protect the structure and strength of true Christian doctrine. One consequence of the Albigensian crusade was a spate of accusations generated by lay people against their neighbors and friends. The ethos that provided justification for such machinations apparently seeped into the Jewish communities in the region as well. Solomon ben Abraham's effort to establish an uncompromising and universal ban on Maimonides' works grew from a sustained examination of the books with which other study-circles in the community occupied themselves.[22] Many who fell under the authority of this *herem* recognized it as an untenable attempt to expand political and social authority beyond the boundaries of local community jurisdiction by unilaterally regulating interpretation and pedagogy.[23] Most Jewish community leaders had grown accustomed to containing local cultural, political, and jurisdictional boundaries within geographically restricted congregations. The everyday practicalities of Jewish life could be considerably different in Paris, for example, than in Barcelona. Definitions of valid interpretive methods, additions of local holidays to the ritual calendar, or pedagogical traditions also varied from one community to the next. The campaign to define a universal orthodoxy by identifying and eliminating elements of heterodoxy or heresy, in contrast, has a decidedly catholic flavor—a fact which was noted repeatedly (whether explicitly or by implication, as in Nahmanides' letter to the French rabbis) in the documents opposing the ban.

The local clergy in Montpellier could have found justification for the censorship of books written by a Jewish author for a Jewish audience in the fact that Maimonides' works contained Aristotelian interpretations of ritual, law, and scripture. Aristotelian interpretation at the University of Paris came under intense scrutiny during the 1230s; in 1231 a papal council condemned and banned the study of Aristotle's natural philosophy for the fourth time.[24] Because Maimonides' *Moreh ha-Nevukhim* and *Sefer ha-Madda* employed Aristotelian interpretive methods, they may have been subject to the general ban on Aristotelian philosophy issued by the Church in 1231.

What may have motivated Solomon ben Abraham and his cohort to initiate an investigation of Jewish texts, and then go to the extreme of using coercive power to discredit anyone who subscribed to interpretations deemed dangerous, is a question worthy of consideration. The political climate in Languedoc was charged during this period. During the first half of the century, the Capetians undertook a strategy of subduing the local nobility by systematically appropriating land, thereby displacing local political and power structures. Even before mendicant friars were sent to Languedoc as a semi-permanent intelligence-gathering organ, the investigation of possible heresy—specifically Catharism—provided the Capetians with a convenient means of separating local landowners from their sources of income and political clout.[25] So, although the mechanisms and technologies of investigation and punishment employed by the inquisition in Languedoc did not reach their full maturation until the second half of the thirteenth century,[26] it is clear that the pattern of inquiry and crusade, the desire to identify and maintain an orthodoxy, were set in motion as early as the first decade of the thirteenth century.[27] It is not unlikely, therefore, that Solomon ben Abraham and his disciples fell under the sway of the same culture of suspicion. Their investigation of Maimonidean interpretive methods ought then to be viewed as a parallel campaign to the one being executed in Languedocian Christendom.

I do not mean to imply that Solomon ben Abraham and his students subscribed to the inquisitors' program of identifying and eradicating opposing opinions.[28] There is no evidence to suggest that they internalized the same conception of power and justice that was orchestrated during the Albigensian crusade. Rather, I would like to suggest that Solomon ben Abraham and his disciples were motivated to identify and weed out any danger in their midst in large part because the tensions of this inquisitorial atmosphere charged cultural and social dynamics throughout Provence and Languedoc, even within the Jewish communities.[29] This is significant for the purposes of this chapter only in so far as Solomon ben Abraham's contemporaries interpreted the extension of the *herem* into disparate communities, not the objection to Maimonides' writings per se, as dangerous. Therefore it was Maimonides' attempt to transcend the boundaries of accepted practice that was viewed as a threat to the coherence of Judaism and the Jewish communities. The political and religious climate in which Solomon ben Abraham and his disciples lived goes some way towards accounting for their willingness to delve into uncharted territories of inter-community government. The note of urgency underscoring Solomon ben Abraham's actions reverberated through each of the responses they elicited, including Nahmanides' carefully orchestrated effort to restore peace to the counter-bans brought against Solomon ben Abraham and his allies and the desperate appeal to Christian authorities.

It should come as no surprise, then, that reactions to the French rabbis' *herem* mirrored, to some extent, the desperation and aggressiveness reflected in the attack on Maimonidean interpretation. The same fundamental questions that propelled the anti-Maimonideans were echoed in the rhetoric of Maimonides' supporters: Could issues of dogma determine who is included in the community of Israel? What methods of interpretation could be considered legitimately Jewish? What defined the boundaries of local Jewish culture and community? And who was in the proper position to distinguish between valid and invalid methods of reading?[30]

The language in many of the circular letters that supported Maimonides' methods was polemical and derogatory, describing Solomon ben Abraham, his disciples, and the French rabbis as traitors beholden to foreign beliefs and powers. The rabbis of Lunel, for example, distributed a letter to the communities of Provence and Aragon in which they defended Maimonides' interpretations. The authors' surprise and dismay at being regulated by rabbis from distant communities is registered by the accusatory, inquisitorial tone expressed in this letter:

> *Who is this who darkens known counsel with* unreasonable *words without knowledge* (Job 38:2)? Since they did so, [this counsel is] *drawn up*

in full and secured (II Samuel 23:5). From this, an interpretation is revealed that is not according to the *halakhah*. And who is this party who furnished the authorities with this [information] and brought forth the meat of divisions and the bread of lies ... and despises and mocks his teachers [*rabbotav*, i.e., the rabbis of the Talmud]? Who is he, who is among the children of Tzaddok and Boetus,[31] a heretic and an *Epikoros* [a skeptic], who settled to destroy *a tower built magnificently high* (Song of Songs 4:4) [i.e., Maimonides' *Sefer ha-Madda* and *Moreh ha-Nevukhim*], in which reside *strength and wisdom* (Job 12:16)? The holy rabbi, the talented leader built it, *for he weighed and investigated and set to order* (Ecclesiastes 12:9). *Who is he, who presumed in his heart to do this* (Esther 7:5). . . ? For he did not pay attention to the Torah or—God forbid—to its honor or splendor.[32]

While the author of this letter referred to the offenders in vague terms, naming no specific names and recommending no punishment, others were less careful about disgracing the honor of respected community members. A group of community leaders from Saragossa wrote a letter referring to the three rabbis of Montpellier by name—i.e., Solomon ben Abraham and his two students, Jonah Gerondi and David ben Saul—as heretics and sinners whose condemnation of Maimonides deserved to be repaid with "excommunication from the diaspora community (*me-kahal ha-gulah*) from now through eternity."[33]

The novelty of an informer in this dispute whose betrayal had serious repercussions on the Jewish community as a whole has attracted similarly diverse responses in the modern scholarship.[34] This is due in part to the availability of evidence. The communications between Solomon ben Abraham and the French rabbis, as well as the French order to ban Maimonides' teachings are lost, although the opinions and actions at least of the Maimonideans are well documented. Moreover, several letters either praising Maimonides' contribution to Jewish textual interpretation or seeking support for an official condemnation of Solomon ben Abraham as well as a number of others by or concerning the reception of Maimonides' interpretation became widely available to scholars in a volume published in 1859 containing legal arguments made by Maimonides.[35] At a more elemental level, the tension between "faith and reason" represents a true continuity in the history of Jews, beginning in the Hellenistic period and continuing in the present.[36] The circumstances surrounding this dispute seem to evoke modern tensions between traditional society and the allure of secular learning and culture, and indeed, between the Jewish historian and the traditional texts she uses as her sources.[37]

In no small measure, the sources invite a dramatic (or even melodramatic) interpretation.[38] Most modern historical depictions of the Maimonidean controversy suggest that Solomon ben Abraham and his students represented a pure Jewish orthodoxy, a view of Judaism untainted by outside influence.[39] Maimonides' followers, on the other hand, represent the counterpoint, individuals who integrated Jewish culture and literature with those grown on "foreign soil." By casting the factions in these terms, historians have infused their narratives with an aura of tragedy or foreboding. Accordingly, the burning of Maimonides' works in 1232 has been read as an early taste of the discriminatory policies implemented later in the middle ages, such as the confiscation, trial, and burning of the Talmud in Paris in 1240 and 1244, or the confiscation of Jews' property and the expulsion of long-standing Jewish communities from European lands.[40] Another common scenario of events reverses the roles of protagonist and antagonist. The followers of Maimonides heroically defended philosophical discourse against Solomon ben Abraham and his faction, portrayed in this version as advocates of a provincial and unsophisticated view of Judaism.[41]

The tragic mode of discourse has been adopted in both of the standard representations of this conflict with particular consistency precisely because the two factions fought so contentiously amongst themselves. From the perspective of many modern historians, this distracted both sides from recognizing the shifting dynamics between the Church and the increasingly powerful kingdoms of Europe, the real dangers facing medieval Jewry.[42]

The Letter and the Law

Both sides in the dispute over Maimonides' works rallied to find support for their respective bans, dispatching letters to rabbis and teachers throughout the Jewish world to back their side in the dispute. Nahmanides was among those who received a request for support of this universal *herem* on Maimonides' teachings. In response, he issued a long missive to Solomon ben Abraham's allies in France intended to facilitate a quick and decisive reconciliation between the two camps. This communiqué established that the dispute over Maimonides' writings fit into an ongoing series of challenges to the integrity of Israel and the corresponding struggle to maintain its continuity during a long and difficult diaspora. Nahmanides' letter indicates that it was precisely this effort to protect Israel's unity from internal and external threats that shaped the Jewish voyage through and experience of history. By placing the controversy over Maimonidean philosophy in the context of a continuing battle against factionalization, Nahmanides provided a model first for making sense of the source of discord, and then for healing the breach. As he did in the handful of shorter and less ornate letters addressed to Maimonides' supporters in the Crown of Aragon and Castile,[43] the letter to the French rabbis represented local contemporary events as essentially linked to events in Israel's shared past. In this letter, Nahmanides based his reading of the common history of the Jews on the historical narrative contained in the canon of traditional Jewish literature which encompassed the biblical period of creation, revelation, and the formation of a nation, an extended period of active prophecy in Israel, and finally the rabbinic period and the inscription of the Talmud. Using examples from the distant past, in which the nation as a whole was strengthened through the resolution of conflicts over leadership or legitimate interpretation, Nahmanides urged the French rabbis to retract their *herem* in order to preserve peace and continuity within and among the Jewish people.

Nahmanides' involvement in the dispute over Maimonides' philosophical writings has made this event particularly interesting for scholars of medieval Judaism. Working with the assumption that reason or philosophy and tradition are fundamentally at odds, Joseph Dan, Daniel Silver, H. H. Ben-Sasson, and Gershom Scholem[44] imply that Nahmanides projected two completely separate, almost contradictory personalities: a flexible public persona intent on forging the middle ground, and a closely guarded private persona characteristic of a mystic and purveyor of a secret tradition. At first glance this seems a satisfying argument. It establishes Nahmanides as a shrewd and capable leader as well as a brilliant scholar and protector of Jewish "orthodoxy." However, it rests on a methodologically and conceptually problematic assumption. Ben-Sasson and Scholem suggest that Nahmanides, as a kabbalist, would *only* have been willing to espouse tolerance for philosophical thought in his capacity as a community leader during times of crisis because Kabbalah and Maimonidean interpretation were fundamentally irreconcilable.⁴⁵ But there is little evidence to be found in Nahmanides' writings, either in the works regarding the Maimonidean controversy or elsewhere, to suggest that he was steadfastly opposed to philosophical methods and reasoning.⁴⁶ Only once in his letter to the French rabbis did Nahmanides express what might be understood as a general distrust of philosophical methods. In that case, he argued that the philosophical reasoning of Galen and Aristotle threatened to weaken the fabric of Jewish tradition and pedagogy if accepted in an unmediated form by Jewish students. But even here, he specified that supervised, studied acceptance of these philosophers was less problematic.⁴⁷

If Nahmanides' objection to Greek philosophy in its pure form is difficult to pin down, it is that much more difficult to categorize his view of Maimonides' works in negative terms. Though Nahmanides was critical of Maimonides in his biblical commentary (as he was of Rashi, Abraham ibn Ezra, and Saadya Gaon), he never condemned Maimonides for applying philosophical interpretation to the standard texts of Judaism.⁴⁸ Indeed, much of the letter to the French rabbis extols the virtue of Maimonides' teachings as an explication of the tradition and as a magnet that might draw back to Judaism individuals who favored philosophical learning over study of Talmud and Torah.

The conceptual framework for Nahmanides' strategy of argument in this letter (and, as I will suggest later in this book, in his role in a public religious disputation with a convert from Judaism in 1263) was a belief that knowledge and understanding of the past and of change could be used as a powerful pedagogical tool. His reactions to contemporary events were shaped by a belief that his own generation held a position of unique importance in the continuum of history. In later works, Nahmanides' periodization of history placed his own generation just on the cusp of a radical historical transformation that would culminate in the messianic redemption. Although Nahmanides wrote his letter to the French rabbis relatively early in his career, the historical notion of change and progress that is so clearly and forcefully articulated in his later writings is already evident here in his interpretation of events and texts.

Nahmanides tackled two distinct though related issues in his responses to the Maimonidean controversy. The first, which saturates each of his letters on this matter, is an overarching concern with the protocols, ethics, and decorum of legitimate leadership in the diaspora. His model of

Jewish leadership preserved local autonomy, but strove towards an ideal of inter-community discussion and interaction. In the event of a dispute, such as the controversy over Maimonides' philosophy, Nahmanides urged leaders to find local resolutions that took into account the health and vitality of the Jewish people as a whole. Only under this umbrella did he turn to his second concern: the consideration of whether Maimonides' *Sefer ha-Madda* and *Moreh ha-Nevukhim* were legitimate Jewish teachings. The *herem* on Maimonides' writings, of course, unilaterally ejected these works from the corpus of valid interpretations of Jewish texts and traditions. Nahmanides attempted to reinstate Maimonides on the basis of his irrefutable mastery of the talmudic sources, his success in reviving Judaism in the eyes of those who seemed to have virtually abandoned their tradition in favor of philosophy, and his canonical stature among the Jews of Yemen.

"Before I answered, I did err. . . ."

The opening line of his letter to the French rabbis, "Before I answered, I did err," set the rhetorical tone of Nahmanides' appeal to the opponents of philosophy. This line is borrowed from Psalms 119: "You dealt well with your servant, Lord, in accordance with your word; Teach me good judgment and knowledge, for I believe in your commandments; Before I answered, I did err, but now I observe your word" (Psalms 119:65–67). The psalmist beseeches God for the strength and wisdom to command a path of justice and righteousness. Nahmanides' reference to the profoundly incommensurate relationship between man and God immediately established a suppliant tone. He used this tenor of discourse to achieve a dual purpose. Addressing the recipients of this letter as his intellectual and spiritual superiors helped endear him to a potentially hostile audience.[49] But this discursive strategy also served to demonstrate that Maimonides' writings could effectively bridge the interpretive divide that seemed to be opening between the Jewish communities of Northern and Southern Europe.[50]

> Today I am like a child who questions[51] his teachers, like a student who insists on understanding his teachers' opinion, for *the bashful cannot learn* (Avot 2:5). I removed the shameful veil from my face, and

I put before my eyes the words of the French rabbis on the written Torah and the oral Torah, in which every student is enveloped, to answer their objections. To increase debate *they asked about things to come* (Isaiah 45:11), and in my objection to their decrees and in my answers to their words, I will ask what, and how, and why?

My spirit is a *willing spirit* (Psalms 51:14), from a loving abode, not a *repulsive spirit* [*ruhi zarah*] (Job 19:17)[52] or one complaining of thought. [But I am] like one who questions with an attentive ear directed at his teacher, and the desire in his heart is as a *flaming flame* (Ezekiel 21:3) and a burnt face. I am full of words and *I did burst like new wineskins* (Job 32:18-19), and my tongue spoke in my mouth, but the words were not uttered by me for I knew nothing. Teach me, my masters and I will be the silent messenger of your judgment and will not dismiss [any portion of it], because you will teach me your verdicts and the wisdom of your ordinance will be known to me, and any true *judgment you determine* (I Kings 20:40) shall be heard by me.[53]

Nahmanides' posture was a direct counterpoint to the leadership strategy that the French faction, and by extension, Solomon ben Abraham's camp, used to bring about the *herem*. By utilizing a vocabulary of praise and honor in addressing his audience, counterbalanced with self-deprecating humility, veneration, and reverence, he interjected a tone of civility and decorum into the already hostile dispute.[54] Rather than negotiate an agreement with the proponents of Maimonides' teachings, the rabbis of Montpellier and later the French rabbis abandoned the decorum of discussion and imposed a universal restriction on the Maimonidean interpretation. The letters exchanged between Solomon ben Abraham's school and the French rabbis have been lost; however, the notorious ban itself suggests that the French authorities were willing to proceed with their condemnation of Maimonides with little regard for legal protocol or the high esteem with which Jews throughout the diaspora regarded both the man and his writings. Continuing his strategy of subservience and praise, Nahmanides cast the French rabbis' ignorance as a virtue. Their failure to take the social and intellectual context in which Maimonides wrote his *Moreh ha-Nevukhim* and *Mishneh Torah* into consideration, Nahmanides indicated, was a direct result of their superior learning and dedication to the study of Torah practiced in French academies ("Teach me, my masters and I will be the silent messenger of your judgment and will dismiss [any portion of it], because you will teach me your verdicts and the wisdom of your ordinances will be known to me, and any true *judgment you determine* [I Kings 20:40] shall be heard by me").[55]

Nahmanides' criticism of both sides in this conflict was based on his concern that an enforced orthodoxy would endanger the social and cultural mechanisms enabling members of diverse Jewish communities to perceive themselves as part of independent cultural groups and simultaneously as part of the ideal of a Jewish people.[56] He wove this view into his argument at three intermeshed layers of exposition, each one more subtle and nuanced than the last. The first occurred at the level of descriptions of Jewish religious life in various diaspora communities at the very historical moment of his composition. At a second level, Nahmanides used historical circumstances to impress upon his audience that the time in which they lived was one of great significance. Finally, he linked the contemporary conflict over Maimonides' writings with past disputes over modes of interpretation or leadership. On the foundation provided by this variegated argument, Nahmanides reconstructed a model of normative Judaism capable of preserving the unique historical and cultural character of dispersed Jewish communities, while providing a single Judaism as the solid ground supporting all of them. Scripture and Talmud established a thread of continuity that transcended time and geographic dispersion and linked dispersed and diverse communities. Since the earliest period of Jewish dispersion, biblical interpretation was the basis for a sustained commentary on the complex patterns of continuity and change inherent in a living religious tradition. This dynamic encounter was played out at length in the canon of rabbinic literature. Nahmanides elevated this process of debate and deliberation to a cultural virtue.

The notion that Jewish culture and society developed on a local basis in concert with the unique dynamics of the societies among which Jews lived is a rhetorical device used to support a complex argument. But it is also much more than this. Nahmanides' historical understanding of Judaism took form as he challenged the French rabbis' unfavorable evaluation of Maimonides' contribution to Jewish law and textual hermeneutics. According to this view, unique cultural and societal conditions necessitated that Jewish communities on the Iberian peninsula develop traditions and methods of reading designed to combat the strong attractive force exercised by court society and its intellectual and artistic pursuits. In particular, he referred to the strong tradition of philosophical writing, conducted in Arabic or Judeo-Arabic, that developed among Jews living in Muslim Spain. In addition, Nahmanides pointed to the tradition among Jews in Yemen of uttering Maimonides' name with each recitation of the *Kaddish* [the sanctification of God recited seven times a day during the prayer services and after the reading of the Bible] as a legitimate custom attesting to the unique quality of local practices as well as an intense respect for Maimonides and his writings.

> *And many from among the peoples of the lands became Jews for a great fear fell upon them* (Esther 8:17), and the fear of [God] was strengthened for all of them; And *here before me,* before my masters are the *sun and the earth testifying* (*Bereshit Rabba* 2, 4) that we heard[57] a true report that in all the lands in the kingdom of Yemen many communities busy themselves with Torah and the Mitzvot for their own sake and they mention the name of the Rabbi [i.e., Maimonides] at each and every *Kaddish.*[58]

The intellectual core of French Jewry provided Nahmanides with a shining example of a Jewish population that followed the opposite cultural and historical trajectory. He suggested that leaders and writers in these communities cultivated a distance from their Christian neighbors and were thus able to preserve a pure Talmud- and Torah-based culture.

The gentle tension between the traditional core of Judaism and customs native to local Jewish communities also provided Nahmanides with a means of legitimizing his own leadership and the specific position he took in the controversy over Maimonides' writings. He framed his challenge to the French rabbis' *herem* in terms of impending danger: the possibility that the attempt by the French rabbis to enforce a universal definition of orthodoxy would cause Jewish communities in the diaspora to break into disparate sects. Because many communities of Jews were culturally and socially engaged with the society that surrounded them, Nahmanides believed there was a danger that Jews might assimilate into the surrounding cultures by adopting the customs, practices, and behavior of their gentile neighbors.[59] Finally, Nahmanides cautioned that any attempt to prescribe a universal definition of Jewish orthodoxy would eclipse the unique local cultures scattered throughout the diaspora.

For the fullest effect, Nahmanides addressed these issues in terms of rabbinic precedent and legal authority. Though references to rabbinic sources appear far less frequently in this letter than do biblical references, a deft application of citations helped him present a polemical argument that derived its resonance from the Talmud, the body of literature that provided both the foundation and the model on which he and other contemporary leaders based their authority.[60]

> The Torah will become like two Torahs, and all of Israel [will become] two opposing groups. . . . [One faction will abide by your decision and the other will not obey your exalted ruling[61]]. . . . If you decree something that, from necessity, [proponents of Maimonidean interpretation] are unable to accept, they will not obey the *herem* of your *minyan* (quorum) (Babylonian Talmud *Hagiga* 3b), and they will say to your faces "I say it is thus." And it will be a net [which will catch] their foot causing [them] to stumble. Moreover, *it is forbidden to declare a ruling on the population unless the majority of the population is able to abide by it* (Babylonian Talmud *Avodah Zarah* 36a). Why, my rabbis and my *geonim*, will you *devour the inheritance of the Lord* (II Samuel 20:19)?[62]

In this passage, and throughout the remainder of the letter, rabbinic citations indicated the importance of diversity of opinion. A multiplicity of interpretations, mediated through discussion and amicable adjudication, provided the foundation for separate and unique local cultural configurations co-existing peacefully within the tradition of Judaism. A talmudic ordinance circumscribing the boundaries of rabbinic jurisdiction in the diaspora grounded his claim in legal terms.

According to his own political philosophy, Nahmanides' solitary voice did not command sufficient authority to challenge a *herem* issued in the name of a rabbinic court, even if the *herem* in question was apparently in violation of the customary power dynamics among dispersed Jewish communities. More importantly, the protocol of government advocated in all his letters concerning the *herem* on Maimonides' works mandated a process of discussion and deliberation involving a majority of community leaders and based on legal and textual precedents from the canon of traditional Jewish literature. Therefore, Nahmanides did not demand a retraction of the *herem*; rather, he attempted to persuade his audience that the *herem* was unjust.

An argument stressing the process of historical development or continuity provided the framework for Nahmanides' advocacy of rapid reconciliation and lifting of the *herem* on Maimonides' writings. He used carefully chosen *exempla* drawn from the Bible and the Talmud to demonstrate that the contemporary conflict over Maimonides' writings was similar in type to events from the distant past of ancient Israel or the rabbinic academies of the talmudic period,[63] but he concealed his personal voice in the language of biblical and talmudic *exempla*. To this end, he used quotations from the canonical texts as a rhetorical device to sway his audience. At the same time *exempla* served as a method of narrative underscoring the significance of continuity and change in Jewish history.[64] Nahmanides' use of these prooftexts was multifaceted. First, using biblical examples drawn mostly from the books of prophets, he implied that a basic agreement among Jews about the essential content of sacred texts was fundamental to the preservation of a unified Jewish people. Then, relying primarily on talmudic citations, he suggested that discussion and disagreement had performed an important role in shaping Jewish tradition throughout Jewish history. On this basis, Nahmanides made a case for diversity as an integral part of the culture and tradition embraced by the Jewish people.

Prophecy and Danger

The trope of imminent danger provided Nahmanides with a historical foundation for his reading of contemporary events. In the letter to the French rabbis, he compared the controversy over Maimonides' writings with the majestic Jewish past and the promised glories of the future by integrating biblical passages with his own original prose. This imposition of an external narrative to shape biblical references into a new work of literature independent of their original context was not unique to Nahmanides. In Hebrew literature, this prose style, known as *shibutz*, was frequently used by Jewish poets and grammarians of medieval Al-Andalus in liturgical and secular poetry to demonstrate the author's capacity for understanding the words and context of biblical verses and their ability to manipulate both for the sake of an original creative expression.[65] Nahmanides used it to the same end, but it also worked in a more subtle register in this text, allowing him to measure the significance of this controversy in biblical terms.

Deliberate selection and use of prooftexts extend the scope of Nahmanides' discussion to include much broader questions about the nature of power and authority in the Jewish diaspora. Who was invested with the authority to pass legally binding rulings? What distinguished between valid and unsound laws? A similar set of questions arose with respect to interpretive authority. What were the components of an authoritative interpretation? To what degree was the validity of an interpretation dependent upon the exegete's social or cultural standing? Finally, did these qualities change through time and space? The final sections of this chapter will explore the subtlety and nuance of Nahmanides' approach to these issues in the context of the Maimonidean controversy through a close examination of one extended passage from his letter to the French rabbis. In this discrete segment of the text, as he did throughout the letter, Nahmanides borrowed passages from the books of prophets to recall times in the distant past when idolatry or a failure to properly obey divine decrees resulted in some sort of crisis. The prophet, giving voice to divinely inspired wisdom, offered the only viable remedy to the nation's illness.

> Why, exalted saintly ones, have you *cast over many communities the net (reshet)* (Ezekiel 32:3) of a *herem*? You did not set out to kill the thorns in the vineyard, but rather, to pluck bunches of young grapes and thus damage the whole. For you gave us *that desolate land* (Ezekiel 36:35), by scorning and destroying their property, *by asking their lives with a curse* (Job 31:30). And you have not given honor to the great rabbi who *built a tower* (Isaiah 5:2) in the Talmud. *The name of the Lord is a strong tower* (Proverbs 18:10) and it sanctifies the masses, the ignorant (*amei he-aretzot*) *rising to the breaches* (Ezekiel 13:5). He raised our house of Talmud, [from] *complete desolation* (Ezekiel 35:9). Among all the *exiled host in Sepharad* (Obadiah 1:20)[66] and in the lands of the west and *to the east and towards the land of beauty* (Daniel 8:9) *there was one who would save them and plead for them* (Isaiah 19:20). How many *outcasts* from faith *has he gathered* (Isaiah 56:8)? How many schools of learning (*betei midrash*) did he tend to? To how many who were hungry for wisdom has he given his bread and given faith from his trustworthy hands? And how many philosophical skeptics (*epikorsim*) and heretics against our Talmud have turned around because of his correct words? If you, faithful ones, are in the bosom of faith *planted in a courtyard fat and flourishing* (Psalms 92:14–15), why do you not pay attention to the *outcasts* [those living on the extremities, *yoshvei pitzaot*] (Psalms 65:9) because he who *returns to the for-*

tress is a prisoner of hope (Zachariah 9:12), and those who were compelled by longing were satisfied with our faith and our traditions; he *satiated their souls* (Jeremiah 31:13).[67]

This complicated and beautifully constructed passage contains three component subsections, each addressing the same overarching concerns, whether implicitly or explicitly, from a different perspective. The first introduces the biblical construct of Israel as a universalizing agent that unites the disparate, independent diasporas. The second confronts the relationship between *Am Yisrael*, or the People of Israel as a whole, and its component communities. In this instance, though, Nahmanides' rhetoric stressed that distinctive Jewish cultures in the diaspora provided the cultural material that gave Israel and Judaism shape as a whole. Finally, this portion of Nahmanides' letter examines the nature of Maimonides' contribution to Jewish textual interpretation. Maimonides earned the author's high praise for making Judaism and the community of Jews stronger and more inclusive. In conclusion, Nahmanides argued that Maimonides' synthesis of rabbinic teaching remained well within the boundaries of legitimate teaching.

The query introducing this passage—"Why, exalted saintly ones, have you *cast over many communities the net* of a *herem*"?—is a clever paraphrase and restatement of Ezekiel 32:3: "This is what the Sovereign Lord says: 'I will throw my net over you in the assembly of many peoples; and they will haul you up in my net. I will toss you on the ground, I will fling you on the open field, I will cause all the birds of the sky to live on you, and I will let all the beasts of the world gorge themselves with you. I will place your flesh on the mountains, and will fill the valleys with your carcass'" (Ezekiel 32:3–5).[68] In the original, the prophet speaks God's words to the Pharaoh warning that God would tear the nation of Egypt apart with his net and leave it to the mercy of wild animals and the ravages of nature.[69] Nahmanides used the general sense of this verse to lay the historical foundation for his criticism of the French rabbis' *herem*. The paraphrase of Ezekiel as a description of an event that already occurred, rather than a future threat, suggests that the French rabbis failed to heed the warning contained in their own prophetic literature. But more importantly, the fact that this particular passage from Ezekiel addresses a nation other than Israel also seems to subtly reassert Nahmanides' criticism of the French rabbis for extending their influence outside the boundaries of their community.

Building on the imagery of Ezekiel 32, Nahmanides exploited a common theme in biblical prophecy: namely, the contrast between violent natural disaster and an idyllic, pastoral agricultural life.[70] Though the words introducing this passage are drawn from a prophecy of the former, Nahmanides used a metaphor likening the people of Israel to vines growing within the vineyard of Judaism to make a quick transition from a prophecy of destruction by nature's fury to prophecy of pastoral redemption. "You did not set out to kill the thorns in the vineyard, but rather, to pluck bunches of young grapes and thus damage the whole." Nahmanides developed the metaphor of the vineyard by alluding to Isaiah 5:1–2. This verse introduces a homily demonstrating that hard work and good intentions are sometimes still insufficient if the effort has not won God's favor: "My love had a vineyard on a fruitful hill; and he dug it, and cleared its stones, and planted a choice vine, and built a tower within it ... and he hoped that it would make [good] grapes, but it made sour grapes" (Isaiah 5:1–2). In despair, the vintner asks of God why his vines produced sour fruit, then resolves to return the hill to its original condition because "the vineyard of the Lord of hosts is the house of Israel and the man of Judah is His pleasant plant" (Isaiah 5:7). In Nahmanides' adaptation, the tower represented Maimonides' writings, while the vintner whose best efforts and intentions failed to bring him sweet fruit ("you did not set out to kill the thorns in the vineyard, but rather, to pluck bunches of young grapes and thus damage the whole") represented Solomon ben Abraham and his allies. And yet Nahmanides reserved criticism for Maimonides and his contemporary supporters as well. In keeping with the homily, Nahmanides' commentary suggested that both parties in the dispute engaged in a worthy struggle, but with a certain disregard for the metaphorical vineyard. With his selection of these particular prooftexts, he registered a note of sympathy for the efforts exerted by both sides in the Maimonidean conflict to protect local interpretations of Jewish tradition and practice, even at the expense of other distinct understandings of Jewish orthodoxy.

The bulk of this passage addresses Maimonides' success in providing a comfortable place within Judaism for people who had immersed themselves in philosophical studies at the expense of intensive Talmud and Torah study. Nahmanides pointed to the conditions of Jewish life and culture in Al-Andalus and North Africa as the setting that made Maimonides' unique interpretations of Jewish tradition both possible and necessary. Maimonides' *Mishneh Torah* and *Moreh ha-Nevukhim* cast the teachings of the Talmud and the central tenets of Judaism in a shape that would appeal to students who had replaced these with a commitment to philosophical methods of thought and discourse. "He raised our house of Talmud [from] *complete desolation* (Ezekiel 35:9). Among all the *exiled host in Sepharad* (Obadiah 1:20) and in the lands of the west and *to the east and towards the land of beauty* (Daniel 8:9) *there was one who would save them and plead for them* (Isaiah 19:20). How many *outcasts* from faith *has he gathered* (Isaiah 56:8)?" According to this rendering, Maimonides served as a redemptive figure who was called to rebuild the weakened superstructure of Jewish faith and cohesion. The healing effect produced by Maimonides' works fortified both locally based Jewish communities and the body of Jewish communities throughout the diaspora. In Nahmanides' view, legitimate power and authority stemmed from an ability to draw a following and influence communal unity over the long term. This view was consistent with the model of prophetic leadership introduced at the beginning of the passage, and indeed, with the approach to leadership he adopted for himself as well as his criticism of Maimonides' detractors.

After rehabilitating Maimonides' textual interpretations as legitimate, Nahmanides turned his attention to the specific accusations of heresy brought by Solomon ben Abraham and the French rabbis against *Sefer ha-Madda* and *Moreh ha-Nevukhim*. To counter claims made by the proponents of the *herem*, he laid the groundwork for an argument that Maimonides' teachings were legally and exegetically conventional. His strategy here was to show that Maimonides made a legitimate and immeasurable contribution to Jewish legal interpretation which was also supported by the opinions and writings of other well-regarded authorities.[71] He addressed two such issues at length: Maimonides' commentaries on the nature of punishment and redemption[72] and his argument that anthropomorphic descriptions of God in the Bible and rabbinic works were metaphors for, not physical descriptions of, the divine.

> I heard others who said that you seized upon the *Sefer ha-Madda*, where it says there is no image or physicality on high. Why, our masters, did you take hold of this particular issue, for as all the *Geonim* [show] in their books, and all our wise predecessors in Spain and Babylon in their liturgy, they would think of one who deviates from this [view] as one who pursues vanity; they called one who believed the opposite [of Maimonides' view] a trouble-making separatist. This

is written in the Torah, and a second time in the prophecies, and a third time in the writings, and it is explained in the *lovely and edifying* (II Kings 1:23) homilies and exegesis (*midrashim*). For the Cause of Causes has blessed all blessing and prayers. None describe him as matter or form and they do not contain Him in boundaries. How can one comprehend Him as [being contained within] boundaries, and how could one describe Him in terms of place and dimension when the heavens, and the skies of the heavens cannot contain Him?[73]

In both cases, Nahmanides presented strong textual evidence to show that Maimonides contributed to an ongoing discussion that had occupied generations of scholars. He suggested that these interpretations represented a welcome addition to the tradition, clarifying an essential principle that had remained obscure in the corpus of rabbinical teachings.[74] Since the tradition contained no conclusive statements as to the nature and possible duration of punishment and repentance, Maimonides violated no tenet of belief.

On the other hand, Maimonides' argument that neither physical form nor image could be attributed to God was supported by a long tradition of commentary, primarily among Jews living in Spain and North Africa.[75] As the final strategy in his appeal to the French rabbis, Nahmanides placed Maimonides among a small group of commentators whose innovations in interpreting the law transcended the local communities for which they were written and had a lasting impact on the understanding and practice of Judaism throughout the Jewish world.[76] Nahmanides suggested, based on this evidence, that Judaism must necessarily change with the demands of the time and place. However, attention to the proper protocol and decorum for introducing new interpretations was fundamental not only in determining the quality of these changes, but also in preserving the character and well-being of the tradition over the long term.[77]

Nahmanides' Leadership: Action and Reaction

It is difficult to determine precisely when Nahmanides wrote his letter to the French rabbis condemning the *herem* on Maimonides' writings. A comparison of the content and tone of Nahmanides' letter to the French rabbis with other sources pertaining to the controversy suggest that Maimonides' works had not yet been consigned to flames at the time this missive was penned. Unlike many of the letters from other rabbis throughout the diaspora, Nahmanides' rebuke of the French rabbis never challenged their authority in matters of teaching or law; neither did it accuse them or their associates in Languedoc of having involved Christian authorities in a dispute among Jews.[78] On the other hand, there is some indication that Nahmanides knew of the Christian involvement but elected to address exclusively the issues that spawned the struggle among Jews. The letter to the rabbis of France includes no explicit reference to Christian involvement in the controversy per se, however, images of fires, sparks, and destructive flames recur throughout the text.

> [I am] a hated servant, *despised in his eyes* (Psalms 15:4). His innermost heart will have melted, *in order that the great fire should consume us* (Deut. 5:22), *with the rising blaze* (*Shabbat* 21a). For the words of the Torah are as joyous to those who busy themselves with [the words] for their own sake, as for those who received them on Mount Sinai. But in the original place those sparks and that flame burn as a fire which rises towards the wide open blackness (Babylonian Talmud *Baba Metziya* 95b), and surely one would hide his face from his appointed purpose behind a speculum that shines, for *there God was revealed to him* (Genesis 35:7) *these are the powerful gods who smote them with all the plagues* in the wilderness (I Samuel 4:8), and with a *consuming fire in their mouths, by which coals were burnt* (Psalms 18:9), and *over their heads hung a likeness of the firmament* (Ezekiel 1:22).[79]

If Nahmanides intended the symbolism of fire as a reference to the campaign to destroy all of Maimonides' writings, his rhetoric is quite subtle. For Nahmanides, the fire scorched those who did not immerse themselves in Torah, though it threatened to devour all of Israel.

Eloquent and carefully considered as his letter to the French rabbis is, it does not appear that Nahmanides' voice of authority in this dispute was responsible for resolving the conflict. The extant documents do not include a response from the French rabbis, nor is there reference to such a letter that is now missing. It seems that the blow of Church involvement in an internal Jewish dispute was a more powerful and convincing deterrent to the formation of a Jewish orthodoxy than a letter from any teacher could be. In the wake of the bonfire, the French *herem* on Maimonides' writings was eventually lifted. Jonah Gerondi, who had been the intermediary between Solomon ben Abraham and the French rabbis, recanted his opposition to philosophical interpretation, and suddenly the struggle for a definition of interpretive norms abated.

But whether or not Nahmanides' appeal for leniency was crucial to the outcome of this dispute is less important for the purposes of this study than the understanding of Judaism as a set of dynamic texts and practices that he articulated in his contribution to the debate. His letters concerning the *herem* represent a highly nuanced evaluation of how changing historical and cultural circumstances altered the configuration of Jewish communities and traditions. Containing, as it does, a carefully constructed, insightful commentary on the history and intellectual life of contemporary Jewry, Nahmanides' letter to the French rabbis reveals the author to have been a politically and historically astute social theorist who was able to demonstrate, while at the same time to promote, a model of Jewish leadership. To this end, he underlined the importance of scholarly humility, precedent, and proper collegial behavior.

In addition to his letter to the French rabbis, Nahmanides penned a series of letters about the struggle over Maimonides' writings which he addressed to communities in Provence, Aragon, and Castile.[80] The first letter Nahmanides circulated on this matter, which was written prior to the French rabbis' ban on Solomon ben Abraham and his followers, implored community leaders in Aragon, Castile, and Provence not to subscribe to the first ban placed by students of Maimonides' interpretations on the anti-Maimonidean activists. In this letter, as in those circulated following the French *herem*, Nahmanides asked his audience to preserve legal precedent and unity. His rhetorical strategy underplayed the differences between the two sides by professing equal admiration for the teachings of both. He argued that under no circumstances should one court register dissatisfaction with a ruling issued in another court by placing a *herem* on the first. Instead, legal decorum required that the two parties resolve the conflict either through negotiation, or by calling upon a third court to pass judgment: "Two sects are contradicting each other so you must bring your *bet din* to unity and *come to a judgment that the judges may rule on them* (Deut. 25:1), *execute true judgment* (Zachariah 7:9) and in their hands *Zion will be redeemed with judgment* (Isaiah 1:27) and you will be worthy to foresee pleasant returns and the tower will emerge from the house of the King on high, as per your desire and your students' desire."[81]

The demands Nahmanides placed on Maimonides' defenders were similar to those he so eloquently articulated in his appeal to the rabbis of Northern France. Questions of legal precedent and inter-community relations shaped the rhetoric in his criticism of the French rabbis. However, these concerns are more succinctly stated in this collection of shorter notes to the opposite side in the dispute. In contrast to the relative restraint displayed in his letter to the authors of the initial *herem* on Maimonides' works, his letters to the Maimonideans exude a deep rancor at the use of a subsequent *herem* to bring their dispute with Solomon ben Abraham into the public realm. Three of these letters reprimanded the community leaders in Provence, Aragon, and Castile for demonstrating an explicit disregard for the French rabbis' authority as the authors of the initial *herem*. According to the rule of precedence, the French *herem* was binding until revoked. Nahmanides was forced to respect the authority of the French ban to preserve order and continuity of legal tradition. He criticized the defenders of Maimonidean interpretation because they chose to excommunicate the rabbis of Montpellier and the French rabbis rather than commence discussion and negotiation with the authors of the universal ban.

In a fourth letter to the rabbis and community leaders of Béziers, Nahmanides addressed personal as well as halakhic grievances against these staunch supporters of Maimonides' method. Following the burning of Maimonides' writings, the leaders of Béziers circulated a letter suggesting that Jonah Gerondi's family line had been tainted by an illegitimate birth resulting from an affair between his great-grandfather and a married woman. These allegations called into question both the family purity and possibly the standing in the community of Jonah Gerondi and his extended family. Since Nahmanides and Jonah Gerondi were cousins, the claims challenged the purity of Nahmanides' birth and that of his family as well. He was therefore obliged to respond. Since Jonah Gerondi was of course an important figure in this controversy, the rabbis of Béziers no doubt hoped to use this challenge to his stature in the community to undermine his legitimacy as an interpreter of text and tradition.[82]

Once again, Nahmanides responded to these allegations by first questioning whether the grounds for their accusation were legally admissible. To make the case that the leaders of Béziers relied on rumors and hearsay rather than valid legal evidence, he brought evidence from specific judges and courts who ruled during his great-grandfather's lifetime that the family line remained intact.[83] This strategy laid the foundation for a model of proper conduct that could be applied in any controversy: the parties must research the legal precedent, appeal to contemporary authorities, and attempt to resolve disagreements through private negotiations before turning to the public sphere. Careful attention to the conventions of the *bet din* assured that justice could be served.

Letting History Take Its Course

Nahmanides' attempt to forge a reconciliation between Northern European Talmud-based Judaism and the philosophical interpretation that had taken root in Spain and North Africa was rooted in a nuanced rendering of the relationship between the past and present and local and universal traditions. His consistent attention to the nature of historical change in the letter to the French rabbis, in combination with his appeal for legal protocol, constituted, in part, an organized statement by the author about his time and place in history. Unlike David Kimhi[84] and others who defended Maimonidean philosophic interpretation against the French *herem*, Nahmanides rarely inserted himself as an unmediated voice into his correspondences about this dispute. When he, as author, did address his audience in the first person he frequently did so through the voice of biblical prophets: "*Before I answered, I did err* (Psalms 119:67), I will speak before my heart dissolves from fear, and *the purposes of* thought *are broken* (Job 17:11)." Nahmanides thus used the words of the prophets to express divine will to the Jewish people—filtered, though this message may have been, through at least two layers of oral and textual tradition and the lens of history. In this sense, he argued on behalf of and for the well-being of the Jewish tradition, a tradition capable of surviving the challenges imposed by time and dispersion, but which was nevertheless driven by the forces of history and change.

Nahmanides' portrayal of himself as a leader reflects an almost historicist opinion of how Jewish leaders in the diaspora ought to conduct themselves. This is most apparent if we read his response to the French rabbis as a general commentary on the responsibilities of Jewish leaders during his lifetime. Nahmanides suggested that interpreters of Jewish law, teachers of Jewish tradition, and those entrusted with the authority to govern Jewish communities were expected to guide their own generation from the past into the future. What emerges from this discussion is a linear understanding of the present as resting between a known beginning and progressing toward a clear and anticipated end. Nahmanides' representation of the controversy over Maimonides' writings as an event in recent history reflects a deep yearning for continuity and stability of leadership and authority, a demand that leaders conduct themselves in a proper and acceptable manner, a desire to record and acknowledge the sequence in which decisions were made and communications sent. Especially in his letter to the rabbis of France, Nahmanides achieved a sense of timeliness in the present by conflating the present conflict with other conflicts, disputes, and periods of political unease in the past. He accomplished this by manipulating canonical works to express his views, a technique used to great advantage in every aspect of his appeal to the French rabbis. Each statement or argument thus made a multiplicity of arguments signifying several levels of meaning and superseding the boundaries of time and space. In Nahmanides' hands, biblical and talmudic citations served as a critical reading of the uses and meaning of history.

For Nahmanides, the present was historically significant as one moment in the ongoing process by which the Jews as a people reinterpreted and renegotiated what it meant to be a fragmented and dispersed nation. But because he acknowledged that each generation contended with unique historical and cultural conditions, his conception of the present as a historical period was more complicated than this. Forces of change—such as local history and traditions, struggles for authority, new interpretations of texts—posed a threat to continuity. Each generation needed to clear these hurdles in order to arrive at the point of redemption promised by the prophets. According to Nahmanides, the past provided the lessons necessary for maintaining continuity between the past, present, and future. In the aggregate, his letters to the French rabbis and the communities of Provence, Aragon, and Castile regarding the crisis of leadership around the Maimonidean controversy suggest that he believed the exchange between past and present tradition had suffered a significant breakdown. All of the parties in this dispute had apparently abandoned the rules and traditions of leadership that had supported the notion that Israel constituted a single people, in spite of one thousand years of dispersion. The subtle rhetoric in his appeal to the French rabbis recommended a method of reading whereby events in the distant past helped elucidate the shape and meaning of conflicts in the present. Nahmanides' representation of recent events thus offered an example of how Jewish leaders ought to integrate historical knowledge into their response to changes in the present.

Nahmanides viewed contemporary events, conflicts, and resolutions as meaningful indications that the time and place in which he lived were fundamental to the unfolding story of history represented in the Bible and Talmud. However, Nahmanides also struggled to maintain a balance in his response to the controversy over Maimonides' writings between the specificity of recent events and the extended timeline of Jewish experience. His commentary on Solomon ben Abraham's proposed *herem* submitted historical explanations for the unique practices and cultures in diaspora communities. He made every effort to reconcile the divisive, fragmentary character of independent Jewish communities in the diaspora with the national unity of the distant past sealed by a shared literature, and the promise of redemption for all Jews in the future. His response to the *herem* vitalized this romantic view of Israel's past as a potentially unifying force by persistently adopting the words and ideals of the prophets.

Prophecy is perhaps the most temporally complex genre of literature in the canon of Jewish texts. The prophets convey to the reader a promise of redemption in a vague and undisclosed future through a critique of Israel the prophet encountered in his daily life. For Nahmanides, the prophets were historical figures, firmly situated in the distant past. Yet prophets also spoke (or wrote) for the future generations. Their specified audience was therefore always in question. Nahmanides used the temporal ambiguity inherent in prophecy to bolster his political argument. By quoting the words of the prophets, he invested contemporary events with an epochal quality. Changes in the structural and circumstantial conditions of independent Jewish communities in the diaspora played a crucial role in shaping Nahmanides' conception of distinct styles of leadership suitable to each given community. This interest in the vicissitudes of change is unparalleled in the other letters generated during this dispute, most of which were framed in overtly partisan terms. Nahmanides, however, evaluated historical examples—the challenges posed by philosophy and Greek science, the messianic movement and hostility to Jewish autonomy in Yemen, pietism in France and Germany—to interpret the contemporary struggle and to comment on the possible consequences that could result from a failure to reconcile opposing views. He mobilized a relatively fluid conception of community in order to preserve the unity of Israel as well as the autonomy of Jewish communities. This view recognized the validity of diverse political practices and leadership strategies, provided they met the widely accepted standards of halakhic procedure.

A clearly formed ideal of leadership as a process of guidance, rather than compulsion, emerged in Nahmanides' response to this struggle for interpretive and political primacy. Since Nahmanides held no official office in the *aljama* of Girona (the royally sanctioned and self-governed Jewish community) it was essential that he present his views as authoritative but not binding. He achieved this by conflating two models of leadership that were commonly recognizable in medieval Catalonia: the distinguished teacher or scholar and the *beror*, the elected or appointed political leader who had close contact with Christian authorities and with Jewish leaders throughout the diaspora. Though Nahmanides never presented this model of leadership in definitive or systematic terms, he related his conception of leadership in a clear critique of the strategies employed by leaders on both sides of the dispute. Biblical and talmudic sources provided a historical precedent for his approach to inter-community leadership, but Nahmanides' letter to the French rabbis offered perhaps the clearest demonstration of this model at work. His tone of address is uniformly respectful and balanced, offsetting the hostile, superior tone of Solomon ben Abraham's alliance with the French rabbis as well as various of the letters supporting Maimonidean interpretation. Moreover, each of his arguments was set against a broad historical vision, connecting actions in the present with their causes in the past and possible future consequences.

CHAPTER TWO

Timely Matters

Nahmanides' Historical Reading of Genesis

NAHMANIDES' CONTRIBUTION TO THE MAIMONIDEAN CONTROVERSY offers an early illustration of his understanding of the interplay between tradition and innovation in the ongoing project of Jewish legal thinking. In the context of this dispute he presented an argument allowing for halakhic innovation suited to contemporary needs and circumstances, but regulated by accepted practice and precedent. The approach to interpretive and legal innovation that Nahmanides articulated in his response to the French rabbis' *herem* finds echoes in his biblical exegesis as well.[1] Though he wrote his biblical commentary some time after the Maimonidean controversy there is a clear continuity between Nahmanides' early leadership strategies and his great exegetical work.

Medieval Jewry produced several schools of exegesis with a variety of approaches and concerns. Beginning in the late eleventh century, there was a groundswell of Torah study and commentary among European Jews. Nahmanides' exegesis is one among several comprehensive interpretations of the Torah that was completed and circulated during the middle ages by prominent teachers. Yet, his systematic biblical commentary stood at the crossroads of several fundamental developments in medieval Judaism, bridging classical midrashic commentary with medieval innovations including philosophy, Kabbalah, and a concern with seeking the *peshat* or the simple meaning of the text derived from Northern European exegetes who were influenced by Rashi's school.[2] Nahmanides' exegesis is systematic and comprehensive. In keeping with the great medieval exegetical works, he followed the narrative structure of Torah and included commentary on each of the five biblical books.

Nahmanides framed his commentary with a methodological introduction, which laid out the way he conceptualized human reception and understanding of divine revelation as well as some of the tools he deemed necessary for grasping the sense and structure of biblical literature. This introduction established the tone and intent of the commentary as a work. The method of interpretation presented here was designed to extract obscure or hidden meanings from the sacred text, while reconciling those with more widely accepted understandings. In the process, Nahmanides identified the story of creation as the epicenter of Jewish faith, practice, and community, the point at which Israel's relationship with God was formalized and structured. Thus, he suggested, the early chapters of Genesis demanded careful explication. Nahmanides' chief exegetical concerns included: 1) the correlation of events as they occurred with the sequence of events represented in revelation as a whole and in the creation narrative in particular; 2) the link between the extended process of divine revelation to Israel; and 3) the meaning and structure of Israel's history. Throughout, he presented Torah as a tangible and dynamic expression of the many faces of divine will.

Nahmanides' concern with direct questions of sequence and history emerging from the creation story illustrates a more fundamental characteristic of his conception of the process, limitations, and objectives of interpreting (and applying) divine revelation. His approach to biblical exegesis, and particularly to Genesis, was rooted in a belief that Torah contained revelation of law and important information about the distant past, but also a map of the structure and duration of human experience from the time of creation until the messianic redemption. In other words, according to Nahmanides the biblical narrative represented, albeit in rough form, the superstructure of changes and events, the duration, rhythm, and purpose of the historical experience of the Jewish people. Change, disruption, and (perhaps paradoxically in the context of this discussion) uncertainty were thus fundamental components in the fulfillment of the historical drama. As a result, methods of interpreting Torah and the means of understanding conceptual and causal links between events or people in the past, present, and future also changed over time.

From a human perspective, processes of historical change occur at a snail's pace; social and cultural shifts only gain clarity in retrospect. Similarly, according to Nahmanides' view of history and Torah, methods of extracting meaning from Torah unfold incrementally over the course of many generations, as does the meaning itself. Meanings that had been hidden from one generation offer themselves as transparent to later generations.[3] The assumed logic of sacred history would not allow for God to permit this slow unfolding of meaning to continue indefinitely. Rather, Nahmanides understood such processes of change to be contained between a clearly defined beginning and end: between creation and redemption. He perceived those processes of historical change and understanding to be speeding towards a conclusion which he expected within the century following his lifetime. Nahmanides employed a method of "reading in," whereby he counterbalanced and compared several layers of interpretation, both traditional and innovative, allowing a timely interpretation to emerge.[4] An engagement with questions concerning the shape, duration, and meaning of time as it is played out in the relationship between human beings and their God is a leitmotif throughout his biblical exegesis, liturgical writings, and epistles.[5] The temporal complexity of creation which Nahmanides excavated in the course of his exegesis set the foundation for his systematic exegesis of the biblical corpus.

In her recent study of Nahmanides' conception of time and revealed texts, Haviva Pedaya demonstrates that notions of temporal cyclicality, divine intent, and human apprehension of this intent through prayer, ritual, and mystical meditation were fundamentally linked in the varied corpus of his writings.[6] Much of the scholarship on Nahmanides' exegesis has focused on classifying the nature of the relationship between the *peshat* and *sod*, or the plain and secret sense of the Torah, in his interpretation and his teaching of Kabbalah. Many agree that Nahmanides' unprecedented juxtaposition of *peshat* and *sod* provides an essential clue about the architecture of his mystical interpretation.[7] Departing from this relatively circumscribed emphasis, Pedaya's study is a holistic survey of the multiple senses and methods of interpretation that comprise Nahmanides' approach to text, revelation, traditional and mystical practice, and human history. Her analysis lingers on the layer of *derash*, or expository interpretation, in Nahmanides' commentary, as well as the integration of kabbalistic premises in his sermons and legal findings. Pedaya argues that Nahmanides understood 'cosmic' time and historical time to be distinct in purpose and shape but still fundamentally connected: according to this model, human society in its relationship with God was constantly pressing forward in a linear historical sense toward the redemption, but the sense of 'cosmic time' was a drive towards a primordial return to divine origins. As she demonstrates, much of this finds expression in Nahmanides' understanding and valuation of creation.

While the present study shares both conceptual and material commonalities with Pedaya's work, the basic assumptions and objectives of our projects are quite different. We both explore Nahmanides' exegesis of creation and the central role of creation in his thought; however, Pedaya presents a comprehensive reading of Nahmanides in his capacity as a leading teacher and innovator of Kabbalah. It is not my intention here to enter the debate about Nahmanides' role in shaping Kabbalah or to examine in what ways his interpretation was a mystical exercise. Instead, I will focus on the structure of his interpretive method and how the layers of meaning he uncovered informed his understanding of historical processes and earthly affairs.

One objective of Nahmanides' method (and model) for interpreting Torah was the explicit reconciliation of style, content, and form in Torah. In the process, he subjected the interpretations of his exegetical forefathers, including the midrashic literature, Rashi, and Abraham ibn Ezra, to a critical review based on the unique interpretive demands of his time. Among the guiding principles behind his analysis of exegetical models was a drive to uncover the *peshat* or plain sense of the scriptures. The *peshat*, he argued, should be universally accessible as long as the reader approached the text after having previously arrived at the appropriate hierarchy of interpretive sources (i.e., the Midrash, Talmud, and later biblical commentaries, including Saadya Gaon, Maimonides, Abraham ibn Ezra, and Rashi).

Begin at the Beginning

In the introduction to his commentary on Genesis, Nahmanides referred to the creation story as a fundamental tenet of Judaism: "It was essential that the Torah should begin with '*bereshit bara Elohim* . . .' (In the beginning God created . . .) because it is the root of faith, and he who does not believe in this and who thinks that the world is eternal denies an essential principle of Judaism (i.e., that the world was created from nothing at the beginning of time) and he has no *torah*."⁸ With this declaration, Nahmanides revealed several essential assumptions that shaped his understanding of divine revelation and the interpretive framework necessary for explicating revealed text and its particular significance for the Jewish people. Embedded in this statement was a deep conviction that the Torah possessed a single, logical, and meaningful narrative structure. It was necessary for Torah to begin with The Beginning, according to Nahmanides, because in addition to the fact that Torah represented revelation, it was also a story. The Beginning provided symmetry, context, order.

With the shift towards comprehensive and systematic biblical exegesis during the middle ages, exegetes turned their attention to explaining the form, content, and sequence of the story of creation. Systematic exegesis aspired to preserve the unity of the Torah in its narrative and legal senses. In this project, medieval exegesis closely followed examples set in the *Midrash Rabbah*. The midrashic view of creation is impressionistic and variegated, showcasing the diversity of opinion and the interplay of ideas. Since Midrash as a whole is a pastiche of commentaries organized around and sequentially replicating biblical text, it makes no claim to presenting a unified interpretive voice or a cohesive, systematic exegesis. The questions and solutions posed in the Midrash leave the entire exegetical problem open to discussion. A single question—what is the significance of the fact that the Torah begins "*bereshit bara Elohom . . .*"—prompted a wide variety of discussions that range from conjecture about which element of ritual was honored by the word *bereshit* to why the Torah began with a *bet*, the second letter in the alphabet, rather than the first, *aleph*. However, these issues took on a new significance in the hands of medieval exegetes, especially after the twelfth century, across the Pyrenees and throughout the Iberian peninsula in the shadow of Christian interpretations and with the increasing influence of Aristotelian and neo-Platonic philosophy.

Formally and structurally the first two chapters of Genesis give the appearance of a complete and sequential catalogue of the acts of creation. Yet, as much of the exegesis produced from late antiquity through the middle ages illustrates, a good number of details in the brief creation narrative seem to demand clarification. Even as a complete narrative, the creation story posed interpretive challenges for systematic, sequential exegesis. The text appears to provide an exhaustive, point by point account of creation, enhanced by the formal structure of the story. Bracketed by a clearly delineated beginning and end, and laid out in an unmistakable sequence of richly detailed action in which the significant transitions were listed numerically, the structure of the creation story suggested narrative comprehensiveness. Nevertheless, upon closer inspection the systematic exegete found the story to be peppered with sequential inconsistencies and lacking some apparently essential details.[9]

Nahmanides' claim that knowledge of creation is essential to Jewish faith responded to a common question in Jewish commentaries on Genesis, namely why does the Bible begin with a story that has no practical application in ritual or worship and does not provide an example of the relationship between Jews and their God? The answer Nahmanides offered reframed the traditional mode of inquiry in terms of historically determined questions that loomed large on the cultural and religious horizon of contemporary Iberian Jewry. With his claim that the creation story was fundamental to Jewish faith, and indeed throughout his exegesis, Nahmanides' terms of discussion, the questions he posed, the prooftexts he brought to support his interpretation, even his understanding of revelation as an ongoing process, seemed uniquely suited to address the cultural and religious conditions of thirteenth-century Aragonese Jewry.

One of the primary goals of biblical exegesis as an expository genre is to render difficult texts accessible, comprehensible, and meaningful to human readers; this task is, of course, rendered more difficult by the assumption of divine authorship.[10] Jewish exegetes embarked upon this interpretive process guided by the belief that a unique relationship between the Creator and the chosen few among human beings necessitates that each generation expound upon the language and sense of the Torah.[11] In terms of both practice and convention, biblical interpretation socializes members of religious communities into ideals of intellectual development, and ethical and behavioral standards of group identification and responsibility.[12] Exegetical methods must therefore be malleable enough to allow both the sacred text and its interpretation to speak across time and space. Throughout the rabbinic period as well as much of the middle ages, biblical interpretation analyzed and compared legal, moral, ethical, or historical precepts pertaining specifically to the people of Israel in order to better serve and honor God.[13] The structure of biblical literature facilitates this very mode of interpretation. As Michael Fishbane has shown, the process of redaction interwove a constant intertextual commentary into the very fabric of biblical narrative, so that the biblical form was the basis for legal commentary and ethical typologies.[14]

The story of creation posed unique formal and narrative exegetical challenges. Because it fits no generic legal or ethical paradigm, the creation epoch is subject to a different set of intertextual exchanges. The first two chapters of Genesis are formally and thematically distinct from all that follows. Most of the first chapter of Genesis is devoid of human characters or historical action (though humanity is of course indicated by the process of creation and its narration). Instead, this portion of the text describes God's creative actions, which are by definition inscrutable and beyond human comprehension. As no other biblical text is completely barren of human characters, a comparison based primarily on contextual similarities with other biblical passages becomes virtually impossible. Even the narrative style of this chapter is sparse and compact, leaving little (or perhaps, to the contrary, far too much) room for extrapolation and speculation. Certainly, other portions of biblical text are rendered in similarly terse or compact language, but the sequential position of the creation story in the biblical corpus and its unique content mark it as incomparable. Since the creation story yields few hints as to the underlying meaning, the proper method for extracting meaningful information appears similarly veiled.

Nahmanides responded to and juxtaposed traditional exegetical opinions and interpretations throughout his own commentary.[15] His frequent interjection of critical remarks about Rashi (Rabbi Solomon ben Isaac, 1040–1105 c.e.) and Abraham ibn Ezra (1092–1167 c.e.) both challenged and solidified a new canon of methodical biblical exegesis. Bernard Septimus has observed that Nahmanides perceived his own biblical commentary as an important contribution to and defense of a tradition of Judaism grown in Andalusia.[16] By bringing together two distinct bodies of exegetical literature—Northern European or French exegesis, represented by Rashi, and the Sephardic tradition, represented by Abraham ibn Ezra and Maimonides[17]—and using these traditions as a foil for his unique reading of the text, Nahmanides constructed a delicate fabric composed of literal readings (*peshat*) and symbolic readings which teased out hidden secrets from the deep recesses of the scripture (*sod*).[18]

Rashi, the author of one of the earliest and arguably the most prominent comprehensive and systematic commentary of the Bible produced in the European middle ages, provided a three-tiered reading of Genesis 1.[19] His commentary rested on the assumption that the story of creation was not intended to teach the strict order of creation. For the substance of this discussion, Rashi drew from a Midrash which set out to answer the question: "Why does the Torah begin with the story of creation?"[20] The answer contained in this Midrash was simple and satisfying: the creation story provided the Jews with scriptural proof that the world humans inhabit was exclusively the domain of God, who could therefore give it to whomever He pleased.[21] Rashi accepted the interpretation offered in *Midrash Tanhuma*, but also chose to pursue an alternative understanding based on the grammatical configuration of the first verse. The phrase *bereshit*, or "in the beginning," consists of a noun (*reshit*, beginning) preceded by the prepositional prefix, "in" (*be*). *Bereshit*, however, lacks the vocalization denoting a definite article. Although "the" is implied and is therefore usually inferred, the first word of this verse represents a grammatical enigma. Further complicating interpretation of this verse is the fact that *bereshit* appears in the grammatical form of a noun in a dependent or construct clause. The most obvious reading would seem to be: "in the beginning of . . .," but the word that follows, "created" (*bara*), is neither a noun nor a gerund, as construct clauses usually demand, but instead, a verb in the perfect past tense. To implement the standard rules of comparative exegesis, in which a verse with an analogous grammatical construct or contextual setting provides a prototype for explaining the text in question, the exegete must locate cases in which the same or similar textual properties are in evidence. There is no exact parallel in the biblical corpus.

The awkward syntax of this verse inspired Rashi to ask what subject was modified by *bereshit*. To the beginning *of what* does this verse refer? His answer complemented the historical interpretation he offered from the outset. Rashi read Genesis 1:1 as an extended dependent clause: "In the beginning of the creating of [the] heavens and [the] earth . . . God said 'Let there be light'" (*Bereshit briyat shamayim ve-aretz, ve-yomer Elohim yahi or*)" (Rashi *Bereshit* 1:1a). This shifted the case of the verb, *bara*, from past perfect (God created . . .) to imperfect verbal noun (creating), suggesting an ongoing action, rather than a complete or final one. According to this reading, the remainder of the verse described the conditions prior to God's command for light, the first definitive act of creation related in Torah. Rashi finally concluded that the process of creation was ruled by the divine attributes of judgment and mercy. His effort to link the enigmatic creation story with the divine attributes of judgment and mercy forged a conceptual link between the creation story—the only biblical unit entirely devoid of human characters—and stories which revolve around human characters.

The conceptual discontinuity between the factual list-like quality and the sparse detail provided in the creation narrative inspired Rashi to interrogate the purpose and meaning of the story of creation as the gateway to sacred history and the covenant. In his view, the Torah was essentially a guide book containing explicit instructions and moral examples intended to help the people of Israel organize life and society around the single goal of serving God.[22] Unable to reconcile the creation story with this understanding of Torah, Rashi repeated a midrashic interpretation that supported his presuppositions about the meaning and purpose of scripture. Because the biblical narrative failed to make an explicit link between the creation narrative and the history of the Jewish people since the time of Moses, Rashi stressed the unusual grammatical construction in the first verse to provide a textual basis for the historical or polemical interpretation with which he opened his commentary.

Like Rashi, Abraham ibn Ezra began by asking what the story of creation was meant to teach. Also like Rashi, ibn Ezra argued that *bereshit* formed part of a dependent or construct phrase. But while they shared similar points of departure, Rashi and ibn Ezra adopted two very distinct methods of interpreting sacred text. Whereas Rashi generally sought rabbinic interpretations before offering his own unique solution to the problems raised by the biblical text, ibn Ezra wove an alternative narrative, frequently without offering prooftexts. In the case of the creation story, ibn Ezra rooted his alternative reading in the argument favored by philosophers that the physical world is eternal. To soften the philosophers' blow to God's omnipotence, ibn Ezra suggested that matter itself was eternal, but that the reshaping of that matter into a world fit for human habitation occurred at the precise moment in time described in the first two chapters of Genesis.

Ibn Ezra began his biblical exegesis with an introduction formulated as a critical review of four methodologically flawed Jewish exegetical techniques that were widely used in rabbinic and medieval biblical commentary. This survey of conceptually unsatisfactory approaches to biblical exegesis allowed ibn Ezra an opportunity to promote a unified and systematic alternative. The first, the "broad and wide" approach (*arukhah ve-rahavah*), which ibn Ezra associated with the tenth-century Jewish philosopher, Saadya Gaon, is characterized by a tendency to make judgments about text and meaning based on broad assumptions for which there is little textual evidence. The second is a "confused or convoluted" exegetical method (*pitlatulim*), which expects the biblical text to provide absolute consistency and leave no narrative gaps. Practitioners of this method devise long explanations accounting for the purpose or meaning of apparent omissions or gaps. To illustrate this point, he cited the large body of literature that grew in an attempt to explain the absence of a clearly constructed calendar of months in the Bible. The third method of interpretation, the "dark and shadowy" approach to Torah (*hoshekh ve-aphelah*), finds secrets in every verse and reads each statement as a hint to a great or small commandment. Finally, the fourth offers an allegorical reading that oversteps the boundaries of reason (*karovah al nekudah*). This method appears frequently in talmudic interpretation. In contrast to each of these methods Abraham ibn Ezra presented an alternative approach, melding technical, grammatical, and textual analysis. The true sense of the Torah, according to ibn Ezra, could be found by first conducting a careful philological and etymological analysis of the individual words, followed by an evaluation of their meaning as part of complex grammatical groupings, such as sentences and phrases in the context of a given verse.[23]

Ibn Ezra found what he believed to be the true meaning of the creation story in the relationship between light and the transformation of watery chaos into organized matter and dry land. He argued that the first two verses of Genesis describe an unformed proto-matter unimportant to the subsequent verses except in so far as it set the stage for the process of creation. According to Abraham ibn Ezra, the biblical creation story did not present an exhaustive representation of every step in the process of creation *ex nihilo*. Rather it taught about the orderly transformation of preexistent matter into an environment suitable for human life. If the reader put aside the assumption that creation was a process of bringing something from nothing, a proposition for which, he argued, there was no support in the text, then the problem of sequence would evaporate.

Nahmanides situated his commentary as a response to and completion of these earlier interpretations. His view was informed not only by the teachings of his predecessors, but also by his belief that he lived in a time ripe for the clarification of previously concealed meanings. By positioning his own reading of the creation narrative against the accepted wisdom of the Midrash, Rashi, and ibn Ezra, Nahmanides emphasized the essential conceptual differences between his own interpretation of the scripture and those of his predecessors. Indeed, he often drew attention to the novelty of his approach by summarizing or quoting from Midrash, Rashi, or ibn Ezra before presenting a controversial interpretation or one that challenges or alters accepted tradition.

Since Nahmanides made no effort to explicate the novelty of his exegetical reading of the creation story in any systematic way, it will be helpful here to thematize the innovative nature of his approach in terms of the sense of temporality it presents. First, Nahmanides read the book of Genesis, especially the first two chapters, as the narrative description of the creation of space, time, and history—all of which were inextricably linked—from a primal nothingness. His approach suggested an essential connection between the biblical narrative (in the sense that it is a story that was told time and again in different times and places, and in the sense that the Torah is a physical document whose textual content does not vary) and the events it describes. Nahmanides' view of creation was a departure from the approach taken by other medieval commentators. Rashi and ibn Ezra made every effort *not* to read the first two chapters of Genesis as a literal catalogue of the actual process of creation as it occurred. However, Nahmanides accepted a literal reading of Genesis 1–2 as a list of God's creative acts. His approach was innovative in that it combined this literal reading with a symbolic and temporally rich understanding of creation which claimed that increasingly sophisticated exegetical methods would reveal themselves over time.

> There is a great need that the Torah begin with '*bereshit bara Elohim*' because it is the root of faith, as he who does not believe in this and who thinks that the world is eternal is essentially an agnostic and he has no torah. The answer is that the story of Genesis is a deep secret that cannot be understood only from the verses and it cannot be known in its entirety except from the tradition given to Moses our master from the mouth of the Lord, and those who know it must conceal it. Thus, Rabbi Isaac[24] said that the Torah did not need to begin '*Bereshit bara*,' or the story of what was created on the first day, or what was done on the second day and the remaining days, or the detail of the creation of Adam and Eve and their sin and punishment, or the story of the garden of Eden and Adam's expulsion from there, because none of this is wisdom that can be understood in its entirety from the verses and all the more so with regards to the generation of the great flood since there is no great need for them at all. It would be sufficient for the people of the Torah to believe in all that is contained for them in the ten commandments without these writings, because "God created the earth and the sky and everything they hold in six

days and rested on the seventh" (Exodus 20:11) and this wisdom would continue with certain individuals familiar with the oral law that was given to Moses on Sinai with the Torah.[25]

There was a very practical side to Nahmanides' literal or historically oriented sense of time in creation. He found the tools used to measure history and its starting point at the exact moment in which God created the world inhabited by man. God even provided the sun, the moon, and the constellations to supply human beings with a natural technology for measuring their existence on earth.[26] According to Nahmanides, the story of creation in Genesis did not represent a completed work, but rather it portrayed the beginning of an ongoing process, the completion of which would be heralded with the resurrection of the dead.[27] The religion and history that belonged to and defined the Jewish people were, in the very deepest sense, contained in the narrative of creation. Nahmanides sustained this view in his typological interpretation of biblical narrative. As a result, his interpretive method presents Genesis, more than the other books in the Pentateuch, as containing numerous historical and moral meanings. Nahmanides' drew from an extensive and diverse body of interpretive sources. By providing so broad a base for his interpretation, Nahmanides addressed this commentary to a general audience, regardless of the readers' possible association with secret study groups (mystical or philosophical) or other such factions within the Jewish communities throughout the diaspora.[28]

Three distinct layers of historical meaning can be discerned in Nahmanides' interpretation of the creation narrative. The first level is an examination of the sequence of events as they were presented in Genesis. This mode of exposition built from an interrogation of each act of creation, emphasizing the order of creation, the quality and substance of language with which it is expressed in the text, and the degree to which one act of creation provided a foundation for the next. Second, Nahmanides posited the Torah as God's formal plan for human history. As such, it necessarily predated and prefigured creation itself. In this sense, according to Nahmanides, the beginning of creation *ex nihilo* was synonymous with the beginning of measurable cosmic time, which provided the key for understanding human history. And finally, Nahmanides established a typological reading of human history, using tropes established early in the biblical narrative to make sense of later events.[29]

Nahmanides interpreted biblical narrative in accordance with a linear view of time in which one event or action necessarily had a causal link to the next. This approach is distinctive. The methods of exegesis employed by the vast majority of authorities who preceded him, including the Midrash and medieval commentaries, rarely acknowledge sequential continuity of action in the biblical narrative. Quite to the contrary, there is an active attempt to disrupt the conventions of timelines and historical specificity in the Midrash. *Aggadot,* or the non-legal narrative portions of the Midrash, frequently depict biblical characters in historically anachronistic settings: in one instance we find the patriarchs attending and adjudicating in rabbinic academies of law.[30] According to the ethos of traditional Jewish exegesis the ability to determine whether the biblical narrative conforms to the demands of logic and chronology is far less important than a talent for discerning legal precedent or identifying useful prooftexts. Rules of talmudic biblical exegesis supported this preference, formally relieving the exegete of any responsibility for imposing on the narrative chronological consistency or continuity.[31] One rabbinic exegetical dictum which played an important role in Nahmanides' exegesis is of particular interest in this regard: "There is no before and after in the Torah" (*ain mukdam ve-me-akhar be-Torah*).[32] Through such dicta we glimpse an important element of the rabbinic conception of man's relationship to divine revelation. A belief that God's motivations for shaping the biblical narrative as it is are beyond human comprehension supports these interpretive principles: Torah speaks the language of man because man could not possibly understand the language or logic of God. Questions of agency in matters of composition and sequence are thus shunned, leaving questions of consequence and content open for discussion.

Nahmanides' exegesis was self-consciously pioneering in so far as it relied on the language and methods of the Midrash and medieval commentators, such as Rashi and Abraham ibn Ezra, while at significant points subverting traditional interpretive guidelines. This is especially true of the distinctly linear conception of narrative time that Nahmanides superimposed on traditional approaches throughout his biblical commentary. As Yaakov Elman has shown, the talmudic exegetical rule "there is no before and after in the Torah" acquired a fresh meaning in Nahmanides' commentary.[33] In its original sense, this formula eliminated the interpreter's responsibility for explaining sequential or temporal inconsistencies. For Nahmanides, however, it signaled a demand to account for each narrative inconsistency or incongruity. "There is no before and after in Torah" instead served to open an extrapolation based on the data provided in the biblical narrative in order to account for narrative gaps.[34]

Nahmanides' demand for consistency in interpreting the biblical text and his insistence on a clear articulation of the questions and concerns that guided his interpretation were the foundation, according to Elman, for biblical commentary organized around the search for "omni-significance," the goal of identifying and understanding the significance of every detail, inconsistency, or letter in the Torah in the service of making a single, unified point.[35] Programmatic statements concerning the nature of sequential narrative, Elman notes, abound in Nahmanides' commentary on the 'historic' portions of the Torah containing Jewish law and ritual. However, he claims that such concerns are conspicuously lacking in Nahmanides' commentary on Genesis, which, as the name denotes, provides the 'prehistory' or mytho-history of the Jewish people.[36]

While Elman's reading of Nahmanides' exegesis elucidates one of the central organizing principles in Nahmanides' exegesis, I would like to test his claim that an interest in sequence is lacking in Nahmanides' interpretation of Genesis. Nahmanides focused his attention on the order of creation, which provided the basis for his reading of the plain sense of the text, or *peshat*. He read creation as a sequential process in which one step followed in a logical manner from the previous one. For instance, in his explication of Genesis 1:26 he asked why the statement "Let us make man in our image," was pluralized. In posing this question, Nahmanides responded to the frequent use of this verse by Christians to support the claim that the God of the Torah was the same as the Christian trinity. But he also did much more than this. The plain sense of the text, according to Nahmanides' reading, was determined by the sequence of events described: namely, the "we" invoked in Genesis 1:26 includes the elements of earth because it is the material God used to shape man.

> The correct simple meaning of "let us make" is as it was shown to be, that the Lord created something from nothing on the first day only. Afterwards, He formed and created from the elements that were created [on the first day]. And when He gave the water the power to breed crawling living souls, "and the waters will crawl" was the commandment given to them; "and let the earth bring out" was the commandment for the cattle; and He said concerning man, "let us make," that is to say, "the aforementioned earth and I will make man,"

that the earth will bring forth the body from its elements, just as it made the cattle and the animal, as it says, "and the Lord formed the man from dust of the land" (Genesis 2:7). And He, may He be blessed, gave the spirit from His mouth on high, as it is written "and He breathed in his nostrils the breath of life" (Genesis 2:7). And He said, "In Our image and in Our likeness" since he would resemble both of them: in the composition of his body, in the capacity of his body he would resemble the earth from which we will take [material]; and he resembles in spirit the higher beings, since they are bodiless and do not die.[37]

In this passage, Nahmanides took stock of the order in which things were created or formed, the syntax and terminology used to describe each act of creation, and the objects created. On this basis, he suggested that the creation of living creatures was a two-part process. It began with the shaping of matter and was completed when the bodies were animated. This "plain" meaning of the text was based on a deliberate cataloguing of events in the order they occurred combined with a directed interpretation of that data.

Establishing the exact sequence of creation had both theological and historical implications since Nahmanides read the biblical narrative as a document that embodied the past, future, and present in more than just symbolic terms. This reading of the plain sense represented a radical departure from his inherited tradition. By stressing the dual nature of creation, Nahmanides also drew attention to the flow of narrative and events even in cases like this one, in which the text would seem to present little exegetical difficulty. According to the logic driving Nahmanides' interpretive method, the true meaning of the events described in the Torah became apparent only once the reader apprehended the placement of the creative acts in time and the causal relationship between them.[38]

This concern with marking the order of events as an issue worthy of examination and explication, whether or not the sequence might possess an obvious internal logic, was a hallmark of Nahmanides' approach to biblical exegesis that had a significant influence on later kabbalist interpretation. Thus, for example, the symbolic or figurative interpretation of biblical text employed in *Sefer ha-Zohar*, in keeping with Nahmanides' reading, used the sequence of events established in the opening chapters of Genesis as a framework on which to build deeply textured interpretations resonating with multiple levels of meaning.[39]

Writing, Prophecy, and the Unfolding Meaning of Torah

The questions Nahmanides' exegesis posed point to a belief that creation was a gradually unfolding process. This rendering of creation and its telling were linked with a series of exegetical questions pertaining to the historical setting in which creation was given narrative structure and later preserved in written form. The tension for Nahmanides developed from a difficulty in determining where and when the story began and how this beginning corresponded to the textual form the story took. The hermeneutic difficulty associated with a primarily sequential reading of this Torah portion led Nahmanides to examine the series of events linking revelation, story, and storyteller: the revelation to Moses, Moses' agency as the scribe who recorded this revelation, and the hypothetical limits of any human experience of God. His explanation of sequential events presented in Genesis begins with the suggestion that the order represented in the canonical text replicates exactly the narrative related to Moses by God on Mount Sinai.

> Moses our teacher wrote this book with the Torah in its entirety [based on words that came] from the mouth of the Holy one, may He be blessed. And it seems that he wrote it on Mount Sinai, since it was there that it was said to him "Climb to me on the mountain and be there, and I will give you the stone tablets and the Torah and the commandments that I wrote so you may teach them" (Exodus 24:12). Then the written Torah included the tablets and the epistle, that is to say, the Ten Commandments, and the commandment from the *Sefer Mitzvot* in its entirety, including positive and negative injunctions. If this is true, the phrase "and the Torah" includes the story that begins "*bereshit*," since it instructs the people on the way in the matter of faith, and when he descended from the mountain he wrote the Torah from the beginning to the end of the story of the tabernacle, and he finished writing the Torah at the end of the fortieth year, when it says "take this book of teaching and make for it an ark [honoring] the covenant with God, your Lord" (Deut. 31:26).[40]

Nahmanides' line of argument brought questions related to narrative and the textual nature of revelation to the foreground. The implication is that before one could understand the demands of the covenant or the most appropriate means of serving God, one must master the narrative structure of revelation.

The next pressing question for Nahmanides concerned authorial responsibility: why did Moses decline to add an introductory statement at the beginning of Genesis explaining its narrative and liturgical purposes? An acknowledgment by Moses that he had received the creation story through divine revelation would have gone a significant distance towards explaining why the creation story did not follow sequentially from the verse which introduced God's revelation to Moses: "Climb to me on the mountain and be there, and I will give you the stone tablets and the Torah and the commandments that I wrote so you may teach them" (Exodus 24:12). The moment of time represented in Exodus 24:12 is also the exact moment at which Moses became conscious of his responsibility as the man through whom God gave the Torah. The narrative logic of a prophetic testament or historical chronicle would dictate that the author tell the story as a sequential testimony, beginning with the author's first experience of the episodes described, followed by a realistic depiction of precisely what happened and when.

In Nahmanides' view, one might be puzzled by the fact that Moses, in his role as biblical narrator, reported events that were certainly beyond his personal experience. In each of the other prophetic works, the prophet stepped out of his story, identifying himself and situating himself in temporal and spatial terms recognizable to the reader.[41] Moses, however, willfully disregarded this "narrative covenant,"[42] effectively shunning even the claim of prophetic authority. Instead, he inserted himself into the story only at that moment when his life or accomplishments became significant to the people of Israel or to the narrative of revelation. And even in these instances, he never introduced himself in the first person as a narrator. According to Nahmanides, Moses understood his role in crafting the textual record of God's revelation and covenant to be that of a scribe rather than an original author because he understood that the story presented in the Torah preceded even the creation of the world. Moses chose to begin the Torah with the story of God's creation, this argument holds, because he feared that dissenters might one day question his authority as a prophet and law-giver, thus bringing devastating consequences upon Israel. The chain of transmission linking the act of creation, the divine revelation of this story to a human audience, and interpretation of the story by a human author is invisible in the creation story as it appears in the Torah. Rather, the reader encounters a fully formed narrative, the author of which remains thoroughly concealed.

The sequence of creation as told in Genesis represented, in Nahmanides' view, the *real* sequence of creation, divine revelation to Moses, and Moses' inscription of this revelation. Acting as God's scribe, Moses recorded the story recounted in Genesis in the exact manner it was told to him on Sinai. Yet this exegetical turn called attention to a temporal gap between creation and revelation on Sinai, thereby throwing the sequence of both revelation and its telling into question once more. Nahmanides added an additional hermeneutic element to the creation story by suggesting that Moses formulated this narrative in its current form in order to impose a linear structure on divine revelation, connecting the beginning with a continuum of Israelite history. Thus, the book Moses produced included all the information necessary for organizing and governing human society, including history and natural philosophy. But most importantly, it contained the necessary information for generations of Jews to imagine a material link between their own history as a people and the God of creation.

In his guidelines for reading and interpreting the biblical story of pre-human history, Nahmanides identified three crucial moments or steps in the transformation of Torah from revelation to holy text. His formulation implied that Moses received the complete Torah—from Genesis through Deuteronomy—through divine revelation, a non-textual, experiential encounter. Moses reproduced every detail of this revelation in textual form, then finally presented the text to the people of Israel at a discrete moment in history. The moment of revelation to the people of Israel occurred at the end of the clearly defined period of forty years during which time the nation wandered through the desert. According to Nahmanides, the time spent in the desert and the revelation were both, of course, revealed, and later inscribed, in the Torah itself in sequential order.

> And the reason for writing the Torah in this language is that it [the Torah] is more ancient than the creation of the world, and, needless to say, the birth of Moses. As it has come to us through tradition, it [the Torah] was written in black fire on a background of white fire.[43] Thus Moses is like a scribe who copied from an ancient book, so he wrote anonymously. It is true and clear that all the Torah, from the beginning of Genesis until "in the eyes of all of Israel" (Deut. 34:12) is

told from the mouth of the Lord, blessed is He, to the ears of Moses. As it is said elsewhere, "From His mouth He called to me all these words and I wrote in the book with my hands" (Jeremiah 36:18). [God] told [Moses] to start [the Torah] with the creation of the heavens and the earth and all their legions, that is to say, the creation of all created things, both upper and lower, and also all those things mentioned in prophecy and in the matter of the *Merkavah* (the divine chariot)[44] and the mysteries of creation and the tradition about them held by the sages, as well as the history of the four forces that are below, the force of minerals, of vegetation in the earth, the soul of motion, and the rational soul. [Knowledge about] all of these things was told to Moses our teacher, their creation, their essence, their powers and their actions and of the cessation of diminishment from them, and it is all written in the Torah, either explicitly or by implication.[45]

Nahmanides fluctuated between exacting temporal precision (i.e., his argument that Moses actually wrote or transcribed his revelation during the forty years in the wilderness, a creative process which concluded at the end of this period when Moses presented the textual rendition to his people) and a theory of authorship in which textuality, experience, and apprehension merged at an ambiguous, unspecified time. The revelation of Torah to Moses contained a past hitherto unknown to human beings. The creation story thus represented Israel's pre-history, or the absolute beginning of the nation's relationship with God. However, the Torah and the complete story it contained, existed, Nahmanides argued, prior to the creation of the physical world. This formulation implied a sequentially intriguing chain of causation: 1) the Torah preexisted the creation of the physical world as text made of fire on fire, and therefore 2) it served as a blueprint for creation itself; 3) following the expulsion of Adam and Eve from the Garden of Eden, the flood, the time of the patriarchs, and the twelve tribes, the Israelite people were enslaved in Egypt, until 4) they were liberated under the leadership and guidance of their God via Moses; 5) after four decades wandering in the wilderness they received God's revelation from Moses and they ultimately settled in God's country, where they built religious and political structures based on—even determined by—the story contained in the text revealed to Moses.

Nahmanides' treatment of Moses' authorial agency drew from and adapted several themes from traditional commentary.[46] The claim, for example, that Torah predates creation appears also in rabbinic sources.[47]

However, it serves a distinct purpose in Nahmanides' exegesis in so far as the early date of Torah undergirds an elaborate construction of the temporal relationship between the story, its teller, the scribe or prophet, and all those who have interpreted it over the generations. For Nahmanides a careful interpretation of the creation story was a prerequisite for entering into a true understanding of the biblical narrative. It also illuminated the structure necessary for fitting together the symbolic and plain meanings of events, national calamities and victories, and important individuals in the continually unfolding story of the people of Israel. By linking creation and history in this way, Nahmanides rendered the narrative of creation pertinent primarily to a nationally specific epoch. Genesis 1–2 became the story of Jewish time. He located the symbolic and material connection between the history of Israel and God's creation in the following sequence of beginnings: first, Torah as an a-temporal, non-physical document that existed prior to creation as "black fire on white fire;" second, God's acts of physical creation as related in the story with which the Torah begins; third, the revelation of Torah to Moses on Sinai; and finally, the symbolic sense that the six days of creation set the precedent for the structure of history. According to Nahmanides, an appreciation for the temporal and narrative complexity of the creation story can serve as a passage to the practical or historical meanings of scripture, as well as more deeply encoded meanings.

From Revelation to Torah

Nahmanides wrestled with a fundamental problem of representation and narrative in his commentary on Genesis. Storytelling necessitates a process of distinguishing between consequential and incidental narrative details, such as people, places, circumstances, etc. When discussing an event the storyteller is faced with the difficulty of determining where or when that event began. That beginning may vary greatly depending on who tells the story and to whom it is being told.[48]

Not surprisingly, the difficulty of distinguishing the important moments in a narrative continuum becomes necessarily much greater in the case of the incomparable story of divine creation. Nahmanides' argument that a perpetual cycle of beginnings was encoded first in the revelation and later in the narration of Torah represents an attempt to address this interpretive difficulty. The entire Torah, including the historical portions of Genesis, according to Nahmanides, preexisted creation in the form of "black fire written on white fire." With the creation of the physical world, God established the stage on which the human drama would be played out. According to this reading, the course of human history (at least until the time of Moses' death) was already mapped out before the beginning of time. The narrative structure of Torah both in its particular form, which dictated the form and details of biblical texts, and in its general form, which imposed a direction on history, thus transcended authorial agency.

The mode of interpretation presented by Nahmanides seems to throw biblical temporality and the time of its revelation to Moses on Sinai into question. Nahmanides took it for granted that God revealed the full story of creation to Moses, who then transcribed the story he received and presented it to the people of Israel. However, his claim that the Torah predated physical creation of the world complicated the time of textual beginning. The dissociation of the creation story as related in the Torah from the historical time and place in which it was revealed to Moses raises some important questions about how Nahmanides chose to interpret the relationship between time and the biblical narrative of creation. How did Nahmanides understand the connection between creation and materiality, and the nature of "before" or "after" in the pre-physical world? For example, if the Torah existed as black fire on white fire before the time of creation, and the Torah contained the story of creation, according to Nahmanides' interpretation when did creation begin? If the story of creation existed before the acts of creation occurred, what is the *peshat*, or the plain sense of this biblical portion? How did Nahmanides understand textuality, and what demands did text, particularly the holy text, make on the reader?[49]

Nahmanides concluded that the Torah was revealed in waves or cycles: as an extra physical or spiritual entity, "black fire written on the back of white fire," it preceded earthly time; as a narrative, containing the stories of creation and the history of the Jewish people, it provided the temporal structure for human life; and as a document written in a specific time and place and narrating events of the recent and distant past (relative to Moses), it preserved historical memory. Each of these temporal constructions and the meanings they signify operate simultaneously throughout the biblical text. For Nahmanides, the creation story provided the marker according to which human existence in general, and the history of the Jews in particular, could be measured, compared, and examined. Nahmanides took this one step further in his commentary on the six days of creation, suggesting that Torah, as a supremely generous gift from God to humanity, provided a means for organizing and structuring human activity, memory, and history. Torah is the narrative that imposes structure on human life, and the story of history, from its beginning until the messianic redemption. He concluded that the six days of creation represented and prefigured the human epoch of history: six thousand years of history followed by one thousand years of messianic redemption, during which conflicts between nations would end. Without Torah there would be no ritual and order linking the people of Israel to their God.[50]

At the same time, the creation story provided insight into the workings of the material world.[51] Accordingly, Nahmanides introduced a universally applicable exegetical method designed to render such texts clear. The exegete had first to identify the narrative structure, the simple story line. Then, having established the plain or simple meaning, one could employ other teachings and traditions to extrapolate deeper, hidden meanings.[52] Frequently interpretations according to *peshat* and *sod* appear neither to parallel or conflict with one another, but rather they seem linked in a material sense, such that an understanding of the former leads to an understanding of the latter. At those points when his commentary does hint at secrets contained in the biblical story—whether they be contained in narrative details, grammatical construction, word choice, or sentence structure—Nahmanides represented them as fundamentally linked to the *peshat*.[53] His commentary on Genesis 1:8 illustrates this method. In this verse, God renames the firmament (*rakiya*) heavens (*shamayim*). Nahmanides was troubled by the idea that God might change the name of something He had already formed without altering its substance. The confusion, he argued, arose from a detail in the flow of narrative which was implied rather than laid out explicitly. Throughout the first two verses the act of naming put the final touches on the thing created. Thus, the heavens (*shamayim*) were created as a watery mass or firmament (*rakiya*), then renamed when they assumed their final shape and substance. The plain sense, Nahmanides argued, was present in the name *shamayim*, which contains the word *mayim* or water. Once it became clear that the plain sense was related in the name of the heavens, information concerning the divine chariot and angels, which had been concealed in the verse, revealed itself.[54]

Nahmanides' treatment of Genesis emphasized an element of constant becoming. Likewise, the process of understanding Torah is constantly self-regenerating, each "way (or road) of truth" (*derekh ha-emet*) leading to another. The doctrine of divine emanations, which garnered only a fairly vague definition in his explication of Genesis 1:1, is by nature a never-ending process of separation and distinction.[55] The deeply textured nature of Nahmanides' reading of creation becomes fully apparent with his introduction of the doctrine of divine emanations as fundamental to the process of creation.

> Rashi wrote "this verse [Genesis 1:1] calls for interpretation. . . ." Our teachers explained that [the story starts this way] for the sake of the Torah, which is called *reshit* (beginning or first), as it says, "The Lord created me as the beginning of his way" (Proverbs 8:23); and for Israel, which is called *reshit*, as it says, "Israel is holy to the Lord, the *first* fruits of his increase" (Jeremiah 2:3). This midrash of our masters is very opaque and mysterious because they found many things that are called *reshit*, and for each of them there is an interpretation, and I am skeptical that they would tell them in their full detail. . . . Their intention here is that the word *bereshit* is a hint, since the world was created in ten emanations, and it refers to the emanation called *hokhmah* (wisdom), for the foundation of all is in it [*hokhmah*], as it is said "The Lord founded the earth by wisdom" (Proverbs 3:19).[56] It is a gift offering and it has no precise measure, for created beings have little understanding of it. And while man counts ten measures and explains one of the ten as a reference to ten *sefirot* so will the wise understand the tenth [emanation] and discuss it.[57]

This passage follows an extended discussion of the rabbinic interpretation of the first word of Genesis, *bereshit*, as corresponding throughout the Torah to the commandment to set aside a part of a larger mass (i.e., the first portion, or the *reshit*) for ritual purposes. Such instances include the ritual separation of a portion of dough for the weekly sabbath *hallah*, the separation of a portion of the harvest for the tithe, and the separation of a portion of the fruit harvest for the first fruit sacrifice, all of which are called *reshit*. In this case, Nahmanides made a symbolic link between creation through divine emanations and rituals of separation for the purpose of sacrifice required of God's people at appointed times. Separation is, by nature, sequential. It entails a methodical process of identification and definition: one must first identify the boundaries of the whole from which the smaller component will be taken before the latter can be removed and formed into a second, independent body. This portion of commentary implies that the doctrine of divine emanations worked in much the same way. The significance of this parallel in temporal terms is more telling when considered as one of a large number of historical renditions of the beginning that appear in his exegesis of Genesis.

The story of creation posed a unique set of difficulties for traditional Jewish exegesis. The early chapters of Genesis (until the revelation to Abraham in Genesis 12, but especially the first three chapters) represent perhaps the only portion of the Hebrew Bible that is necessarily inclusive of all living human beings, at least in the view of the narrative. Lacking active human characters, reference to any nation or group of people as chosen or preferred, or clear narrative parallels in any other portion of Torah, the first two chapters of Genesis open the door for general speculation about the relationship between God and the physical world, between man and nature, and the structure of history.

Nahmanides' biblical exegesis clothed innovative readings in the language of traditional biblical interpretation. His explication of the process and meaning of creation and the book of Genesis more generally stressed the importance of the creation narrative for understanding the complexities of change and development in human history. Using midrashic sources and medieval exegetes such as Rashi and Abraham ibn Ezra as his point of departure for his innovations, Nahmanides presented a method of reading creation which directly linked the divine creation of a human habitat with the dynamic relationship between humanity (in particular, the people of Israel) and God. He connected creation and history more solidly with the introduction of a two-tier typological model for reading historical portions of the biblical narrative. The first tier promoted the seven-day process of creation as the temporal model for the structure of history; while the second offered a typological model as the general rule for interpreting specific historical themes that repeat through the generations.

Casting the creation story as a model for human history, Nahmanides' reading emphasized the temporal complexity of the first biblical book. Telling and retelling the story of creation, revelation, and prophecy in increasingly sophisticated formulations, Nahmanides presented an interpretation he deemed appropriate for his generation. Because the sequential reading of Torah portions over the course of the calendar year liturgically links the story of creation to the transition from one year to the next, Jewish communities reenact the story of creation as a beginning year after year. As such, the creation story bears the distinction of being a pattern that is repeated at the communal and historical level and the inaccessible emblem of divine benevolence and power. Nahmanides captured and reified this paradox in his exegesis of Genesis.

Typological exegesis is a tool generally associated with Christian, rather than Jewish, biblical interpretation. In his ground-breaking article delineating the nature and limits of Nahmanides' typological or symbolic interpretation, Amos Funkenstein has shown that Nahmanides "insists far beyond midrashic reminiscences that the events and persons of which the Torah speaks—not the words themselves—are historiosophical symbols whether or not they are also theosophically relevant. They foreshadow, prefigure, and even predetermine events in the future of Israel."[58] The inspiration for Nahmanides' typological approach to biblical history, Funkenstein concludes, grew from a familiarity or contact with Christian biblical interpretation. The reasoning behind this argument is as follows. The rabbinic principle Nahmanides used to support his interpretation—"whatever happens to the fathers is a sign for the sons" (*kol mah she-ira la-avot simen la-venim*)—is cited only infrequently in the corpus of rabbinic literature. Second, in no earlier Jewish exegetical work was this principle applied as a general rule-of-thumb. Nahmanides set a precedent with his application of this rule to the entire literary body of stories concerning Abraham, Isaac, and Jacob.[59]

In most cases, these typologically relevant texts describe Israel's arrival at or exile from the Holy Land or encounters between Israel and other national bodies. Nahmanides' interpretation of typologies ascribes a material connection between events that share formal or linguistic similarities. For example, the stories relating sibling rivalries between the patriarchs and their brothers provide information about the individuals involved as well as important details about the structure of Israel's history and relationship with other nations. Finding that Nahmanides' typologies assumed more than superficial narrative similarities, Funkenstein questions why Nahmanides limited his application of this hermeneutic to events involving the patriarchs. He concludes that Nahmanides recognized typology to be a useful, if dangerous tool for understanding biblical history and thus his application was relatively restrained, particularly in comparison with Christian typological interpretations. Christian exegesis invokes typological interpretations as a means of accommodating the universalistic principle of Christian theology to the nationally exclusive narrative of the Hebrew Bible. According to Funkenstein, typological interpretation of biblical narrative enabled Christian theologians to demonstrate "the unity-within-diversity of two or more successive revelations."[60] Matching biblical narratives with known circumstances of Christian history thus provided a foundation for the Christian claim that Israel's chosenness had passed from the Jews to the Christians. For Nahmanides, on the other hand, typological interpretation was merely a means of explaining narrative relations within the limited scope of the history of the patriarchs, so that universalizing typologies tend not to explain all of human history. According to Funkenstein, Nahmanides applied typological exegesis only hesitantly because he recognized it as a hermeneutic device preferred by Christian biblical exegetes to demonstrate historical progress within a closely defined paradigm, and to shift the designation of chosenness from the Jews to the Christians.[61]

Funkenstein's question about the degree to which Jews felt comfortable sharing concepts and beliefs with their non-Jewish neighbors is essential. Nahmanides was of course enmeshed in the political and intellectual culture shared by Jews and Christians in the medieval Crown of Aragon. The historical record shows that Nahmanides engaged in dialogue with members of the Christian clergy over theological matters; he thus seems an appropriate measure of the nature of cultural exchange between Jews and Christians in the middle ages. The remainder of this chapter examines Nahmanides' typological model of biblical interpretation. Using typological exegesis, Nahmanides located symmetry and meaning in ancient history and order in recent events as well.

Nahmanides' interpretation of Genesis as a whole is saturated with observations and questions motivated by a deep interest in the shape and content of narrative. His exegetical method emphasized narrative moments representing human actions that had a profound effect on the history of Israel. When properly interpreted, these could provide insight into the structure of society and human interactions in general. According to Nahmanides' reading, the complete book of Genesis chronicled the foundational historical events in Israel's past, but at the same time, it comprised the blueprint for all of human history. Initially, this relationship between future events and their representation in Genesis appears to operate in Nahmanides' exegesis at the symbolic or hermeneutic level alone. At times it seems that the model of typological parallels simply explain biblical narrative in Nahmanides' view, not the vicissitudes of recent (or at least post-biblical) history. However, in conjunction with his interest in historical details, Nahmanides' methods for decoding the narrative significance of biblical stories also played a role in his analysis of the structure of historical change over the longer term in the post-biblical periods.

The sequential narrative of creation concludes with Genesis 2:3: "And God blessed the seventh day and sanctified it, for on [that day] He rested from all His work, which God created and did." This verse marks a moment of distinct narrative and discursive transition. From this point onward human mistakes and triumphs, not the shaping and formation of raw matter, command the attention of both the scriptural narrative and the active divine voice it represents. In his commentary on Genesis 2:3, Nahmanides advanced a general model which he used to interpret portions of Genesis that contained historical data. The hermeneutic challenge in this verse was posed by the repetition in the final clause of words indicating creative work: "which God created and did (*asher bara Elohim laasot*)." As is the case throughout his exegesis, Nahmanides introduced his commentary on the verse with a summary of the authoritative interpretations offered by Rashi and Abraham ibn Ezra: "'The work He would have done on Shabbat, He doubled and did on the sixth day,' as they said, according to Rashi, in *Bereshit Rabbah* (11:10). However, Rabbi Abraham [Ibn Ezra] said in accordance with its simple meaning that His work is the root of all things, that He gave them [i.e., God's creations] the ability to reproduce (*laasot*) according to their type."[62] Both Rashi and Abraham ibn Ezra emphasized doubling or multiplication as the operative meaning implied by the repetition of verbs indicating creative action, *laasot* and *bara*. Nahmanides, however, offered two interlinked alternative readings. The first restated the biblical verse, adding explanatory language where he perceived gaps (indicated in the following with italics): "It appears to me that the [proper] interpretation is that He rested from all His work, which was creating *something from nothing* (*yeish me-aiyin*) to make *from it* [i.e., the matter] *all the things mentioned during the six days*."[63] The added details clarify the purpose and sequence of creation: God made the matter and shaped it into forms during the first six days and then rested. After summarizing the events of creation he clarified the syntax of the creation story. The reiteration or doubling of verbs meaning "to create" or "to do" in Genesis 2:3 alluded to—and concluded—the twofold meaning and enactment of creation which is the subtext throughout the narrative of Genesis 1:1–2:3. This claim built on the observation that the verb "create" (*bara*) appears in only three verses in the story of creation: first in Genesis 1:1, "In the beginning God created the heavens and the earth. . . (*bereshit bara Elohim et ha-shamayim ve-et ha-aretz*)"; three times in Genesis 1:27, "And God created (*yevra*) the man in his image, in the image of God he created (*bara*) him, male and female he created (*bara*) them;" and finally in Genesis 2:3, the closing verse of the creation story, "And God blessed the seventh day, and sanctified it, because in it He rested from all his work which God had created and made." In every other act of creation—from the shaping of the firmament to formation of the animals—the verb "made" (*asah*) signals the reshaping of matter to form important components of the physical environment that would house human beings. Nahmanides' commentary emphasized the verbal distinction between "create," as a purely innovative act, and "make," as the manipulation of existing material. This indicates that the only true act of creation out of nothingness occurred at the first moment of time when God created the primordial matter of the heavens and the earth. The rest of creation was a process of making forms and shaping matter, which were subsequently fixed or completed with the statement "and God saw that it was good."[64] The verbs "to create" and "to make" in the concluding statement of the creation narrative thus reflect the true order and process of divine creation.

At this juncture in his commentary—in his discussion of the final verse of the creation narrative—Nahmanides introduced his model for interpreting history. Each day of creation represented a one thousand year historical epoch; the historical drama would culminate with the messianic redemption in the seventh and final epoch. An acute attention to sequence, a sense that all events must occur at their proper time, is integral to this understanding of the Jewish past, and, one might argue from Nahmanides' perspective, the present and future as well.[65] Nahmanides' reading of Genesis 2:3 preserved the transitional function of this verse, while at the same time reinscribing it as a gloss on all of God's work from the beginning of time to the end of days. It provided the foundation for an interpretive method applicable to the remaining historical biblical portions.

After demonstrating that "to make" (*laasot*) represented something separate from "created" (*bara*), Nahmanides argued that the doubling of verbs in Genesis 2:3 also distinguished between different kinds of actions: *bara* referred to the work of creating and shaping matter, while *laasot* heralded the inscription of formalized historical epochs in the Torah, represented by the days of creation. "Know that something more is included in the word 'to make,' that the six days of creation are all the days of the world, that is, the world will exist for six thousand years. In this regard they (the rabbis) said, 'A day for the Lord is equal to a thousand years' (*Bereshit Rabbah* 9.12)."[66]

Nahmanides developed the symbolism for his historical interpretation of the six days of creation in some detail, linking the physical conditions described for each day with the moral, political, or social conditions most indicative of a corresponding historical period.[67] The first two days, during which the world was covered with water—and, according to Nahmanides, before any act of creation was completed—represented the first two thousand years of history. This period included the lives of Adam and Eve, the antediluvian generation, and the generation of Abraham's birth. Although selected individuals benefited from God's intercession during this period, God did not establish a solid covenant with any nation or individual at this time. The unfinished condition of the world during the first two days of creation paralleled the fluidity of human relations with God before the notion of a chosen people was established under the covenant with Abraham. The third day, characterized by the appearance of dry land and vegetation, corresponded with the lives of the patriarchs and their descendants until the revelation on Mount Sinai. God established a covenant with the patriarchs during this period, which laid the foundation for the revelation of an organized and unique law. The sun, moon, and stars appeared on the fourth day. According to Nahmanides, this day corresponded to the construction of the First and Second Temples, the physical symbols of God's domain on earth, and subsequent years during which the Israelites worshipped there. Like the luminaries, the Temples provided temporal structure to the daily life of Israel. The fifth day, when creeping, crawling creatures freely roamed the earth, represented the one thousand year period of exile following the destruction of the Second Temple "since during this time the nations will rule over them [i.e., the Jewish people] and they will be made like the 'fish of the sea, the crawling creatures that have no ruler over them. . . ' (Habakuk 1:14)."[68] The sixth day, split between the blessing permitting the animals to reproduce with mates of their own kind and the creation of man, represented a period of foreign rule followed by redemption. Finally, the seventh day, when God rested from the work of creation, signified the world to come.

The linkage of the creation week with the structure of world history held an important place in biblical exegesis during late antiquity. In addition to the fact that a six thousand year historical plan is a prominent theme in Christian theology,[69] mention of "the world week" is included also in the rabbinic literature. In Sanhedrin 97a–b, the six thousand year history is one of several possible world chronologies that the rabbis of the Talmud suggest could unfold before the coming of the messiah. "Rabbi Elijah said the [history of] the world will be six thousand years. Two thousand of *tohu*, two thousand of Torah, and two thousand days[70] of the Messiah."[71] However, there are structural and symbolic differences between Nahmanides' use of the six thousand year model and its talmudic application. Rabbi Elijah implicitly placed his generation roundly in the period of Torah. Rabbinic discourse was in large part an effort to iron out the ambiguities of living a life of Torah outside a political institution organized around the rituals of the Temple. During Nahmanides' lifetime, however, the demands and challenges to organized Jewish life in the diaspora were quite different. The institutions of Jewish communal autonomy in the diaspora were long since well established, organized around the practical examples contained in the Talmud.[72] Nahmanides was aware that Rabbi Elijah lived nearly one thousand years before him, which meant that the period of Torah was drawing to a close.

Nahmanides' interpretation of the sixth day is the most complex and well developed. His own generation was, according to this reckoning, balanced near the tail end of the final six thousand year epoch because the most is at stake in the penultimate epoch in God's historical plan. The biblical story of divine creation is laid out incrementally, the work of each day building on the previous day. Human capacity for understanding scripture, for recognizing the significance of historical events, improved with the approach of the six thousand year mark. "On the sixth day in the morning, [God said] 'Let the earth bring forth the animal according to its own kind, cattle and crawling things, and creatures of the earth according to their own kind' (Gen. 1:24). This creation came before the sun rose. . . . Then man was created in the image of God. . . . "[73] The creation of man in God's image signaled a move toward human understanding, in Nahmanides' view, as a step in a long process that had been underway in historical terms since the founding of the covenant.

If historical periods are read as symbolic reflections of the days of creation to which they correspond, then the defining events of each day of creation must be represented as comparable to the dominant features of the corresponding historical epoch. After laying a scriptural foundation for his characterization of the final thousand year epoch of history, he extended this reading to its symbolic representation.

> This is the sixth period of a thousand years, at the beginning of which the animals ruled. They signify the kingdoms that know nothing of God. After a tenth of it, like the portion that the sunrise is to the day,[74] the savior will come
>
> .... This is a son of David created in the image of God, as it is written, "And behold one like a son of man came with the clouds of heaven, and came to the ancient of days, and they brought him near before him. And there was given him dominion, and glory, and a kingdom" (Daniel 7:13–14).

An assumption that this process must rationally follow a progressive trajectory from base to exalted, from primitive to fully matured, supported Nahmanides' entire symbolic system. However, only in the description of the sixth day did he provide clear and precise temporal boundaries within which this transformation would take place. The application of this symbolic method also incorporated the twists and turns of the biblical narrative to account for the complexity of social units and individual motivations.

> It will be one hundred and eighteen years after the fifth thousand year period, that the word of God in the mouth of Daniel will be completed. "And from the time that the daily sacrifice shall be taken away, and the abomination that makes desolate be set up there shall be one thousand two hundred and ninety days" (Daniel 12:11).[75] It appears from the change of days from the creature that swarms in the water and the bird and the animal on the earth that, at the beginning of the sixth period of a thousand years, there will be a new kingdom of ruling people "dreadful and terrible, and exceedingly strong" (Daniel 7:7).[76]

Verses from Genesis and Daniel provided Nahmanides with evidence that the Jewish people should expect redemption at a specific moment in their history. This interpretation demanded that the reader see elements of the scriptural narrative reflected in the vicissitudes of history in the long term and in everyday life. The creation story thus had a double purpose in Nahmanides' understanding of the shape and meaning of history. It was both the prototype for the duration and sequence of events in human history and the key for unlocking the complicated biblical narrative in its entirety. Nahmanides' interpretive method required that the reader remain aware of both elements, allowing both levels of meaning to converge in the messianic promise.

To guide the interpretation of specific historical events, Nahmanides invoked a rabbinic exegetical rule: "what happens to the fathers is a sign for the sons." A variation of this exegetical rule is formulated in the *Midrash Tanhuma*, on Genesis 12 in a discussion of Abraham and the events leading to his name change and his covenant with God. In its original context, the application of this formula is clearly limited to the patriarchs: "It is a sign transmitted from God to Abraham that all that happens to him will be a sign for his sons" (*mah she-ira le-avot simen le-venim*).⁷⁷ This interpretive device thematizes specific or isolated local political, social, and religious conditions. However, Nahmanides introduced it as part of a complex conception of historical time and change.

> *And Abram passed through the land until he reached Shekhem* (Genesis 12:6). I [now] tell you a rule you will use to understand each of the coming verses concerning Abraham, Isaac, and Jacob. This is a great matter that the rabbis mentioned briefly in passing, saying "all that happened to the fathers is a sign for their sons" (*Midrash Tanhuma, Lekh lekha,* 12). Thus, the scriptures elucidate this in the story of the travels [of the patriarchs], the digging of the wells, and the remaining events. Lest one should think that these [stories] are unimportant or of no benefit, all of them are intended to teach about the future, for when an event happens to [one] of the three fathers, it should be understood that such is decreed to come to his offspring (*le-zaro*) as well.⁷⁸

The Midrash makes an explicit rule pertaining to the patriarchs and their sons (*benim*). Rather than replicate this formula, Nahmanides replaced the word "sons" (*benim*) with the openly inclusive term *zaro*—"his seed" or "his offspring." In this case he replicated the language of Genesis 12:7, the story of God's blessing of Abraham: "And God appeared to Abram and said 'to your seed I will give this land.'" By substituting a more general term, Nahmanides expanded the rabbinic formula and transformed it into a statement about the interconnection of events in Jewish history.

Nahmanides applied this rule throughout his commentary on Genesis. He argued, for example, that the struggle for primacy between Jacob and Esau will be repeated indefinitely by their descendants. In his introduction to the Torah portion *Va-yishlah* (Genesis 32) he made this argument explicitly:

> This portion was written to show that the Holy One, may He be blessed, saved His servant and "redeemed him from the hand of one who was stronger than he was" (Jeremiah 31:11), "and sent him an angel who saved him" (Numbers 20:16). Moreover, it is to teach us that he [Jacob] did not trust his [Esau's] righteousness and that he worked for his salvation with all his might. There is another lesson to the generations, which is that everything that occurred between our father and his brother Esau will occur always (*tamid*) to us (in our relations) with Esau's sons. . . . Our Rabbis already saw this allusion in this portion, as I will show.[79]

As Nahmanides himself pointed out, the symbolic representation of Esau as the subjugator or political enemy of the Jewish people was a common theme in rabbinic literature.[80] But as the application of a general exegetical rule, rather than an isolated instance in which a theme makes itself apparent, this observation allowed his reader to speculate about how contemporary changes and events fit into the narrative of Jewish history presented in his commentary on creation.

In his interpretation of the portions of Genesis that follow the creation story, Nahmanides maintained an accurate account of ages and periods of time between events, especially when the narrative provides sequentially inconsistent or confusing details. Biblical accounts of human life-spans, including lists of generations and the details recounting the lives and deeds of individuals in the antediluvian era, provided him with the material for a complete tally of the number of years that comprised each of the first five periods of one thousand years. For example, Nahmanides established a method for decoding genealogical lists in his commentary on the first reference to a biblical human life-span, a chronology of Adam's life (Genesis 5:1–4).[81] The biblical narrative recounts that "Adam lived one hundred and thirty years and bore a son in his own image and appearance, and he called his name Seth; and the days of Adam after he bore Seth were eight hundred and thirty years" (Genesis 5:3–4). According to Nahmanides, the number of years mentioned in this verse represent real years counted on a human calendar. Moreover, responding to Maimonides' claim that only those individuals mentioned by name enjoyed the extraordinarily long life-spans listed in the early genealogies, and then only by virtue of miraculous intervention,[82] Nahmanides argued that the life-span of several hundred years was normal for men of this era; the number of years men lived decreased substantially following the flood.[83] Nahmanides allowed for even the most imprecise temporal information revealed in the Bible, such as "a generation" (*dor*), to be tallied at the greatest possible value. This was of great importance for Nahmanides' extended agenda of counting the exact number of years elapsed since creation or the time destined to pass until redemption. Since his tally was based on the interval of an average human life represented in the Bible, the final sum would vary significantly if the standard of measurement was, for example, a life-span of seventy, rather than 190, years.[84]

Though Nahmanides' interpretation employed rabbinic prooftexts, his adaptation embellished and reformulated the bare outline presented in his sources. What was a mere allusion in Sanhedrin 97 a-b—in fact, one among many—became for Nahmanides the basis for a complete and fully developed mode of reading historical periods and events as singular, unique, and timely. Breaking the periods into six blocks of one thousand years, rather than the model of three two thousand year historical periods suggested by Rabbi Elijah in the Talmud, allowed for more precision in depicting each epoch's historical characteristics and drawing out themes of historical and spiritual change with greater clarity. Using this historiographic pattern as a template, Nahmanides laid the foundation for a hermeneutic that could systematically assign meaning to events and changes in the temporal world. This model provided a method for organizing and making sense of historical data contained in the Torah and Hebrew prophecy and ultimately for constructing a time frame for the messianic era. In his estimation, the period of redemption was due to commence nearly one hundred years after the time he was writing. He developed similar calculations in his account of the Barcelona disputation and *Sefer ha-Geulah* (*The Book of Redemption*), in which he drew out the implications and importance of prophetic allusions to redemption.

Historical Time and the Search for the Messianic Era

The novelty of Nahmanides' approach in Jewish hermeneutics is most apparent in his promotion of a typological method of reading sacred texts as a universally applicable interpretive principle. This universalization was developed to its fullest extent as Nahmanides guided his reader through the narrative transition from Genesis, a book of historical foundations, to Exodus, in which fragments of history were endowed with meaning and structure through the invention of law and government.

> This completes the scripture of the Book of Genesis, which is the story of the original formation of the world (*siper ha-yetzirah be-hidush ha-olam*)[85] and the formation of all creation, and of all the deeds of the fathers, which are like a type of formation for their seed [i.e., offspring], because all their deeds are figures[86] of things alluding to and informing of all the future that will come to them [i.e., their progeny or seed].[87]

He thus concluded his interpretation of the creation story—that is, the portion that chronologically precedes any human drama—by defining the preceding story as the prototype for all human history from the time of Moses' death until the promised redemption.

For Nahmanides, understanding the vicissitudes of history was an essential step in the effort to elicit meaning from the scriptures. His commentary returned again and again to analysis of periods of human history and the rhythm of social, religious, and political change. Whether presented explicitly, as in the case of the history of the patriarchs, or submerged in narrative allusion, such as the six thousand year epochs Nahmanides teased out of the story of creation, the historical layer of the Bible provided a means of actively integrating the story of creation as told in Genesis with the history of God's chosen people and the promise of redemption. He understood the Torah as a single unit consisting of countless inextricably linked individual parts, forming a web of interconnected meanings, and governed by a host of interpretive tools passed orally from one generation to the next since the time of Moses. This rendering of the Torah served an important didactic purpose. Sequential and historically conscious exegesis accounted for and codified Jewish dispersion, the failure of political sovereignty, and the anticipation of future redemption as part of a single, linear process. Nahmanides examined the sequential arrangement of words and text to arrive at the *peshat* or plain meaning in his commentary on the creation narrative. Accounting for the relative sequence of narrative and action also played an important role in his reading and signification of individual historical circumstances and events, such as the patriarchs' behavior and motivations. Amos Funkenstein has shown that Nahmanides' exegesis works at a specifically figurative level. "[J]ust as the more mature Christian exegetes do, [Nahmanides] distinguishes clearly between words and images describing an event on the one hand, and the events themselves on the other: typological analogies rest only on the latter."[88] However, by focusing exclusively on the symbolic aspect of his historical exegesis, Funkenstein effectively negates—or at the least underplays—the fact that practical historical reckoning was a dominant theme throughout Nahmanides' writings. The position Nahmanides took in his public debate with Friar Paul, and later in *Sefer ha-Geulah*, was informed by the view that the quality and quantity of historical time were the byproducts of the divine model established with the six days of creation. Thus, the Bible comprises not just a narrative representation of the shape of historical time, but also the real physical embodiment of the divine plan. Nahmanides called upon the revealed text's narrative flow, grammatical construction, and numerical value of symbols, words, and events embedded in the Torah to confirm this conception of biblical meaning. The crucial element in this view of text and history is the steadfast belief that time itself was purposeful, that it was organized in a manner that provided a qualitative and quantitative rhythm to the generations of human life.[89]

Musings about messianic expectation were certainly not unknown in medieval Jewish exegesis. As Gerson Cohen has noted, Rashi, in his search for the *peshat* or "plain meaning" of the text, could not help but take at face value the precise predictions in Daniel and the Talmud of when the Messiah would arrive.[90] Like many other medieval Jewish exegetes, Rashi took on the question of when messianic redemption might begin only when explicating direct biblical or talmudic references to the issue. However there are some important examples of exegetes who did seek out questions related to the time of messianic redemption. In his *Megilat ha-Megaleh* (*Scroll of the Redeemer*) Abraham bar Hiyya, the early twelfth-century philosopher and scholar, presented a painstakingly argued six thousand year model of world history.[91] In this reading as well, each one thousand year period reflected the tone and content of the corresponding day of divine creation.[92] Although it circulated widely during the period, there is no evidence that Nahmanides was familiar with this work, and he never referred to it in his exegesis. Still, the historical schema outlined by Abraham bar Hiyya and Nahmanides shared a sense of historical direction or purpose, as well as a certain immediacy attached to the need to understand historical change. Both used the parallel between world history and creation as the basis for a messianic theology, the climax of which both believed would commence in the not too distant future. But the similarities end there. Abraham bar Hiyya presented his theosophy with the precision and discipline of a philosopher, using this historical philosophy to gloss the condition of the collective intellect and the role of history as a means of cleansing the stain of sin from the human spirit.[93]

Nahmanides, on the other hand, did not concern himself, at least not overtly, with the same philosophical or metaphysical questions that occupied much of Abraham bar Hiyya's writing. Instead, in Nahmanides' writings on the messianic redemption, the relationship between the Jewish people, their literature of divine revelation, and a theory that a clear historical direction or purpose seeps from these works all become part of a single interpretive framework. He tried not only to understand revelation, but also to guide his reader to discover a direct link between revelation and recent history. Nahmanides' pedagogy utilized the idiom and method of traditional biblical exegesis—constantly calling attention to authoritative interpretations—while advancing innovative methods and interpretations of the prehistory of creation or revelation. His interpretation assigned a prescriptive *and* descriptive power to the story of creation. Genesis 1–2 is a depiction of God's creation, but according to Nahmanides, it also set the course of events and provided the shape for history. Creation, biblical history, and the full history of Israel were molded in narrative form prior to the actual creation of the world (in accordance with the Midrash which described the Torah as an a-temporal text written in "black fire on a background of white fire"). The history revealed to Moses, including the story of creation, was at the same time an enactment of this prehistoric narrative and a blueprint for what would come. Finally, in Nahmanides' view, the story of creation had direct consequences on the way history would unfold in the long term, even until his own day.

It has been well established that Jews have traditionally used sacred narrative as an interpretive paradigm for giving meaning to apparently senseless catastrophe.[94] But in Nahmanides' hands this interpretive process was inverted. Rather than use the biblical narrative as a model to show why history failed to follow another perhaps more appealing path, Nahmanides used the biblical example to demonstrate that Israel had arrived at precisely the historical and temporal moment projected in the creation narrative.

CHAPTER THREE

The Barcelona Disputation

Text, Rhetoric, and Cultural Politics

IN THE SUMMER OF 1263, KING JAMES THE CONQUEROR OF ARAGON (1213–1276) called upon Nahmanides to face a certain Friar Paul Christiani,[1] a convert from Judaism to Christianity, in a public debate at the royal palace in Barcelona. The disputants were to address several questions of immediate consequence to the Jewish claim that their messianic redemption was still imminent. According to the set agenda, Nahmanides was to defend the Jews' continued expectation of messianic redemption against evidence culled from Jewish sources, which showed, Friar Paul claimed, that the rabbis of the Talmud believed the Jewish messiah had already come in the person of Jesus. Arguments based on biblical texts had provided the mainstay for more than one thousand years of religious disputation and disagreement between Christianity and Judaism.[2] However, the novelty of Friar Paul's approach lay in the fact that he drew evidence from the Talmud to support his claim that Jesus was the messiah promised to the people of Israel in the Bible.[3]

The disputation in Barcelona was recorded in two contemporary accounts, one written in Hebrew and the other in Latin. These accounts provide the only extant documentary evidence of the event, but their provenance commands respect. The Hebrew version, written from Nahmanides' perspective, almost certainly by Nahmanides himself,[4] is a detailed narrative in dialogue form.[5] It claims to present an accurate account of the debate including arguments advanced by both disputants and commentary and interjections from the audience. The Latin document, on the other hand, offers only a bare outline of the issues addressed during the debate.[6] The Latin author is unknown, but the text carries the royal seal of the Crown of Aragon.[7] With sparse detail, this version succinctly highlights the rabbi's rapid and irrevocable humiliation.

The Hebrew and Latin accounts essentially agree as to the agenda and topics of discussion. However, they present very different views of the tone and outcome of the discussion between the rabbi and the friar. It is at the points of disparity between the two accounts that they bear witness to the shared and contested currency of historical and exegetical discourse between Jews and Christians.[8] Questions about the reliability or veracity of the documentary evidence have been addressed at length—and to little avail—in the voluminous secondary literature on the disputation. As these accounts naturally represent very different versions of the disputation itself, such issues will not be of concern here. Instead, this chapter will examine the Hebrew narrative with a particular focus on the strategies Nahmanides employed to preserve and document the encounter.

Many of the basic details of the Barcelona disputation of 1263 are already quite familiar to students of Jewish history and Jewish-Christian polemics. Friar Paul converted from Judaism to Christianity as an adult. The details of his life prior to his conversion, however, remain fairly vague. What we do know has largely been pieced together from Jewish responses to his missionizing efforts. He studied with at least two highly reputed rabbis in his native Montpellier, one of whom, Rabbi Jacob ben Elijah of Venice, composed a rejoinder to Paul's arguments against the Talmud and Judaism.[9]

Jeremy Cohen has suggested that Friar Paul's conversion was precipitated by a dramatic disillusionment with the authority of traditional rabbinic sources, and with the *Aggadah* in particular.[10] Though Friar Paul left no testimonial delineating the events and emotions that precipitated his conversion, Cohen's explanation is quite compelling. Friar Paul's early education in Montpellier provides one clue. Maimonidean philosophy and Rabbi Solomon ben Abraham's anti-Maimonidean campaign had both struck deep roots during the first half of the thirteenth century. On the basis of a polemical letter written by Friar Paul's former teacher, Jacob ben Elijah, Cohen suggests that Paul became despondent over the conflict between two very different understandings of how Judaism and its canonical works should be interpreted.[11] In addition, Dominican friars, under the leadership of Raymond de Peñaforte, were represented in great numbers in and around Montpellier. Friar Paul was probably converted by and was certainly a student of Raymond de Peñaforte, who was instrumental in founding language institutes where friars were instructed in Hebrew and Arabic so they could use native sources to demonstrate that the precepts and sacred texts of Judaism and Islam led to Christianity. Under Raymond de Peñaforte's tutelage Friar Paul dedicated himself to Christianity. He brought to his new faith what he believed was a deep understanding of rabbinic literature and religiosity, both of which, he argued, pointed to the veracity of the Christian claim that Jesus was the promised messiah described at length in the Bible and Talmud.

The disputation in Barcelona apparently lasted four days and was attended by many local lay and clerical notables as well as representatives from the Jewish community.[12] Contemporary evidence leaves no reason to believe that the various parties dispersed on terms that were anything but amicable: Nahmanides returned to Girona with a generous monetary gift from King James, and the king also granted the friars permission to continue their missionary work with the Jews in the Crown of Aragon.[13]

But while the disputation itself apparently passed without incident, a controversy immediately erupted around the documents produced in its aftermath. Two Latin documents preserved in the royal chancellery refer to an official accusation of blasphemy brought against Nahmanides by Friar Paul and two of his Dominican brothers, Raymond de Peñaforte and Arnold de Segarra.[14] The first is a report of proceedings that were held in the royal court in 1265.[15] The friars who instigated the disputation submitted a petition to the papal court demanding that Nahmanides be punished for falsely representing the debate and spreading blasphemous statements. They claimed that Nahmanides "said various punishable words about our Lord and about the whole Catholic faith [during the disputation], and made them into a book, a copy of which he gave to the Bishop of Girona."[16] According to the same document, Nahmanides argued in his own defense that he composed his narrative as a favor to the bishop of Girona, who had requested a written account of the disputation between himself and Friar Paul. None of Nahmanides' adversaries contradicted his claim that the bishop requested the rabbi's record of the disputation. The friars' complaint specified that Nahmanides wrote and circulated an account of the debate that framed the rabbi as the clear victor. It is impossible to determine with certainty whether the extant Hebrew text bears any likeness to the document Nahmanides wrote in either Latin or, more likely, Catalan for the bishop of Girona; however, based on the friars' description of Nahmanides' work, it seems unlikely that the Hebrew and vernacular versions were entirely unrelated. Unfortunately, Nahmanides' account remains today only in the Hebrew recension. The second of these documents is a letter from Pope Clement IV to James I of Aragon charging that the outcome of this hearing, a sentence of two years of exile from the Crown of Aragon, was insufficient punishment for the crime of blasphemy.[17]

Approximately two years had passed between the disputation and the controversy over Nahmanides' presentation of his account to the bishop of Girona. This fact, together with the disparity of both style and content between the Latin and Hebrew disputation accounts, the lack of documentary evidence of the Catalan version of Nahmanides' account, and doubt about the amount of freedom Nahmanides claimed to have enjoyed during the debate have given scholars in the modern period ample basis on which to debate the veracity of one or the other document.

The texts recording this controversy shed some light on several of the key issues of the controversy that followed the disputation. The Latin sources, including the Latin disputation account, hint at a taut and complicated web of relations between the king, the pope and the friars, the bishop of Girona, the Jewish community of Barcelona, and Nahmanides. However, the precise details of this conflict are difficult, if not impossible, to discern. Aside from the fact that the punishment meted out by the king was viewed by the authors of the petition and their papal sponsor as insufficient, even the positions adopted by the various players remain unclear.

Rather than add to the already considerable scholarship speculating about what actually happened in 1265 and why, I turn my attention to the mechanism of public memory Nahmanides utilized with his narrative reconstruction of the dispute. The difficulty in understanding or accounting for the relationship between form and content in Nahmanides' account of the disputation seems to have its roots in Nahmanides' failure (or refusal?) to clarify who was his intended audience for this text, and what would have been its desired effect. Nahmanides' disputation account gives voice to several facets of social and cultural exchange between Jews and Christians in medieval Aragon that remain largely unexplored in contemporary scholarship on the disputation and the documents that record it. The present chapter examines the rhetorical structure of this contemporary discussion and of the Hebrew disputation account itself. I aim to depart from the course that much of the scholarship on the disputation has taken, which frequently replicates the tone and tenor of the textual evidence of the event. In this chapter, I will pursue an alternative line of analysis, departing from questions of verisimilitude and authenticity and focusing instead on the styles of social, cultural, and intellectual engagement that are represented in the Hebrew disputation account.

Medieval Polemics and the Politics of Modern Jewish Scholarship

> [I]t is striking to see how often historical work is held hostage to impossible oppositions—say, between truth and fiction, objectivity and partiality, knowledge and ethics, science and art. Historical research and writing are bound to seem intellectually incoherent on one side or another of these alleged extremes.[18]

Carlo Ginzburg has observed that human beings embrace the common practice of forming meaningful narratives around discrete fragments of evidence. "Man had been a hunter for thousands of years. In the course of countless chases he learned to reconstruct the shapes and movements of his invisible prey from tracks on the ground, broken branches, odors. He learned to sniff out, record, interpret, and classify such infinitesimal traces as trails of spittle. He learned how to execute complex mental operations with lightening speed, in the depth of a forest or in a prairie with its hidden dangers."[19] In like manner, historians, physicians, critics have learned to follow 'clues' sprinkled throughout the physical form and countenance or demeanor of the objects of their study to make broad conclusions about the nature of a given community, individual, or event.[20] Historians, of course, piece together unifying narratives and analyses from disparate, often fragmentary textual evidence. This project, especially when applied to the analysis of the premodern world, is characteristically a complex one. Since historical narratives are inevitably informed by a wide array of factors, including historical or social memory—a body of common knowledge about the past as it pertains to a group, whether it be a national, cultural, or social past—the process of interpreting documents, the questions asked of evidence, and the kind of information sources yield to any given scholar will necessarily be shaped by the trajectory of analysis followed by those who interrogated the sources in the past as well as individually determined interests, biases, and bodies of knowledge.

Likewise, scholarship on the Barcelona disputation has been guided by deeply entrenched and contentious patterns of scholarly discourse. A good deal of the research on the debate in Barcelona and the documents that record it tries to gauge the significance and impact the surviving documents had on political and interfaith relations in the Crown of Aragon and throughout Europe during the latter half of the thirteenth century. Much of this literature is apologetic in nature. It is rooted in the conceptually problematic, even anachronistic terminology of victory and defeat; in many cases, modern scholars have attempted to expiate Nahmanides' failure to avoid the awkward and potentially dangerous circumstances of a public debate about issues of faith. There has been a tendency to place the Barcelona disputation at a crucial point in the litany of attacks and humiliations suffered at the hands of Christians, beginning with the Crusades and flowing contiguously and inevitably to the violent persecution inflicted by the Spanish Inquisition.[21] Until now, the dominant strain of this scholarship has replicated the adversarial climate implied by the structure of a politically mandated religious disputation. What seems to elude this mode of analysis, however, is the degree to which culture, language, and even discursive methods were shared by Jews and Christians, making this kind of public discussion possible and, for the Christians, desirable.[22]

The documents that remain from the Barcelona disputation preserve traces of the codes of behavior that governed cultural, social, and political interactions between Jews and Christians. Yet attempts to demonstrate the veracity of one or the other disputation account have diverted attention from the political and cultural nuances that could be gleaned from these documents. Nahmanides' claim that the various Christian authorities in attendance granted him freedom and candor of expression has been the stage for significant contention. Because Robert Chazan has reviewed this secondary literature at length,[23] a full survey is unnecessary here; I will focus instead on three loci of debate in the contemporary scholarship: 1) the veracity of Nahmanides' account; 2) Nahmanides' objective in circulating his disputation account; and 3) the authenticity of the Hebrew narrative.

Many analyses of the Hebrew and Latin narratives pivot on questions of verisimilitude:[24] Which of the two documents is more plausible? Which details were fabricated and why? This thrust in the twentieth-century scholarship can be attributed, at least partially, to the fact that the earliest analyses of the Hebrew and Latin accounts were driven by a polemical effort to expose one medieval author or the other as a blatant liar who intentionally invented details of his report to deceive his reader. Heinrich Graetz, one of the leading figures of *Wissenschaft des Judentums*, articulated this view for the first time in 1865.[25] Based on a comparison of the Hebrew and Latin accounts of the disputation, Graetz concluded that the author of the Latin document deliberately misrepresented the proceedings in hopes of repairing any damage that Nahmanides' successful refutation of Friar Paul's arguments may have caused to the friars' mission to convert the Jews.[26] This analysis largely focuses on the incommensurability between the Latin and Hebrew accounts in terms of style as well as content. Graetz thus used his examination of the disputation documents as an opportunity to imply that powerful men in Latin Christendom, and in the Church in particular, used their position of power to routinely falsify the historical record pertaining to Jewish-Christian relations during the middle ages.

Graetz's article engendered a heated debate with Heinrich Denifle, a noted scholar of the Christian middle ages. Denifle's response was equally polemical. He argued that it was Nahmanides, not the author of the Latin chronicle, who fabricated facts to conceal his miserable failure in defending his faith. The Graetz-Denifle debate set the agenda for subsequent treatments of the disputation. The late nineteenth-century French scholar, Isadore Loeb and, to a lesser extent, Yitzhak Baer reevaluated the verity of Nahmanides' account in relation to its Latin counterpart.[27] Both concluded that Nahmanides' account was less than absolutely accurate.

Since the direction and tenor of the prevailing secondary scholarship plays an important role in shaping the questions addressed by subsequent authors, the issues of comparative reliability and facticity continue to guide disputation scholarship. By the turn of the twentieth century more was at stake in the evaluation of Nahmanides' account than a contest between Jewish and Christian master narratives of medieval history. More recent examinations of the Hebrew narrative move to distance Nahmanides from the details provided in the narrative, even from the document itself. Driving this debate is an effort to make sense of the controversy that followed the distribution of Nahmanides' narrative account. If one of the two accounts can be classified as accurate, then it stands to reason that the other must have deliberately contrived to misrepresent what happened.

Along these lines several studies have considered what may have motivated the politically experienced, savvy rabbi to circulate a potentially volatile work during a period of increased Christian scrutiny of the inner workings of Jewish learning and literature.[28] The form of narrative and the levity of its tone suggest that Nahmanides wrote his disputation account for the purpose of popular distribution. Yet this supposition has garnered a great deal of speculation about what prompted Nahmanides to publicize a text arguing that *aggadot* (non-halakhic—non-legal—portions of the Midrash and Talmud) were not authoritative or binding. Non-legal portions of the rabbinic canon are of little significance for defining the parameters of ritual or behavior. This genre of literature was the target of pointed criticism by Maimonides and the heirs to his philosophical school of rabbinic criticism. Defenders of the traditional and literary value of *aggadot*, however, argued that the historical, moral, and ethical values contained in these stories were essential to Jewish culture and rabbinic scholarship. *Aggadot* also served an important function in the mystical mode of both narrative and hermeneutics represented in the *Sefer ha-Zohar*, the *magnum opus* of the still young mystical movement of Kabbalah.[29] In this context, they were largely interpreted allegorically, deriving from enigmatic hints about the nature of God and redemption. Nahmanides' association with the early kabbalists in Girona is, of course, well known. He played an important role in disseminating and popularizing kabbalistic hermeneutics—or at least making the tools of mystical interpretation accessible to a wide audience of readers—in his biblical commentary.[30]

Nahmanides' argument in the disputation account that *aggadot* are neither binding, nor definitive of dogma—a strategy of argument attested to in the Hebrew and Latin disputation accounts—thus has seemed to several scholars writing in the middle of the twentieth century especially problematic in light of his involvement with the nascent school of kabbalistic interpretation. The assumption of intellectual consistency is itself, perhaps, a modern concern. It presumes clearly drawn ideological commitments and an inherent value placed on linear or systematic thought. The need to account for apparent inconsistencies in Nahmanides' thought has inspired stunning acts of analytical gymnastics. Martin Cohen, for example, has suggested that the events and document records of the disputation reveal that Nahmanides cultivated a sort of split personality in his role as a public persona: on the one hand, he was a representative of the Jewish people in the Christian world, and on the other hand, he was a rabbi whose people relied upon him to lead them through a time of political and cultural difficulty. In the guise of the former, Nahmanides showed his loyalty and obligation to the king by consenting to participate in a contest which he could not possibly have won. According to Cohen, the friar backed him into a corner during the debate, citing a rabbinic text that seemed to indicate that the messiah was born at the time the Second Temple was destroyed. Nahmanides was therefore forced to make the unqualified statement that aggadic literature was not dogma.[31] In the years following the disputation, and in the wake of King James I's continued support of the friars' missionizing efforts, Cohen argues, Nahmanides recognized that the friars could use the position he took during the disputation to weaken the Jews' resistance to their arguments. He therefore strove to clarify his stand in a written account, placing his argument in the full context of a dramatic religious debate.

Cohen's reconstruction of Nahmanides' motivations provides an explanation for the disparity between the Hebrew and Latin accounts and for Nahmanides' classification of *aggadot* as merely edifying literature. This argument also contextualizes the rabbi's apparently poor judgment in distributing the volatile account during a politically and religiously troubled time for the Jews of western Christendom. But while his assessment of the political setting is quite astute, Cohen's effort to explain the rabbi's motivations strains against the evidence of Nahmanides' exegesis. In his biblical interpretation, Nahmanides frequently presented rabbinic Midrash or *aggadah*, only to point out the inadequacies of that interpretation in order to lay a foundation for his own original reading. Although the interpretation he favored was generally also formulated in the style of *aggadah*, it is important to note that his strategy of argument was built upon a fairly systematic process of denying the validity of some rabbinic interpretations.[32]

Marvin Fox argues that scholarship like Cohen's perpetuates a problematic reading of Nahmanides' interpretive allegiances which implicates the medieval rabbi in contemporary disputes about rabbinic authority and theology. Fox suggests that the inclination to explain Nahmanides' emphatic stance that *aggadot* are not articles of dogma reflects an inability to reconcile twentieth-century sensibilities of orthodoxy with medieval sensibilities. "Many scholars dealing with this text find it difficult, if not impossible, to believe that this great pillar of Jewish orthodoxy (as they perceive him) could possibly have seriously held such views. Generally, they take the position that his statement in the context of the disputation was only a ploy which he adopted in order to refute his adversary, but that it in no way represented his own position."³³ Fox's criticism draws attention to one of the most troubling tendencies in the scholarship on Nahmanides and his role in the disputation. All too many of the scholars writing on Nahmanides' contributions to medieval Jewish history and culture stopped short of viewing him as an individual driven by historical, even political circumstances. Instead, Nahmanides comes to represent an essentialized ideal of orthodoxy and Jewishness whose actions and beliefs were, for the most part, unaffected by the strains and turns of history.³⁴

More recently, Robert Chazan reset the agenda, displacing the ideological, polemical thrust that had shaped the scholarly discussion in the past in favor of a more carefully drawn contextual consideration of the two accounts. Responding to many of the same concerns as his predecessors, Chazan argues that Nahmanides codified arguments made in the course of the disputation to provide an effective refutation for a new and profoundly threatening, if not overtly damaging, missionizing strategy.³⁵ According to this interpretation, Nahmanides spent the final years of his life trying to render the friars impotent in their effort to undermine Jewish faith and rabbinic textual authority. Like Martin Cohen before him, Chazan appears to be driven by a desire to reconcile Nahmanides' actions during and following the disputation (including the fact that he circulated his account) with what the accepted historical narrative has represented as a period of gradually shifting attitudes towards Jews and Judaism within the Church. While completely solid in its evidence and logic, Chazan's analysis focuses on one facet of Nahmanides' role as a leader in the Jewish community, while opting not to explore the position Nahmanides and the Jewish community held in Catalan society and culture as a whole.

In Chazan's view, the Latin disputation account, which represents the rabbi's speech as severely constrained, offers the more plausible representation of the debate. Having concluded that portions of Nahmanides' account are obviously fictitious, he is left wondering what might have moved Nahmanides to consciously misrepresent the true nature of the disputation.³⁶ Many of Chazan's forerunners also read the Hebrew disputation narrative as a fabricated account intended to compensate for a job poorly done or to smooth over political tensions.³⁷ But contrary to prior scholarship, Chazan views these "fictional" moments of the account as evidence of a highly orchestrated polemical tract meant to counteract the aggressive new effort to convert Jews to Christianity.

Chazan's study is the first work of systematic scholarship to assess the literary value of Nahmanides' account. He argues that Nahmanides crafted this fictionalized narrative with a twofold purpose: first to reassure Jews that their messiah was still to be expected,[38] and second to provide a working example of an effective response to the friars' line of argument. Yet, the question of whether Nahmanides' account is an accurate or true representation of the disputation remains at the crux of Chazan's analysis.

Chazan's careful distinction between the disputation itself and Nahmanides' account of the proceedings draws attention to the narrative nuances employed in this document. However, Nahmanides' disputation account has yet to be examined in conjunction with literary traditions that developed in the geographic region of Catalonia. The mid-thirteenth century saw the development of a significant body of literature written in the Catalan vernacular, including works written by King James I and Raymond Llull. Prominent themes in the representative works of the tradition include an interest in preserving events of the moment and recording individual accomplishments in dramatic narrative form. The development of a system of literary patronage around King James I's court supported an aesthetic preference for literature dealing with the recent past which would remain for posterity.

Many of the scholarly monographs and articles that have examined the Barcelona disputation participate to one degree or another in the Jewish scholarly discourse Salo Baron so aptly identified as the "lachrymose" view of history.[39] In these cases, the interpretation of Nahmanides' performance in the disputation and his narrative account of the encounter bears the unmistakable mark of the individual scholar's assessment of Jewish life in the medieval diaspora, in Aragon, and under the reign of King James I.[40] What has troubled many of the scholars who studied the Hebrew document is the sense that Nahmanides should have seen as clearly as they did that circulating his account would bring danger upon himself and possibly upon the community of Jews at large. This approach to Nahmanides' leadership assumes that that rabbi possessed a modern understanding of the dynamics of European secular and Church politics. However, these assumptions are frequently supported not by the textual evidence but instead by a meta-narrative that suggests that Jewish history as a whole has been governed by a cyclical pattern of periods alternating between prosperity and acceptance ("Golden" ages) and periods of humiliation, degradation, and violence. These 'types' of historical periods are never represented as being exclusive of qualities or elements of other epochal 'types'; instead, periods of prosperity are frequently marred by violent or unfortunate events, just as examples of protective gentile leaders often punctuate periods of degradation. For example, Yitzhak Baer's argument that medieval Aragonese Jewry was comprised of two distinct factions: 'assimilated' court Jews who engaged in the intellectual, cultural, and economic pursuits of the dominant culture and lower-class 'orthodox' Jews, who fought to preserve a pure form of Jewish life even at the cost of humiliation and degradation.[41] Nahmanides stands out, in Baer's view, because he occupied both worlds simultaneously. His family was powerful and well situated, and yet he protected, according to Baer, a pure expression of Jewish life and ritual. Jeremy Cohen, in contrast, represents Nahmanides and the Jews of Aragon as a profoundly and completely subjugated people.[42]

A different set of evidentiary and narrative concerns sparked Jaume Riera i Sans' interest. Inconsistencies between the Hebrew and Latin disputation narratives brought Riera i Sans to reexamine the manuscript tradition of these texts.[43] Confronted with two contradictory depictions of the same event, Riera i Sans argues that neither of the extant sources is what it appears to be. Though the anonymous Latin document has been generally accepted as a summary of the proceedings written by an observer for the official royal record, Riera i Sans suggests that it was a summary of the disputation arguments written by Friar Paul for King James I, his royal sponsor. In the same vein, he sees the Hebrew text not as a firsthand account of the debate written by Nahmanides, but rather as a fictional representation composed some two to three hundred years following the event.[44]

A close comparative analysis of the accounts of the Barcelona disputation and a comprehensive evaluation of the available manuscript tradition provide the framework for this dating. Fascinated by the disparity between the two accounts (as had been many of the scholars who analyzed the textual remains of this event before him), Riera i Sans took an inventory of the extant manuscripts of the Hebrew recension. The Latin version exists in only one manuscript copy that can be dated to the late thirteenth century; however, there is not a single manuscript copy of the Hebrew text that dates from the thirteenth, or even the fourteenth century. Based on this lack of physical evidence, he suggests the late fifteenth or early sixteenth century as a possible date of composition. This late date of authorship, Riera i Sans argues, also accounts for the unique dramatic and fictional flourishes used in this document. The author's sense of showmanship, ironic sense of humor, and self-consciousness about pomp of court rituals are narrative techniques and themes typical of literary production during the Italian Renaissance, not, according to Riera i Sans, of Jewish authors in the late thirteenth century.[45] Instead, he argues that the Hebrew account was written by an unknown scholar who could not believe widespread reports that the talented exegete and legal authority had faltered so badly and embarrassingly in the public debate with Friar Paul. Riera i Sans superimposes on this anonymous author the same concerns that motivate many scholars today. He thus redeems Nahmanides' name from the charge that he dishonestly represented the disputation and restores his reputation as a great textual authority.

This argument is intriguing. It makes sense of the discrepancy between the two representations of the disputation, but without impugning Nahmanides' authorial integrity. However, the suggestion that the Hebrew documentary evidence of the Barcelona disputation was fabricated *post facto*, literally to change the historical record by transforming a minor and embarrassing event in the life of one of the most important figures of medieval Jewry into a glorious fable, does not raise sufficient doubt about the authenticity of this text. There is a clear thematic continuity between Nahmanides' commentary on the Torah, his *Sefer ha-Geulah* (*Book of the Redemption*, which includes a timetable for the date of the messianic redemption based on biblical sources), and the account of the Barcelona disputation. In addition, as we have seen above, the royal archive contains evidence that some two years following the debate Nahmanides circulated a document recounting his performance in this encounter. These documents indicate that the style and content of Nahmanides' disputation narrative, combined with the fact that Nahmanides presented his account to the bishop of Girona, raised the ire of the Dominican friars and ultimately resulted in his banishment from the Crown of Aragon. Riera i Sans' construction seems to suggest that a Jew living in the fifteenth or sixteenth century had access to the same royal documents modern scholars have used to reconstruct the details of the disputation, including a record showing that King James I borrowed a sum of 300 *dineri* from a Barcelona money lender during July 1263 or that the parallels between the archival evidence and the Hebrew text were purely coincidental.[46] This assumption is untenable, especially in the case of the Latin disputation account, which portrays Nahmanides as inept and incapable of defending his faith.

All of these modes of analysis highlight the interpretive and methodological difficulties inherent in the frequently degraded and at times unreliable medieval (Jewish) archive (this is perhaps especially true in the case of Riera i Sans' analysis and conclusions). Efforts to make sense of Nahmanides' disputation account give voice to a deep ambivalence about how the textual remains of the past speak and what they tell contemporary scholars about the past and present alike. One might argue that this question is especially pressing in the context of Jewish studies, given the relative youth and isolation of the discipline. Like all 'field studies,' the investigation of Jews and Judaism as historical subjects has been, since its inception in the nineteenth century, wedged between the competing demands of 'pure' objective scholarship and the more deeply fraught territory of identity or community politics. But it is also essential not to isolate Jewish studies either topically or methodologically from the more general fields of historical and literary studies.

Source criticism, of course, is crucial to historical research. Conventions of modern historiographic practice insist that documentary evidence, to the degree possible, be reliable and authenticated. In a field like medieval Jewish history, in which the chains of evidence are marked by significant lacunae, the problem of source authentication is an especially troubling one. Even a faint shadow of doubt about the provenance or validity of a widely accepted source can significantly compromise both the document and the historical story it tells. But to what degree must questions about the authenticity of a text be couched in terms of evidentiary proof? Given the methods of storage, transmission, preservation, the notions of authorship and authority practiced during the medieval and early modern periods, modern scholars possess few guarantees that accepted documentary sources are what they started out as, what they appear or claim to be, or, for that matter, what we think they are. The use of source criticism to discredit texts, especially those sources that provide unique, firsthand information, frequently takes place as the final (rather than the initial) stage of extensive, even exhaustive scholarly debates about the value and meaning of the document in question. Riera i Sans' dismissal of the Hebrew disputation account as inauthentic seems a fairly logical step following a decades-long debate about the accuracy and meaning of the Hebrew document. And it is no surprise that his skepticism stems largely from the failure of the archives to provide evidence confirming the ancient provenance of the document.

The goals of radical documentary criticism appear unassailable: this mode of scholarship strives in the name of historical truth to clarify the textual record, to provide an accurate representation of the past. But is this an unquestionably valuable practice? Dominick LaCapra has suggested that a rigidly documentary approach to historical analysis drains the practice of history of intellectual vitality.[47] He criticizes the 'fetishization' of archival discovery and recommends instead a more "interactive model of discourse that allows for the mutual—and at times mutually challenging—interchange of 'documentary' and 'rhetorical' dimensions of language."[48] Sources that come under this sort of close examination have typically occupied a crucial place in our reconstruction of the historical past. Attempts to discredit accepted sources can have the additional consequence of refocusing subsequent scholars' discourse exclusively on the merits of this source criticism. The absence of evidence to confirm or refute such claims is sufficient to highjack critical discourse, forcing subsequent scholarship to begin by reclaiming the provenance of central documents.

It is fitting to pause here and ask whether consideration of this event or its documentary evidence represent a worthy scholarly pursuit. The eminent scholar and rabbi Solomon Schechter remarked that Jewish-Christian disputation literature makes for repetitive, predictable, boring reading unworthy of scholarly attention. He proceeded to argue that

> the polemics between Jews and Christians were barren of good results. If you have read one, you have read enough for all time. The same casuistry and the same disregard for history turn up again and again. Nervousness and humility are always on the side of the Jews, who know that, whatever the result may be, the end will be persecution; arrogance is always on the side of their antagonists, who are supported by a band of Knights of the Holy Cross, prepared to prove the soundness of their cause at the point of their daggers. Besides, was there enough common ground between Judaism and thirteenth century Christianity to have justified the hope of a mutual understanding?[49]

Schechter's observation that medieval disputation literature is redundant in theme, style, and content is indisputable; however, precisely those recurring textual elements that he regards as valueless for measuring how deep were the cultural and social sympathies between Jews and Christians during the middle ages offer the most promising paths of analysis. Public disputations were necessarily conducted in an atmosphere tinged with adversity and discord. But this is just part of the picture.

Disputations could be successful *only* if sufficient common ground existed between the two sides to enable a clear expression of the difference between the disputants' interpretations. At the linguistic level, this is merely a statement of the obvious. But at the level of politics, culture, and religion the points of intersection and divergence are more fundamental and at the same time, more difficult to pin down. In the controlled atmosphere of a public disputation, issues that were not likely the stuff of everyday intercourse either among Jews or between Jews and their Christian neighbors were explicitly addressed. And since victory in a debate with an opponent who was either mute or incompetent was a hollow victory, each party needed to present his arguments in a manner that would elicit discussion and response from his adversary. The process of building rhetorical boundaries between Judaism and Christianity, therefore, might also have had the unexpected and perhaps contradictory result of reaffirming the points of contact between the two traditions. The same general considerations apply to the production of textual records or narrative representations of such debates. It can be taken for granted that no medieval religious disputation account is devoid of partisan biases. As a rule, the authors of such documents intended to reproduce, or at the very least to recall, the air of tension that gave the discussion gravity in the first place.[50]

As this brief survey of the secondary literature has shown, considerations of the Barcelona disputation have been directed by efforts to claim contested or hidden meanings, and the authentication of Nahmanides' authorial voice in the Hebrew account. At stake in these debates are attempts to claim ownership of the sense, form, and content of the documents attesting to the Jewish past, indeed ownership of the Jewish past and its meaning. The remainder of this chapter examines the nuances of rhetoric and discourse in Nahmanides' Hebrew account of the Barcelona disputation. Nahmanides composed his disputation account, in part, as a means of establishing his version of the event in public memory. What will be of particular interest here is Nahmanides' estimation of the relationship between apostates and the Jewish community. I approach this issue through a close reading of two discrete portions of the text: the first instance is the homiletical frame which introduces the Hebrew account, and the second is his representation of a debate concerning Jewish and Christian periodizations of history and attempts to predict the time of redemption. Nahmanides' choice of narrative tools and allusions to past controversies provides a glimpse into his conception of the role played by apostates in Jewish culture and society.

Framing the Narrative

Nahmanides' desire to preserve a record of the disputation for posterity is apparent in the very structure of the Hebrew text. His effort to demonstrate a correspondence between the narrative report and the event itself is especially evident in the role he inscribed for himself as storyteller. Nahmanides appears throughout in two separate voices: first as the narrator and commentator, who speaks always in the definite past tense ("I said," "he replied," etc.); and second as the subject, whose speech is constantly animated in the present tense. And it is precisely this nod towards veracity that has impelled modern scholars to approach the Hebrew document with caution and even distrust.[51] The contrast between the author as narrator and as subject preserves the memory of the encounter in a perpetually dynamic temporality. Nahmanides' audience thus arrives with him at convincing arguments, working with the proper prooftexts under the pressure of the moment. Indeed, the very identification of completely formulated arguments as belonging to one or another individual seems to flag the author's concession to the rigorous demands of maintaining accuracy in his narrative. In this way, Nahmanides exploited the credibility that came with presenting an eye-witness account without compromising the integrity of the dispute as a dynamic exchange witnessed by a host of political and religious leaders.

The structure and style of the narrative are nearly as important as the content for Nahmanides in his presentation of the disputation as an important event in the history of Jews in the diaspora; yet, he also provided a more direct, if not entirely forthright, statement about his authorial intentions at the beginning of the text. The Hebrew disputation account opens with an introductory preamble which explains Nahmanides' purpose in writing this document. He justified his effort to establish a textual record of his encounter with Friar Paul by drawing a comparison with events from the Second Temple period. Nahmanides established a sense of thematic and historical continuity by quoting a passage from the Babylonian Talmud, tractate *Sanhedrin* (43a):

> Jesus of Nazareth had five students, Matai, Nakai, Netzar, Buni, and Todah. When Matai was brought forward he asked, "should Matai be killed? It is written 'when (*matai*) I will come and see the face of God' (Ps. 42:3)." They responded, "No, Matai should be killed, as it is written 'when (*matai*) will he die and perish' (Ps. 41:6)." When Nakai was brought forward he said, "should Nakai die? For it is written 'the innocent (*naki*) and righteous shall not kill you' (Ex. 23:7)." They said to him, "this is not so, Nakai should be killed, as it is written 'in secret places he slays the innocent (*naki*).'" When Netzar came forward he said, "shall he be killed? It is written 'and a shoot (*natzer*) will grow from his roots' (Isaiah 11:1)." They responded, "this is not so, Netzar will be killed, as it is written 'and you are cast out of your grave like a despised offshoot (*natzer*)' (Isaiah 14:19)." When Buni came forward, he said "shall he be killed? For the scripture says, 'Israel is my son, my firstborn' (Ex. 4:22)." They said, "no, Buni will be killed, it is written 'behold, I kill your son (*benkha*), your firstborn' (Exodus 4:23)." When Todah came forward, he said, "shall Todah be killed? for the scripture says, 'a song of thanksgiving (*todah*)' (Ps. 100:1)." They said to him, "this is not so, Todah will be killed, as it is written, 'whoever offers a sacrifice of thanksgiving (*todah*) honors me (Ps. 50:23).'"[52]

In this passage, members of a rabbinical court weigh evidence in the cases of treachery and heresy against five disciples of Jesus: Matai, Nakai, Netzar, Buni, and Todah (the first two correspond to Matthew and Luke, respectively, though the other three have no known historical parallels). The talmudic passage makes its point through word play based on the names of the accused. In each case, the court offers scriptural precedents defending a lenient sentence of acquittal; and in each case the court of judges finds in favor of biblical prooftexts that support the strictest legal penalty possible—execution.

The entire preamble takes place outside the historical time and place of the disputation itself. It recalls a long historical experience of exile and the complex and even precarious position of rabbinic courts in the diaspora. And the reader immediately wonders why this passage is of relevance to Nahmanides' first person disputation narrative. The author quickly addresses this question by citing a commentary by the important eleventh-century French rabbi, Rashi, on the same talmudic passage: "Rabbi Solomon wrote that they [the apostles] were close to the government, and thus they [the Rabbis] needed to answer all of their vain arguments." In anticipation that readers might raise similar concerns about his disputation narrative, the preamble concludes with a justification for his literary endeavor and an assertion that this account was an accurate representation of the proceedings: "It is for this purpose that I record the arguments with which I responded to the delusion[s] of Friar Paul, who publicly disgraced his education before our lord, the King, and his wise men and counselors."[53]

Perhaps because Nahmanides' introductory frame appears tangential to the narrative itself, most scholarship on the Barcelona disputation has ignored it. The only extended treatment of this portion of the text is presented by Hyam Maccoby, who categorically dismissed the preamble as inauthentic.[54] In an introduction to his abridged translation of Nahmanides' narrative, Maccoby argues that the opening passage was not originally part of the Hebrew document as Nahmanides wrote it, but was added some centuries later by a scribe. It then became integral to the text as future scribes included it without question. His conclusion is based on a set of assumptions about what Nahmanides would or would not have felt he was at liberty to commit to writing during a period of increased Christian scrutiny of Jewish literature. The most persuasive of his arguments points to the systematic review and censorship of rabbinic literature—including the very passage in *Sanhedrin* cited by Nahmanides—undertaken during the same period by the Dominicans. But Maccoby's argument is not entirely convincing. For, if we apply his criteria to the introduction of the narrative, it follows that we must apply the same logic to the entire account, since Nahmanides presented several arguments that would have appeared similarly offensive according to these standards. It would then be necessary to conclude that Nahmanides played no role in the production of this text, whether in Hebrew or in the vernacular, because he feared punishment.[55]

The preamble deserves attention since it sets the stage for an overall narrative and rhetorical strategy that Nahmanides maintained throughout the work. Nahmanides' reference to this talmudic passage adds a complex layer of social and cultural commentary to his highly dramatic literary representation of the proceedings. Three central points will emerge in the course of this discussion. First, this talmudic text provides the typological model by which Nahmanides invested the Barcelona disputation with historical meaning. By framing his narrative with this passage, Nahmanides constructed a historical continuum in which the disputation easily fit. Second, through the citation of this passage, Nahmanides offered a concealed commentary on Jewish apostasy, suggesting that Christianity was, at its deepest core, infected by idolatry. Finally, Nahmanides represented himself and Friar Paul as opposing examples of how Jews who worked in the orbit of Christian political power might conduct themselves. The Hebrew narrative also depicts an internal Jewish conflict, the tensions between Jews and apostates to Christianity.[56] The introductory frame lays the foundation for a subtle commentary on the web of social and cultural relations between Jews, apostates, and Christians in the Crown of Aragon.

Rashi considered the story of the apostles' trial in *Sanhedrin* to be problematic, on the one hand, because it did not seem to provide sufficient legal justification for the execution of these men, and on the other, because the trial of Christian apostates did not immediately seem to warrant inclusion in the corpus of Jewish historical or legal records. Rashi's extrapolation that the apostles conspired against the Jews superimposes a social and political commentary onto this talmudic passage. Nahmanides recognized this. By citing both the talmudic story about Jesus' disciples and Rashi's interpretation of it, Nahmanides established a point of reference for his reader to keep in mind throughout the narrative. It frames the account and enables the author to make a link between the Barcelona disputation and similar events in the Jews' past. Building on Rashi's interpretation, Nahmanides implied that conflicts with treacherous apostates always merited inclusion in the historical or legal record. Nahmanides, then, represented his narrative as a contribution to a venerable tradition of literature that portrays apostates who used their understanding of the Jewish canon, legal practices, and traditions to benefit themselves while at the same time damaging the Jews' standing as a political and religious minority. The implication is that records of previous confrontations of this nature provided the clearest models according to which one could form an effective response to accusations lodged by hostile apostates. According to this logic, therefore, it was necessary to record and preserve all of the details of the disputation, including Friar Paul's possibly dangerous claims, in an accurate and precise record of the event.[57]

The Boundaries of Local Culture

Nahmanides' introduction provides a reader's guide, setting the tone for the work as a whole. With the very act of writing an account that strives for realism, Nahmanides deliberately inserted himself and Friar Paul into the historical record as counterexamples of how Jews wielded and exploited power in the diaspora. Friar Paul provides a negative example of Jewish alliance with secular government, in contrast to the positive example of Jewish interaction with Christian authority in the disputation narrative represented by Nahmanides. Like the apostles in the talmudic story, who remain subject to the rabbinic court, he portrayed Friar Paul not as a Christian, but rather as a Jew who was seduced by the promise of power and fame to betray his faith, his education, and his community. In contrast, Nahmanides himself filled the role of a Jewish leader who was able to maneuver with ease through the labyrinth of court society, while remaining sufficiently detached from political power that he was still able to criticize its contradictions. Nahmanides fashioned himself as an emissary in the royal court who was able to balance his apparent alliance with the ruling government with his image as an independent and strong Jewish leader. He did so in part by giving the king an important and active role in his narrative. As the moderator of the debate, the king granted the rabbi the liberty to speak freely, but with the stipulation that Nahmanides refrain from making explicitly blasphemous statements about Jesus, the holy family, or Christianity.[58] In contrast to the value-laden representation of Nahmanides and Friar Paul in the Hebrew document, the characters who were Christian by birth are generally represented in neutral, even positive terms. Nahmanides represented King James, for example, as a captive audience for a detailed lesson on the historical differences and the complex affinities between Judaism and Christianity.[59]

This subtle commentary on the type of public behavior that was appropriate for learned Jews in Christian society is perhaps most clearly represented in the struggle between Nahmanides and his adversary to establish interpretive primacy. The Barcelona disputation was staged, the textual evidence indicates, to spotlight Friar Paul's innovative arguments concerning the time of the messiah's advent. Disagreement about how to interpret the authoritative texts is therefore fundamental to the drama. Because Nahmanides figured him as a Jew, Friar Paul's failure to bring sound interpretations and prooftexts in support of his claims reflected poorly on his training in rabbinic texts; this, in turn, would logically reflect poorly on Jewish learning as a whole, since Friar Paul's faulty understanding of talmudic methods made it possible for him to misrepresent the tradition before the king.

> Friar Paul answered: "... But today you no longer have the form of ordination known in the Talmud, so this form of government has also ceased among you. Indeed, there is no one among you today who merits the title 'Rabbi.' And what they call you today, *maestri*, is a mistake. Through a lie you appropriate that title."
>
> I responded to him mockingly: "This is not pertinent to the disputation, but you do not speak the truth. *Rabbi* is not equivalent to *maestri*, rather *rav* corresponds to *maestri*, and without a *semikha* (ordination) one could be called *rav* in the Talmud. But I agree that I am neither a *maestri* nor a *talmid tov* (good student)." I said this by way of an example. I continued and said to him: "I will demonstrate to you that it was not the intention of our rabbis, may their memories be for a blessing, to interpret this verse except to mean kingship in general, but you do not understand law or justice (*din ve-halakhah*), only a small portion of the *aggadot* with which you familiarized yourself."[60]

Nahmanides' condemnation of Friar Paul's public persona here cuts two ways. He first criticized Friar Paul for exploiting his training in talmudic literature to gain prominence within Christian society. In this respect, Paul's ability to read rabbinic literature devalues the tradition of talmudic training in so far as it becomes a commodity, a means of gaining access to prominent ecclesiastical and secular figures. But at the same time, Nahmanides reviled Friar Paul for demonstrating to his Christian patrons that the training he received in Montpellier allowed him to form arguments that could not be substantiated either historically or allegorically; the weakness in Friar Paul's approach is all the more damaging to the status of Jews in the Crown of Aragon, since he presented these arguments to his Christian patrons as *views contained in the canon of Jewish learning*. Nahmanides' careful, thoughtful lesson to the king and his courtiers about rabbinic learning stands in sharp contrast with Friar Paul's haphazard methods. He criticized Friar Paul not as a Christian who used Christian interpretive methods, but as a Jew whose learning failed him.

But by framing the account with this talmudic citation, Nahmanides also introduced a more nuanced commentary on Jewish-Christian social and cultural relations. James C. Scott has argued that dominated peoples use a vocabulary of signs, language, and references believed to be opaque to the ruling class as a means of perpetuating traditions that those in power would deem subversive.[61] This mode of discourse, which Scott labels 'hidden transcript,' allows the dominated community to participate in daily life in a potentially hostile atmosphere, while building internal barriers to protect against complete cultural domination. Nahmanides' use of the story of Jesus' disciples at the beginning of his disputation record, in conjunction with his realistic mode of representation, seems to work in this fashion, although the Hebrew document skirts issues of controversy and explicit blasphemy. The talmudic passage framing the Hebrew disputation account enabled Nahmanides to present a carefully disguised identification of the historical Jesus, his early followers, and contemporary apostates as idolaters. In this regard, the example Nahmanides chose as the preamble for his disputation account warrants closer examination.

In its original context of *Sanhedrin* 43, the story of the five apostates immediately follows an ongoing discussion about the rabbinical court's deliberations over the case against Jesus himself:

> On *Erev Pesah* [the first evening of Passover] they hanged Jesus of Nazareth. Forty days before a crier came forth and said: "Jesus of Nazareth will be stoned for sorcery and for inciting [public disturbances] and leading the people of Israel astray. Anyone who knows he is worthy of acquittal should come forward and defend him." But they found nobody to defend him, and hanged him on *Erev Pesah*. Ulla asked, "is it logical that Jesus of Nazareth was one for whom redeeming evidence was sought?" [They answered], "he was a rebel, and the Merciful one said, 'have no compassion for him, do not shield him' (Deut. 13:9). For it is taught that Jesus was close to the temporal government."[62]

Deuteronomy 13, the prooftext that provides proper legal precedent here for the decision to execute Jesus, addresses the problems that arise when members of the Israelite community turned to idolatry.[63] More specifically, it highlights the fear that idolaters would maintain ties with the community whose beliefs and practices they eschewed. Through continued relations, they might encourage family or friends to break the covenant by producing or even worshipping idols. Since the Torah marks idolatry as taboo, contact with idolaters is strictly regulated by both biblical and talmudic injunctions. The legal and cultural apparatuses that governed Jewish life in the diaspora reiterated this view, though the challenges of maintaining self-sufficiency when Jews lived as a minority community in lands populated by pagans, and later by Christians, made a modification of this principle necessary. According to the Babylonian Talmud, Jews were permitted to conduct social and business relations with idol worshippers only on days when their associates were neither preparing rituals nor participating in them.[64] The idiosyncrasies of the Christian liturgical calendar, in which nearly every day commemorated a saint, dictated the need for further revision of these standards. Productive Jewish life within the closely inscribed social and economic environment of medieval Christian Europe was made legally feasible due only to an early medieval rabbinic argument which distinguished Christianity as a non-idolatrous faith.

The talmudic example Nahmanides chose seems to suggest a blurring of the lines of distinction between conversion from Judaism to Christianity and the practice of idolatry. He represented Friar Paul as a particular type of apostate, one who betrayed Jewish communities to the ruling government in order to lure other Jews away from their faith and practices and who was foolish enough to overlook the rabbis' clear disdain for Jesus and his followers. This categorization had a deep resonance in the cultural and social climate of thirteenth-century Jewish Catalonia, where outspoken converts to Christianity were a valuable commodity in the effort to fully Christianize the Iberian peninsula.[65]

Also striking is the fact that Nahmanides' language seems to imply that according to rabbinic and biblical standards, Jesus was himself an idolater. The description of Nahmanides' verbal promise to the Christian authorities that he would refrain from blaspheming Jesus, Joseph, Mary, or any sacred doctrine of Christianity sets the dramatic scene for his detailed and forthright arguments contra Friar Paul's interpretations of rabbinic tradition. And while there is no point in the account at which he makes an overtly blasphemous statement, any knowledgeable student of the Talmud would easily link the story of the five disciples with the justification for Jesus' punishment. The message is bold. Nahmanides hints that Jesus was the archetype of an idolatrous traitor who was discovered and duly castigated for his crime. Jesus and his disciples were punished to the most extreme letter of the law because they colluded with the ruling authorities. Because Nahmanides did not figure Christianity itself or Christians, for that matter, as idolatrous, I would not go so far as to say that this was meant as a commentary on contemporary Christianity. Rather, it was apostasy from Judaism that troubled Nahmanides and that he wrestled with in this document.

Apostasy and Jewish Society

The apostate held a unique place in medieval Jewish society.[66] By choosing to adopt Christianity, the apostate abandoned the familial, social, economic, religious, and legal apparatuses that had structured his or her daily life until the moment of conversion. According to Jewish law, apostasy resulted in the absolute exclusion of the individual from nearly all of the protections and, by extension, the judicial control exerted by the Jewish community.[67] By this logic, the apostate would be excluded from the earthly Jewish community and from the world to come. However, the relationship between the Jewish community and the apostate was more complicated and ambiguous than this. Sacha Stern has suggested that rabbinic perceptions of idolatry and apostasy underwent a significant shift with the development of Christianity and rise of martyrdom. This change, he argues, is registered in tractate *Avodah Zarah* of the Babylonian Talmud, which prescribes a host of regulations on interactions—both social and economic—between Jews and *ovdei avodah zarah* (those who practice idolatry). While the label *oved avodah zarah* had previously been a distinction which applied to individuals, whether Jewish or pagan, who participated in specific idolatrous practices, tractate *Avodah Zarah* referred to everyone who was not Jewish as an idol worshipper.[68] The legal status of converts according to talmudic tradition reflected this stark categorical distinction between Jews and non-Jews. *Halakhah* viewed apostates as being legally and spiritually deceased; family members marked their departure from the Jewish world with mourning rituals.[69] Nevertheless, converts remained subject to Jewish law in matters of marriage, property rights, and inheritance.[70] When these injunctions were followed strictly, apostates resembled ghosts, both legally and emotionally for the community they departed, and especially for their families.

In so far as the allusion to idolatry in Nahmanides' disputation account comments on the complex relationship between Jews or Jewish culture and converts from Judaism, it brings an additional question into focus: according to Nahmanides' record of the disputation, what were the boundaries of the Jewish community? Or, to phrase the question slightly differently, in what ways does Nahmanides' account figure Jewishness in the Crown of Aragon? Based on the theological issues raised and discussed in the course of his disputation narrative—many of which focus on the nature and time of Jewish redemption—it is difficult to pinpoint a clear expression of how he thought Jews should behave qua Jews in their relations with Christians, but as I have suggested above, a model of behavior can be extracted from the literary style and legal examples Nahmanides employed in telling this story.

One might presume, based on the example of proper Jewish conduct that Nahmanides represented in the introduction to his disputation, that he avidly shunned contact with gentiles, and with the government in particular. However, Nahmanides' portrayal of the disputation itself indicates that this was not the case. Nahmanides' close association with members of the royal and ecclesiastical courts registers as legitimate precisely because he conducted himself there in the capacity of a diplomat. His relationships with the king and the bishop, then, were not comparable with Friar Paul's collusion with the government because Nahmanides forged, then maintained these connections for the good of the Jews of Girona and the Crown of Aragon as a whole.

He represented himself as being on very friendly terms with the king—indeed, so close, that he claimed to have accepted a sizable monetary gift from the monarch as a reward for his impressive performance in the disputation.[71] But the royal archives also tell us that during the decade preceding the disputation, Nahmanides had received at least two royal grants in his capacity as rabbi of Girona.[72] He was also on close enough terms with the bishop of Girona to have written an account of the disputation in Catalonian or Latin and presented it to him as a gift.[73] So, if Nahmanides implied that the gravest crime committed by Jesus and his apostles was the commission of idolatry through collusion with the temporal government, how did he legitimize his own close association with the secular and ecclesiastical officials?

In his disputation account, Nahmanides made a clear distinction between apostates and Christians. Those who chose to convert from Judaism to Christianity, in his estimation, voluntarily broke the covenant by abandoning the commandments. Even more degraded were those apostates who curried favor with the ruling government, like Friar Paul, Jesus, and the apostles. In his view, they exchanged their faith, education, and customs to indulge their hunger for power. In contrast to these apostates, Nahmanides' contemporaries who were born into Christianity were raised and nurtured on a tradition that had long before abandoned the *mitzvot*. They were not to be blamed for their beliefs, since they never knew any better. Nahmanides made this point explicitly near the middle of the disputation account in a remark directed specifically to the king:

> I said: "... the division between the Jews and the Christians is, as you have said, at the divine foundation a very bitter thing (*be-ekar he-alehut devar mar meod*). And you, our lord king, are a Christian, son of a Christian mother and a Christian father and you heard all your days Christian priests and their sermons and interpretations and stories about the [miraculous] birth of Jesus and they filled your brain and the marrow of your bones with this belief and you always return to the same point of faith. But this matter in which you place faith—and it is the very root of your faith—does not appeal to the rational intellect [i.e., defies logic]...."[74]

This passage seems to suggest that contemporary Christians were not idolaters because they did not purposefully betray their covenant with God. Anyone who was born and trained in Jewish tradition, practice, and law was held to another standard. Thus, Friar Paul and the apostles were fundamentally blameworthy because they willfully deviated from the path that revelation and tradition had taught them was true. With this distinction, Nahmanides added a shade of nuance to the Tosaphists' blanket classification of Christians as practitioners of a non-idolatrous faith. This approach allowed ample space for cultural, social, and intellectual exchange between Jews and Christians, even for discussion of the respective religious traditions. While Nahmanides made a moral distinction between native Christians and converts, it is clear that he viewed contemporary Christians with ambivalence. Although he sanctioned a thorough knowledge of and conversation about the tenets of Christianity on the part of Jews (and presumably, a knowledge of Judaism on the part of Christians), as his disputation account demonstrates, he marked as taboo immersion in and adoption of the beliefs and traditions fundamental to the other faith. His scorn for apostasy was by no means radical; however, the example he set in the disputation account for intellectual exchange between

Jews and Christians does set a precedent. I do not wish to suggest that Nahmanides' disputation account advocates an exchange resembling a modern inter-faith discussion, but rather, that he provided an example for exchange that was designed to maintain both the possibility of informed discourse and a clear boundary between Judaism and Christianity which conversation could not bridge.

The Hebrew disputation account engages in a multi-layered commentary on the condition of contemporary Jewish society. At one level, it underscores the ongoing struggle within the Jewish diaspora to maintain internal coherence once individuals turned to apostasy. Nahmanides made use of a typological parallel between Friar Paul and other famous converts in the Jewish past to demonstrate that the threat of apostasy warranted attention and record. To make this point more strongly, Nahmanides used a narrative of allusion which placed Friar Paul on par with Jesus and his early followers. Finally, in contrast to Friar Paul, Nahmanides represented his own conduct as the model of Jewish behavior in the Christian world. The connection between these three layers of social commentary brings into relief an ambivalence towards Christianity and towards his own association with individual Christians. Nahmanides' commentary on the place of Jewish culture in the Latin West seems to echo the mixed emotions with which the Tosaphists in the twelfth century reaffirmed the designation of Christianity as non-idolatrous faith: "regarding our idolaters, they are not idolaters."[75]

Shared History, Disputed Tradition

A shared biblical heritage provided fertile ground for deeply complex Jewish-Christian relations during the middle ages characterized by violent disagreement in the worst cases and ambivalence in the best. Legal and spiritual leaders in both communities claimed legitimate authority to interpret the practical and religious meanings of the shared texts for their followers, and both communities saw biblical prophecy in its many guises as applying directly to their own history. Under any circumstances, the process of interpreting historical events has political overtones. It involves reducing complex series of occurrences to a handful of salient details, which in turn come to represent 'an event.' The components of any given event consist of countless individuals, memories, circumstances, and locations prior to this filtration process. Separating important strands from this complex web to form a narrative of significance for any single community necessarily invests the evidence used with a privileged value. Details of the resulting story become fundamentally meaningful; in contrast, the details and evidence that were set aside or neglected are thus rendered insignificant. Signification of evidence is all the more value-laden when the source of evidence is divine revelation or prophecy, especially, as in this case, prophecy contested by the powerful Christian authorities and the more vulnerable and less powerful Jewish minority. In the context of a religious disputation the participants were forced to stake out and ferociously guard the textual domains over which they could not afford to risk sole or at least privileged interpretive authority.[76] Consequently, and not surprisingly, the attribution of significance to historical events and timelines is a prominent theme running through late antique and medieval Jewish-Christian religious polemics.[77]

Integral to Nahmanides' defense of the Jewish reading of biblical history and prophecy in his disputation account was a demonstration of his mastery over the sources as well as the chronological data they contain. He achieved this by presenting his adversary's interpretation (or, in Nahmanides' view, misinterpretation) of biblical and talmudic sources in full detail. Both accounts of the disputation related that disputants were expected to address a series of theological issues salient to the historical foundations of both Christianity and Judaism: 1) whether the messiah had come already, as the Christians believed, or was yet to come, as the Jews believed; 2) whether the rabbis of the Talmud believed the messiah had appeared already in the person of Jesus; 3) whether the messiah was (or would be) essentially human or divine; 4) an analysis of the political condition of the Jews vis-á-vis the statement in Genesis 49:10, "the staff of Jacob will not depart from between his feet"; and 5) an examination of the reference to the suffering servant in Isaiah in relation to the tradition of Jesus.[78]

The format and content of the Barcelona disputation proved ideal for Nahmanides' representation of a defense of Jewish primogeniture, chosenness, and interpretive authority. Nahmanides' narrative account attempts to reconcile the Jews' state of continued exile with the Christian interpretation of biblical history and prophecy and with his own interpretation of history. The method he proposed examined the vicissitudes and contours of history to extract patterns encoded in the Torah, writings, and prophecy.

Following a description of the opening conventions, where the ground rules of the disputation are laid out,[79] Nahmanides' account opens with a debate concerning the relationship between prophecy and historical circumstance or causality. This theme, which recurs repeatedly during the Hebrew disputation narrative, is depicted as a site of considerable importance in establishing a strong, credible argument for both parties.

Friar Paul's first argument concerning the status and interpretation of biblical prophecy is a christological reading of Jacob's blessing of Judah in Genesis 49:10:

> He [Friar Paul] began and said: "The scripture says, *the staff shall not depart from Judah, etc., until Shiloh comes* (Genesis 49:10), for he is the messiah. Thus, the prophet says that power will forever remain with Judah until [the time of] the messiah, who will come from him [i.e., the tribe Judah]. If this is the case, then on the day that you no longer have one tribe and you have no law giver, then [you will know] the messiah has already come and he was from his [Judah's] seed, and government is his."[80]

The question demanding clarification in the discussion of Genesis 49:10 is whether Jacob's blessing of Judah is a prophecy of the Christian messiah. According to Nahmanides, Friar Paul framed the question with a logic which suggested that clear historical causes and consequences had brought an end to the era of Jewish chosenness. The historical demise of the kingdom and destruction of the Temple resulted in the passing of Jewish chosenness to the Christians.

Nahmanides expanded upon the two disputants' efforts to claim the authoritative interpretation of this verse because Genesis 49:10 trains the spotlight on fundamental issues of historical and interpretive disagreement between Judaism and Christianity over their shared textual origins. Was biblical prophecy universal or did it address only the Jewish (i.e., chosen) people? Was Jewish chosenness static, or could it be transferred to another people were the Jews deemed unworthy? How and to whom was the authority to interpret prophecy conferred? By what method could historical events be interpreted as prophecies fulfilled? And finally, what was the proper method for interpreting and counting the time of history and prophecy? These questions became especially urgent in the context of religious polemics, since the understanding of the past has considerable impact on the way circumstances and events appear in the present.

Like the religious communities they represented in the disputation, Nahmanides and Friar Paul both looked to biblical prophecy to make sense of how and why civilization had arrived at that time and place without realizing the promise of redemption. Nahmanides prescribed a systematic evaluation of historical data, a precise definition of terms, historical personages and locations, and methodical contextualization of events in both time and place. It is with this subtle advancement of an analytical method that Nahmanides laid the cornerstone of his argument against Friar Paul's claims: a systematic effort to discredit Christian biblical and historical analysis which avoids the rhetorical and politically problematic challenges of explicitly debasing or insulting the fundamental tenets of Christianity.

Supplementing his initial argument, Friar Paul drew prooftexts from rabbinic sources to demonstrate that even in the eyes of reputed rabbinical authorities the power to rule and the authority to interpret texts allocated to the tribe of Judah in Genesis 49:10 had passed long ago from the Jewish community to the Christians, who recognized and followed the true messiah.[81] In fact, Friar Paul's interpretation finds strong support in rabbinic authority. Traditional exegesis identifies the reference to Shiloh in this verse as the messiah. In the words of *Midrash Rabbah*, "'Until Shiloh comes,' that means the king who is messiah" (*Bereshit Rabbah* 98, 8). Using the very texts that gave Nahmanides' interpretation and practice of Jewish law validity, Friar Paul took the first step in an attempt to systematically discredit the traditional and practical basis of rabbinic Judaism. The reason for this strategy of argument on the part of the friar, Jeremy Cohen has suggested, was political. Had Friar Paul been successful in dismantling the structure of Jewish interpretive authority, he could also have undermined the basis for Jewish self-government in the Crown of Aragon. Since the disputation was conducted in the presence of King James I, who granted the Jews political autonomy and who viewed Jewish law as a valid and authoritative legal structure, this was a conceivable outcome.[82]

Friar Paul's interpretation of Genesis 49:10 is typical of the method he exploited throughout the disputation, according to Nahmanides' representation, to transform portions of the vast corpus of Jewish sacred texts into evidence demonstrating that Jesus was the Jewish messiah. Genesis 49:10 had been used frequently by Christian polemicists to support Christian primacy.[83] Because the Christian argument opened with this verse, any reader who was familiar with traditional Christian polemical tactics might assume that the discussion would follow a course of attack already quite familiar to Jews who lived among Christians. However, rather than proceed with what the Jewish polemical sources indicate was a typical christological interpretation of this text,[84] Friar Paul's argument immediately followed a new track which challenged the authority of contemporary Jews to interpret sacred text.[85] This line of argument is played out in Nahmanides' account in a dispute over the proper interpretation of Genesis 49:10. But simultaneously, during the debate over this verse, and indeed throughout the remainder of the disputation narrative, the Hebrew account represents the disputants haggling over the more significant question of what constitutes legitimate interpretive authority and on what basis the rules dictating legitimacy might change.

Friar Paul's neatly constructed argument based on Genesis 49:10 that Jewish chosenness had expired rests on historical data. Jesus' lifetime was contemporaneous with an extreme and catastrophic change in the Jews' political status. After the fall of the Second Temple the Jews were completely and forever subjugated to outside powers. Yet it is precisely Friar Paul's appeal to historical evidence to decode prophecy that allowed Nahmanides to interrogate the depth of the friar's understanding of the history and tradition shared by Jews and Christians and the authoritative basis for his interpretation.

Nahmanides presented a multifaceted response to Friar Paul's interpretation of Genesis 49:10. First, he addressed the meaning of the verse, arguing that the right to govern the people of Israel was granted to the tribe of Judah unconditionally during times of Jewish political self-determination: "I answered and said: 'it is not the prophet's intention to say that there would not be a time when the rulership of Judah would cease. Rather, he said that the right to rule would not pass from him. The meaning is that at all times that Israel has a kingdom, it is designated for the tribe of Judah. If their kingdom is abolished because of sin, it will return to Judah.'"[86] After directly challenging his opponent's ability to interpret prophecy, Nahmanides turned his attention to Friar Paul's historical data and the way he used it. Friar Paul read "Judah" as a generic term denoting the Jewish people as a whole. Based on this understanding, the prophecy of Genesis 49:10 is easily transformed into a commentary on the status of the Jews as a chosen people. However, Nahmanides called for a more constrained reading of this text and the historical events and circumstances to which this prophecy assigned meaning. According to a more historically precise view, Judah refers first to the tribe and then to the kingdom of the same name, which must be distinguished initially from the other eleven tribes, and later, from the kingdom of Israel. A survey of the historical data pertaining to the limited sense of Judah, Nahmanides claimed, reveals that this prophecy could not possibly have any bearing on the status of the Jews as a chosen people.

> The proof for my words is that already many years before (*haiyu yamim rabbim kodem*) Jesus the kingdom fell from Judah, but not from Israel; and for several years the kingdom ceased for Israel and Judah. For seventy years, during the time of the Babylonian exile, there was neither a kingdom of Israel nor a kingdom of Judah. And during the Second Temple there was no king in Judah, just Zerubavel and his sons [ruled] for several years. And they stood after that for 380 years until the destruction, when the priests ruled through the Hasmonains and their servants.[87]

With this argument, Nahmanides established the foundation for what he viewed as an historically accurate method of interpreting the practical implications of biblical prophecy. Unique historical events, like the blessing of Judah, were important in and of themselves, but also as part of the historical drama as the age of redemption drew near.

Aggadah, *History, and the Struggle for Textual Authority*

Friar Paul's second line of historically based argument drew from rabbinic as well as biblical sources to show that the messiah had already arrived. This strategy built upon an *aggadah* from *Midrash Lamentations,* which describes an incident that purportedly occurred at the moment the Second Temple was razed.

> Friar Paul responded and argued that in the Talmud they said that the Messiah already came, and he brought with him a *haggadah*[88] that is in *Midrash Eikha,* which states "a man was plowing, and his cow lowed, an Arab passer-by said to him, bar Yehudai, bar Yehudai, untie your cow, untie your plow, untie your plowshare, for your Temple has been destroyed. He untied his cow, untied his plow, and untied his plowshare. [The cow] lowed a second time. [The Arab] said to him,

tie up your cow, tie up your plow, tie up your plowshare, for your Messiah was born."[89]

This *aggadah* offers consolation for the destruction of the Temple, mitigating the resulting social and religious humiliation with the promise of timely messianic redemption.[90] Friar Paul used this example to support his argument that the rabbis of the Talmud knew and believed that the messiah had already come in the person of Jesus.

Friar Paul's use of this *aggadah* elicited Nahmanides' most pointed attack on the christological interpretation of talmudic sources. The Latin and Hebrew disputation accounts agree about basic details of this exchange: according to both, Friar Paul cited a rabbinic text, the authority of which Nahmanides subsequently denied. The difficulties Nahmanides faced in refuting this argument were great. In his narrative representation, he needed to present the friar as an incompetent interpreter of rabbinic texts. He also had to cast doubt on the source itself while protecting the value and status of rabbinic literature as a whole as the foundation for Jewish life in the diaspora. Nahmanides formulated an argument that enabled him to reclaim interpretive authority over his texts. He contended that the corpus of rabbinic literature consisted of a hierarchy of interpretive methods, and each one uncovered different layers of meaning. *Aggadot* or non-halakhic rabbinic tales, Nahmanides argued, rested at the bottom of this hierarchy. They provided edifying moral tales, but not law or dogma.

The first strategy presented in Nahmanides' account is a blanket refusal to subscribe to the historicity of Friar Paul's prooftext: "I do not believe this *aggadah* at all, although it provides evidence for my argument."[91] The method for identifying the correct dating and interpretation of historical events and evidence are once again crucial to Nahmanides' record of this debate. He presented his argument in two parts. First he subjected the details of the *aggadah* and Friar Paul's interpretation of it to close scrutiny; then he returned later in the text to clarify his claim about the truth-value of the story in question.[92] A lecture on the three distinct classes of Jewish sacred literature provides the narrative structure for this reprise. At the highest level, and accepted by all Jews without question, is the Bible, followed by the Talmud, which explains and comments on the 613 commandments contained in the Torah, and finally, the Midrash, which he described as comparable to Christian *sermones,* or illustrative commentaries on biblical stories and historical themes.[93] Acceptance or rejection of the truth in this final class of literature, he argued, fell to the individual's personal discretion and could vary from one *aggadah* to the next. In the dramatic flow of the narrative, Nahmanides' assessment of Jewish literary genres serves as a brief lesson for his Christian audience in the categories and hierarchy of Jewish sacred literature. It was also calculated to undermine Friar Paul's attack by demonstrating that the convert lacked the training necessary to prioritize and decode these difficult texts.

The *aggadah* from *Midrash Lamentations* provided Friar Paul's missionizing strategy with significant rhetorical leverage.[94] The eager, vocal apostate from Judaism, who was an influential force directing anti-Jewish policy, added a new dimension to the Jewish-Christian religious confrontation in the middle ages.[95] Of course, the convert who argued for the truth of his new belief, while at the same time enthusiastically showing the shortcomings of the old, is a *topos* in Christian polemical literature that can be traced back as far as Paul.[96] Until the thirteenth century, however, official sponsorship of this kind of confrontation was relegated primarily to the literary realm of polemical treatises. Several tracts dramatizing either fictional debates or, less frequently, the conversion process were written in Latin for a Christian audience.[97] In the case of the Barcelona disputation, however, Friar Paul claimed to possess the key necessary for unlocking the secrets of Jewish tradition and interpretation contained in the Talmud, both of which, he suggested, had been controlled and concealed since the time of the Talmud by rabbis and Jewish teachers. His conversion to the truth, his unquestioning acceptance of Christian dogma as the proper interpretive apparatus enabled him—at least in the eyes of his fellow Christians—to wrestle interpretive authority away from Nahmanides.[98]

The Hebrew and Latin accounts of the disputation agree that Friar Paul's interpretation of this story was quite convincing to the Christian audience.[99] The destruction of the Second Temple was roughly contemporaneous with the historical moment at which Jesus was born. Nahmanides' response trains a critical eye on Christian interpretation of historical facts. By identifying well-known temporal markers against which events in the narrative time frame could be compared, Nahmanides provided the historical context that allowed for a proper understanding of this rabbinic tale. In particular, he referred to the destruction of the Temple, which occurred in the Hebrew year 3828 (68 c.e.), and the birth of Jesus, according to the chronology of *Book of the Life of Jesus* (*Sefer Toldot Yeshu*),[100] which locates Jesus' birth in 3671 (89 b.c.e.), as the correct markers in this instance. His exertion of control over precise events and periods of history is overt.

> I said: "Truly, I know and believe that the messiah was not born on the day of the Destruction (*he-hurban*). Perhaps this *haggadah* is not true, or perhaps it has another meaning from the secrets of the sages. However, I will accept the plain [literal] meaning you quoted, for it provides evidence for me. The *haggadah* says that the messiah was born on the day of the Destruction, just after the Temple was razed. If this is so, then Jesus was not the messiah, as you claimed, because he was born and died before the Destruction. According to the truth (*be-derekh ha-emet*),[101] he was born close to two hundred years prior to the Destruction, and according to your own calculations, 73 years [before the Destruction]." The man [i.e., Friar Paul] was thus quieted.[102]

The distinction between the "true" chronology of events according to Jewish sources and the less exact one presented by Friar Paul provides Nahmanides with strong evidence impugning the Christian reckoning of time and thus, the place of Christianity in human and cosmic history. He intimates that in their effort to date the age of the world, Christian authorities misread the biblical sources. As a result, the traditional Christian chronology misrepresented the number of years that passed since creation, thus providing ample support for christological reinterpretations of Jewish history.

As the editor of a first person account, Nahmanides took full advantage of the dramatic tension produced by the spectacle of an impassioned public exchange. He presented himself and Friar Paul advancing conflicting arguments about the connections between the history of the Jewish people and their prophecy. Explicating these arguments, he demonstrated that historical and textual primacy of Judaism is reflected in the continued drama of Jewish experience in the diaspora. The Christian reading of the shared biblical past, in contrast, failed to make sense of biblical prophecy that history would culminate with political redemption of the Jewish people.[103] Nahmanides' Hebrew narrative of the Barcelona disputation is thus in conversation not just with Jewish readers who held views similar to his own, but also with Christianity. This conversation takes place at several levels. At the most superficial, the rabbi's fictionalized dialogue with Friar Paul captures the anxiety engendered by a shared sacred tradition. But since Nahmanides' disputation account also previews an interpretive method which he used and developed with great success in various of his other works, including his Bible commentary, it is not difficult to imagine that his confrontation with Christian biblical interpretation infused his understanding of the very core of his tradition.

CHAPTER FOUR

At the Threshold of Redemption

*Daniel and Messianic Discourse in
Thirteenth-Century Catalonia*

AND I HEARD, BUT I DID NOT UNDERSTAND; THEN I SAID, "MY Lord, what will be the end of these things?" He said, "Go Daniel, for these words are secret and sealed to the time of the end. Many will be purified and purged and refined; the wicked will act wickedly and none of the wicked will understand; but the knowledgeable will understand. From the time the regular offering is abolished, and an abomination is set up—it will be a thousand two hundred and ninety days. Happy is he who waits and reaches one thousand three hundred and thirty-five days. But you, go to the end; you shall rest and arise to your destiny at the end of the days." (Daniel 12:8–12)

Building from the final verses of the book of Daniel, Nahmanides formulated a bold prediction that the messianic age would begin by 5118 (1358 according to the Christian calendar). This argument, which he asserted in his commentary on Genesis, his disputation account, and *Sefer ha-Geulah* (*The Book of Redemption*, an extended reflection on the historical meaning of prophecy), identified the destruction of the Second Temple as the epochal transition indicated in the prophecy of Daniel. His interpretation of this portion of Daniel as prophecy of the messianic age was not entirely innovative. Rashi, writing in the late eleventh century, interpreted the very same verses as a prophecy that the messianic redemption would begin in the mid-fourteenth century.[1] But Nahmanides' interpretation of Daniel 12:11–12 is notable within the constellation of medieval Jewish commentators for the proximity of the date he projected, the certainty with which he made his claim, and (perhaps most importantly) the centrality of this precise and foreordained date of messianic redemption in his conception of prophecy, divine redemption, and of the process of Jewish history as unified and self-contained.

Nahmanides' commentaries on redemption provide an invaluable tool for observing and examining the complexities of messianic discourse in thirteenth-century Catalonia. As one of the most important Jewish teachers, scholars, and leaders of medieval Aragon, Nahmanides was a prolific commentator on law and practice. Throughout his works he forged a middle ground between a traditional, even conservative reception of rabbinic interpretation and fresh innovations informed by and suitable to the political and social circumstances which confronted him locally on a daily basis. Nahmanides presented his conclusions about the approaching time of redemption most forcefully and systematically in *Sefer ha-Geulah*. In this work, as in his other writings, Nahmanides used biblical sources to demonstrate that the time of redemption could be expected within a few decades from the time of his old age. But here he also clarified an issue that remained vague in earlier works. He argued that the meaning of biblical revelation unfolded slowly over time, becoming clearer and more transparent for each successive generation. According to this view, revelation and prophecy remained dynamic in the sense that fresh layers of meaning revealed themselves in accordance with the needs of the particular age. Thus, Nahmanides believed that he and his contemporaries by accident of their time possessed precise information about the messianic era, information that had been hidden from previous generations. Nahmanides' view of redemption informed his understanding of contemporary events and his view of history, of which redemption was the final phase, the culmination of a process that was initiated at the moment of creation. His prediction of the time of redemption therefore reflects a deep engagement with Torah, on the one hand, and with contemporary concerns and historical change on the other.

The integrated method Nahmanides used to interpret Torah, prophecy, and history did not emerge in a cultural and intellectual vacuum, nor did his interest in the time of messianic redemption. As Jeremy Cohen, Moshe Idel, Harvey Hames, Robert Lerner, and others have shown, both Jewish and Christian intellectual and spiritual leaders in late thirteenth-century Catalonia fully embraced the notion that knowledge of when and how redemption would occur was available to the contemporary generation.[2] Christian exegetes, such as the Franciscan followers of Joachim of Fiore, and Jewish commentators like Abraham ben Levi Abulafia, presented fully developed schemas representing the shape of history and the time of redemption.[3] Although Nahmanides never formulated his view of temporality in systematic philosophical terms, his historical sensibility was the fruit of a protracted discourse among and between Jews and Christians in Catalonia that likely was performed in every mode of social encounter, from casual conversation in the marketplace to highly ceremonial, carefully orchestrated religious disputations and forced sermons. A familiarity with the interpretive strategies, theology, history, and imagery of Christianity played a part in shaping the interpretations and self-perceptions formed by Nahmanides and his peers; on the other side of the same coin, Christians who were familiar with Jewish interpretations absorbed and processed them, transforming them into Christian interpretations.

The present chapter examines Nahmanides' participation in and contribution to this Catalonian discourse on the time of messianic redemption. As a student and authority of *halakhah* and the Bible, Nahmanides drew from and rooted his writings in the long tradition of Jewish literature on the question of redemption. This chapter will first juxtapose his speculations about the messianic era with the conservative or cautious strain in talmudic and medieval Jewish writing about counting to the time of redemption. Nahmanides' willingness to engage this issue was a product of his finely honed understanding of Jewish history as a process leading towards the goal of return to the holy land, repair of the nation, and redemption.[4] According to this view, the shape and structure of this journey can be found by the discerning reader in the books of divine revelation. In the remainder of this chapter I will turn to the broader context of late thirteenth- and early fourteenth-century Catalonia. Focusing on the writings of Arnau of Vilanova, I draw a parallel between Nahmanides' reading of the concluding verses of the book of Daniel and Christian interpretations of the same verses.

Traditions of Messianism

Though post-biblical Judaism incorporates messianic longing into the long-term view of Jewish history, the consensus in rabbinic and medieval Judaism discourages active messianic hopes in favor of a passive acceptance that redemption would occur in the distant future. Still, expectation of messianic redemption, supported by biblical hints about Israel's future, is a tradition deeply embedded in rabbinic literature. Born from what appears to be a radical chasm between chosenness and the historical reality of subjugation and humiliation, speculations about the timing, duration, and quality of redemption are sprinkled among legal discussions (*halakhah*) in the Talmud. While narrative homiletic or moral writings (*aggadot*) on redemption seem to stand in stark contrast to legalistic talmudic discourse in their projection into the future, a clear dogma of messianic expectation never emerges in rabbinic literature, nor are there clearly stated guidelines for interpreting biblical promises of redemption. *Masekhet Sanhedrin* in the Babylonian Talmud contains a rich and varied selection of reflections on the messianic era, including comments on the shape and duration of world history, classifications of the sorts of events that must transpire before the redemption will occur, denials that the messiah would ever come, as well as many others.[5] Rabbinic approaches to end-time speculation are generally subdued. Descriptions of redemption as glorious are counterbalanced in this list by a catalogue of the possible dangers that could arise if active speculation were to become a popular pastime.

Because they feared that those who engaged in such speculations might abandon the covenant, the rabbis of the Talmud took the cautionary effort of discouraging active speculation about when the messiah would arrive. In this context the rabbis extended a grave warning: "May the bones be blown away of those who calculate the end."[6] This cautionary note does not represent a legal injunction against voicing such calculations, but it laid the foundation for a conservative approach to messianic expectations that was taken up by many medieval authorities: one was expected to maintain faith that redemption would come, but investing this promise with too much significance was considered dangerous. Maimonides, for example, carefully outlined the dangers of calculating the messianic era in his letter to the Jews of Yemen. This letter, addressed to a beleaguered community that struggled against persecution from without and failing faith within, encouraged Jews in the diaspora to immerse themselves in the practice of Judaism and to resist messianic pretenders and end-time speculations.

> First of all, it devolves upon you to know that no human being will ever be able to determine it [the date of redemption] precisely, as Daniel has intimated: *For these worlds are secret and sealed* (Daniel 12:9). Indeed many hypotheses were advanced by scholars who fancied they had discovered the date. This was anticipated in his declaration: *Many will run to and fro, and opinions will be multiple* (Daniel 12:4), that is, there will be numerous views concerning it. Furthermore, God has communicated through His prophets that many people will calculate the time of the advent of the Messiah, but they will be disappointed and fail. He also cautioned us against giving way to doubt and distrust because of these miscalculations. The longer the delay the more fervently we hope.[7]

Maimonides further warned that fervent messianic expectation would promote sectarianism and undermine the legal and community basis of Judaism in the present. His letter to the Jews of Yemen responded to a specific incident in which a messianic pretender had drawn a considerable following, yet the rhetoric of his letter reinscribes the sense of danger associated with active messianism while preserving the hope for redemption in the remote future.

A similar ambivalence between hope for messianic redemption and wariness that any given prediction of a specific time of redemption might fail is reflected in *Sefer Hasidim*. Leaders of the late twelfth-century pietistic movement looked with contempt upon those who speculated about or calculated the time of redemption.[8] In the context of a discussion classifying respectable versus unseemly conduct among scholars, *Sefer Hasidim* offered the following colorful admonition against calculating the time of redemption:

> If you see one making predictions about the Messiah, you should know that he deals with deeds of witchcraft and deeds related to demons or with deeds related to the divine name. And because [... these deeds] bothered the angels, they tell him about the Messiah so that it

will be revealed to the world that he bothered the angels and at the end he will be shamed and despised by the world because he bothered the angels or demons, who come to teach him the calculations and the secrets to his shame and to the shame of those who believe in him, for no one knows anything about the coming of the Messiah.⁹

Sefer Hasidim reflects a concern for presentist practice and ritual which would ultimately establish the conditions for messianic redemption. While it is beyond doubt that messianic movements and longing for redemption periodically captured the imagination of communities and groups within medieval Jewry, prevailing opinion, especially among the intellectual elite, viewed clear expression of immediate messianic hopes with suspicion.

Against this background of restraint, Nahmanides' unreserved prediction that the messianic age would begin in the relatively near future seems at odds with the traditionally conservative attitude toward discussion and speculation of the time of redemption. Modern scholars have therefore questioned the sincerity of the calculations that Nahmanides made public in his disputation account, *Sefer ha-Geulah,* and his biblical commentary.¹⁰ Robert Chazan, for example, has argued that *Sefer ha-Geulah,* a work largely devoted to predicting the time of redemption, was intended to provide a desperately needed boost to the Jews' waning hope that redemption would ever come, not to articulate Nahmanides' personal convictions.¹¹ As a leader who was concerned that the continuity of Judaism was in doubt, Chazan suggests, Nahmanides felt it was necessary to cater to the desire for reassurance. Chazan pays close attention to the broad context of medieval Jewish-Christian relations. He explains Nahmanides' interest in messianism and redemption as the necessary product of an encounter with the Dominican friars and their newly developed missionizing programs, which employed talmudic sources to support their claim that Jesus was the Jewish messiah. According to Chazan, Nahmanides believed that the Dominicans' success in weakening the Jews' faith in their covenant demanded unusual measures to strengthen the Jews' defenses. *Sefer ha-Geulah* and Nahmanides' account of the Barcelona disputation, he concludes, were intended to do precisely this.

In his effort to find external motivations for Nahmanides' assertion of a messianic time frame, Chazan undervalues the role played by expectation of redemption as an interpretive strategy throughout Nahmanides' writings. I will argue here that Nahmanides' attribution of a precise date to the time of Jewish redemption was not merely a defensive, reactionary line of argument made necessary by the success of Christian polemics. Rather, the imminence of messianic redemption is a consistent theme that courses through Nahmanides' biblical exegesis, sermons, and letters, reflecting a programmatic conception of time, history, and change.

Prophecy and a History of the Future

Had Nahmanides introduced his bold claim that the messianic redemption would occur at a definite point in the foreseeable future for the first and last time in a commentary on the book of Daniel itself, it might have been possible to disregard his interpretation as little more than an attempt to make sense of a troubling biblical verse or to reassure fellow Jews about the future redemption. However, an interpretation of Daniel 12:8–12 provided the foundation for Nahmanides' conception of Jewish history as a whole. To frame his biblical commentary, Nahmanides presented a theory of history in its entirety which provided, in his view, the key for making sense of events and conditions in the present and future. Nahmanides represented the Torah as God's blueprint for history.[12] According to this interpretation, the complete narrative of history is bracketed between divine creation and messianic redemption. The patterns and rhythms of historical change, the dynamics of relations between nations, the contours of Israel's relationship with God and the holy land throughout history were emplotted either explicitly or through veiled hints in the revelation to Moses on Mt. Sinai. Nahmanides read the six days of creation as a symbolic prefiguration of the sequence and duration of human history: the complete process would consist of six one thousand year epochs, followed by the seventh era, the age of redemption. This system of interpretation assumed a unity of scriptural purpose and meaning. Thus, the knowledge that time and history were organized in accordance with the structure of creation informed his interpretation of prophecy and post-biblical history.[13]

The meaning of time and units of time in prophecy is a recurring theme also in Nahmanides' disputation account. In particular, he made a concerted effort to establish guidelines for interpreting references to specific units of time. The issue took center stage during a discussion of how to interpret numerical symbolism in prophecy. In a lengthy discussion occupying a significant portion of the narrative, Nahmanides and Friar Paul debated the correct method of formulating a symbolic translation of biblical references to specific time units (i.e., days, weeks, or years). A christological interpretation of the final verses of Daniel 9 provided the foundation for this dispute. In Daniel 9:21–27, the prophet recounts the message he received from the angel Gabriel during a vision. As is typical, the prophecy is couched in slightly vague symbolic terms. Long spans of time are grouped in periods of "weeks," each of which, according to exegetical convention, was considered to be equivalent to seven years. Friar Paul cited Daniel 9:24 to substantiate his claim that both the historical circumstances in which Jesus lived and his personal accomplishments fit the description of the messiah central to Jewish tradition.

> [Friar Paul] responded, saying: "'*Seventy weeks are decreed for your people, and for your holy city, to complete the transgression and to bring an end to sins, and to atone for wrong doings, and to bring eternal righteousness, and to seal a vision and prophecy, and to anoint the holy of holies*' (Dan. 9:24). The 'seventy weeks' are [periods] of years, and it is the 420 years that the Second Temple stood, with another ninety years of the Babylonian exile, and the holy of holies refers to Jesus."
>
> I said to him: "Did Jesus not [live] more than thirty 'weeks' before that time, according to our calculations, for it is the truth which his contemporaries who knew him and recognized him told of him. And even according to your calculations, [he lived] more than ten 'weeks' before [the destruction of the Second Temple]."[14]

Nahmanides readily accepted a reading that grouped clusters of years into 'weeks.' What he objected to was the friar's application of this formula to Christian history. According to Nahmanides' representation, Friar Paul's rendering of this verse was haphazard, sloppy, and over-determined. Returning to a theme he introduced earlier in the disputation account, he compared the Christian reckoning of years, which set Jesus' birth in the year 3755 of the Hebrew calendar, seventy-three years, or "more than ten 'weeks,' before the destruction of the Second Temple," with the chronology accepted by Jews, corroborated by *Sefer Toldot Yeshu* (*The Book of the Life of Jesus*).[15] In his representation of pointed, almost leading questions attributed to Friar Paul, Nahmanides supplemented this line of attack by substituting what he considered a more accurate historical narrative over the chronology derived from Daniel 9:24: the "anointed one" was Zerubavel, the Prince of Judah who resettled Jerusalem before the Second Temple was erected.[16] As such, from the perspective of the Nahmanides' lifetime, Daniel 9 conveyed historical information, rather than predictions of the messianic future.

As this reading demonstrates, Nahmanides insisted that scriptural interpretation follow a precise and painstaking process.[17] This was consistent with the exegetical preferences delineated in his biblical commentary. Exegesis, according to this model, was the product of systematic reflection, at the end of which multiple layers of meaning came to light individually. The biblical verses had first to be read according to the plain sense within the larger frame of the story or text. Only thereafter did hermeneutic devices drawn from other scriptural, rabbinic, or more recent authorities such as Maimonides, Rashi, or Abraham ibn Ezra apply.[18] The counter-argument to Friar Paul's interpretation of Daniel 9:24 illustrates Nahmanides' interpretive method as well as his methodological objection to Friar Paul's interpretation.

> He [Friar Paul] said: "Yes, it was [Jesus who fulfilled the prophecy in Daniel 9:24 that the messiah would arrive 490 years after the destruction of the First Temple]. But in one verse it says *and you will know and understand from the going forth of the decree: 'to return and build Jerusalem' until an anointed prince* (Daniel 9:25). The anointed one is the same as the prince, and he is Jesus."
>
> I said: "This too is a common mistake. For the verse divides the seventy weeks that it mentions, and counts from them seven weeks *until [the time of] the anointed prince,* and then sixty-two weeks for a building with *broad places and a moat,* and then it counts one week [and a half], [at which time] he extended the covenant to the masses, then the seventy weeks were completed. Jesus, whom you call messiah and prince, did not come after seven weeks, but after more than sixty weeks, according to your calculation."[19]

Nahmanides' response to the friar's interpretation of Daniel 9:24–25 scrutinized some fundamental Christian historical claims, but without blaspheming or denigrating the trinity, the holy family, or the Christian saints.[20] He superimposed well-documented events known to have occurred between the destruction of the First Temple and the construction of the Second Temple over the circumstances described in Daniel 9:24–27 to illustrate his point.[21] The anointed prince, Nahmanides argued, was Zerubavel, and the conditions of the prophecy (i.e., resettlement of Jerusalem, reconstruction of the Temple etc.) fit precisely with this time schema. On this basis, Nahmanides posed a solid challenge to the Christian reading of biblical history. This is an important argument for Nahmanides' representation of the disputation, for it was on a christological reading of biblical history and ancient tradition that the Christian claim for the title *Verus Israel* was based. He accepted that Jesus was a historical figure in the Jewish past, but he also made an effort to undercut the weight and validity of historical evidence which fit Jesus into the Jewish historical chronology as the messiah.

However, it was not only Friar Paul's use of biblical verses to decode or make sense of historical events to which Nahmanides objected. He also condemned the friar's apparently capricious selection and explication of the single verse that seemed to confirm the Christian claim, a method which showed little regard for the place of the verse in the complete literary work, or even the discrete series of verses within which it appears. A careful reading of Daniel as a complete literary unit, Nahmanides argued, revealed that only once does the book of Daniel make an explicit reference to the definite time of redemption and reward. This prediction is found in the final chapters of the book, Daniel 12:11–13: "And from the time that the daily sacrifice is removed, and allows for an abomination that lays waste, there will be 1,290 days. Happy is he who waits, and arrives at 1,335 days. For you must continue until the end, and you will rest and then stand for your lot at the end of days." As in his commentary on Genesis, Nahmanides' treatment of this issue began with a careful analysis of the narrative structure, the sequential order, and the rhetorical form of the text as a whole. On this foundation, he argued that Daniel 9:24 did not promise final messianic redemption. Instead, the anointed one indicated in this verse assured the reader that historical figures and events would pave the way to the messianic redemption spelled out at the end of the book. Nahmanides showed that by the time Jesus was born, these conditions had already been fulfilled in the history of Israel. He concluded that true understanding of the prophecy offered in Daniel was available exclusively to those who read Jewish history as a narrative in progress. The historical circumstances of the reader, then, shaped the meaning of the text.

Nahmanides' assumption that the meaning of prophecy was dynamic, regulated in part by the historical time and place in which the reader lived, warrants closer examination. A similar characterization of sacred text supports his interpretation of Genesis 1-2. Nahmanides understood the creation story to contain several layers of meaning, each one temporally specific. In other words, the story of creation was a description of events that occurred at the beginning of time, and at the same time it is an archetype for the history of the Jewish people and the history of the world in general until the time of messianic redemption.[22] The argument advanced in his account of the disputation indicates that Nahmanides understood prophecy, and particularly the portions of Daniel that provide temporally specific information, to serve two functions in the continuing project of Jewish self-narration. Explicit predictions indicate important historical moments in the Jews' sometimes troubled relationship with their God. Prophecy guided the interpretation and explication of historical events and more generally, change. Nahmanides' identification of Zerubavel as the anointed one indicated in Daniel 9:25 is a gesture in precisely this direction. Nahmanides presented his interpretation of Daniel as a demonstration to both Christians and Jews that temporally specific prophecy is binding and exact.

The second line of argument in Nahmanides' discussion of Daniel 9:24 led him to the difficult question of prophetic temporality. Nahmanides argued that when references to specific temporal periods—such as a day, week, or year—appeared in prophecy their meaning must automatically be translated into symbolic terms. In this case, the terms *shavua* (week) and *yom* (day) must each refer to the temporal unit of a year if a greater historical and cosmological significance can be read in the verse. Specific references to time, according to this interpretation, must be understood symbolically in order that the information be endowed with meaning beyond the strict time, place, and significance of the biblical story.

Nahmanides' argument relies on scriptural evidence that the Jewish messiah was to be expected at a specified point in the future. Careful demonstration of his interpretive method was therefore crucial. He focused attention on the hermeneutic difficulty of accurately determining the symbolic meaning of time references via a dispute over the proper meaning of *yom* (day). In defense of his interpretation, Nahmanides brought several biblical examples in which *yom* or its plural, *yamim*, had been generally accepted to mean a full year (or years).[23] He explained that "in the language of the Bible *yom* refers to time [in general]. For example *at the time (ba-zeman) that I afflicted all the firstborn* (Numbers 3:13). The plural form, *yamim*, means years."[24] Thus, the singular, *yom*, denoted for

Nahmanides a specific point in time defined in the context of the narrative by the event or events that transpired then. It is not the *quantity* of time consumed by the event that Nahmanides defined as important here, but instead, the quality which the historical record associated with a set of events, the image imprinted by these events on the memory of any period of time (the duration of which could be unspecified).

The correlative of *yamim,* on the other hand, *shanah* or *shanim* (year or years), indicated the definitive period of a year or clusters of that precise measure. When the Scripture qualified *yamim* with a specific numerical value, Nahmanides argued, the period acquired an exact measure.[25] Daniel 12:11–13 is the example on which he built this argument. These final verses of Daniel contain what Nahmanides regarded as the only information in the entire book of Daniel on which one could legitimately base a prediction of the time between the destruction of the Second Temple and the coming messianic redemption. On this basis, Nahmanides stated with resolve that the time of reward would begin ninety-five years hence, in 5118 according to the Hebrew calendar (1358 c.e., according to the Christian calendar).

In *Sefer ha-Geulah,* Nahmanides undertook the task of distinguishing the biblical prophecies or declarations that had already occurred from those that were still expected and to determine on this basis when messianic redemption would begin.[26] Guiding this argument throughout was the assumption that the temporality of revelation was multidimensional. Revelation—and prophecy in particular—was shaped by and directed to the unique time, place, and circumstance inhabited by the prophet. As such, divine revelation must be understood to be addressing the prophet's immediate political, religious, and cultural environment as well as a contemporary audience. At the same time, from the moment prophecy was committed to writing and later canonized, the message contained in revelation must necessarily transcend the immediate context in which it was given and speak to future generations. Thus, for future generations of Jews, prophecy contained historical records as well as possible information about the present and the future.

Nahmanides confronted the temporal complexity of prophecy in *Sefer ha-Geulah.* He divided this work into four chapters or gates (*shaarim*), each addressing a different layer or dimension of biblical prophecy. In the first chapter, Nahmanides argued that the Hebrew scriptures contain both time-bound, historically specific prophecy, and prophecy that transcended specific historical periods and events. The latter category would include assertions that apply at all times to the possibility of redemption occurring if or when the people of Israel successfully conquer sin and the evil inclination (*yetzer ha-ra*) as well as to information regarding historical patterns which recur through time, such as the tensions between Esau and Israel.[27] Nahmanides used the criteria of consistency of historical context and narrative sequence to distinguish prophecy that was still to be expected from that which the historical record had shown was already fulfilled.

Sefer ha-Geulah opens with the observation that "our Torah is not [replete with] sayings about the future or puzzles, as are the books of Prophets and the Writings."[28] This distinction between classes or genres of biblical literature was crucial to Nahmanides' analysis. It provided an apologetic explanation for entering into a potentially unpopular, even dangerous explication of revealed text. The Torah established the historical and interpretive foundation for the subsequent biblical books. Implicitly, this assertion about the temporal and territorial circumstances represented in the various categories of biblical writings also had some bearing on when, where, and by whom prophetic biblical texts may be read as pertinent in the prophetic sense at any given time and place. In Nahmanides' view, the circumstances and events promised in divine prophecy were unique—they could occur only once in history. As a result, any interpreter intent on distinguishing between outstanding and already fulfilled prophecies must necessarily take into consideration whether the information contained in a particular biblical portion was circumstantially suitable not just to a particular time in history, but also to all other moments in history. Such a systematic evaluation of history and prophecy would ultimately lead to a matching of the events represented in the various portions of biblical literature. On the basis of this comparative reading one could determine with certainty whether a prophecy revealed in Genesis, for instance, had been fulfilled during the time of David, or was still expected.[29]

The details of the narrative that fall between creation and the pending messianic redemption, Nahmanides argued, would only fit into a coherent and meaningful order after first having been measured against the known historical record. For example, the first suggestion that Israel would suffer grave punishment for breaking the covenant with God appears in Leviticus 26:15–56: "If you despise my statutes, or if your soul abhor my judgments, so that you will not do all my commandments, but that you break my covenant: I also will do this to you: I will even appoint over you terror, consumption, and fever that will consume the eyes and cause sorrow of the heart...." In turn, Nahmanides determined that the first egregious violation of the covenant to be punished in the severe manner described in the verse resulted in the first exile.[30] A systematic review of the historical circumstances of the exile in comparison with the conditions of the prophecy led him to conclude that all the conditions of Leviticus had been fulfilled, and therefore they could not be doubled in a subsequent period of history.

Nahmanides drew much of his historical valuation from *Seder Olam Rabbah*, a midrashic chronicle which recites events in the history of Israel from the creation of Adam through the Second Temple period based on biblical and early rabbinic sources. This is also the first rabbinic text to synthesize history and account for the number of years that had passed since the moment of creation. *Seder Olam Rabbah* is innovative in that it arranges discrete events in chronological order governed by causality and continuity. But while Nahmanides borrowed the basic time-line and valuation of events from *Seder Olam Rabbah*, he went one step further than his source in interpreting the data in that he superimposed an analysis on this chronology. The distinction is subtle. In *Sefer ha-Geulah* historical data provide the basis for conclusions about symmetry, direction, and simultaneity of events in history. Nahmanides built on this, elevating the question of redemption to a position of immediate contemporary importance for his own and subsequent generations. Even simple chronology forces events into an order replete with meaning endowed by the mere fact of arrangement. Events must be arranged in the proper sequence before a meaningful story can be extracted from apparently random or unrelated details. For Nahmanides, the priority given to various events changed from one generation to the next.

A brief review of Nahmanides' analysis of the narrative continuity between the books of Chronicles, Ezra, and Nehemiah will help illustrate his method.[31] What commanded Nahmanides' attention in the case of these texts was the question of whether the return from Babylon and the construction of the Second Temple constituted the full redemption promised to Israel, as Friar Paul claimed, or merely one among many significant events leading to that point.[32] Nahmanides argued that this process of resettlement was incomplete because it included descendants of only seven of the ten tribes. The events chronicled in these books are fundamental for Nahmanides' argument that the messianic redemption could be foreseen in biblical literature as imminent for his generation because they explicitly recorded the first return to Israel from exile and could potentially include a key for interpreting contemporary circumstances.

> It is written in the Chronicles in connection with Benjamin: "And all of Israel was accounted for according to their genealogies, and behold, they are written in the books of days:[33] and Judah was exiled to Babylonia for their transgressions. And the first ones who settled in their possessions in their cities were the Israelites—Cohenim, Levites, and Netinim; and [those who] settled in Jerusalem were of the sons of Judah, the sons of Benjamin, and the sons of Ephraim and Manasseh," and so forth (I Chronicles 9:1–3). Thus, the explanation of these verses is that Ezra wrote this book as our sages noted, and he did this to instruct us of the relationship of those who returned with him to Jerusalem.[34]

The portion from Chronicles supported what Nahmanides presented as a precise and irrefutable historical fact remembered and corroborated in the Scriptures. This prooftext specified that the descendants of the Israelite monarchy were allowed to resettle their ancestral lands after accounting for their genealogies. The extensive genealogies provided in I Chronicles and Ezra demonstrate that even among the tribes who returned, the redemption was only partial. Only the return of *all* the tribes in their entirety would have fulfilled necessary conditions for complete redemption.

> I explain this verse in accordance with the opinion of our Rabbis, may they be blessed: of those who erected the Second Temple, a few were refugees from the remaining tribes, and [these refugees] do not represent all the tribes, but only the sons of Ephraim and Manasseh.[35] It is not appropriate to refer to them as 'tribes' [i.e., complete tribes] or even as 'parts of tribes.' They simply joined as a minority with two tribes and lived in their cities, for this redemption was designated for them [i.e., for the sons of Ephraim and Manasseh].[36]

He thus concluded that the prophecy of return was fulfilled for the tribes of Manasseh and Ephraim, but the construction of the Second Temple did not (and was not intended to) fulfill the promise of complete redemption for all Israel, since the return was only partial.

This survey of the history of the return from the Babylonian exile laid the foundation for Nahmanides' assessment of both the past and future of the Jewish people. According to his typological understanding of history, key patterns in Israel's history could be expected to repeat.[37] Using traditional sources, he showed that none of the periods of political or cultic redemption extended to the people of Israel in the past and related in the Bible encompassed the entire nation. Although portions of the nation were rewarded, the moment of true political and historical deliverance for Israel had not yet occurred. *Sefer ha-Geulah* contains many comparative assessments of the relative significance of past events for shaping the outcome of later events. Nahmanides' method of evaluating and determining whether the circumstances related in historical and prophetic literature truly fulfilled the prophecy of national redemption suggests that he deliberately assembled a specifically historical set of evidentiary criteria. For example, he focused on an examination of Ezra 2:1–58, which provides exact numbers of people from various tribes and families who returned to Jerusalem with Ezra, to determine whether the historical circumstance of the return from Babylonia fulfilled the promise of redemption.[38] The evidence provided in Ezra, Nahmanides concluded, demonstrated that this was not the messianic redemption of Israel. Although the historical record shows a national return en masse to the ancestral homeland, this resettlement was partial, and the political sovereignty attendant to it encompassed only those who returned to the Land of Israel. The historical trajectory of the Jewish people, therefore, continued to point towards the ultimate goal of a complete national redemption.

The second and third chapters of *Sefer ha-Geulah* address constructions of national redemption in the books of Isaiah and Daniel and in the Talmud. The approach here is synthetic, aimed at demonstrating a continuity and consensus of opinion among the authorities about what was meant by messianic redemption. Nahmanides argued that redemption would result in the complete restoration of all of the tribes of Israel to the Holy Land as a single political and cultic entity. Building from this principle, Nahmanides concluded that the vast majority of prophecy had already been fulfilled in the course of history; the only prophecy whose domain lay entirely in the future was contained in the final three verses of Daniel: "From the time the regular offering is abolished, and an abomination is set up—it will be a thousand two hundred and ninety days. Happy is he who waits and reaches one thousand three hundred and thirty-five days. But you, go to the end; you shall rest and arise to your destiny at the end of the days" (Daniel 12:11–13). Using this projection as a formula for counting the time of redemption, Nahmanides concluded that the messianic age would begin in less than a century from the time he wrote this book. Since the messianic age would last for several generations, this prediction supported his claim that human history would last for 6,000 years. Nahmanides confirmed his calculations with the interpretive method *gematriah*, interpretation based on the sums of the numerical value of the Hebrew letters contained in a word, phrase, or verse in the fourth and final chapter of the book.

Nahmanides' emphatic prediction that the dawn of the messianic age was on the horizon was rooted in three fundamental assumptions about the relationship between revelation and history. The first of these assumptions is that a unity of meaning, intention, and purpose can be extracted from divine revelation with the application of methodical and systematic exegesis. Attention to the sequence of narrative and the context (in the textual and historical sense) from which verses or passages are drawn were essential to Nahmanides' method of interpretation. The second assumption is that a slightly varied dimension of this meaning revealed itself to each generation or time in history. And finally, that Nahmanides' knowledge of when redemption would occur was an accident of time. His generation was poised on the cusp of the messianic age, so knowledge of when it would occur had been made available to them. As a result, he considered himself obliged to reveal this information to his contemporaries and future generations and to provide responsible, accurate interpretation of the prophecy.

Nahmanides' method in this work scrutinized and compared historical details contained in the biblical narrative in order to eliminate extraneous details and already fulfilled prophecies from the pool of prophecies relevant to the time of redemption. By matching prophecies with events, he claimed, one could determine which circumstances had yet to be fulfilled. His approach was inherently time-bound. Because the greatest sages of the Talmud lived in relatively close temporal proximity to events Nahmanides disregarded as already fulfilled in his own time, the rabbis were unable to see clear of the extra details of prophecy and historical narrative. This final conclusion left Nahmanides in the uncomfortable position of challenging, at times even contradicting the authority of the rabbis in matters of redemption.[39]

Nahmanides understood that his attempt to reconcile an assortment of biblical projections of Jewish redemption with the time frame presented at the conclusion of Daniel was likely to be viewed as radical and potentially dangerous. He addressed this problem directly, taking pains to justify both his engagement in the discourse itself and the range and detail of his speculations.

> Before we open our mouths to discuss the topic of the end, we need to defend ourselves against what was said by the Rabbis of blessed memory: *May the spirits of those who calculate the end be blown away* (Babylonian Talmud *Sanhedrin* 97b).[40] One might say, as we did, that the intent of this [curse] is to show that among them [the rabbis] of blessed memory there were some who knew the end would come only a long time after them, as they said to Rabbi Akiva: *grass will grow on your cheek and still the son of David will not have come* (Jerusalem Talmud *Taanit* 24a). They did not want the matter revealed to the common men for fear that it would weaken their already weakened hopes.[41]

Nahmanides' self-perception as an interpreter of Talmud and Torah was shaped by the sense that his time was one of significance and change. Noting that the rabbis of the Talmud discouraged definitive statements regarding the specific time of redemption, Nahmanides suggested that this stand was driven by a combination of many historical factors, some of which no longer applied in his time. For instance, although the rabbis had the same textual sources at their disposal as he did, Nahmanides argued that the rabbis were both unwilling and unable to draw more concrete conclusions about when this redemption might begin. Their hesitation resulted from a knowledge that complete redemption would occur at the end of the historical cycle, which, as the same passage in *Sanhedrin* revealed, loomed several hundred years in the future. Accurate predictions at that time would only cause the people of Israel to despair that redemption was too remote even to hope for. The fact that the rabbis failed to find clear references to a precise date of redemption in the distant future, Nahmanides argued, was an indication that the time in which he lived was significantly different than theirs. Whereas the rabbis of the Talmud recognized that their time in history fell at the beginning of an excruciatingly long period of exile, Nahmanides claimed that his own generation was blessed to be born just prior to the time of redemption. "And now this reasoning no longer applies to us, for we are at the end of days. Already there are a good many other adherents to our Torah who composed books on this topic, thus there would be no harm done to the people if we too were to express our opinion on this matter, perhaps it will add a positive influence for them and a consolation if our words, with the help of God, agree with knowledge and unite with the intellect."[42]

While he suggested that the talmudic prohibition on speculation about the end of days had expired, Nahmanides at the same time assembled an elaborate argument appealing to historical and specifically temporal qualifications to justify his actions. The rabbis possessed the painful knowledge that they stood before a great historical abyss, a future that would be characterized by extended periods of disappointment and humiliation. The danger posed by exuberant messianic hope at a time when redemption remained a distant promise took a toll even among the great men of the rabbinic era. Rabbi Akiva, who placed his faith in Bar Kokhba, the messianic figure and leader of the failed rebellion against the Romans, illustrates that the rabbis' warning was at that time highly necessary. According to Nahmanides, the rabbis' wisdom applied specifically to their own generation and their descendants, and, at least in this case, their authority to define what was permissible diminished with time. As the moment of redemption drew closer, it became less likely that such speculation might be fraught with the risk of unnecessarily raising and dashing the common man's expectations for the messiah's arrival.[43] Moreover, he argued, the biblical verses could not have revealed to the rabbis of the Talmud the same information that they revealed to him. God had hidden that information from them because they were too far from the target date.[44]

Nahmanides' projection of an impending messianic redemption seems to be rooted in a sincere personal conviction that an outline of the process and duration of history could, with the proper interpretive tools, be extracted from divine revelation. According to this view, the messianic age is the closing bracket of human history, a closed cycle defined by the prescribed duration of 6,000 years. The final verses of the book of Daniel play a crucial role in this formulation. Whereas the story of creation maps out the structure of human history, the prophecy in Daniel 12:8–12 points to that history's resolution and conclusion.

Messianism in Catalonia, an Interfaith Discourse

Thus far, I have argued that Nahmanides' interpretation of Daniel represents a sincere effort to engage the issue of the messianic age. In the remainder of this chapter, I will suggest that this issue provided the basis for a discourse in which Jewish and Christian exegetes engaged each other's interpretations and conclusions. The question of timely redemption had percolated to the fore in thirteenth-century Catalonian intellectual and interfaith discourse, not merely as a reaction to interfaith polemics *per se*, but as an element of Catalonian culture that transcended the boundaries of religious faith. Nahmanides was not alone in his view that the final verses of Daniel shed light on the conclusion of human history. In this respect, he contributed to a more widespread discourse which transformed the final verses of the book of Daniel into prophecy aimed directly at the time in which the exegetes lived. This discourse did not always take place on a personal or interlocutory basis, although the Barcelona disputation was one occasion in which we know these issues were discussed candidly.[45] Jewish and Christian exegetes struggled to assert interpretive authority over scriptural revelation, and over the book of Daniel in particular, as a means of locating the thirteenth and fourteenth centuries in a crucial position on the map of human history. But it is more important to note that both Jews and Christians seemed to engage, if not always acknowledge, timely readings of scripture and prophecy presented by exegetes from the other faith.

Robert Chazan concluded that Nahmanides' calculation of the time of redemption for a public audience was primarily a stop-gap effort meant to reassure members of his community that the messianic era was within reach. He suggests that Nahmanides' unguarded interpretation of Daniel 12:8–12 was intended to reinvigorate the faith of those whose resolve to withstand the trials of dispersion had been shaken by the proselytizing efforts of the friars. While an interfaith dispute over the meaning of Jewish history and prophecy was instrumental in motivating Nahmanides to formulate this argument, it is not self-evident that this was a belief to which he did not personally subscribe. Chazan's assertion that a Jewish-Christian dialogue regarding the time of messianic redemption influenced Nahmanides' thinking on history, prophecy, and redemption is not incorrect—indeed, this was surely a useful by-product of Nahmanides' argument. But it will be fruitful to pursue a new line of questioning, shifting attention from public polemics and proselytizing to more subtle intellectual and cultural currents in thirteenth-century Catalonia.

During the latter half of the thirteenth century, Jews and Christians in Catalonia saw numerous controversies around messianic expectation and speculation.⁴⁶ The writings of Joachim of Fiore played an important role in shaping this messianic or apocalyptic fervor especially among Christian authors.⁴⁷ Joachim's symbolic interpretation of scripture was rooted in the notion of constantly unfolding meaning contained in scripture.⁴⁸ He argued that historical and scriptural symmetry made it possible for an understanding of the time of the Second Coming and the battle between Jesus Christ and the Antichrist to be granted to him, a monk living less than a century prior to the specified time of redemption.⁴⁹ The understanding of scripture as a unified, self-referential system of meaning was a very compelling notion in medieval Catalonia. In the decades immediately following Joachim's death, members of the newly founded Franciscan order—many of whom resided in the northern region of the Iberian peninsula—widely adopted and disseminated his understanding of history and prophecy as a prescriptive system mapping out a very clear order of life and authority to be followed by those living at the moment before redemption.

A good deal of scholarship has been dedicated to unraveling the historical and exegetical methods employed by these friars, many of whom adopted and, in several cases, expanded the apocalyptic leanings of Joachim's teachings.⁵⁰ The vast majority of this scholarship has focused on the Christian or Joachite origins of or impetus for apocalyptic activism, while leaving Jewish messianic expectation beyond the frame of consideration. Typically, Jews enter such discussions only in a very circumscribed capacity: primarily, indeed almost exclusively, as the virtually silent and passive audience for Franciscan and Dominican preaching or as a lingering obstacle to the time of Christian redemption.⁵¹ The body of scholarship on the Dominican response to Nahmanides' disputation account, much of which speculates about why the friars responded with such hostility, can be folded into this category.⁵² While this approach highlights discursive continuity and/or development within Christian exegesis, it necessarily obscures the richly textured cultural and intellectual exchange between Judaism and Christianity as a factor informing the present-centered apocalyptic speculation that became so prominent in certain circles in late thirteenth- and early fourteenth-century Catalonia. Neither has there been any concerted effort to track the influence Nahmanides' interpretation of the time of messianic redemption may have had on Christian exegetes in the wake of the controversy around his first person disputation account beyond the limited circle of friars.⁵³

Arnau of Vilanova (ca. 1238–1311), a royal courtier, medical doctor, and Joachite exegete, actively promoted messianic fervor around the final verses of Daniel using an approach very similar to the one Nahmanides employed. In particular, Arnau's conception of history, temporality, and redemption bears a striking structural likeness to the interpretation of Daniel 12:8–12 Nahmanides publicized in his disputation account, his exegesis of Genesis, and in *Sefer ha-Geulah*. I would like to suggest that the formal and rhetorical correspondence between Nahmanides' and Arnau's methods of interpretation is indicative of a reciprocal conceptual and methodological exchange between Jews and Christians. It seems quite likely that Nahmanides' disputation account, perhaps even his *Sefer ha-Geulah*, was known and taught in Dominican schools where Arnau and others learned it.

Trained at the University of Montpellier, Arnau of Vilanova earned his reputation within the late medieval intellectual world as a physician who treated, among other notables, King James II of the Crown of Aragon and three successive popes.[54] He wrote, taught, and lectured extensively on questions of medicine throughout his lifetime, but in the late 1280s Arnau turned his attention to religious issues. He initially engaged theological questions and biblical exegesis in *Tractatus de tempore adventus Antichristi*.[55] Inspired by Joachim of Fiore's exegetical method, which read a concordance or intertextual linkage between the Hebrew Bible and the New Testament, Arnau turned to the book of Daniel to find crucial information regarding the time of the Antichrist, whose arrival would signal that the Second Coming was near at hand.

One of Arnau's original contributions to Christian exegesis was his application of identifiably Jewish exegetical methods to interpret key historical events that would lead to the Christian apocalypse and redemption. This interest in Jewish exegesis was, in part, a product of Arnau's affiliation with the Dominican *studium* in Barcelona, where he studied Hebrew under the tutelage of Ramón Martí from 1281 to 1285.[56] It was in this context that Arnau began to pursue a method of interpreting Christian scripture and history in a manner that would account for and resolve the theological tensions posed by the continued existence of Jews at a crucial juncture in Christian history. It was also in this setting that Arnau was likely exposed to interpretations advanced by Nahmanides.

In his polemical guide, *Pugio Fidei*, Ramón Martí, who was himself a student of Raymond de Peñaforte, reproduced and improved upon several of the arguments used by Friar Paul at the Barcelona disputation and responded to a good number of the objections to Paul's exegetical methods raised by Nahmanides in the disputation accounts. A product of well-orchestrated teamwork under Martí's direction, the *Pugio Fidei* represents a nearly exhaustive catalogue of Jewish texts and interpretations drawn from the Talmud as well as later authorities concerning the messiah and messianic expectation assembled to refute Jewish objections to Christian biblical exegesis.[57] Although Arnau discontinued his affiliation with the Dominicans, and later came into direct conflict with them,[58] his early education by and association with the Dominicans provided him with the tools for utilizing Hebrew biblical interpretation. These included the linguistic skills to navigate the Hebrew Bible and possibly the Talmud as well, but more importantly, it appears that he developed a critical sense of the rhythms, aesthetics, and hermeneutic preoccupations of contemporary Jewish interpretation. And though Arnau denied that he made use of Jewish sources or interpretive methods, partially to defend himself against accusations that his works were Judaizing, his *Tractatus de tempore adventus Antichristi* and *Allocutio super tetragrammaton* both reflect at least a rudimentary familiarity with Jewish interpretive methods.[59] His engagement with Jewish exegesis is most apparent in his discussion around the book of Daniel as evidence that the arrival of the Antichrist, followed by the Second Coming, was imminent. Daniel had been used before as a key for interpreting the signs of the apocalypse and the shape of redemption. Joachim and his followers, for example, used the four kingdoms to determine when the human historical struggle would end. They used the book of Daniel to reify the generally accepted belief that the drama of Jesus' life and death stood at the pivotal point in human history.[60] In contrast to Joachim, whose interest in the book of Daniel remained focused on structural or figural allusions to the qualities of historical epochs in this prophetic work, Arnau used the final verses of Daniel, "From the time the regular offering is abolished, and an abomination is set up—it will be a thousand two hundred and ninety days. Happy is he who waits and reaches one thousand three hundred and thirty-five days" (Daniel 12:11–12), as the formula with which a well-informed exegete could predict the date of the Antichrist's arrival. End-time speculation as a genre of interpretation necessarily demands both a hermeneutic apparatus and a justification. Arnau arrived at Daniel as the key to understanding the advent of the Antichrist through the book of Matthew, which clearly projects the prophecy of Daniel into the future:

> So when you see the *abomination of desolation*—spoken about by Daniel the prophet—standing in the holy place (let the reader understand).... For then there will be great suffering unlike anything that has happened from the beginning of the world until now, or ever will happen. And if those days had not been cut short, no one would be saved. But for the sake of the elect those days will be cut short. Then if anyone says to you, 'Look, here is the Christ!' or 'There he is!' do not believe him. For false messiahs and false prophets will appear and perform great signs and wonders to deceive, if possible, even the elect. (Matthew 24:15–25)

This passage from Matthew builds upon a fairly rudimentary linkage in Daniel between an economy of punishment and redemption and divinely appointed human agents who represent God's interests on earth. The New Testament established a typological and symmetrical concordance between the distant past and the future. In keeping with the eschatological model proffered in the book of Revelation, Arnau used the allusions to national punishment and devastation in Daniel to pinpoint when and under what circumstances the Antichrist, who would inaugurate the final judgment and lay the foundation for the Second Coming, would arrive. This intertextual approach to prophecy was rooted in the assumption that explicit information about the future could be extracted from prophecy that appeared to speak to a precise time and place in the past.

To support his argument that portions of Daniel contained prophecy of events that had not yet occurred, Arnau first set out to establish that several of the temporally specific passages in Daniel could only be understood to apply to the future—relative to the prophet as well as to Arnau himself—in a literal sense.

> Indeed, in the forty-second year after the passion of the Lord the Romans under Titus and Vespasian destroyed Jerusalem and under a settled agreement allowed Jews to remain on the available promised territory, but they themselves, three years later, violated the pact; thereupon the Roman people, again contrary to what they prepared for, ejected them from the promised land in its entirety in the middle of the fourth year and dispersed them throughout all the world and the regular sacrifices of the Old Testament ceased completely, because the second Law does not permit them to sacrifice except in the prom-

ised land. Therefore, Daniel declared that the beginning of the previously named reckoning ought to be from the middle of the fourth year following the destruction of Jerusalem, since the fourth year was the forty-six years from the death of Christ.[61]

The interpretive challenge he faced was not dissimilar to the one that occupied Nahmanides in *Sefer ha-Geulah* and elsewhere. Both arguments rested on a careful review of the historical record in conjunction with a running tally of which prophecies had already been fulfilled. In both cases, the author found it necessary to establish a convincing rationale for identifying a certain date or event as the time from which to count.

Like Joachim and Nahmanides, Arnau viewed time as a cleansing force slowly clearing away obstructions that had hidden information about history and redemption contained in the scriptures since the time of revelation.[62] According to this view, time was a closed process, contained between a definite beginning and end, which enveloped all of human history from the time of creation to redemption. But as a hermeneutic device for estimating when redemption would begin, discrete units of time—days, years, generations—became important as keys for deciphering previously hidden information about the future. One difficulty inherent in this exegetical method was in locating a defensible and logical point in history from which temporal or numerical calculations should commence. The book of Daniel contains several allusions to symbolically significant temporal units, and a variety of different dates and meanings could be derived from these depending upon the point of beginning chosen.[63] Focusing on the historical context described in the final verses in Daniel, Arnau lighted upon the cessation of sacrifice in Jerusalem and the destruction of the Second Temple. His choice of the destruction of the Second Temple as the starting point is thus quite telling. The historical component in this passage had a dual meaning for Arnau. The first stratum is a symbolic correlation between the 'abomination' described in Daniel and the Antichrist; this link confirmed the Christian story of severe moral degradation followed by redemption.[64] The second layer of meaning made a direct historical connection between the redemption promised to the Jews in the book of Daniel (which was directly associated through Christian exegetical tradition and historical circumstance to the dissolution of the Jewish kingdoms and the destruction of the Second Temple) and Christian redemptive history.

Arnau counted 1,290 years from the time that the daily sacrifice was finally halted, some years following the fall of the Temple, and arrived at the decade between 1366 and 1376 as the time indicated. He supported his conclusion with a clear and fully argued exegetical justification for reading the 'days' mentioned in Daniel as 'years'.[65]

> There are two prooftexts where the Sacred Spirit intends that [the meaning of] year can be gleaned through the word 'day.' The first, as Ezekiel himself explains in chapter four, says: "I have assigned for you one day for each year." The second, according to the revelation of the vision, in which the angel in the same chapter [in Daniel] added after this verse, as it says: "Know, son of man, that the vision pertains to the end of time" (Daniel 8:17). Thus, since the end has not yet come, one understands that 'days' does not mean day in the ordinary sense. For instance, do not 2,300 days usually make six years and 110 days? If so, then the time [indicated] in Daniel's vision would have already been completed, which is false, the words of the angel elucidate as much; as it says: "And when the scattering of the band of the holy people shall be accomplished, all these things shall be finished" (Daniel 12:7).[66]

Anchoring his argument in scriptural authority, Arnau then suggested that all temporally specific prophecy must be rendered in symbolic terms. This approach made the verses at the conclusion of Daniel immediately significant to the time and place in which he lived.[67]

Arnau's claim that 'days' meant 'years' in the prophecy of Daniel bears a strong resemblance to the argument Nahmanides laid out in his account of the Barcelona disputation. There Nahmanides explained that the word day (*yom*) had three meanings in the Bible: the literal meaning, referring to the period between sunset and sunset; a generic meaning, referring to a period or span of time; and a figurative meaning in prophecy and revelation meaning a year.[68] In this context, Nahmanides presented his argument as a response to his opponent's claim that the time of Jesus' incarnation corresponded to the time projected for redemption in Daniel, but the same interpretive device also supported his interpretation of Daniel in *Sefer ha-Geulah* and his biblical commentary.

This similarity between Arnau's and Nahmanides' styles of argument sheds light on a current of suspicion running through Catalonian society about the authority supporting apocalyptic speculation. Both Nahmanides and Arnau invoked canonical authorities to support their refusal to abide by admonitions against apocalyptic speculation. In *Sefer ha-Geulah,* Nahmanides framed his interpretation of Daniel with a defense against rabbinic prohibitions on calculating the time of redemption. In similar manner, Arnau addressed concerns that his opponents might raise about conflicts between his interpretation of prophecy and history and authorities such as Augustine, who condemned avid speculation about the advent of the Antichrist and the turmoil he would cause. Arnau defended the legitimacy of his interpretation, arguing that Augustine's prohibition had been misunderstood and that careful and well-grounded speculations about when the Antichrist would arrive were viable as long as they did not resort to gruesome descriptions of the chaos that was expected to arise.[69]

Arnau's understanding of the destruction of the Temple was innovative in the context of Christian exegesis. The fall of the Second Temple was traditionally viewed as evidence that God no longer viewed Judaism, with its legalism and regular sacrifices, as an acceptable form of worship; the proximity between the destruction and the rise of the Jesus cult served Christian polemicists as historical proof that the conclusion of the Jewish era gave rise to the Christian era. By looking to pre-Christian history, rather than the birth, crucifixion, or resurrection of Jesus, for milestones in the Christian historical epoch, Arnau advanced a view of history which was rooted in a sense of continuity within history as a whole, rather than the radical break between the old and the new suggested by the traditional Christian narrative, and even by the Christian method of reckoning time.

Whether Arnau arrived at his utilitarian reading of Daniel on his own or came to it through contact with Nahmanides' interpretation, either via Ramón Martí's *Pugio Fidei* or through direct exposure to Nahmanides' writings, is not the crucial question. What is both more interesting and more important is the fact that Jews and Christians developed a shared vocabulary for discussing the economy of salvation as well as methods of interpreting prophecy as the harbinger of historical transformations in the near future. As presented in these two readings of Daniel and the time of redemption, this discourse reflected two seemingly contradictory modes in Aragonese culture. It revealed a culture capable of facilitating the production of aesthetic and interpretive norms that transcended the barriers erected by religious authorities and the fundamental power imbalance that characterized even the most open of medieval societies. At the same time, though, the means by which these concepts traveled among members of the Jewish and Christian religious and intellectual elite illustrates the degree to which the ambivalence of similitude and proximity marked this cultural exchange.

It should come as no surprise that the book of Daniel played a key role in Jewish-Christian theological dialogue in the middle ages,[70] as this text contains temporally specific references to the time and shape of redemption. Nevertheless, the parallels between Nahmanides' and Arnau de Vilanova's interpretations of these verses point to a very interesting moment in medieval Jewish-Christian relations. Polemics, whether officially sponsored or informal, provided the forum for an exchange of ideas and interpretations. At times, this exchange was purely hostile, but it also fostered a discourse in which Jewish and Christian exegetes seriously wrestled with the challenges posed by alternative sacred meta-narratives. Nahmanides' interpretation of Daniel 12 was arguably shaped in response to Dominican polemics, but this interpretation also acquired a life of its own in all of Nahmanides' later works, and as such was absorbed into Jewish culture.

Intimate exchange between Jews and Christians took a variety of forms during this period, covering a full spectrum of social, economic, and intellectual relations. Literature on medicine and natural philosophy in the late thirteenth and early fourteenth century, for example, developed through an exchange of interpretations and translations of key texts among the leading Christian and Jewish figures in the field.[71] Yet, in contrast to such 'positive' examples of intellectual interchange, the discourse around interpretation of Daniel as the basis for end-time speculations developed in large measure in tandem with the emergence of an increasingly adversarial polemical exchange. Religious and intellectual leaders thus participated in a tendentious contest. In the process of struggling against the cultural and textual blurring between Jewish and Christian interpretive practices, Nahmanides, like Arnau and other Christians engaged in similar enterprises, utilized the very tools that made this blurring possible. Nahmanides brought a familiarity with Christian interpretations as well as personal experiences and a sense of history as a continuum to his own reading of the Torah and tradition. Contemporary Christian interpretation stands as an unnamed authority against which his exegesis argues.

Events surrounding the Barcelona disputation illustrate that familiarity born of physical proximity, as well as shared cultures and sacred texts, planted the seeds for religious tensions. Increasingly aggressive missionizing campaigns among the Muslims, Jews, and heretics by mendicant friars throughout the Crown of Aragon fostered a greater sense of cultural identification through the acquisition of Hebrew and Arabic and a mastery of interpretive methods as tools for the mission. The friars' commitment to the practical necessity of using rational argument rooted in knowledge of the mistaken theology and interpretations of Jews, Muslims, and heretics, for example, also had the unintended consequence of bringing these unsanctioned interpretations to life in the writings and arguments produced by the mendicants.[72]

As Robert Lerner has shown, this intimacy had a particularly important influence on the Franciscan theology.[73] Intensified scrutiny of Jewish interpretation and practice in conjunction with Joachite-influenced hermeneutics provided the necessary building blocks for millennial scenarios in which Jews *as Jews*—rather than as an abstinent perfidy or as potential Christians—played a crucial role. It is at this point of intersection where Jewish interpretive methods became an invaluable tool for understanding Judaism, but more importantly for making sense of the Christian past and future as well. At the same time, however, this very discourse served to emphasize the theological and ritual differences that distinguished outsiders in late medieval western Christendom, a process that periodically found expression in regulations on Jewish economic activity as well as programs of forced sermons and scrutiny of Jewish books and traditions.[74]

As the Church utilized a growing familiarity with Jewish practices and interpretations to encourage Jewish conversion, exegetical themes, specific biblical verses or passages, and methods of decoding patterns in the revealed text favored by Jewish interpreters began to play an increasingly significant role in Christian exegesis during the thirteenth and fourteenth centuries. The deeply ambivalent texture of this exchange, through which increased understanding of Judaism was deemed both valuable and dangerous, takes especially interesting shape in the broad dissemination of the arguments Nahmanides advanced during the disputation.

CHAPTER FIVE

Language and Literature

Nahmanides' Disputation Account and Narrative in the Catalonian Vernacular

FRIAR PAUL SAID THAT THERE IS NO JEW IN THE WORLD WHO would not confess that [the word] *yom* means a real day. Otherwise, he changes the meaning of words to match his desire. And he complained to the king, so they brought in the first Jew they found on the street and asked him, 'what does *yom* mean in your language?'
He said: "*Diu* (day)."¹

... anyone should be able to declare under oath: I have only one language and it is not mine; my "own" language is, for me, a language that cannot be assimilated. My language, the only one I hear myself speak and agree to speak, is the language of the other.²

Midway through the description of the second day of debate at the Barcelona disputation, Nahmanides interrupted the flow of dialogue and narrative to introduce a surprising narrative digression. In the wake of a heated disagreement between the disputants about whether the Hebrew word *yom*, or day, must be interpreted literally or symbolically in the prophecy of Daniel, Friar Paul complains that the matter can only be resolved by an impartial party. The first Jewish passerby (*ish yehudi*) is brought in from the street and asked to define *yom* for the audience of community notables. He responds to their question in the Catalan vernacular, saying that *yom* means "day."

Symbolic rendering of temporal expressions, such as *yom, yamim* (day and days) and *shevua* (week) in the prophecy of Daniel 9:21–27 provided the basis for an extended argument during the disputation. At stake for the disputants was the appearance of control of or mastery over the biblical passages and the ability to define their meaning for the present day. Friar Paul advocated an interpretation which matched the sense of the prophecy in the book of Daniel with specific events of Jesus' life. Nahmanides, on the other hand, argued for a symbolic rendering of temporal expressions, which would then yield specific information about the future time of messianic redemption for the Jewish people.

Linguistic expression, an author's choice of words, can be a useful indicator of cultural identity. Yet it is just one in a widely varied set; local culture is fluid, and therefore consists of more than a common language, shared idioms. Shared experiences of political, economic, and climatic circumstances, modes of expression, physical comportment, manners, gestures, traditions, aesthetics—not to mention rituals and expectations—are all important components as well. As Anne Norton has noted, "[w]ords are not simply vessels into which one pours meaning or tools used to transmit internal apprehensions—thoughts, passions, needs, desires, opinions, insights—to another. Words and grammars shape the meaning they convey."[3] The insertion of a Catalan-speaking Jew at this dramatic point in the disputation narrative seems to point to an anxiety on Nahmanides' part about how porous the boundaries between Jewish and Christian culture could be.

The disputation in Barcelona was presumably conducted in Catalan, the shared language of everyday intercourse in Barcelona.[4] In the extant version of Nahmanides' account, however, the entire disputation is rendered in Hebrew, the language of Jewish ritual, law, and intellectual production, so that all of the characters—from the king of Aragon to the rabbi of Girona—expressed themselves in the Jews' sacred language. The anonymous Jew from the street is one notable exception.[5] By preserving the anonymous Jew's response in the vernacular Nahmanides made a nod toward the impossibility of translation. As Jacques Derrida has argued, the feeling of belonging in a language is in some sense native—one grows into it from early childhood. Individuals think, speak, breathe in the language that expresses their most mundane as well as their most intimately personal thoughts. The brief interchange between the anonymous Jew, the Christian sponsors of the disputation, and Nahmanides' reader unwittingly demonstrates two things about the language of medieval Jewish Catalonian culture: first, that Catalan was the language in which Jews of the region most naturally expressed the verbal nuances of everyday experience. Hebrew was reserved for the communication of religious or cultural ideals and norms.[6] As the language of Jewish prayer and ritual most Catalonian Jews had at least a rudimentary knowledge of Hebrew. Thus, in the midst of a narrative that self-consciously transposed a series of conversations about meaning from one language to another, it is significant that clarity was represented by the local vernacular. The intrusion of the Jew from the street reaffirms the author's conceit of dramatic and narrative realism, reminding the reader that Nahmanides' disputation account did not represent the monovocal perspective of a biblical commentary or a sermon, for example, but rather, a debate, the content over which Nahmanides had only limited control.[7]

Second, the inclusion of an outside (albeit unidentified) voice reminded Nahmanides' reader that the issues of debate were complex, weighty, and of great importance for Jews and Christians both. In the narrative and in the imagined event represented there, this affirmation of meaning—*yom* is a day—is meant to introduce a set of terms that established a common frame of reference that could be understood by all, from ordinary men on the street to intellectuals in the great Jewish and Christian academies of Aragon. But more importantly for the purposes of this chapter, Nahmanides' introduction of an unnamed character who spoke in the common vernacular reminded the reader that the conversation recounted in this text took place in historical time in the *galut* (exile). The exile, as Nahmanides presented it, was a place and time marked by challenges great and small to Jewish interpretation, ritual, practice, and autonomy.

By reading both the event of the disputation and the texts produced to represent it as a dramatic and literary spectacle, rather than a site of Jewish persecution, the questions addressed to the Hebrew disputation narrative may yield some new information about the currency of Jewish-Christian cultural relations.[8] The question of language—in which language and how Nahmanides was able to speak during the disputation or in which language he chose to write his account—is important, for through the examination of language it becomes possible to engage the disputation account as a work of literature. Nahmanides wrote at least two versions of this account; one in Hebrew, which remains as a complete document, and another as a gift to the bishop of Girona, most likely in Catalan, which is no longer extant. The two texts—distinct but likely not unrelated—represent the author's engagement in the politics, aesthetics, and rhythms of the respective languages and their literatures.[9] In their study of Franz Kafka, Gilles Deleuze and Félix Guattari have illustrated the potential cultural force that can be exerted by minorities through literary production—a creative process that also marks a territory both rooted in the time and place of the author and transcendent of it.[10] They argue that one of the things that made Kafka's voice and literary production both novel and essential was the fact that in German, rather than Czech or even Yiddish, he produced a unique and rich "minor literature." "The three characteristics of minor literature are the deterritorialization of language, the connection of the individual to a political immediacy, and the collective assemblage of enunciation. We might as well say that minor no longer designates specific literatures but the revolutionary conditions for every literature within the heart of what is called great (or established) literature."[11] The choice, or rather, the necessity Kafka faced in his choice to use German as the creative language signals to the reader the author's disassociation from the dominant culture and a mastery of a language and technology of literature—creation for the sake of art, not utility. For Kafka, a resident of Czech-speaking Prague, German was a deterritorialized language, a language which reflected the double, even triple dislocation of Jewish culture and society in the diaspora, and a language which distinguished its users as allied with the superpower of German cultural, economic, and political dominance. Because Kafka contributed to a "minor literature," his writing was thus political and could be seen as representative of a collective, rather than solely an individual voice.

The qualities of a minor literature as laid out by Deleuze and Guattari will be helpful for reading the relationship between the Catalan and Hebrew versions of Nahmanides' disputation account. In both the (lost) Catalan and the Hebrew incarnations, Nahmanides' textual record of the Barcelona disputation contributes to a minor literature. In the case of the former text, Nahmanides entered the fray of a newly burgeoning vernacular literature, much of which celebrated the cultural values of the region. In the case of the latter, he self-consciously assumed a voice and language of interpretive authority. Like Latin, the language of Christian law, theology, and prayer, Hebrew was used by Jews throughout the diaspora as a language of correspondence, business, prayer and ritual, and literature. But Hebrew was not a cipher comprehensible solely to Jewish readers. As the disputation itself shows, Christian authorities were increasingly interested in gaining access to (and regulating) the exclusive world of Hebrew letters. By producing a highly stylized and aesthetically oriented representation of a recent historical event, Nahmanides marked a very clear political territory. Like Deleuze and Guattari's Kafka, Nahmanides wrote as a representative of deterritorialized culture in two deterritorialized languages.

Nahmanides' disputation account is richly adorned with stylistic and substantive clues that expose him as an author navigating in two connected, though distinct political and cultural arenas. To establish his own domain of authority during the disputation spectacle, as the Latin account suggests, Nahmanides exhibited a command of the sources and master narrative of Jewish history and scriptural interpretation.[12] The substance, style, and structure of his disputation account attest to a mastery of the aesthetic and structural demands of contemporary literary production and historical narrative as well. His replication of the dynamic structure and rhythm of the debate by preserving the dialogue form in his disputation account, for example, made use of a literary form with a long and treasured history in Christian and philosophic writing.[13] The effort to achieve narrative realism is evident at several levels in Nahmanides' disputation account, especially in his role as storyteller.[14]

Because he faced a vocal and hostile adversary who enjoyed the encouragement and support of the Christian religious and royal authorities, it was essential that Nahmanides use this text to establish his own authority as a commentator on Jewish literature and tradition (whether his reader was Christian or Jewish), while thoroughly debunking his opponent's profession of superior knowledge. The dramatic literary format of dialogue or disputation provided an ideal setting for this strategy. It brought to life the intense exchange and the process of reasoning involved in religious disputation and polemics.[15] In terms of both style and content, this text is a product of and commentary on the Jewish state of exile and dispersion. The effort to record in realistic dramatic form a challenge to the historical and theological legitimacy of diasporic Judaism is an effort to reaffirm precisely this condition as both necessary and temporary.

The very notion of (medieval) Jewish culture is highly complicated. Exile or diaspora culture is, by definition, a composite or hybrid of the tradition, practices, memories, hopes, literature, and language of the originary culture and those of the 'host' society. Language, ritual, historical perception, and culture are in large measure fluid, in perpetual conversation with other histories and cultures. In other words, diaspora culture is comprised of some constant qualities, but those must be malleable enough to accommodate countless individuals spread over vast stretches of time and space. It is thus very difficult to isolate the subtleties of what is fundamentally *Jewish* in Jewish culture. Even Jewish ritual is marked by the historical circumstances of specific times and places. At the same time, determining the limits of a unique, local culture in the Jewish diaspora is a similarly challenging endeavor. What were the crucial factors that distinguished medieval Catalonian Jewish culture from northern French Jewish culture, for example? Was it that the members of these communities spoke different languages? That they lived under different political patrons? That they developed distinct traditions of interpretation? Is the identification of one such factor sufficient to make a distinction, or is the combination of several factors necessary?

In his treatment of the cultural spaces defined by diasporas, James Clifford argues that diasporic cultural forms "are developed in transnational networks built from multiple attachments, and they encode practices of accommodation with, as well as resistance to, host countries and their norms."[16] Members of diaspora communities are both implicated in and at the same time self-consciously alienated from the dominant culture in which they live. The boundaries of a minority culture, in this case, a diaspora culture with numerous known cousin communities but lacking a viable center or place to which to return (or more precisely, a home abandoned in recent memory), are necessarily porous. Yet, to remain distinct, minority cultures must continually reaffirm and reassert their difference. This is an economy of negotiation that was well practiced by Jews throughout their history. The vast bodies of Jewish literature—written in Hebrew as well as in Jewish dialects of local vernaculars (such as Judeo-Arabic)— that participate in the genres and styles of the dominant cultures illustrate this cultural adaptability.

The textual records of the Barcelona disputation provide a rare glimpse at the way these cultural negotiations were conducted. The case of Nahmanides' disputation account was distinctive in that the interplay and tensions between Jewish and Christian Catalonian culture were played out just below the surface in the Hebrew text and the corresponding Latin records of the disputation. Because the vernacular version of this text is no longer extant, the dual facts of the friars' citation of this work as justification for charging Nahmanides with blasphemy and Nahmanides' claim that the bishop of Girona commissioned him to compose it must stand as evidence to support several assumptions about the texts: 1) that such a text existed and that Nahmanides did write it and present it to the bishop; 2) that the rabbi's account fundamentally differed from the friars' recollection of the same event; and 3) that the very act of composing an account and circulating it among powerful Christian readers was considered a fundamental breach of etiquette on Nahmanides' part. Though none of these suppositions can be 'proven,' entertaining the possibility that acceptance of the friars' charges yields this information presents a fresh view of Jewish-Christian cultural relations in Catalonia. Nahmanides' venture into Catalan letters may represent an early contribution to a body of poetry and prose written by Jews either in the Catalan, Provençal, or Castilian vernacular, or in a Jewish dialect of the vernacular beginning in the early fourteenth century.[17] Vernacular literatures in Aragon and Castile flowered during the late thirteenth and early fourteenth centuries. It has not been questioned that Nahmanides' Hebrew account contributed to an informed Jewish history and culture. It is important at this juncture to ask to what extent his Catalan account likewise contributed to Jewish culture. The remainder of this chapter places Nahmanides' literary representation of the Barcelona disputation in this regional cultural expansion.

History and the Art of Narrative in Thirteenth-Century Catalonia

The dramatic flair, the dynamic quality of the exchange, distinguishes Nahmanides' account from the vast majority of contemporary historical accounts from the Jewish middle ages. A handful of chronicles (in the technical sense) were produced by Jewish authors in the middle ages. These include the *Chronicle of Ahimaaz*, probably written in the late ninth century, and *Sefer ha-Kabbalah*, written by Abraham Ibn Daud in the twelfth century.[18] Yosef Hayim Yerushalmi has grouped both of these works in the same category as the colorful and highly dramatic narrative descriptions of Jewish martyrdom during the Crusades.[19] For his purposes, this parallel is helpful: each author believed wholeheartedly that he witnessed a dramatic shift in the fortunes of Jews in the diaspora. The Crusade narratives, on the other hand, fit more comfortably in the genre of dramatic narratives, which I will address below. More frequently, however, descriptions of important events were transmitted by witnesses in letters to friends or relatives who lived in distant communities.[20] The events described in such letters could be characterized in general terms as disasters in which lives or community autonomy were lost, or near brushes with disaster, from which the community narrowly escaped destruction thanks to the intervention of local authorities. Such events were frequently commemorated with local holidays or festivals.

Hebrew accounts of Jewish-Christian disputations provide a notable exception to this general rule. The historical narrative most closely resembling Nahmanides' account of the Barcelona disputation in both form and content is the Hebrew account of the Paris disputation of 1240. This text records the polemical exchange between Rabbi Yehiel ben Joseph of Paris, one of four rabbis called to defend his faith before King Louis IX of France, and Nicholas Donin, a Jew who converted to Christianity after dabbling with Karaism.[21] The parallel between Barcelona and Paris is not exact. Rabbi Yehiel and Nahmanides were faced with very different challenges by their apostate opponents. Whereas Friar Paul used talmudic literature as proof for the Christian claim that Jesus was the messiah, Nicholas Donin claimed first that the Talmud contained blasphemous references to the historical Jesus and Mary, and second, that the Talmud was designed to blind the Jews to the Christian truth. Finally, this public disputation did result in a communal disaster: after the Talmud was deemed blasphemous, hundreds of volumes of the Talmud and talmudic commentary were consigned to flames.

In contrast with the Paris disputation, where the responses Jewish disputants were allowed to offer were severely restricted, Nahmanides was permitted to respond and, even according to the Christian account, develop his responses at length. The Paris disputation was little more than a session of the papal inquisition seeking and stamping out heresy and blasphemy. Indeed, in this way, the proceedings of the disputation in Paris of 1240 were of a completely different nature. More importantly, the textual representations of these events appear to have been crafted with significantly different aesthetic and narrative tools. The tone of the Paris disputation account reflects anger and helplessness on the part of the author. In contrast Nahmanides embedded his polemic message in an entertaining, at times humorous, work of literature.

Putting aside the similarities or differences between the two disputation accounts, or even between the two events, it is interesting that both authors chose to preserve the formal structure of the original encounter in their accounts. It is precisely this truth claim that has caused modern scholars to question the veracity of Nahmanides' account.[22] Moreover, in view of the Church's increased interest in and censorship of sacred Jewish books during the thirteenth century, some have viewed Nahmanides' decision to write and distribute a text—whether in Hebrew, Latin, or Catalan—that was likely to be viewed by the sponsors of the debate as contentious to be an act of desperation.[23]

The formal charges of blasphemy point to three grievances against Nahmanides: Nahmanides' favorable portrayal of his performance in the debate, his representation of carefully drawn arguments that Jesus was not the messiah, and the fact that he presented a copy of this misrepresentation of the debate to the bishop of Girona.[24] That the friars objected to Nahmanides' assessment of his own arguments and performance at the disputation should come as no surprise; only the last item on this list warrants close attention. How did Nahmanides come to present a copy of this document to the local bishop? Why did the friars object so vociferously to this gift? Scholarly discussions of Nahmanides' text and his authorial objective and motivations have largely underplayed or even neglected the bishop's role as an impetus for Nahmanides' composition of this text. This may be due to the fact that the state of textual evidence has made a conclusive answer to these questions impossible. There is no record of the bishop's request, of his response, or even of the Catalan text itself. Nevertheless, by introducing the bishop of Girona as a significant force shaping the literary history of the Barcelona disputation I hope to present a more modulated image of Jewish-Christian relations and the intersections between Jewish and Christian culture.

Among the many scholars who have commented on this text, only Robert Chazan has inquired with any degree of seriousness about the meaning or significance of the relationship between the bishop of Girona and Nahmanides' narrative of the Barcelona disputation. Chazan, however, does not seem fully comfortable with the notion that Nahmanides composed this text for an audience that may have extended beyond the

Jewish community. Giving some credence to Nahmanides' claim that the bishop requested a narrative account of the disputation, Chazan concludes that it is unlikely that the document Nahmanides presented to the bishop was a Catalan rendering of the now-familiar Hebrew account.

> *While it is not clear at all what the bishop of Gerona might want with a Jewish report of the Barcelona proceedings,* such a request cannot be ruled out. That the Hebrew narrative we possess is the report made for the bishop or a Hebrew translation of that report is most unlikely. Careful examination of the Nahmanidean narrative... reveals it to be a brilliantly crafted work, clearly meant for a Jewish audience. That this was the document written for the bishop of Gerona, however friendly he might have been to the rabbi, is untenable. It seems to me likely that a report for the bishop was written by the rabbi, but it could not have been the narrative that we now possess.[25]

Chazan's discomfort with the possibility that the rabbi and bishop shared their intellectual work is palpable here. In the very act of crediting Nahmanides' claim that the bishop of Girona requested a first person account of the exchange in Barcelona, Chazan negates the suggestion by questioning why the bishop might have been interested in the rabbi's reconstruction of his encounter with Friar Paul in Barcelona. This response is largely shaped by his belief that Nahmanides' account was intended not primarily as entertainment or art, but explicitly to reinforce Jewish faith. Chazan concludes that Nahmanides wrote two substantially different accounts, the first a polemical tract intended for a Jewish audience and the other intended for a Christian audience. As noted above, Chazan has shown that Nahmanides responded to the friars' attack on the Talmud, which he viewed a grave threat, by circulating an alternate account. This latter account was designed to ring true in tone, style, and content, so it could be used as a polemical guide by others to counter the friars' arguments. For this purpose Nahmanides utilized sophisticated narrative and dramatic devices to construct a fictionalized representation of the disputation. The controversy that resulted in Nahmanides' expulsion from the Crown of Aragon was a response to his disputation account.

The argument presented by Chazan seems to imply that a Hebrew account could have circulated throughout the dispersed communities of the Jewish diaspora without official consequence. However, because Nahmanides gave the Catalan document to the local bishop, the account was clothed in a veneer of legitimacy and substance. Whether strictly accurate or not, the publication of these two literary accounts inscribed Nahmanides' version in local memory. Even in the absence of the original document, the circumstances that precipitated the publication of the vernacular account provide a convenient point of departure for evaluating the intellectual milieu and the body of literature to which it contributed. But it is necessary here to ask what motivated Nahmanides to circulate two versions of this text, and how he conceived of the role he wrote for himself in this narrative.

There is no reason to suspect that the bishop of Girona was deeply familiar with rabbinic literature and methods (indeed, he may have been offended by them if he were). At first glance, as Chazan's response indicates, it seems surprising that the bishop of Girona would have derived the same amusement from a first person narrative penned by Nahmanides. However, the evidence that literary culture throughout Aragon, and particularly in Catalan, flourished during the second half of the thirteenth century under the guiding force of a developed patronage network is quite strong. In this light, the literary value of Nahmanides' disputation account, even outside the Jewish community, appears slightly less problematic. By granting credence to the friars' report that Nahmanides professed to have written and distributed the account in compliance with the bishop's wishes, I hope to present an alterative explanation for the genesis of Nahmanides' account and, more importantly, the form it ultimately took. The fact that the friars prosecuted Nahmanides for blasphemy following the publication of his disputation account shows that he moved, however tentatively, in the same intellectual circles as King James I and Raymond Llull, two of the most notable figures associated with the rise of medieval Catalan literature. As the records from the royal court proceedings indicate, Nahmanides' account became offensive and threatening to the friars only after it came into the possession of the bishop.

It is by now a commonplace to observe that Jewish culture in the diaspora developed and changed partially as a result of a dialectical engagement with the people and cultures among which Jews settled. But the act of articulating a connection stops short of suggesting a method of reading which might accentuate the variegated quality of Jewish cultural specificity represented in texts produced in the diaspora. This is particularly so in the case of works in which the author engages issues of a specifically religious nature, such as biblical exegesis or *halakhah*. Unlike his works of religious or ritual substance, Nahmanides' account of the disputation in Barcelona directly confronts culture at the intersection between Jewish and Christian, and between lay and clerical.

Protocols of Jewish-Christian Relations

The King, our lord, ordered me to debate in his palace before him and his council in Barcelona with Friar Paul.

I answered: "I will do as you commanded me my lord, the King, if you give me permission to speak as I wish. And I request [this] permission be granted by the King and by Friar Ramon de Peñaforte and his entourage with him here."

Friar Ramon de Peñaforte answered: "Only if he does not speak blasphemous words."

I said to them: "I do not want to break your law on this matter. But I must be able to say what I wish during the debate, just as you say whatever you wish. As for me, I understand I must speak according to the guidelines, but it must be as I wish." And they all granted me permission to speak freely.[26]

The medieval Crown of Aragon was a multicultural, multilingual society. As a result of the successful conquest of Valencia and Majorca under King James I a considerable population of Arab-speaking Muslims fell subject to the Crown of Aragon. This political, demographic, economic, and territorial shift proved beneficial to the Aragonese Jews. Jewish deputies were a great asset to King James' expansionist policies. In Valencia, members of newly charted Jewish communities were often entrusted with the sensitive business of overseeing and collecting taxes from recently conquered Muslim populations. According to Robert I. Burns, James I colonized newly conquered land in Majorca with Jewish and Muslim settlers because their power base was, at best, negligible and they were uniquely obliged to the Crown. In this sense, Jews played a central role in financing (through taxes) and securing the expanding political, territorial, and cultural boundaries of the Crown of Aragon.[27]

King James I was quite generous in his treatment of his Jews. In keeping with Aragonese Jewish policy of his predecessors, he permitted self-government, freedom of religious practice, and protection from overly hostile or dangerous missionizing practices.[28] Jewish leaders were permitted to collect taxes within the *aljama*, which were then allocated to the payment of duties and fees to the royal *fisc* and to support the central institutions of the Jewish community—i.e., courts of law, houses of worship, schools, the cemetery, and ritual baths. Most important, Jewish communities chose their own leaders who oversaw the operation of self-government and served as an intermediary between the communities and the Christian authorities. King James I benefited from an alliance with the Jewish population of Aragon and therefore cultivated the relationship by making allowances for Jewish religious freedom, economic autonomy, and self-government.

Jewish communities played a central role in the development of Catalonian urban culture and economies. Wills, deeds, and business contracts show that Jewish intellectuals and businessmen figured prominently in the development of urban society during the thirteenth century. Members of the Jewish community in various Catalonian cities availed themselves of the services of Christian courts of law as well as the Jewish court, the *bet din*.[29] This is indicative of a relatively high degree of Jewish integration in the institutions and workings of Catalonian urban life, including the king's principle domain of Barcelona. Courtiers, including the king, employed Jewish physicians. Jews held official administrative posts in many of the central cities in the Crown of Aragon through the thirteenth century, and Catalonian Jews continued to hold significant portions of their family wealth in land well into the fourteenth century.

Royal privilege and protection, social acculturation, and integration did not, however, free the Jews of Aragon from being subject to organized sermons and aggressive missionizing efforts. Following the disputation in Barcelona, for example, King James I gave the Dominicans permission to enter Jewish communities and preach to the residents. There was no inherent contradiction in the policy. King James was as secure in his knowledge that Christianity was the true and correct faith as he was in his knowledge that Judaism was inherently wrong and misguided. It was therefore his duty to make an honest effort to convince the Jews of the truth of Christianity, even while he supported the autonomy of Jewish communities. Yet, his Jewish policy took shape in the context of an expanding empire covering vast territory and containing relatively sizable Jewish and Muslim populations. The Jews of Aragon were an important asset to James I, and the implications of this fact, both positive and negative, were well understood by Jewish leaders.[30] Ruling over a kingdom comprised of three religious faiths and multiple cultures meant establishing a clear social, cultural, and religious hierarchy. Therefore, in keeping with the rules of conduct established in the Crown of Aragon, Jewish leaders were permitted "to answer the allegations that their books contained anti-Christian passages"[31] when King James I saw fit to take an active role in the internal functioning of the Jewish community. Along with the other reigning kings of Christian Europe during the thirteenth century, King James I faced considerable pressure to do whatever was necessary to reshape the Catholic Church in his realm to conform with the increasingly rigid definition of Christian orthodoxy laid out in the Fourth Lateran Council.[32] As was the case throughout Latin Christendom, this meant employing recently developed technologies of discipline and enforcement in the Crown of Aragon, such as the mendicant friars and the papal inquisition to nudge Christian, Jewish, and Muslim dissenters towards the orthodox center. At times the execution of these dictates meant working at cross purposes with policies designed to meet specific local needs.

Analysis of the public nature of Nahmanides' disputation account and the event it represents brings several cultural and social dynamics of medieval Aragon into sharp relief. To a certain extent, what is illuminated in this literature is a complex of power struggles:[33] between the king and his nobles, between the friars and the clergy, between the Jews and the friars, between the king and the pope, and between the authorities in various Jewish communities.[34] By participating in the disputation, Nahmanides performed a service for the king, his political patron, in exchange for the continuation of privileges granted to Jewish communities in the region. Indeed, the act was not inconsequential. Had his performance failed to please the king, the results, for him personally as well as for the community he represented, could have been dire. However, it seems that Nahmanides' performance was pleasing: the king reciprocated by continuing privileges granted to the Jewish communities and, according to the Hebrew account, thanked the rabbi personally with a gift. King James I, of course, maintained a much more complicated net of obligations. At least five royal patronage links—between the friars, the pope, the local clergy, King James I's entourage, local nobility, and the Jewish community—can be discerned between the Hebrew and Latin disputation narratives.[35] None of these relationships was uncomplicated or unidirectional. The friars, sponsored by the pope, petitioned the king for the right to stage a public disputation with his Jews. By granting this favor, King James I demonstrated his respect for the pope and the friars, while at the same time keeping in motion a cycle of mutual obligation.[36]

The position Nahmanides held in the orbit of Christian society during and after the disputation is an issue which the textual evidence hints at without providing sufficient clarity. King James I and the bishop of Girona invited Nahmanides to perform the role of a Jewish leader. Had the friars succeeded in convincing him that Christianity, not Judaism, was the true and righteous faith, the achievement would have been a celebrated added benefit. However, given the pomp in which the disputation was set, the subsequent reward that was apparently paid to Nahmanides by King James I, and the controversy that followed surrounding Nahmanides' account, he was very likely expected to act precisely as he did: as a faithful Jew who argued valiantly in favor of a worldview that was in the eyes of his sponsors blatantly false.[37] Nahmanides' behavior during and following the debate in Barcelona was informed by the dual factors of being a savvy and experienced leader of the Jews in Girona and a cautious though well-positioned client of both King James I and of the local aristocracy of Girona—including the bishop. A reading of Nahmanides' disputation account as a work of literature that self-consciously embraced and manipulated aesthetic and cultural nuances, rather than one that merely reacted to them, brings to light the relationship between the author and his contemporary audience.

Patron-client alliances flourished only as long as the more powerful member of the partnership found the alliance beneficial. The intended reader's expectations, beliefs, assumptions could not help but inform the author's composition. Though it is necessarily a highly speculative avenue of analysis, an effort to locate traces of the patron in the extant version of Nahmanides' disputation account shifts the terms and focus of discussion. The consequence of suggesting that aesthetic or political preferences held by the bishop of Girona as literary patron may have influenced Nahmanides' composition is that the modern reader must revise expectations about the purpose and form of the work. Perhaps the dramatization, even the clear fictionalization in Nahmanides' disputation narrative can be read as a product of his desire to provide his patron with a compelling and entertaining narrative. Acceptance of this proposition demystifies Nahmanides' apparent disregard for the danger posed by Christian interest in

Jewish texts—even taking into account that the text available today is no doubt more scandalous than the one the bishop commissioned. In short, this line of inquiry moves the objective of analysis from the realm of personal motivations to the cultural domain. The fact that the bishop's interest in Nahmanides' performance has been essentially concealed, or at least overlooked in the scholarship, can be traced back to commonly held assumptions about Jewish political powerlessness, on the one hand, and cultural autonomy on the other.[38]

While the systems of patronage in medieval royal courts were less elaborate than in their early modern offspring, many of the same dynamics governed the negotiation of power and culture in both settings. Nahmanides' ostensible involvement in Catalonian court culture is impossible to reconstruct with any precision. Nevertheless, it is necessary to fill in as much of the background as possible. The social and political complexity of Jewish life in Christian lands during the middle ages meant that any risks Nahmanides took in his relationships with Christian patrons could have severe repercussions on his own life and on the entire community.[39]

Nahmanides' participation in the public disputation in Barcelona, his demand for and receipt of freedom of speech (at least according to the Hebrew document), and the cash gift that King James I apparently bestowed upon Nahmanides appear to be part of a delicately orchestrated exchange of favors.[40] In his account of the disputation, Nahmanides seems also to be responding to and engaged in the literary impulse to capture recent events in stylized narratives that emerged in Catalonia during the thirteenth century. His account reflects a concerted effort to record and publicize his role in the disputation in a dramatic, linear, highly orchestrated narrative. The Hebrew version of Nahmanides' account that is available to us today represents the significance of recent events in literary form, preserving a record of events for posterity and perpetuating Nahmanides' performance indefinitely. Nahmanides paid homage to the drama or spectacle acted out during the event, while imposing the artificial markers 'beginning' and 'end' on the structure of the narrative. The form of a literary artifice provided Nahmanides with an opportunity to demonstrate his control of the exegetical methods and practices as well as his mastery of contemporary literary aesthetics.

The form of disputation is a classic stage on which matters of authority and intellectual right were tested. Ritualized demonstration of intellectual and rhetorical prowess was an important aspect of medieval aristocratic culture—in the court and in the university, whether written or performed. Already, by the mid-thirteenth century, the titles Doctor of Theology and Doctor of Philosophy were awarded based on the completion of a formal public or discursive *disputatio* in which candidates presented and defended complex proofs of theological or philosophical arguments.[41] The schools founded by Dominicans and Franciscans also emphasized a culture of dispute and argument. Part and parcel of the training of friars was instruction in exegesis, rhetoric, and dialectic.[42] When placed in the literary genre of *disputatio*, a literary form and practice which shaped standards of representation and authority across linguistic and religious lines, Nahmanides' textual representation of the Barcelona disputation finds its place within a body of medieval literature motivated by broad aesthetic, exegetical, and social norms.

By the end of the twelfth century, medieval royal courts throughout Europe had become important loci of vernacular literary production. The French aristocracy cultivated a genre of vernacular prose historiography which self-consciously posited an unbroken line of descent from the Greek and Roman historical epochs and medieval French nobility.[43] That this historiography was composed in the French vernacular was neither accidental nor inconsequential. The vernacular facilitated a translation of the events of antiquity into the chivalric aesthetic of the high middle ages. It also laid the foundation for an aristocratic culture that was distinct from, even in direct opposition to the French culture defined by the royalty.

The royal courts of thirteenth-century Iberia actively cultivated literary innovation and production. The method of using original narrative strings to join stories or arguments collected from extant documents was in vogue in Castilian literature during this period under the strong influence of Alfonso X of Castile.[44] This method was favored among court historians who began converting chronicles into prose or poetry. A trend along similar lines took place in Catalan letters during the same period and King James I played an active role in this movement both as author and as literary patron.[45] In addition to composing a memoir recounting his accomplishments as king, James I also promoted this literary tradition in his court by building universities in the territories that were under his domain, supporting Franciscan academies as well as individual friars involved in the culture of letters, and facilitating troubadour competitions in the court.[46]

James I's investment in Catalonian literary production is best represented by his memoir, *Llibre dels feyts*.[47] There is some disagreement about authorial motivations and about whether James or his collaborators bore primary responsibility for the shape and content of the text. It is also important to note that the original Catalan manuscript of this text is lost. The version available today is likely based on a translation from the original into Latin.[48] Nevertheless, this work stands as one of the most significant works of thirteenth-century Catalonian (historical) narrative. According to Martí de Riquer, the style and content of this text are driven by a sincere effort to represent events, emotions, and changes in realistic terms.[49] This finds expression in a wide variety of narrative and linguistic devices. Much of the text is narrated in the first person plural, a direct and intentional nod towards the king's agency as both author and historical actor. In addition, in tribute to the king's worldly sophistication and to his multilingual kingdom, the narrator occasionally inserts foreign words into the dialogue of James' diverse conversation partners—an occasional Latin or Italian word uttered by the pope in the course of a conversation with the king, or an Arabic word in the mouth of a Muslim.

Reading the *Llibre* primarily as a work of *Catalan* literature, Antoni Badia i Margarit views even the infrequent intrusion of foreign words into the Catalan narrative as frivolous, even distracting.[50] But the disruption of the Catalan in this text is calculated; indeed, it is a product of the larger project of creating a vernacular literature. It signals the author's command of the languages as well as the power dynamics that made yielding linguistic control, even for a brief moment, a sign of power and authority rather than weakness. James' instinct to record his exploits in the vernacular, rather than in Latin, was a calculated decision. Building upon a tradition that can be traced back at least to the twelfth century, James used the local dialect to chronicle and explain military exploits undertaken in the name of the county of Barcelona, the king's ancestral territory. The narrative style, which includes detailed descriptions of battles as well as more personal or intimate vignettes, highlights the dramatic, suggesting that this work was intended not only to inform but to entertain as well.

Among the distinctive qualities of King James' memoir is the frequent use of Arabic phrases, especially descriptions of combat, negotiations, or physical geography. In certain cases, this shifting between languages served to locate the reader and the drama in contested territory—on a battlefield, for example. Arabized terms naturally filled the martial lexicon during the conquest of Valencia and Majorca and were used interchangeably with Catalan words.[51] The use of Arabic phrases or Catalan words built on Arabic roots also reflected a naturalization of commerce with Muslims. By integrating these phrases into a work that self-consciously made use of the local vernacular King James made a clear and pointed statement about the political and military policies of his government, while at the same time reinforcing a realism of expression and setting. Structural and formal similarities between King James' *Llibre* and Nahmanides' account are more suggestive of an overarching literary aesthetic. Both authors used dialogue, personal tensions, and dramatic tension about the outcome to establish realism in the narrative and move the narrative through a series of similar situations that might otherwise become monotonous and dull. For example, to depict one of several instances in which James was forced to persuade his forces to follow the course of action he chose, the narrator inserted a speech about the balance between personal well-being and sacrifice for the love of God and kingdom.

> And they told Jimeno de Urrea that he should speak first. And he said: "In this land, lord, we do not know what *bovatge* is;[52] and I say to you that, when they heard this thing said, all cried with one voice that they would have none of it."
> And we said: "We greatly wonder at you: you people are too stubborn to listen to reason. You ought to think well on what the business is and you ought to consider whether we do it for good or bad reasons. Because we certainly believe that nobody would be able to consider what we do to be evil, since we do it in the first place for God, in the second place to save Spain, and in the third place so that we and you might win great fame and renown for together having saved Spain, through you and us."[53]

Here, as in the passage from Nahmanides' Hebrew disputation account this chapter opened with, the drama developed around a failure to agree upon the meaning and significance of a seemingly common term. In each case, the author provided an aura of realism by reporting complete, dynamic verbal exchanges as personal recollections.

While King James' memoir is not the only work of medieval Catalonian literature to stress the dramatic in its storytelling, it offers a standard of narrative and discursive techniques employed in mid-thirteenth–century vernacular literature with which to compare Nahmanides' disputation account. By drafting their works in the literary vernacular, both authors addressed a self-selected audience; a limited literary community of readers who could navigate their way through cultural allusions, narrative flourishes, and metaphors in a language that may or may not have been intelligible to clerical literary elites. Framing their narratives in the first person, both established a fairly intimate relationship with their readers while presenting the narrator as the arbiter of cultural values. In Nahmanides' case, establishing this voice demanded more organized and crafted literary license, since maintaining a veneer of realism demanded that he incorporate his position of relative powerlessness in the face of clerical and royal powers as a prominent thread in the narrative.[54]

Many of Nahmanides' arguments amount to commentaries on the Christian conception of (Jewish) history, the time of the messianic redemption, the effect this redemption would have on the plane of history. But, as the disputation was both a spectacle, performed before an audience of political and religious leaders, and a literary work available to an unspecified audience through the ages, it is necessary also to consider how Nahmanides' text might be situated in a wider body of literature. If his presentation of a version of the narrative to the bishop of Girona is evidence for this, then it may be that the disputation account represented a discloser of Jewish interpretation to the outside (i.e., Christian) world. The practical reality of power negotiations, such as notions of literary and political patronage and the ideal of Jewish religious freedom, are very difficult to recognize decisively in any sources dating from this period. However, the documentary evidence relating to the Barcelona disputation contains substantial enough clues to facilitate an analysis of the points of intersection between Jewish and Christian culture, interpretation, and behavior—at least in the limited context of the disputation and events that followed as its consequence.

A CONSTELLATION OF CULTURAL SHIFTS TOOK PLACE IN CATALONIA during the late thirteenth and early fourteenth centuries. These found expression in various literary forms, including, though not limited to, the development of a vernacular literature, as well as efforts to strengthen and centralize royal authority, and increasing Christian involvement and interest in Jewish literature and practice. The narrative aesthetic and the conceptualization of history and redemption that Nahmanides articulated in his disputation account contributed to a discourse that played a significant role in shaping cultural, religious, and political dynamics during the fourteenth and fifteenth centuries in the Crown of Aragon and Catalonia. Nahmanides' participation in the Barcelona disputation and the subsequent controversy over the texts reflect a direct and interpersonal exchange between Jewish and Christian exegetes.

A more subtle dialectic between Jewish interpretations and Christian political, religious, and cultural norms can be discerned in many of Nahmanides' written works. Throughout this study, I have suggested that Nahmanides' engagement with Christian culture was highly ambivalent in nature. His use of typological exegesis, which had recognizable Christian parallels, in service of a specifically Jewish view of history and redemption entertained an interpretive method that Jews and Christians could share, while at the same time, offering a corrective to the Christian application of these readings. Similarly, Nahmanides' rendering of the need for ritual and cultural accommodation to different diasporic settings seems to render interaction and exchange with the gentile world—whether it be Christian, Muslim, or even Babylonian—as both necessary and fruitful steps in an unfolding process leading to historical and spiritual redemption of the people of Israel. Ambivalent though it was, Nahmanides' engagement with Christianity and Catalonian culture was significant to his interpretation and conception of Judaism, and to the way he fashioned himself as a leader, a teacher, and an exegete.

Notes

Notes to the Introduction

1. Nahmanides has been characterized by modern scholars as the rare leader who could maintain amicable relations with Christian leaders and with multiple factions within the Jewish communities. Three dominant themes emerge in this literature: Nahmanides' contribution to and interpretation of Kabbalah, a comparison between Nahmanides' and Maimonides' interpretive and leadership methods, and Jewish-Christian relations and polemics. Some recent examples of the former two include the following (I will address the final category separately): Henri Atlan, "Rationalisme et théologie: Maïmonide et Nahmanide," *Les nouveaux cahiers* 118 (1994): 5–14; Menachem Lorberbaum, *Politics and the Limits of the Law: Secularizing the Political in Medieval Jewish Thought* (Stanford, CA: Stanford University Press, 2001); Josef Stern, "The Fall and Rise of Myth in Ritual: Maimonides versus Nahmanides on the *Huqqim*, Astrology, and the War against Idolatry," *The Journal of Jewish Thought and Philosophy* 6 (1997): 185–263; Elliot R. Wolfson, "'By Way of Truth': Aspects of Nahmanides' Kabbalistic Hermeneutic," *AJS Review* 14, no. 2 (1989): 103–178; Elliot R. Wolfson, "The Secret Garment in Nahmanides," *Da'at* 24 (1990): xxv–xlix; P. Christopher Smith, *The Hermeneutics of Original Argument: Demonstration, Dialectic, Rhetoric* (Evanston, IL: Northwestern University Press, 1998); Haviva Pedaya, *Ha-Ramban: Hitalut—Zeman Mahzori ve-Tekst Kadosh* (Tel Aviv: Am Oved, 2003).

2. In particular see Yom Tov Assis, *Jewish Economy in the Medieval Crown of Aragon, 1213–1327: Money and Power* (Leiden: E. J. Brill, 1997); Yom Tov Assis, *The Golden Age of Aragonese Jewry: Community and Society in the Crown of Aragon, 1213–1327* (London: Littman Library of Jewish Civilization, 1997); Leila Berner, "On the Western Shores: The Jews of Barcelona during the Reign of Jaume I, 'el

Conqueridor,' 1213–1276" (PhD dissertation, University of California, Los Angeles, 1986); Mark D. Meyerson, *A Jewish Renaissance in Fifteenth-Century Spain* (Princeton, NJ: Princeton University Press, 2004); Mark D. Meyerson, *Jews in an Iberian Frontier Kingdom: Society, Economy, and Politics in Morvedre, 1248–1391* (Leiden: Brill, 2004); Jonathan Ray, *The Sephardic Frontier: The Reconquista and the Jewish Community of Medieval Iberia* (Ithaca, NY: Cornell University Press, 2006). For a similar approach to Jewish communities in Castile, see Nina Melechen, "Loans, Land, and Jewish-Christian Relations in Archdiocese of Toledo," in *Iberia and the Mediterranean World of the Middle Ages: Studies in Honor of Robert I. Burns*, ed. Larry J. Simon (Leiden: E. J. Brill, 1995); Nina Melechen, "The Jews of Medieval Toledo: Their Economic and Social Contacts with Christians from 1150 to 1391" (PhD dissertation, Fordham University, 1999).

3. María Rosa Menocal's recent study of medieval Iberian culture straddles the line between popular and scholarly analysis. While her understanding and interpretation of the literary culture of medieval Al-Andalus are unassailable, her tendency to apply the same interpretive paradigm to politics, social life, and economics perhaps overly romanticizes interfaith relations in medieval Iberia. See María Rosa Menocal, *The Ornament of the World: How Muslims, Jews, and Christians Created a Culture of Tolerance in Medieval Spain* (Boston: Little, Brown, 2002).

4. Perhaps the best example of this can be found in Yitzhak Baer's work. Though he objected to Americo Castro's formulation of the dynamics as *convivencia*, Baer mobilizes a very similar set of assumptions in his work on medieval Spanish Jewry. At the very foundation of his argument is the claim that Jewish comfort or acculturation in medieval Christian Spain—especially among the political and economic elite—provided the very conditions that made the persecution and later expulsion of Jews from Spain seem necessary to the Christian authorities in the late fifteenth century. See Yitzhak Baer, *A History of the Jews in Christian Spain: From the Reconquest to the Fourteenth Century*, trans. Louis Schoffman, 2 vols. (Philadelphia: Jewish Publication Society of America, 1961), 2:444–456.

5. Esther Benbassa and Aron Rodrigue, *Sephardi Jewry: A History of the Judeo-Spanish Community, 14th–20th Centuries* (Berkeley: University of California Press, 2000), xxv–liv; Jane Gerber, *The Jews of Spain: A History of the Sephardic Experience* (New York: The Free Press, 1992), 59–144; Menocal, *The Ornament of the World*.

6. By now there are numerous critical analyses of the assumptions and methods of *convivencia* studies. Many of these critiques call for moderation and objectivity in the portrayal of medieval Iberia. Since 2001, what is at stake in responsibly representing the medieval Iberian past has changed dramatically. During a period when the phrase 'conflict of civilizations' is regularly used in the popular media to describe relations between the (Christian) west and the (Muslim) east, it is a worthy effort to subject historical studies in which interfaith relations are portrayed as

largely peaceful and mutually beneficial to close and critical scrutiny. Many of these critiques begin by interrogating the very notion of 'tolerance' in the medieval setting. See Ross Brann, *Power in the Portrayal: Representations of Jews and Muslims in Eleventh- and Twelfth-Century Islamic Spain* (Princeton, NJ: Princeton University Press, 2002), 1–21; Thomas F. Glick, "Convivencia: An Introductory Note," in *Convivencia: Jews, Muslims, and Christians in Medieval Spain*, ed. Vivian Mann, Thomas F. Glick, and Jerrilynn D. Dodd (New York: George Braziller, 1992), 1–9; Thomas F. Glick, *Islamic and Christian Spain in the Early Middle Ages*, 2nd rev. ed. (Leiden: Brill, 2005), xi–xxii; Jonathan Ray, "Beyond Tolerance and Persecution: Reassessing Our Approach to Medieval *Convivencia*," *Jewish Social Studies* 11, no. 2 (2005): 1–18; David Nirenberg, *Communities of Violence: Persecution of Minorities in the Middle Ages* (Princeton, NJ: Princeton University Press, 1996) (Nirenberg's complete work represents a revision of the conception of *convivencia* in that he reframes the interfaith cultural exchange that took place in northern Iberia and southern France in terms of violence and animosity rather than cultural development); Alex Novikoff, "Between Tolerance and Intolerance in Medieval Spain: An Historiographic Enigma," *Medieval Encounters* 11, no. 1–2 (2005): 7–36. For a general history of the conceptualization and application of 'tolerance' in Europe during the middle ages and early modern period, see István Bejczy, "*Tolerantia*: A Medieval Concept," *Journal of the History of Ideas* 58, no. 3 (1997): 365–384; Perez Zagorin, *How the Idea of Religious Toleration Came to the West* (Princeton, NJ: Princeton University Press, 2003).

7. It is not surprising that this narrative is most prevalent as the frame for histories of the Inquisition and the events that led to its establishment. See, for example Baer, *A History of the Jews in Christian Spain*; Ha'im Beinart, "Order of the Expulsion from Spain: Antecedents, Causes, and Textual Analysis," in *Crisis and Creativity in the Sephardic World, 1391–1648*, ed. Benjamin Gampel (New York: Columbia University Press, 1997), 79–94; and Benzion Netanyahu, *The Marranos of Spain, from the Late 14th to the 16th Century, According to Hebrew Sources*, 3rd ed. (Ithaca, NY: Cornell University Press, 1999).

8. On the lachrymose view of history, see Salo W. Baron, "Ghetto and Emancipation," *Menorah Journal* 14 (1928): 515–528.

9. Much recent scholarship makes a significant dent in the viability of this tragic narrative frame, even as it applies to the late middle ages. See Meyerson, *A Jewish Renaissance*; Meyerson, *Jews in an Iberian Frontier Kingdom*; Nirenberg, *Communities of Violence*.

10. On cultural symbiosis between Jews and Christians, see Talya Fishman, "The Penitential System of Hasidei Ashkenaz and the Problem of Cultural Boundaries," *The Journal of Jewish Thought and Philosophy* 8, no. 2 (1999): 201–229; Ivan G. Marcus, *Rituals of Childhood: Jewish Acculturation in Medieval Europe* (New Haven, CT: Yale University Press, 1996); Nirenberg, *Communities of Violence*; Israel Jacob Yuval, *Two Nations in Your Womb: Perceptions of Jews and*

Christians in Late Antiquity and the Middle Ages, trans. Barbara Harshav and Jonathan Chipman (Berkeley: University of California Press, 2006).

11. *Halakhah* is the legal apparatus that was first formalized in the Mishnah and then in the Talmud. It is a constantly evolving system which addressed the changing conditions of Jewish life and community. As halakhic thinking has its roots both in stable biblical foundations and in an exchange between learned discussions concerning the form and structure of biblical passages and applications of legal innovations in the diaspora, it is fundamentally a dynamic form. In so far as this study deals with *halakhah,* it is primarily interested in the way that Nahmanides maintained a balance between precedent and novel interpretations.

12. Haim Dov Chavel, *Kitvei Rabbenu Moshe ben Nahman,* 2 vols. (Jerusalem: Mosad Ha-Rav Kook, 1964), 1:336–351; Joseph Perles, "Nachträge über R. Moses ben Nachman," *Monatsschrift für Geschichte und Wissenschaft des Judentums* 9 (1860): 184–195.

13. Chavel, *Kitvei Rabbenu Moshe ben Nahman,* 302–320.

14. Amos Funkenstein, *Perceptions of Jewish History* (Berkeley: University of California Press, 1993), 112–121; Gershom Scholem, *Origins of the Kabbalah,* trans. Allan Arkush (Princeton, NJ: Jewish Publication Society and Princeton University Press, 1987), 449–454.

15. Funkenstein, *Perceptions of Jewish History,* 117–121.

16. Ibid., 112–119. Gershom Scholem makes a similar argument, suggesting that Nahmanides' interpretation of Genesis was influenced by Christian exegesis. "Nahmanides also used Christian sources elsewhere, as in the parallel drawn between the week of creation and the week of the worlds (derived from Isadore of Seville) and in his doctrine of the purificatory nature of Purgatory (in *Sha'ar ha-Gemul*)" (Scholem, *Origins of the Kabbalah,* 449).

17. See, for example, Robert Chazan, *Barcelona and Beyond: The Disputation of 1263 and Its Aftermath* (Berkeley and Los Angeles: University of California Press, 1992). Also, although arguments are not configured in precisely these terms, the scholarship on the esoteric in Nahmanides' teachings and writings follows a similar pattern: Daniel Abrams, "Orality in the Kabbalistic School of Nahmanides: Preserving and Interpreting Esoteric Traditions and Texts," *Jewish Studies Quarterly* 3, no. 1 (1996): 85–102; Moshe Idel, "Rabbi Moshe ben Nahman: Kabbalah, Halakhah and Spiritual Leadership" (Hebrew), *Tarbiz* 64, no. 4 (1995): 535–580; Wolfson, "'By Way of Truth'."

18. For an extensive and detailed account of the political and economic history of Barcelona, see Stephen P. Bensch, *Barcelona and Its Rulers, 1096–1291* (Cambridge: Cambridge University Press, 1995). David Abulafia, *A Mediterranean Emporium: The Catalan Kingdom of Majorca* (Cambridge: Cambridge University Press, 1994) is a study of the unique economy which developed on the island of Majorca, which was ruled by the house of Barcelona.

19. Bensch, *Barcelona and Its Rulers, 1096–1291,* 282–288. On the Jewish contribution of economic development in the Crown of Aragon, see Assis, *Jewish*

Economy. Some of Assis's pioneering findings have come under revision in three more recent works. David Abulafia, Elka Klein, and Jonathan Ray all suggest that less emphasis should be placed on the role Jews played in money lending and credit-based businesses. See Elka Klein, *Jews, Christian Society, and Royal Power in Medieval Barcelona* (Ann Arbor: University of Michigan Press, 2006), 143–148 and 163–191 and Ray, *The Sephardic Frontier*, 54–74.

20. For a brief overview of demographic changes from the early thirteenth through the fourteenth centuries, see Robert I. Burns, *Jews in the Notarial Culture: Latinate Wills in Mediterranean Spain, 1250–1350* (Berkeley: University of California Press, 1996), 11–22.

21. Jean Régné, *History of the Jews in Aragon: Regesta and Documents, 1213–1327*, ed. Yom Tov Assis and Adam Gruzman (Jerusalem: Magnes Press, Hebrew University, 1978), doc. #36, 7. In particular, this invitation names Solomon ben Ammar and a certain Jucef, distinguished residents of Fez. For discussion of Jewish communal life in the newly conquered Valencia, see Robert I. Burns, "Jaume I and the Jews of the Kingdom of Valencia," in *X Congreso de Historia de la Corona de Aragón: Jaime I y su época* (Zaragoza: Institución Fernando el Catalico, 1979), 245–322.

22. On the formation of a historical, political, and cultural identity among the nobility of Catalonia, see Thomas N. Bisson, *Tormented Voices: Power, Crisis, and Humanity in Rural Catalonia, 1140–1200* (Cambridge, MA: Harvard University Press, 1998) and John C. Shideler, *A Medieval Catalan Noble Family: The Montcadas, 1000–1230* (Berkeley: University of California Press, 1983). On the class system within Catalonia, see Paul Freedman, *The Origins of Peasant Servitude in Medieval Catalonia* (Cambridge: Cambridge University Press, 1991), especially 119–153.

23. Thomas N. Bisson, *The Medieval Crown of Aragon, A Short History* (Oxford: Clarendon Press, 1986), 76. Also, Klein, *Jews, Christian Society, and Royal Power*, 142–161.

24. Elka Klein's recent study of the Jewish community of Barcelona destabilizes some standard assumptions about the processes of Jewish settlement and organization. She suggests that Jews organized as autonomous communities not because the Talmud instructed them to, but rather because it was desirable and convenient for royal and local leaders that they do so. See Klein, *Jews, Christian Society, and Royal Power*, 26–51.

25. This discussion is largely based on extensive research conducted by Yitzhak Baer, Yom Tov Assis, and Elka Klein. Baer's work is a highly detailed and complete sketch of Jewish life and culture throughout the Iberian peninsula based on Jewish and Christian sources. Among its shortcomings, however, is a tendency to paint in very broad strokes, minimizing the distinctions between Castile and Aragon or subtle changes over time. Assis's representation of Jewish life in medieval Aragon is not significantly different, but he contributes a far more nuanced and responsible use of sources. He is careful throughout to underscore when and where changes occurred. Moreover, he focuses his research and conclusions on

the Crown of Aragon. Although Jewish self-government was in effect in the Crown of Aragon at least since the twelfth century, Hebrew and Latin documentation dealing with Jewish community organization in the Crown of Aragon is quite sparse until the latter half of the thirteenth century. Assis primarily relies on the writings of Solomon ben Adret (Rashba, 1235–1310) for his reconstruction of Jewish leadership. The Rashba was an important intermediary between the king, the representatives on the *aljama*, and the lower classes during a bitter dispute concerning the structure and inequity of Jewish community government. Because the changes in Jewish self-government had such a profound impact on Jewish life (or at least on the documents recording Jewish life) Assis takes Adret at his word in his description of conditions of the *aljama* throughout the thirteenth century. On the genesis of political structures within Jewish communities in the diaspora, see Yitzhak Baer, "The Origins of the Organisation of the Jewish Community of the Middle Ages" (Hebrew), *Tziyon* 15 (1950): 1–41; on the development of Jewish political institutions on the Iberian peninsula, see Baer, *A History of the Jews in Christian Spain*, 1:212–236. On the specific case of Aragon, see Assis, *The Golden Age*, 70–71 and 91–92. (The vast majority of Assis's footnotes, throughout the book, refer to Solomon ben Adret's writings.) For a more general discussion of Jewish community organization, see Daniel J. Elazar, "The Kehillah," in *Kinship and Consent: The Jewish Political Tradition and Its Contemporary Uses*, ed. Daniel J. Elazar (New Brunswick, NJ: Transaction, 1997), 233–276, especially 242–255, and Baer, "The Origins," 1–41. On Barcelona in particular, see Berner, "On the Western Shores," and Klein, *Jews, Christian Society, and Royal Power*.

26. Royal documents apply the same term (which is of Arabic derivation) to autonomous Muslim communities within the Crown of Aragon. See L. P. Harvey, *Islamic Spain 1250 to 1500* (Chicago: University of Chicago Press, 1990), 98–137. Also see Abulafia, *A Mediterranean Emporium*, 56–74 and Robert I. Burns, *Muslims, Christians, and Jews in the Crusader Kingdom of Valencia: Societies in Symbiosis* (Cambridge: Cambridge University Press, 1984), 9–51.

27. Local specificity was often determined by an order or privilege issued by the king. For example, in 1258 King James I granted permission to the Jews of Girona and Beslau to elect five representatives to collect and disperse revenue. This privilege granted the tax-collecting body the right to collect revenue in the form of products—agricultural goods, household utensils, or oil—when debtors had no other means of payment. See Régné, *History of the Jews in Aragon*, docs. #97–98, 18–19; Baer, *A History of the Jews in Christian Spain*, 186–235.

28. Yom Tov Assis lists twenty-seven different titles used with some consistency in Hebrew and Latin sources, though it is not always clear that their meaning was consistent. See Assis, *The Golden Age*, 122–128.

29. Ibid., 91.

30. Ibid., 80–85.

31. Régné, *History of the Jews in Aragon*, doc. #1–657, 1–111. According to Assis, King James I and his heirs to the throne frequently saw to it that their fa-

vorites, those who served in the court or as trusted administrators in the government of the Crown, were appointed to serve as *dayyanim*. See Assis, *The Golden Age*, 101.

32. King James I consulted Nahmanides in 1232 about the potential benefits of allowing the Alconstantini family to assume the title of *dayyanim* for the entire Crown of Aragon. Following Nahmanides' advice against this step, King James withheld this title, though the Alconstantini family continued to hold considerable power among Aragonese Jews until the end of the fourteenth century when popular uprisings resulted in a royally supervised effort to restructure Jewish community leadership. See Régné, *History of the Jews in Aragon*, doc. #1852, 331, doc. #1857, 331–332, doc. #1863, 333, doc. #1865, 334, doc. #1871, 335; Assis, *The Golden Age*, 165–167 and 237–241. Also see Baer, *A History of the Jews in Christian Spain*, 212–231.

33. Babylonian Talmud *Avodah Zarah* 36a.

34. Assis, *The Golden Age*, 132–135; Elka Klein, "The Widow's Portion: Law, Custom, and Marital Property among Medieval Catalan Jews," *Viator* 31 (2000): 147–163; Elka Klein, "Splitting Heirs: Patterns of Inheritance among Barcelona's Jews," *Jewish History* 16, no. 1 (2002): 49–71. Also see Robert I. Burns, *Diplomatarium of the Crusader Kingdom of Valencia, the Registered Charters of Its Conqueror Jaume I, 1257–1276*, 2 vols. (Princeton, NJ: Princeton University Press, 1985), 1:29–32 and 125–133; Burns, *Jews in the Notarial Culture*.

35. Klein, "Splitting Heirs"; Assis, *The Golden Age*, 274–278.

36. It is important to note here that a larger number of Latin wills remain than Hebrew wills. The mass riots of 1391 and the subsequent expulsion of Iberian Jewry may partially account for this imbalance, since the extant wills remain in Christian archives. See Klein, "Splitting Heirs," 51–57; and Burns, *Jews in the Notarial Culture*, 22–31.

37. On efforts to reform Jewish law in keeping with local practices, see Jacob Katz, *Exclusiveness and Tolerance: Studies in Jewish-Gentile Relations in Medieval and Modern Times* (Oxford: Oxford University Press, 1961), 37–63; Gideon Libson, "Halakhah and Reality in the Gaonic Period: Taqqanah, Minhag, Tradition and Consensus—Some Observations," in *The Jews of Medieval Islam: Community, Society, and Identity*, ed. Daniel Frank (Leiden: E. J. Brill, 1995), 67–99.

38. Chapter one of the present study contains a detailed discussion of this controversy and the modern scholarship on it. In another dispute over valid legal jurisdiction, the community of Saragossa taxed Jews from other cities who set up trade in their city. See Assis, *The Golden Age*, 166.

39. It was also a possibility that a philanthropist would pay educational fees for the poor; see ibid., 308–314 and 327–334.

40. Burns, *Jews in the Notarial Culture*, 46–48; David Nirenberg, "A Female Rabbi in Fourteenth-Century Zaragoza?" *Sefarad* 51, no. 1 (1991): 179–182.

41. The position of rabbi became an official position administered by the king in the Crown of Aragon around the turn of the fourteenth century. This shift

in the structure of Jewish leadership was not well received outside of aristocratic circles. "Some of the communal or regional rabbis were appointed by the king. The Jewish communities throughout the kingdom resisted attempts by the king or his entourage to impose on them rabbis whom they had not chosen themselves.... The court rabbis did not owe their position to their expertise but rather to their influence in the court" (Assis, *The Golden Age*, 141).

Chapter 1   The Maimonidean Controversy

1. On the interpretive methods Maimonides applied in the *Mishneh Torah*, see Isadore Twersky, *Introduction to the Code of Maimonides (Mishneh Torah)* (New Haven, CT: Yale University Press, 1980), 97–142.

2. Maimonides, *The Guide of the Perplexed*, trans. Shlomo Pines, 2 vols. (Chicago: University of Chicago Press, 1963), 524. On Maimonides' treatment of the practical purposes of the commandments (*taamei ha-mitzvot*), see Amos Funkenstein, *Perceptions of Jewish History* (Berkeley: University of California Press, 1993), 131–147. Also see Josef Stern, *Problems and Parables of Law: Maimonides and Nahmanides on Reasons for the Commandments (Ta'amei ha-Mitzvot)* (Albany: SUNY Press, 1998), 15–48.

3. On the mechanics of Jewish community government and the authority of the *herem*, see Gerald J. Blidstein, "Individual and Community in the Middle Ages: Halakhic Theory," in *Kinship and Consent: The Jewish Political Tradition and Its Contemporary Uses*, ed. Daniel J. Elazar (Washington, DC: University Press of America, 1997), 327–369; Aryeh Graboïs, "The Use of Letters as a Communication Medium among Medieval European Jewish Communities," in *Communication in the Jewish Diaspora: The Pre-Modern World*, ed. Sophia Menache (Leiden: E. J. Brill, 1996), 93–105; Samuel Morell, "The Constitutional Limits of Communal Government in Rabbinic Law," *Jewish Social Studies* 33, no. 2–3 (1971): 87–119.

4. Jonah Gerundi played a significant role in several portions of this story. As a disciple of Solomon ben Abraham, he actively pursued a policy of censorship. Because he spent some time in a *yeshivah* in Northern France, he was also an ideal conduit for translating the teachings of Maimonides from the south to the north. Finally, his involvement in the Maimonidean controversy will also be important as we consider Nahmanides' response to the French rabbis' universal *herem* and to the later relations on the part of Maimonides' defenders because Jonah was Nahmanides' cousin (the son of his mother's brother). For biographic information on Jonah Gerundi, see Abe Tobie Shrock, *Rabbi Jonah ben Abraham of Gerona: His Life and Ethical Works* (London: Edward Goldstein, 1948), especially 21–41 on his education and 134–145 on his role in communal leadership. Also see Israel Ta-Shma, "Rabbi Yonah Girondi: Spirituality and Leadership," in *Jewish Mystical Leaders and Leadership in the 13th Century*, ed. Moshe Idel and Mortimer Ostow (Northvale, NJ: Jason Aronson, 1998), 155–177.

5. The text of the French rabbis' order of *herem* is no longer extant, however it is possible to piece together the tone of the order from the responses on both sides of the controversy. Primary documentation of this conflict is contained in a series of letters that circulated throughout the Jewish communities of Europe in 1232, most of which were written by the supporters of Maimonidean interpretation. These are reproduced in A. L. Lichtenberg, ed., *Kovetz Teshuvot ha-Rambam ve-Egerotav* (Leipzig: 1859), Section III. (The enumeration in this volume is peculiar. The entire volume is in Hebrew with text printed on both sides of each page, but the front and back of each page bears the same number, the first an Arabic numeral and the second the Hebrew letter corresponding to the numerical value. To preserve clarity I refer to the first of the printed pages as 'a' and the second as 'b': i.e., 1a.) In addition, Joseph Shatzmiller has published three letters from the communities of Narbonne and Lunel to the "sons of the exile from Jerusalem in Spain" expressing confusion about the nature of the French rabbis' charges against Maimonides. See Joseph Shatzmiller, "Towards a Picture of the First Controversy over Maimonides' Writings" (Hebrew), *Tziyon* 34, no. 3–4 (1969): 126–144. Because the record of Solomon ben Abraham's correspondence with the French rabbis and their response has been lost, an exact reconstruction of the opinions and chain of events is difficult at best. For example, as Joseph Shatzmiller has noted, based on the available sources, it is impossible to know which French rabbis proclaimed the *herem*, whether they represented rabbinic authorities in France at large, or how Solomon ben Abraham came to contact this particular group from the outset. The most complete and cohesive reconstruction of the events was published by Azriel Shohat, "Concerning the First Controversy over the Writings of Maimonides" (Hebrew), *Tziyon* 36, no. 1–2 (1971): 25–60.

6. Several other Hebrew sources report on this unprecedented intervention of Christian authorities in Jewish intellectual life; however there is no parallel Christian source. For a brief summary of these sources, see Yitzhak Baer, *A History of the Jews in Christian Spain: From the Reconquest to the Fourteenth Century*, trans. Louis Schoffman, 2 vols. (Philadelphia: Jewish Publication Society of America, 1961), 1:398–399. In a discussion of Hillel of Verona's lamentation for the works of Maimonides that were burned in 1232, Susan Einbinder shows that burning offensive books may have been a mode of rabbinic social control that was exercised more frequently than scholars have believed. See Susan L. Einbinder, *Beautiful Death: Jewish Poetry and Martyrdom in Medieval France* (Princeton, NJ: Princeton University Press, 2002), 84–90, especially 88.

7. Lichtenberg, ed., *Kovetz Teshuvot*, Section III, 4b. Informing the ruling authorities of the transgressions of fellow Jews was considered an egregious crime in the Jewish diaspora. As a result, scholars have been wary of accusations pointing to Solomon ben Abraham and his disciples as the informers—in spite of David Kimhi's direct reference to them as the culprits. The most compelling reason to throw the responsibility to men other than Solomon ben Abraham and his students is the fact that all three returned to be active members of the Jewish community,

which would have been impossible had they been identified as informers. For the full text of David Kimhi's letters concerning the *herem,* see Lichtenberg, ed., *Kovetz Teshuvot,* Section III 1a–1b, 3a–4b. Discussion of Kimhi's accusation that Solomon ben Abraham and his circle informed the Christian authorities can be found in Jeremy Cohen, *The Friars and the Jews: The Evolution of Medieval Anti-Judaism* (Ithaca, NY: Cornell University Press, 1982), 57–58; Idit Dobbs-Weinstein, "The Maimonidean Controversy," in *History of Jewish Philosophy,* ed. Daniel H. Frank and Oliver Leaman (London: Routledge, 1997), 331–349 (especially 334, where she argues that although there is no evidence that Solomon ben Abraham and his students were the informers, they can be held accountable for the circumstances that led to the burning of Maimonides' works); José Faur, "Anti-Maimonidean Demons," *Review of Rabbinic Judaism* 6, no. 1 (2003): 50 (he argues that only the so-called 'heretical' portions of Maimonides' *Moreh Nevukhim,* or *Guide of the Perplexed,* were burned, and not at the instigation of Solomon ben Abraham); and Shohat, "Concerning the First Controversy," 35 and 45–60. Finally, E. Urbach suggests that the French rabbis never actually banned Maimonides' writing. Rather, he argues, the defenders of Maimonides' interpretive methods invented the ban as a polemical device meant to discredit Solomon ben Abraham; see Ephraim Urbach, "The Role of French and Spanish Rabbis in the Dispute over Maimonides and His Writings" (Hebrew), *Tziyon* 12 (1947): especially 156–159.

8. Klein has shown that Jewish community leadership and government transformed in tandem with or as a result of changes in the ways that Aragonese kings conceptualized and oversaw Jewish autonomy. By the end of the thirteenth century, the kings of Aragon gave official endorsement to Jewish autonomy while at the same time taking an active role in matters of justice. She argues that Nahmanides was instrumental in facilitating this shift in Barcelona by rallying respected and powerful allies and by example of his own behavior. See Elka Klein, *Jews, Christian Society, and Royal Power in Medieval Barcelona* (Ann Arbor: University of Michigan Press, 2006), 116–141. On the legacy of this political transformation within the Jewish community, see Menachem Lorberbaum, *Politics and the Limits of the Law: Secularizing the Political in Medieval Jewish Thought* (Stanford, CA: Stanford University Press, 2001), 93–149. Also see Baer, *A History of the Jews in Christian Spain,* 1:94–100.

9. Menachem Kellner captures this dynamic in his politically resonant description of the conflict as a debate about "who is a Jew." See Menachem Kellner, "Heresy and the Nature of Faith in Medieval Jewish Philosophy," *Jewish Quarterly Review* 77, no. 4 (1987): 299–318, especially 299–301.

10. For a general discussion of the mechanisms and demands of local Jewish authority, see David Biale, *Power and Powerlessness in Jewish History* (New York: Schocken Books, 1986), 34–86; Yitzhak Baer, "The Origins of the Organisation of the Jewish Community of the Middle Ages" (Hebrew), *Tziyon* 15 (1950): 1–41; Louis Finkelstein, *Jewish Self-Government in the Middle Ages* (New York: Jewish

Theological Seminary of America, 1924); Jacob Katz, *Exclusiveness and Tolerance: Studies in Jewish-Gentile Relations in Medieval and Modern Times* (Oxford: Oxford University Press, 1961); Klein, *Jews, Christian Society, and Royal Power*; Lorberbaum, *Politics and the Limits of the Law*, 93–124.

11. Blidstein, "Individual and Community," 327–369; Kellner, "Heresy," 299–318; Morell, "The Constitutional Limits," 87–119.

12. In his study of the conflict over Maimonides' writings during the early fourteenth century, Marc Saperstein argues that a political analysis of this controversy must begin with the question of local political autonomy of local Jewish communities. According to Saperstein, Solomon ibn Adret's theory of law precluded his intervention—even if outside parties requested his opinion—in a matter of controversy in another Jewish community. "The general rule is that one community may not impose its will on another, the only exceptions being a ban issued by a Nasi or an Exilarch, or an emergency *gezerah* of one community that the majority of the second community are capable of obeying. When a political boundary divides the two communities, the jurisdiction of one over the other is even more strictly curtailed. Adert argued that one kingdom has no jurisdiction over the subjects of another even if they are living temporarily in the first. As a legal authority, he clearly recognized the right of the local Jewish community to govern its own affairs free from the threat of outside interference from powerful neighbors." See Marc Saperstein, "The Conflict over the Rashba's Herem on Philosophical Study: A Political Perspective," *Jewish History* 1, no. 2 (1986): 28. Adret's final ban on philosophical works was limited to his own community.

13. Thomas N. Bisson, *Medieval France and Her Pyrenean Neighbours: Studies in Early Institutional History* (London: Hambledon Press, 1989), 351–374; James B. Given, *Inquisition and Medieval Society: Power, Discipline, and Resistance in Languedoc* (Ithaca, NY: Cornell University Press, 1997); William Chester Jordan, *The French Monarchy and the Jews: From Phillip Augustus to the Last Capetians* (Philadelphia: University of Pennsylvania Press, 1989); Marc Gregory Pegg, *The Corruption of Angels: The Great Inquisition of 1245–1246* (Princeton, NJ: Princeton University Press, 2001).

14. Thomas N. Bisson, *The Medieval Crown of Aragon, A Short History* (Oxford: Clarendon Press, 1986), 38–83; Bisson, *Medieval France*, 351–374; James B. Given, *State and Society in Medieval Europe: Gwynedd and Languedoc under Outside Rule* (Ithaca, NY: Cornell University Press, 1990), 80–90 and 134–147; Jordan, *The French Monarchy*.

15. The depth of the tension that characterized relations between leaders of these communities is palpable in the letters that circulated in response to Solomon ben Abraham from the communities of Narbonne and Lunel. See Shatzmiller, "Towards a Picture," 139–144. For discussion of the broader ramifications of this dispute in matters of inter-community politics, see Shohat, "Concerning the First Controversy," 40–45.

16. Baer, "The Origins," 29–41; Saperstein, "The Conflict," 27–29; Sophia Menache, "Communication in the Jewish Diaspora: A Survey," in *Communication in the Jewish Diaspora: The Pre-Modern World*, ed. Sophia Menache (Leiden: E. J. Brill, 1996), 20–22.

17. Blidstein, "Individual and Community," 215–256; Morell, "The Constitutional Limits," 87–119.

18. Questions about whether Maimonidean philosophy represented an appropriate method of interpretation arose again during the first decade of the fourteenth century. In this case, though, in which the orbit of debate concerned public preaching versus private study, the resulting ban on the study of Maimonidean works was limited to the community of Barcelona. It is not coincidental that Rabbi Solomon ben Adret, a student of Nahmanides, issued this *herem* within local geographic boundaries. He issued this ban first on a wider scale, encompassing the Jewish communities of Spain and Provence. For the purposes of this discussion, the fact that Solomon ben Adret chose to maintain a limited scope for his ban is more important than whether he feared reprisals from Christian or Jewish authorities. See Ram Ben-Shalom, "Communication and Propaganda between Provence and Spain: The Controversy over Extreme Allegorization (1303–1306)," in *Communication in the Jewish Diaspora: The Pre-Modern World*, ed. Sophia Menache (Leiden: E. J. Brill, 1996), 171–224; Ram Ben-Shalom, "The Ban Placed by the Community of Barcelona on the Study of Philosophy and Allegorical Preaching—A New Study," *Revue des Études juives* 159, no. 3–4 (2000): 387–404; Lorberbaum, *Politics and the Limits of the Law*, 11–123; Saperstein, "The Conflict."

19. Jeremy Cohen traces the trajectory of the Church's perceptions of Jews and Judaism from Augustine's pioneering call for Christianity to tolerate Judaism so that the Jews could witness the second coming of Jesus Christ, one of the conditions necessary for ushering in the final redemption, through the late middle ages when the Church saw fit to regulate the practice of Judaism. See Jeremy Cohen, *Living Letters of the Law: Ideas of the Jew in Medieval Christianity* (Berkeley: University of California Press, 1999).

20. See Given, *Inquisition and Medieval Society*; Jordan, *The French Monarchy*, 105–127; Jacques Madaule, *The Albigensian Crusade: An Historical Essay*, trans. Barbara Wall (London: Burns & Oates, 1967); R. I. Moore, *The Birth of Popular Heresy* (New York: St. Martin's Press, 1976), especially 99–155; Marc Pegg, *The Corruption of Angels*; Jeffrey Burton Russell, *Dissent and Order in the Middle Ages: The Search for Legitimate Authority* (New York: Twayne, 1992), 43–67; Joseph R. Strayer, *The Albigensian Crusades* (Ann Arbor: University of Michigan Press, 1992), 123–142; Walter L. Wakefield, *Heresy, Crusade, and Inquisition in Southern France, 1100–1250* (London: George Allen & Unwin, 1974), 96–152.

21. For a detailed discussion of the friars' role in implementing changes in the treatment and perception of Jews and Judaism during the thirteenth century, see J. Cohen, *The Friars and the Jews*, 33–76. Cohen revisited this issue some years

later; see Cohen, *Living Letters of the Law*, 313–363. See also Funkenstein, *Perceptions of Jewish History*, 172–207. Also Daniel Jeremy Silver suggests that there is a direct connection between the involvement of the friars in this controversy and the subsequent investigations of the Talmud during the disputations in Paris (1240) and Barcelona (1263). Daniel Jeremy Silver, *Maimonidean Criticism and the Maimonidean Controversy, 1180–1240* (Leiden: E. J. Brill, 1965), 5.

22. Nahmanides attests to this in his letter to the French rabbis. See Haim Dov Chavel, *Kitvei Rabbenu Moshe ben Nahman*, 2 vols. (Jerusalem: Mosad Ha-Rav Kook, 1964), 1:343.

23. Earlier conflicts over Maimonides' writings were played out over the more explicit issue of interpretive authority: if Maimonides did not possess the political and religious authority granted by title *gaon* or *nasi* did his rulings on issues of tradition and practice carry any weight? See Dobbs-Weinstein, "The Maimonidean Controversy," 334–335; Moshe Carmilly-Weinberger, *Censorship and Freedom of Expression in Jewish History* (New York: Sepher Harmon, 1977); Raphael Jospe, "Faith and Reason: The Controversy over Philosophy," in *Great Schisms in Jewish History*, ed. Raphael Jospe and Stanley M. Wagner (Denver: University of Denver, Center for Jewish Studies, and Ktav Publishing, 1981), 73–117; Silver, *Maimonidean Criticism*, 23–104.

24. Study of Aristotle's writings on natural philosophy and commentaries on them were first banned at the University of Paris at the Council of Sens in 1210. The ban was subsequently renewed in 1215, 1228, and 1231. In the final instance, Pope Gregory IX specified that these works should be reviewed and any damaging content removed before their use would be permitted. For a discussion of the opposition to Aristotelian science among Christians, see Luca Bianchi, *Censure et Liberté Intellectuelle à l'Université de Paris (XIIIe–XIVe siècles)* (Paris: Les Belles Lettres, 1999), 110–124. See also Gordon Leff, *Paris and Oxford Universities in the Thirteenth and Fourteenth Centuries: An Institutional and Intellectual History* (New York: Wiley, 1968); Hilde de Ridder-Symoens, ed., *Universities in the Middle Ages, A History of the University in Europe* (Cambridge: Cambridge University Press, 1992), 319–328.

25. Given, *Inquisition and Medieval Society*, 108–111.

26. Ibid., 25–90 and 141–165.

27. J. Cohen, *The Friars and the Jews*, 51–99; Given, *State and Society*, 80–88, 104–113, and 224–243; Wakefield, *Heresy, Crusade and Inquisition*; Russell, *Dissent and Order*; Moore, *The Birth of Popular Heresy*, 101–154.

28. Joseph Sarachek has suggested that Maimonides' interpretation of tradition and authority had a rough parallel in Cathar beliefs. My argument is slightly different. While Sarachek is concerned primarily with similarities in the content of their Jewish and Christian 'heretical' views, I am interested in the mechanisms through which authority was expressed and power executed. See Joseph Sarachek, *Faith and Reason: The Conflict over the Rationalism of Maimonides* (New York:

Hermon Press, 1935), 5–8. According to Edward Peters, centralization of authority for categorical legal classifications in the hands of a small number of trained experts was one of the most important things at stake in the investigation of heresy. Here too we see a corollary in Solomon ben Abraham's effort to restrict authority to define legal principles to a handful of legal experts; see Edward Peters, *Inquisition*, 2nd ed. (Berkeley: University of California Press, 1989), 1–58.

29. For discussion of the sociological and mass psychological impact of the inquisitorial atmosphere on the ethos of the general community under investigation, see John H. Arnold, *Inquisition and Power: Catharism and the Confessing Subject in Medieval Languedoc* (Philadelphia: University of Pennsylvania Press, 2001); Miriam Bodian, *Hebrews of the Portuguese Nation: Conversos and Community in Early Modern Amsterdam* (Bloomington: Indiana University Press, 1997), 76–84; Carlo Ginzburg, *Ecstasies: Deciphering the Witches' Sabbath*, trans. Raymond Rosenthal (New York: Penguin, 1991).

30. Kellner, "Heresy," 299–301.

31. Both were leaders of famous Jewish sects during the rabbinic period. See Elias J. Bickerman, *From Ezra to the Last of the Maccabees: Foundations of Postbiblical Judaism* (New York: Schocken Books, 1962); Gedaliah Alon, *Jews, Judaism, and the Classical World: Studies in Jewish History in the Times of the Second Temple and Talmud*, trans. Israel Abrahams (Jerusalem: Magnes Press, 1977).

32. Shatzmiller, "Towards a Picture," 140. The authors went on to accuse the individuals who instigated the *herem* in France of collaborating with the Christian authorities, though the letter does not refer to Solomon ben Abraham et al. by name. David Kimhi employed a similar rhetorical tone in his letter to Judah Alfakhar. See Lichtenberg, ed., *Kovetz Teshuvot*, Section III, 4b.

33. Lichtenberg, ed., *Kovetz Teshuvot*, Section III, 6a.

34. Much has been written about the dynamic and consequences of the Maimonidean controversy of 1232 over the past century. I refer here primarily to authors who thematize this dispute as a decisive moment in medieval Jewish history: Baer, *A History of the Jews in Christian Spain*, 1:100–110; David Berger, "The Great Struggle: Provence and Northern Spain from the Late Twelfth to the Early Fourteenth Century," in *Judaism's Encounter with Other Cultures: Rejection or Integration?* ed. Jacob J. Schacter (Northvale, NJ: Jason Aronson, 1997), 85–108; J. Cohen, *The Friars and the Jews*, 51–60; Carmilly-Weinberger, *Censorship and Freedom*, 29–77; Dobbs-Weinstein, "The Maimonidean Controversy," 331–349; Julius Gutmann, *Philosophies of Judaism: The History of Jewish Philosophy from Biblical Times to Franz Rosenzweig*, trans. David Silverman (New York: Holt, Rinehart, and Winston, 1964), 183–186; Jospe, "Faith and Reason," 73–117; Sarachek, *Faith and Reason*, 73–127; Shatzmiller, "Towards a Picture," 126–144; Shohat, "Concerning the First Controversy," 25–60; Silver, *Maimonidean Criticism*, 147–198; Charles Touati, "Les Deux Conflits autour de Maimonide et des Études Philosphiques," in *Juifs et judaïsme de Languedoc*, ed. Bernard Blumenkranz and Marie-Humbert

Vicaire (Toulouse: Cahiers de Fanjeaux, 1977), 173–184; Schmuel Trigano, "The Conventionalization of Social Boundaries and the Strategies of Jewish Society in the Thirteenth Century," in *New Horizons in Sephardic Studies,* ed. Yedida K. Stillman and George K. Zucker (Albany: SUNY Press, 1993), 45–66; Urbach, "The Role," 149–159. More recently, Elka Klein has argued that the dispute over Maimonides' philosophy marked the beginning of a longer term effort to restructure Jewish community leadership and government in terms that favored centralized local authority. See Klein, *Jews, Christian Society, and Royal Power,* 116–141.

35. Lichtenberg, ed., *Kovetz Teshuvot,* Section III.

36. This narrative strategy is evident particularly in Baer, *A History of the Jews in Christian Spain,* 1:96–110 and Baer, "The Origins," 1–41.

37. Trigano, "The Conventionalization of Social Boundaries," 60–63.

38. For an analysis of the literary genres of historical discourse, see Hayden White, "The Value of Narrativity in the Representation of Reality," *Critical Inquiry* 7 (1980): 5–27 and Hayden White, *The Content of the Form: Narrative Discourse and Historical Representation* (Baltimore: Johns Hopkins University Press, 1987).

39. Baer, *A History of the Jews in Christian Spain,* 1:96–108; J. Cohen, *The Friars and the Jews,* 51–60; Joseph Dan, "Ashkenazi Hasidim and the Maimonidean Controversy," *Maimonidean Studies* 3 (1992–1993), 29–47; Shatzmiller, "Towards a Picture," 126–144; Shohat, "Concerning the First Controversy," 25–60; Silver, *Maimonidean Criticism*; Urbach, "The Role," 149–159. It is interesting that the historians who interpret the controversy in this way also read Nahmanides' letter to the French rabbis as an explicit condemnation of Maimonides and philosophy. It will become clear later in this chapter that I consider such a reading to be impossible to sustain. For a demonstration that Nahmanides' views on the topic of philosophy were more complicated than Baer and others argue, see Y. Tzvi Langermann, "Acceptance and Devaluation: Nahmanides' Attitude towards Science," *Jewish Thought and Philosophy* 1 (1992): 223–245.

40. For a critical discussion of the way medievalists have interpreted isolated violent incidents—such as attacks on individual Jews or Jewish communities during Holy Week—as precursors to later incidents of more widespread violence and antisemitism, see David Nirenberg, *Communities of Violence: Persecution of Minorities in the Middle Ages* (Princeton, NJ: Princeton University Press, 1996), 217–230. Though Nirenberg examines historical events of a very different nature than the ones under consideration here, the critical apparatus he applies is relevant in this case as well.

41. Dobbs-Weinstein, "The Maimonidean Controversy," 331–349; Graboïs, "The Use of Letters," 93–105; Gutmann, *Philosophies of Judaism,* 183–208; Jospe, "Faith and Reason," 73–117; Kellner, "Heresy," 75–82.

42. This view is most apparent in Silver, *Maimonidean Criticism,* 6–17 and 137–198.

43. These are reproduced in Chavel, *Kitvei Rabbenu Moshe ben Nahman*, 1:330–332 and 1:353–364.

44. Dan, "Ashkenazi Hasidim," 31–32; Silver, *Maimonidean Criticism*, 149–151 and 159; Haim Hillel Ben-Sasson, "The Maimonidean Controversy," in *Encyclopedia Judaica* (Jerusalem and New York: Macmillan, 1971–72), 11:749; Gershom Scholem, *Origins of the Kabbalah*, trans. Allan Arkush (Princeton, NJ: Jewish Publication Society and Princeton University Press, 1987), 404–414. Menachem Fisch complicates the commonly held perception that rabbinic Judaism scorned rationalism. See Menachem Fisch, *Rational Rabbis: Science and Talmudic Culture* (Bloomington: Indiana University Press, 1997), 51–110.

45. See the nuanced analysis of Nahmanides' leadership in this dispute in Harvey J. Hames, *The Art of Conversion: Christianity and Kabbalah in the Thirteenth Century* (Leiden: Brill, 2000), 39–54. For a more general discussion of the conflict between "traditional" and philosophical interpretations, see Jospe, "Faith and Reason," 73–117. Chavel adopts a similar view in his notes concerning Nahmanides' role in the controversy: Chavel, *Kitvei Rabbenu Moshe ben Nahman*, 1:352. In contrast, see David Berger, who suggests that Nahmanides' response to this debate was more complicated than a simple acceptance or rejection of the arguments of either side. "What, then, did Nahmanides propose in order to resolve the Maimonidean controversy? First, the ban on the *Sefer ha-Madda*, which is a wonderful book, must be lifted. Second, the ban on the *Guide*, a ban which currently applies to private as well as public study, must be lifted as well. Third, a ban on group study of the *Guide* should be instituted. Fourth and finally, the study of philosophy should be entirely discouraged, but gently and without a ban" (David Berger, "How Did Nahmanides Propose to Resolve the Maimonidean Controversy?" in *Me'ah She'arim: Studies in Medieval Jewish Spiritual Life in Memory of Isadore Twersky*, ed. Ezra Fleischer et al. (Jerusalem: Hebrew University, Magnes Press, 2001), 145. Berger's assessment hangs on a comparative analysis of the published editions of Nahmanides' letter to the French rabbis. He concludes that Chavel's edition, the most commonly referenced printed version of the text, is based on the least reliable, most problematic early modern printing of the letter, which, according to Yitzhak Baer, was assembled with other sources on the controversy by a member of the Maimonidean camp. Berger shows that though Chavel's edition of the letter is the most recent and most easily accessible, the 1860 edition by Perles is the more responsible and reliable scholarly edition. I will cite both versions in references to Nahmanides' letter to the French rabbis and draw attention to significant differences between the two. For a discussion of the manuscript and printed traditions of this text see Mauro Perani, "Mistica e filosofia: la mediazione di Nahmanide nella polemica sugli scritti di Maimonide," in *Nahmanide, esegeta e cabbalista: Studi e testi*, ed. Moshe Idel and Mauro Perani (Florence: Giuntina, 1998), 115n 34.

46. A notable exception to the factionalist approach of much of this scholarship can be found in James H. Lehman, "Polemic and Satire in the Poetry of the Maimonidean Controversy," *Prooftexts* 1, no. 2 (1981): 133–151, especially 142–148. Lehman traces the rhetorical interchange between Nahmanides' letter to the French rabbis and the polemical poems of Meshullam da Piera, one of the more strident advocates of the anti-Maimonidean stand. He argues that Meshullam da Piera modeled his polemical defense of Solomon ben Abraham on Nahmanides' letter to the French rabbis, mimicking, satirizing, and overstating Nahmanides' defense of Maimonides to bolster his own argument. Even as Lehman glosses da Piera's travesty of the letter to the French rabbis, he is also careful to highlight Nahmanides' measured defense of Maimonides' contribution to rabbinic learning.

47. Joseph Perles, "Nachträge über R. Moses ben Nachman," *Monatsschrift für Geschichte und Wissenschaft des Judentums* 9 (1860): 186; Chavel, *Kitvei Rabbenu Moshe ben Nahman*, 1:339.

48. For a clear demonstration of Nahmanides' appropriation and adaptation of Maimonides' philosophical interpretation of Jewish tradition, see Josef Stern, "Nachmanides's Conceptions of Ta'amei Mitzvot," in *Commandment and Community: New Essays in Jewish Legal and Political Philosophy*, ed. Daniel Frank (Albany: SUNY Press, 1995), 151–163. Stern extended and developed the argument in this article in his book *Problems and Parables of Law*. Elliot Wolfson also draws attention to methodological and hermeneutical parallels in Nahmanides' and Maimonides' exegetical approach. See Elliot R. Wolfson, "The Secret Garment in Nahmanides," *Da'at* 24 (1990): 122.

49. In his analysis of the language and etiquette in early medieval Christian petitions and political negotiations, Geoffrey Koziol demonstrates that the supplicatory tone was a crucial ingredient in negotiations at all levels of the power hierarchy. "The vocabulary of petition was remarkably consistent over time; but the consistency cannot have been due to the rote copying of ancient formulas, since the formulas do vary significantly according to period, region, and the status of the benefactor. Rather, the durability of the formulas is a sign of the continuing importance of etiquette in medieval society, and of the formulas' flexibility, their ability to shift meanings to accommodate a variety of interactions. Thus, at all levels of society inferiors beseeched superiors. . . . But great men would also beseech their equals, since to do otherwise would have been rude. As a demonstration of their magnanimity they might even beseech inferiors" (Geoffrey Koziol, *Begging Pardon and Favor: Ritual and Political Order in Early Medieval France* [Ithaca, NY: Cornell University Press, 1992], 37). Though it is not my intention to do so here, a systematic examination in this vein of customary language use in Jewish power negotiations would contribute a great deal to our understanding of the extent to which Jewish leaders shared the conventions of the cultures that surrounded them.

50. That the anti-Maimonidean camp saw through this rhetorical strategy is clear in the mockery to which Meshullam da Piera subjected it in one of his polemical anti-Maimonidean poems. "Da Piera's use of Nahmanides soon becomes apparent when we compare the arguments of Poem 49 and the Epistle [to the French rabbis]. In the letter Nahmanides opens with a great show of humility before the French rabbis. In da Piera's poem, the opening consists of a corresponding show of humility; the difference is that the voice bows, indeed grovels, before Maimonides. Thus, Nahmanides' bowing before the rabbis is shown by the *sha'ir as-sargatiyyin* to be a bowing before Maimonides: *Shiflut ani 'oseh lerov hitnatslut* (I humble myself in profuse apology). And line 11 of the poem could be spoke to the rabbis or to Maimonides: *'atah tevo'eni mehilah megevir/ lo ehyeh miposh'im ne'enashu* (May I be forgiven by the Master / May I not be punished a sinner)" (Lehmann, "Polemic and Satire," 144).

51. The Saraval edition published by Perles includes the adjective *pasuq* to modify the questioning child (Perles, "Nachträge," 185).

52. In the original context, *ruhi* refers to Job's breath in a physical sense, which marks his spiritual, personal, and physical alienation.

53. Perles, "Nachträge," 184–185; Chavel, *Kitvei Rabbenu Moshe ben Nahman*, 1:337.

54. For example, he took the anti-Maimonidean camp to task for addressing and describing their adversaries in disrespectful, insulting terms: "*Prostitutes praise one another, students of wise men do not likewise* (Babylonian Talmud *Shabbat* 34a). You spoke to us with words and a voice that we heard. The eye of our community shed many tears as a result of them. According to your statement, there is a great one among us who has behaved like a Sadducee. In this matter you have not acted righteously [but] I will reply to you. Why, my masters, *would you distract* the great rabbi *from his tasks* (Exodus 5:4), while you would disgrace the mighty great. *Did you not question the passers by* (Job 34:17) *who stretch out their tongue* (Isaiah 57:4), [use] exaggerated rhetoric, and *who use parables* (Micah 2:4)? In the great rabbi's prayer, the extent of his wisdom, the formidability of his faith, the essence of his modesty, the generosity of his pocket, his marvelous deeds, his constant fear of God, love for our Talmud, and his love and kisses for the words of our rabbis. They are beloved to his eyes and darling to his soul, the crown on his head" (Perles, "Nachträge," 187).

The manuscript copy reproduced in Chavel and Lichtenberg inserts the following even stronger condemnation following "a voice that we heard": "*Words of arrogance escaped from your mouths* (I Samuel 2:3), terrible words of fanaticism and hatred were spoken; it is forbidden to listen to them when they are uttered and all the more so when they are written. You said and wrote these things about this holy man, while in all the diaspora of France and Spain there did not arise another like him" (Chavel, *Kitvei Rabbenu Moshe ben Nahman*, 1:340; Lichtenberg, ed., *Kovetz Teshuvot*, Section III, 8b).

55. Perles, "Nachträge," 185; Chavel, *Kitvei Rabbenu Moshe ben Nahman,* 1:337. He also made a specific point of arguing that the rabbis of France had reached an elevated level of pure scholarship and piety which made Maimonides' fusion between rabbinic and philosophical thought unnecessary for their students: "If you, faithful ones, are in the bosom of faith *planted in a courtyard fat and flourishing* (Psalms 92:14–15), why do you not pay attention to the *outcasts* (those living on the extremities, *yoshvei pirtzot,* Psalms 65:9) because he who *returns to the fortress is a prisoner of hope* (Zachariah 9:12), and those who were compelled by longing were satisfied with our faith and our traditions; he *satiated their souls* (Jeremiah 31:13)" (Perles, "Nachträge," 186; Chavel, *Kitvei Rabbenu Moshe ben Nahman,* 1:339). This portion appears in largely the same form in these printed versions.

56. This strategy was also at work in his letters to the communities of Provence, Narbonne, and Saragossa in response to the counter-ban against Solomon ben Abraham, Saul ben David, and Jonah Gerundi. The topos of praise and, by extension, self-deprecation in his letter to the French rabbis is however more effusive. There are several possible reasons for this, but I think it is most likely a product of Nahmanides' sense of legal protocol. The Maimonideans exhibited a clear breach of etiquette by disregarding the French rabbis' *herem* without engaging in the proper legal dialogue. See Chavel, *Kitvei Rabbenu Moshe ben Nahman,* 1:330–332 and 353–364, especially 360–364. In Nahmanides' letter to the community of Béziers he utilized the same rhetorical style while defending his family honor.

57. In Perles, "I heard from true report that in all the lands in the kingdom of Yemen many large communities . . ." ("Nachträge," 187).

58. Ibid.; Chavel, *Kitvei Rabbenu Moshe ben Nahman,* 1:341.

59. According to Nahmanides, Maimonides' teachings impeded the process of complete assimilation into Gentile culture. "For *the sons were expelled from their fathers' table* (Berakhot 3.1) and they *defiled themselves with the delicacies of the king and the wine they drank* (Daniel 1:8). They intermixed with the [gentile] nations and learned their practices, in spite of the sword of apostasy which remained as a result of our sins throughout the *captivity of Jerusalem that is in Sepharad* (Obadiah 1:20). It was permitted for those who were close to the government to learn the wisdom of the Greeks to understand the medical profession, to reflect on every principle, and to know all the forms, and the remaining [forms of] wisdom and their trickeries to revive their souls in the kings' courts and palaces. Although these forms of wisdom are permitted, our rabbis, may their names be for a blessing, enlightened us about them and bequeathed them to us. And as they lost our books of wisdom in the *destruction of our kindred* (Esther 8:6) it was necessary for them to learn them [i.e., the medical arts] from the works of the Greeks and from other nations. They continued in their hearts in pursuit of the apostasy, and they began with praise and ended in slander. Thus the rabbi (Rambam) gave

his books as a *shield against calamity* (Mishneh, *Masekhet Avot* 4:11)" (Perles, "Nachträge," 186; Chavel, *Kitvei Rabbenu Moshe ben Nahman,* 1:339).

60. For Nahmanides' description of Maimonides' dedication and indebtedness to the Talmud that makes use of rabbinic citation in the same manner, see Perles, "Nachträge," 187; Chavel, *Kitvei Rabbenu Moshe ben Nahman,* 1:340–341.

61. This sentence is omitted from the Perles text.

62. Perles, "Nachträge," 188; Chavel, *Kitvei Rabbenu Moshe ben Nahman,* 1:341–342.

63. Jacques Le Goff has shown that by the thirteenth century, Christian preachers were using biblical quotations in an innovative manner. This change, he argues, reflects a significant shift in perceptions and interpretations of time and history. Until the early thirteenth century, citation of *exempla* was used primarily as a rhetorical device necessary to persuade the audience of an argument. By the end of the twelfth century, preachers, principally in cities, used biblical citations more frequently to convey a message about the place of present time in history. "Interest in the exemplum was connected with the vogue for narrative in literature, especially brief narrative forms such as the lay, the fabliau, and the tale. All of these forms reflect the new importance attached to narrative time, that is, historical time." Nahmanides uses his prooftexts in a very similar manner. As I will argue in the coming pages, his selection and use of texts for this purpose was self-conscious and calculated. See Jacques Le Goff, *The Medieval Imagination,* trans. Arthur Goldhammer (Chicago: University of Chicago Press, 1988), 78.

64. See chapter two in the present work for a discussion of Nahmanides' effort to establish the proper sequence in biblical narrative in his exegesis of Genesis. Yaakov Elman has also shown that a concern with sequence was one of the innovations in Nahmanides' biblical exegesis, however Elman argues that Nahmanides sought to establish sequence only in his commentary on the historical portions of the Bible. I argue that his interest in preserving sequence and continuity is the driving and organizing force in Nahmanides' biblical commentary. See Yaakov Elman, "'It Was No Empty Thing': Nahmanides and the Search for Omnisignificance," *The Torah U-Madda Journal* 4 (1993): 1–83; Yaakov Elman, "Moses ben Nahman/Nahmanides (Ramban)," in *Hebrew Bible / Old Testament: The History of Its Interpretation,* ed. Magne Sæbo (Göttingen: Vandenhoeck & Ruprecht, 2000), 1:416–432.

65. Ezra Fleischer argues that the tradition of Hebrew poetry was revitalized in Girona during the thirteenth century. The art of Hebrew poetry, which had been essentially linked to the culture in the courts of Muslim Spain, suffered an irreparable blow during the twelfth century when the court life of Jews essentially ceased in Al-Andalus. According to Fleischer, Nahmanides and some of his contemporaries were responsible for building a new tradition of Hebrew poetry from the ruins. "Remodeling secular poetry was part and parcel of the tremendous effort displayed in Ramban's Gerona in reassessing (should we say: reforming?) the

Jewish way of life in Spain, against the cultural and spiritual breakdown forecast, maybe already represented, by the Maimonidean controversy in the fourth decade of the thirteenth century. . . . Both Ramban and R. Meshullam were aware of [poetry's] efficiency, and, unlike the professional poets of the time, they also had important things to say and strong emotions to express. On the other hand, they had no allegiance whatsoever to the courtly poetics and no respect at all for any of its sacred rules. . . . They remolded Hebrew poetry in almost all its aspects and opened a new path for literature" (Ezra Fleischer, "The 'Gerona School' of Hebrew Poetry," in *Rabbi Moses Nahmanides (Ramban): Explorations in His Religious and Literary Virtuosity*, ed. Isadore Twersky (Cambridge, MA: Harvard University Press, 1983), 47–48. For a more general discussion of the aesthetic and formal qualities of medieval Hebrew poetry, see Dan Pagis, *Hebrew Poetry of the Middle Ages and the Renaissance* (Berkeley: University of California Press, 1991), especially 1–23; Adena Tanenbaum, *The Contemplative Soul: Hebrew Poetry and Philosophical Theory in Medieval Spain* (Leiden: Brill, 2002), especially 222–223.

66. *Sepharad* is also the Hebrew name for Spain.

67. Perles, "Nachträge," 186; Chavel, *Kitvei Rabbenu Moshe ben Nahman*, 1:338–339.

68. In addition to "ban" or "excommunication," the noun *herem* can also mean "net." In the verse from Ezekiel, it carries the latter meaning. Nahmanides, however, does not specify which meaning he intends, and thus allows the word to carry both meanings.

69. For an analysis of the relationship between prophecy and poetry in the medieval Hebrew poetic tradition, see Dan Pagis, *Ha-shir davur al ofanav: Mehkarim ve-masot ba-shirah ha-Ivrit shel yemei ha-benayim* (Jerusalem: Magnes Press, Hebrew University, 1993), 277–285.

70. Hurbert Irsigler outlines four interpretations proposed in modern exegesis of the balance between function and intention in the 'song of the vineyard': a) the prophet announced the approaching disaster, or woe-oracle, as an accusation of the people of Israel, which then justifies the pronouncement of judgment; b) the judgment serves as a call for repentance; c) the accusations stand as proof for the already determined guilty verdict in a case against the people of Israel; d) the accusations are evidence against the people of Israel by God, their accuser, in an ongoing trial proceeding. See Hurbert Irsigler, "Speech Acts and Intention in the 'Song of the Vineyard' Isaiah 5:1–7," *Old Testament Essays* 10, no. 1 (1997): 39–68. Marjo Korpel suggests that Isaiah 5 and Isaiah 10:1–6 constitute a single commentary on tensions in the relationship between the nation and its leaders. See Marjo C. A. Korpel, "Structural Analysis as a Tool for Redaction Criticism: The Example of Isaiah 5 and 10:1–6," *Journal for the study of Old Testament Studies* 69 (1996): 53–71, especially 55–66.

71. "If you saw his books, if you examined his pamphlets, you might have [justly] proclaimed him to be trampling on the restrictions, based on *qal ve-homer*

(if in a minor case, all the more so in a major case); if he had omitted every decision and ordinance having failed to make *a fence around the Torah* (Mishneh, Masekhet Avot 1a); if he closed his eyes to *eruvin* (the boundaries within which Jews can travel and transport items on Shabbat) and *yadayim* (regulations concerning defilement and purity of the hands) (Babylonian Talmud *Eruvin* 21b); if he forgot (where to find the laws about practices concerning) a *sheaf on the threshing floor* (Mishneh *Peah* 5:8), or on [eating] *fowl and cheese* (Babylonian Talmud *Hulin* 104b) as they are eaten by infidels. However, he demands greater restrictions on these matters than are required by the law. It is not for you, our teachers, to *treat him with contempt because he is from the east* (Babylonian Talmud *Barakhot* 54a and 61b)" (Perles, "Nachträge," 187; Chavel, *Kitvei Rabbenu Moshe ben Nahman*, 1:340–341).

72. "For we heard that you said he was like an infidel who denies the judgment of Gehenna (hell), because he said: 'there is no punishment above the severance (and destruction) of the soul' this is its punishment. But I, who am young, do not believe this pronouncement because you called fully after him, and in *accordance with these words* (Exodus 34:27). Our rabbis, may they be remembered for a blessing, remarked using the language of *Sifra*: 'Although it refers to being cut off in many places [in the Bible],' I do not know what it means when [the Bible] says *I will destroy the soul* (Leviticus 23:30) unless it teaches that being cut off is nothing more than being destroyed" (Perles, "Nachträge," 189; Chavel, *Kitvei Rabbenu Moshe ben Nahman*, 1:344). To show that Maimonides' significance as an interpreter encompassed the whole canon of Jewish learning, Nahmanides also pointed out that Maimonides frequently ruled on the conservative side in questions of practice. See Perles, "Nachträge," 188; Chavel, *Kitvei Rabbenu Moshe ben Nahman*, 1:342.

73. Perles, "Nachträge," 190–191; Chavel, *Kitvei Rabbenu Moshe ben Nahman*, 1:345–346. In addition, Nahmanides defended Maimonides' condemnation of anthropomorphic representations of God by drawing a parallel with treatments of the same matter by Eleazar ben Judah of Worms of the pietistic movement *Hasidei Ashkenaz*. Thus, Nahmanides used Eleazar ben Judah as a cultural and hermeneutic bridge between the French rabbis and the Maimonideans in Provence and the Crown of Aragon. "On this matter I say in truth that one who believes in God's divinity will understand that the spirit has no limbs protruding from His holy spirit [from the throne of His holiness, according to the Chavel edition]. Thus the Creator has no body and no image or form at all. . . . Moreover, he of blessed memory [Eleazar ben Judah of Worms] wrote more in the same book: 'and when the prophet knows that he has a vision in glory it is according to the desire of the Creator of the same light, as it says *and I saw God* (Isaiah 6:1); and *my eyes beheld the Lord, the King of hosts* (Isaiah 6:5) so that he [the prophet] knew that God desired him to be a visionary, thus it says, *I have used similes by means of the prophet* (Hosea 12:11). It would not be their intention [to imply] that the thing that appears to the eye of messengers or to the eye of the prophets is the appearance of

God, for (how could) the Creator of all, who has no figure and no limit, be in His existence and in His unity *within* the world and *outside* the world...' And I know that this book exists in your land" (Perles, "Nachträge," 19; Chavel, *Kitvei Rabbenu Moshe ben Nahman*, 1:347–348).

74. "What will they say about *Sefer ha-Madda*, and about the *writing that was the writing of God* (Exodus 32:16) that they displaced? The introduction to the great rabbi's books (may his memory be for a blessing) on the Talmud and the introductions to all of his books, he counts the positive and negative commandments of God, teaches students honor and instructs them in the *Laws of Talmud and Torah. He teaches sinners the way* (Psalms 25:8) in the laws of repentance, and with patience and penance and without questions and disputes, or *pouring forth pearls* [i.e., eloquence] (Babylonian Talmud *Kiddushin* 39b), for we do not find words of repentance in the Talmud, just scattered and dispersed amongst *halakhot* and *aggadot* without clarification. And in all the books of the early and late Geonim we do not find these matters; *they are needed by those who wait* (Psalms 111:2) for them and are ready. While these are delineated and explained in this book [i.e., *Sefer ha-Madda*] which is filled with pearls and set in sapphires" (Perles, "Nachträge," 189; Chavel, *Kitvei Rabbenu Moshe ben Nahman*, 1:343).

75. See Perles, "Nachträge," 190–191; Chavel, *Kitvei Rabbenu Moshe ben Nahman*, 1:345–346.

76. Nahmanides explicitly referred to Saadya Gaon and Eleazar ben Judah of Worms as authorities of the same order. See Perles, "Nachträge," 191–192; Chavel, *Kitvei Rabbenu Moshe ben Nahman*, 1:346–347.

77. "And if you our rabbis (of France) agree with the wise men of Provence, and we also follow on your heels, you will harden this matter with the *herem* and curse. *(Judgment will come) with thunder, an earthquake and 'a great tumult'* (Jeremiah 11:16) *and a consuming flame of fire* (Isaiah 29:6). In an offensive war the aggressor pays the appropriate penalty, *whether it be death or banishment* [lit. uprooting] *or confiscation of property* (Ezra 7:26). Surely there is enough in this regulation and order. In the pasture of peace you will lead the flock and in the pasture of love you will cause the flock to lie down. Furthermore, it is appropriate for you to gently caution everyone and lay the matter to rest entirely. The God-fearing man will return and guard the written and oral law, for it is our life and with this our honor will increase. *Who ever listens, let him hear and who ever refuses [to listen], let him refuse* (Ezekiel 3:27). For it is impossible for you to compel all of Israel to be constantly friends [*haverim*—in Chavel *hasidim*, or pious, replaces this word]" (Perles, "Nachträge," 193–194; Chavel, *Kitvei Rabbenu Moshe ben Nahman*, 1:349).

78. The circumstances here are more complicated than they appear at first glance. Jonah Gerundi, Solomon ben Abraham's disciple and sponsor of the ban, was Nahmanides' first cousin. This family connection added fuel to the conflict when their family history became an issue of discussion. An opponent of the *herem* from Béziers recalled to public memory a charge that Jonah Gerundi's

grandfather (who was also Nahmanides' grandfather) was the product of an illegitimate union. Nahmanides was thus placed in the difficult position of defending his cousin, while demonstrating that the family line was untainted. He argued that the matter had been resolved at the time in his grandfather's favor by a *bet din* (court) of community notables. Nahmanides cleared the family name, while at the same time calling into question the political ethics and decorum of the rabbi from Béziers. See Chavel, *Kitvei Rabbenu Moshe ben Nahman*, 1:353.

79. Perles, "Nachträge," 184. A slightly different version appears in Chavel, *Kitvei Rabbenu Moshe ben Nahman*, 1:336. and Lichtenberg, ed., *Kovetz Teshuvot*, Section III, 8a.

80. Chavel, *Kitvei Rabbenu Moshe ben Nahman*, 1:330–332, 353–364. Nahmanides also addressed some specific concerns about conflicts within communities in the Crown of Aragon in the letter to the French rabbis: "*Natives of Jerusalem who are in Sepharad* (Obadiah 1:20), ministers of Aragon, noblemen of Narbonne, masters of Castile, those who *stand on generosity* (Isaiah 32:8) are students and teachers, and interpreters of letters and singers at [religious] gatherings in the [threat] of emergency are as the *tail of the lions* (Mishnah *Avot* 4:5 [in the original, 'be a tail to lions, not a head to jackals'; i.e., better to follow wise men than to lead fools]. They gave you counsel and a suitable word and to the residents of this place [i.e., *Sepharad*] you will answer in peace. I already saw *those who make a man a sinner with a word* (Isaiah 29:21) who traveled to us, and in their hands were divisive letters, winning hearts and defaming ideas. I was forced to reveal to you the substance of the matter, lest you heed the words of the *Zephites* [referring to the false report related to Saul by the people of Ziph about David, I Samuel 23:19] and *allow for the excommunication and defilement of Jacob and Israel* (Isaiah 43:28). I am your student. For days I researched this matter, these words of hearsay [i.e., the accusation that Solomon ben Abraham and his students had done something punishable by *herem*] and I saw the evidence of the sanctimonious faction that is before you. It captures souls and it is like a rebellious wife. If the rabbis of France, from whose hands as their students we drink, told the sun that in half of the sky it will be hidden beneath wings, and the moon, which shines, they commanded to be concealed and sealed for the sake of the stars, would there not be a transgression upon the rabbi who declared his judgment before you because he opposed a colleague. And that in contrast to him, his dissenter would denounce his misdeed. The prophet *did not accuse God of impropriety* (Job 1:22) and *he did not attribute praise to the angels* (Job 4:18). And you, my teachers (*rabbotai*), should not listen to the words of the proponent of discord [i.e., those who supported the *herem* on Solomon ben Abraham et al.], *do not place faith in a friend, do not trust a companion* (Micah 7:5) until such time as you hear a reply from the mouth of the author of the judgment. For *the first to plead his case seems just, then his neighbor comes to cross-examine him* (Proverbs 18:17)" (Chavel, *Kitvei Rabbenu Moshe ben Nahman*, 1:331–332).

81. Chavel, *Kitvei Rabbenu Moshe ben Nahman*, 1:332.

82. Early in the controversy, Jonah Gerundi traveled to France on behalf of Solomon ben Abraham and hand-delivered copies of the *Moreh ha-Nevukhim* and *Sefer ha-Madda* to the French rabbis. He likely directed the French rabbis' attention to egregious passages in the texts, since they had been until that time unfamiliar with the works Maimonides wrote in Judeo-Arabic.

83. "It has been more than 130 years since the *ketubot* [marriage contracts] were issued, and how many like them and like the promissory notes were advanced from a woman and her husband with the signatures of the great men of the city: Saul and Moses, the assistants to the ministers of the city. And in the second generation all the notables of the city [and] masters of Torah [wrote] in the language of the court: 'the tradition of our fathers teaches that fear of vanity brings vanity, and according to the *bet din* (court) the remainder is for her husband.' Apart from this ruling, rav Meir, my father and my teacher Nahman (may he rest with honor), and the great Nasi Yitzhak, and the rabbi. Avigdor and five wise men who investigated the matter in our records and in their records and found the charge was false, and they heard as much from the Nasi R. Kalonimos of Narbonne" (Chavel, *Kitvei Rabbenu Moshe ben Nahman*, 1:353).

84. See Frank Talmage's biography of David Kimhi, *David Kimhi: The Man and the Commentaries* (Cambridge, MA: Harvard University Press, 1975). For an example of Kimhi's reasoning, see Frank Talmage, ed., *Sefer ha-berit ve-vikueh RaDaK em ha-Natzrut* (Jerusalem: Hotza'at Mosad Bialik, 1974). Also see Moshe Kamelhar, ed., *Perushe rabbi David Kimhi (Radak) al ha-Torah* (Jerusalem: Mosad ha-Rav Kook, 1970).

Chapter 2   Timely Matters

1. Moshe Halbertal has argued that Nahmanides provided the foundation for a dramatic shift in the halakhic thought which supported Jewish community government in Catalonia during the late thirteenth and fourteenth centuries. According to Halbertal, Nahmanides was the first to formulate the "constitutive view" of *halakhah*, which is rooted in the assumption that God gave law for Israel's leaders to interpret. This approach represents a radical departure from a more traditional "retrieval" approach to *halakhah*, which is based on the assumption that human understanding of the law suffered greater and greater degradation with each successive generation since the great rabbinic sages of the Mishnah. See Moshe Halbertal, "The History of Halakhah, Views from Within: Three Medieval Approaches to Tradition and Controversy" (paper presented at the Harvard Law School Gruss Lectures, Harvard University Law School, Cambridge, MA, 1994, http://www.law.harvard.edu/programs/Gruss/halbert.html). For a discussion of transformation in Catalonian Jewish political life during this period

see Menachem Lorberbaum, *Politics and the Limits of the Law: Secularizing the Political in Medieval Jewish Thought* (Stanford, CA: Stanford University Press, 2001), 93–123, and Elka Klein, *Jews, Christian Society, and Royal Power in Medieval Barcelona* (Ann Arbor: University of Michigan Press, 2006), 26–69.

2. This shift was offset by a traditional concern with mastering and commenting on the Talmud. For a discussion of the difficulties of maintaining a balance between Torah and Talmud study among medieval Jews, see Frank Talmage, "Keep Your Sons from Scripture: The Bible in Medieval Jewish Scholarship and Spirituality," in *Understanding Scripture: Explorations of Jewish and Christian Traditions of Interpretation*, ed. Clemens Thoma and Michael Wyschogrod (New York: Paulist Press, 1987), 81–101.

3. On Nahmanides' application of this type of argument in legal tradition, see Moshe Halbertal, "The *Minhag* and the History of Halakhah in the Teaching of Nahmanides" (Hebrew), *Tziyon* 67, no. 1 (2002): 25–56.

4. In his study of rabbinic exegesis, David Weiss Halivni describes rabbinic *derasha* (the applied meaning of the scripture determined by the rabbis as support for rabbinic theology and practice) as "timebound." He uses this term to indicate interpretive rules and methods that were defined in a unique time and place to meet the religious needs of the moment. This analysis is framed as a defense of rabbinic interpretive methods against the claims of medieval philosophers, Reform Judaism, and participants in the *Wissenschaft des Judentums* that rabbinic exegesis robs the scripture of its "natural" or plain sense (*peshat*). Halivni's study provides a comprehensive and sophisticated presentation of the genesis of rabbinic interpretation. However, his discussion evolves into an apologetic defense of rabbinic exegesis. For Halivni, the fact that historical circumstance bound the forms of biblical interpretation is a means of accounting for the differences between modern and pre-modern notions of evidence and argument. See David Weiss Halivni, *Peshat and Derash: Plain and Applied Meaning in Rabbinic Exegesis* (Oxford: Oxford University Press, 1991), 3–22.

5. See, for example, his *Derasha le-Rosh ha-Shannah*, in Haim Dov Chavel, *Kitvei Rabbenu Moshe ben Nahman*, 2 vols. (Jerusalem: Mosad Ha-Rav Kook, 1964), 1:211–252.

6. Haviva Pedaya, *Ha-Ramban: Hitalut—Zeman Mahzori ve-Tekst Kadosh* (Tel Aviv: Am Oved, 2003).

7. Amos Funkenstein argued that *peshat* and *sod* inhabited completely separate interpretive worlds in Nahmanides' exegesis, to the degree that they frequently seem incommensurable. "On the deepest level of scriptural understanding, 'the way of truth' (*bederech ha'emet*), the Pentateuch is a code of kabbalistic mysteries. So considered, it contains theosophical mysteries only: it neither narrates events nor prescribes laws but reflects the interactions and counteractions between the divine emanations or forces (*sefirot*)." This argument responds to two distinct and apparently divergent interpretations of Genesis 1:1 offered by Nah-

manides as the 'true sense' of the scripture. In the first place, Nahmanides read the verse in its plain sense to mean that God created matter out of absolute nothingness at the beginning of time and being. In the second place, however, Nahmanides seemed to argue that an entity, *Bereshit* (which corresponds with *hokhmah*, or the second emanation), created or emanated (*bara*) another being, *Elohim* (the third emanation in the kabbalistic model, corresponding with *binah*). Funkenstein points out that this interpretation is cited as heretical in the Babylonian Talmud *Megillah* 9a. He concludes that Nahmanides willfully employed a questionable mode of interpretation for the purpose of "rescuing suspicious readings and investing them with higher mysteries." Nahmanides' recognition that various levels of meaning co-existed in Torah, according to Funkenstein, does the work of reconciling apparently contradictory readings. See Amos Funkenstein, *Perceptions of Jewish History* (Berkeley: University of California Press, 1993), 108. Responding to Funkenstein, Elliot Wolfson argues that in Nahmanides' hermeneutic "there are two distinct but parallel ontological levels that correspond to two levels of meaning in the text." Wolfson suggests that Nahmanides saw these meanings as parallel, coexistent, even complementary, not incommensurable, as Funkenstein suggests. As such, he argues, Nahmanides did not present this principle as a tool to be used exclusively in the case of Genesis, but rather as a general hermeneutic rule. A more important signifier in Nahmanides' kabbalistic interpretation, in Wolfson's estimation, is the formula *be-derekh ha-emet* (in the way of truth), which, he argues, signals a radical departure from the traditional mode of interpretation. See Elliot R. Wolfson, "'By Way of Truth': Aspects of Nahmanides' Kabbalistic Hermeneutic," *AJS Review* 14 (1989): 121. David Berger, on the other hand, suggests that for Nahmanides, *peshat* and *sod* are one and the same. See David Berger, "Miracles and the Natural Order in Nahmanides," in *Rabbi Moses Nahmanides (Ramban): Explorations in His Religious and Literary Virtuosity*, ed. Isadore Twersky (Cambridge, MA: Harvard University Press, 1983), 112–113. Finally, Moshe Idel argues that Nahmanides was fundamentally a conservative kabbalist. Nahmanides' assertions about the nature and attributes of God, Idel argues, are made only on the basis of oral tradition passed through kabbalist teachers or through written sources, such as *Sefer Bahir* or *Sefer Yetzirah*. This distinguishes Nahmanides in Idel's view from other mystics of this period, including the author of *Sefer ha-Zohar*, Moshe de Leon. Idel's observation about Nahmanides' reverence for authority is very important for understanding the development of Kabbalah as a shift from an esoteric method or reading restricted to a small group of initiates to that of a widely disseminated system of interpretation and theology. However, to my mind, Idel's emphasis first on Nahmanides' role as a transitional figure in the development of Kabbalah, and second on the comparison between Nahmanides and some of his contemporaries seems to distract from the innovative use to which Nahmanides put traditional sources. See Moshe Idel, "'We Have No Kabbalistic Tradition on This'," in *Rabbi Moses Nahmanides (Ramban): Explorations in His Religious and Literary Virtuosity,* ed. Isadore Twersky (Cambridge, MA: Harvard University Press, 1983), 51–73.

8. Haim Dov Chavel, *Perush ha-Ramban al ha-Torah,* 2 vols. (Jerusalem: Mosad Ha-Rav Kook, 1959), 1:9; Jacob Newman, *The Commentary of Nahmanides on Genesis* (Leiden: E. J. Brill, 1960), 29. This is an undisguised jab at philosophers who argued that time, like the world, is eternal and without beginning or end. I chose to translate *kofer,* which carries the markedly polemical connotation of "heretic," in relatively benign terms ("he denies . . ." or, more awkward, "he is a denier . . ."). As I indicated in chapter one, Nahmanides' attitude towards Maimonides, the Jewish philosopher *par excellence,* was by no means uncomplicated. During the Maimonidean controversy Nahmanides declined to make a judgment about Maimonides' standing in the community united by a dedication to the traditions of Judaism based solely on his beliefs on individual matters of tradition or belief. Instead, Nahmanides insisted on reading Maimonides' entire body of writing as a single unit, and on that basis judging his contributions to the corpus of Jewish belief.

9. For example, Genesis details the formation of earth and its inhabitants but fails to account for the creation of the angels who appear in the lives of the patriarchs.

10. For a general discussion of the purpose and practice of Jewish exegesis, see Michael Fishbane, *The Exegetical Imagination: On Jewish Thought and Theology* (Cambridge, MA: Harvard University Press, 1998); Halivni, *Peshat and Derash,* 3–51.

11. "The purpose of *derasha* is not to interpret Scripture on the basis of objective, verifiable data, but to *generate* meaning from the text of the Scripture on the basis of the linguistic, cultural, and psychological factors binding the coexisting terms of Judaism. From the perspective of this axis the Tora has a wholly valid existence apart from its specific history or diachronic axis. The rabbis saw themselves and the Jewish people as 'the linguistic community' who 'spoke' and actually 'lived' the Tora" (José Faur, *Golden Doves with Silver Dots: Semiotics and Textuality in Rabbinic Tradition* [Bloomington: Indiana University Press, 1986], xv).

12. See Alan Cooper, "On the Social Role of Biblical Interpretation: The Case of Proverbs 22:6," in *With Reverence for the Word: Medieval Scriptural Exegesis in Judaism, Christianity, and Islam,* ed. Jane Dammen McAuliffe, Barry D. Walfish, and Joseph W. Goering (Oxford: Oxford University Press, 2003), 180–193.

13. Halivni, *Peshat and Derash,* xii–xv.

14. Michael A. Fishbane, *Biblical Interpretation in Ancient Israel* (Oxford: Clarendon Press, 1985); Michael A. Fishbane, *The Garments of Torah: Essays in Biblical Hermeneutics* (Bloomington: Indiana University Press, 1989).

15. Jacob Newman argues that this is Nahmanides' primary motivating purpose in his exegesis (Newman, *The Commentary of Nahmanides,* 4–5). Indeed, if we were to characterize in schematic terms Nahmanides' criticism of Rashi's exegesis, we could say that he objects to Rashi's tendency to view the Torah exclu-

sively as a basis for the ritual code, on one hand, and on the other, to his use of aggadic material, which embellishes and writes over the narrative, instead of clarifying either the plain or the hidden meaning. On Nahmanides' view of *aggadah*, see Robert Chazan, *Barcelona and Beyond: The Disputation of 1263 and Its Aftermath* (Berkeley and Los Angeles: University of California Press, 1992); Marvin Fox, "Nahmanides on the Status of Aggadot: Perspectives on the Disputation at Barcelona, 1263," *Journal of Jewish Studies* 40, no. 1 (1989): 95–109; Funkenstein, *Perceptions of Jewish History*, 108; Bernard Septimus, "'Open Rebuke and Concealed Love': Nahmanides and the Andalusian Tradition," in *Rabbi Moses Nahmanides (Ramban): Explorations in His Religious and Literary Virtuosity*, ed. Isadore Twersky (Cambridge, MA: Harvard University Press, 1983), 16.

16. Septimus, "'Open Rebuke and Concealed Love'," especially 12–19 and 26–30.

17. Rashi and his school emphasize the "plain sense" of the text (*peshat*), an exegetical method rooted in contextualization and narrative logic. The Sephardic tradition, on the other hand, is strongly influenced by Greek philosophical categories and rationalism.

18. Chazan, *Barcelona and Beyond*, 37–38.

19. On Rashi's contribution to medieval Jewish exegesis, see B. J. Gelles, *Peshat and Derash in the Exegesis of Rashi* (Leiden: Brill, 1981); Sarah Kamin, *Rashi, His Exegetical Categorization in Respect to Peshat and Derash* (Hebrew) (Jerusalem: Magnes Press, 1986). Also see R. Loew, "The Plain Meaning of Scriptures in Early Jewish Exegesis," *Papers of the Institute for Jewish Studies London* 1 (1964): 140–185.

20. *Midrash Tanhuma, Bereshit*, 1, 11:59, *Midrash Tanhuma al Hamushah Humshe Torah*, ed. Shlomo Buber (Vilna: ha-Almanah veha-Ahim Rom, 1885), 7–8.

21. "And what does it mean that it opens with '*bereshit*'? It is for the following reason: *He proclaimed to his people the power of his works in giving them the heritage of the nations* (Psalms 111:6). For if the nations of the world say to Israel 'you are thieves, because you conquered the lands of seven nations,' they [Israel] say to them [the nations of the world]: 'All the earth belongs to the Holy One, blessed is He. He created it and gave it to whomever seems worthy in his eyes. When he desired he gave it to them, and when it suited Him, he took it from them [i.e., the nations of the world] and gave it to us'" (Rashi on *Bereshit*, 1:1).

22. Michael A. Signer, "*Peshat, Sensus Litteralis*, and Sequential Narrative: Jewish Exegesis and the School of St. Victor in the Twelfth Century," in *The Frank Talmage Memorial Volume*, ed. Barry Walfish (Haifa: University of Haifa Press, 1993), 203–216; Michael A. Signer, "Restoring the Narrative: Jewish and Christian Exegesis in the Twelfth Century," in *With Reverence for the Word: Medieval Scriptural Exegesis in Judaism, Christianity, and Islam*, ed. Jane Dammen McAuliffe, Barry Walfish, and Joseph W. Goering (Oxford: Oxford University Press, 2003), 70–82.

23. David Biale, "Exegesis and Philosophy in the Writings of Abraham Ibn Ezra," *Comitatus* 5 (1974): 42–62.

24. This refers to the *Midrash Tanhumah* as well as Rashi's citation of it.

25. Chavel, *Perush Ha-Ramban*, 1:9.

26. Ibid., 22–23. Newman, *The Commentary of Nahmanides*, 47–49.

27. See the discussion of his messianic interpretation in chapter four of this book. Nahmanides addressed this issue in his extensive treatment of the legal stipulations concerning health, death, and resurrection, *Torat ha-Adam*, in Chavel, *Perush Ha-Ramban*, 2:9–311. In particular, see the final section, *Shaar ha-Gemul* (*The Gate of Redemption*), ibid., 2:264–311. Also, see his *Sefer ha-Geulah*, in Chavel, *Kitvei Rabbenu Moshe ben Nahman*, 1:261–95.

28. The clearest evidence of this can be found in the introduction to his biblical commentary. "Now, know and see how I answer those who question me about writing an interpretation of the Torah. I will conduct myself like the early leaders and bring to rest the opinion of the students, exhausted by the exile and the troubles, those who read in the *Seder* about the sabbath and the festivals, and to perpetuate their hearts in the plain meaning, and to a small measure, things that are pleasant to the listeners and to 'those who know grace' (Ecclesiastes 9:11). . . . Now I enter into a covenant of faith and it gives wise counsel for all who gaze at this book not to reason or think a thought about the hints which I write about the mysteries of the Torah, because I make it known to him faithfully that my words will not be known or understood at all by wisdom and understanding. Only from the mouth of a wise bearer of tradition to the ear of an understanding recipient. Reasoning on them is foolish, misdirected thought [brings] many dangers, and prevents healing. . . . But they will see in our interpretation novelties in the plain sense of the text and in explanations, and they will take a moral lesson from our holy teachers: 'do not investigate that which is greater than you, do not examine that which is stronger than you, do not desire to know what is more wondrous than you, do not ask about what is concealed from you; contemplate that which is permitted to you and do not concern yourself with mysteries' (*Bereshit Rabbah* 8:2)" (Chavel, *Perush Ha-Ramban*, 1:7–8; Newman, *The Commentary of Nahmanides*, 28–29).

29. Amos Funkenstein, "Nahmanides' Typological Reading of History" (Hebrew), *Tziyon* 45, no. 1 (1980): 35–49; Amos Funkenstein, "Nahmanides' Symbolic Reading of History," in *Studies in Jewish Mysticism, Proceedings of Regional Conferences Held at the University of California, Los Angeles and McGill University in April 1978*, ed. Joseph Dan and Frank Talmage (Cambridge, MA: Association of Jewish Studies, 1982), 129–150; Funkenstein, *Perceptions of Jewish History*, 98–121.

30. Yosef Yerushalmi references some examples of this narrative strategy in his discussion of biblical and rabbinic sense of the past. In particular, *Bereshit Rabbah* 46:4, in which Abraham renders judgment on legal opinions in a rabbinic academy; Yosef Hayim Yerushalmi, *Zakhor: Jewish History and Jewish Memory*

(New York: Schocken Books, 1989), 16–22. Also see Funkenstein, *Perceptions of Jewish History*, 2–21.

31. See Babylonian Talmud *Menahot* 29b, which argues that Moses and God agreed that Hebrew letters should be adorned with crowns for the sake of the academy of Rabbi Akiva. See Yerushalmi, *Zakhor*, 16–22.

32. For example, see Babylonian Talmud *Pesahim* 6b, *Sanhedrin* 49b; and Jerusalem Talmud *Shekalim* 25b; *Pesahim* 31b; *Suta* 37a; and *Midrash Tanhuma*, 8. According to José Faur, this is a product of the midrashic conception of the relationship between the Jewish people and their holy texts. See Faur, *Golden Doves with Silver Dots: Semiotics and Textuality in Rabbinic Tradition*, xiv–xvi. For Nahmanides' application of this principle, see Chavel, *Perush Ha-Ramban*, 1:185, also 1:198 on Genesis 35:28, 1:282 on Exodus 2:1, and 1:299–300 on Exodus 4:19.

33. Yaakov Elman, "'It Was No Empty Thing': Nahmanides and the Search for Omnisignificance," *The Torah U-Madda Journal* 4 (1993): 30–48; Yaakov Elman, "Moses ben Nahman/Nahmanides (Ramban)," in *Hebrew Bible / Old Testament: The History of Its Interpretation*, ed. Magne Sæbo (Göttingen: Vandenhoeck & Ruprecht, 2000), 1:416–432. Avraham Grossman also points out that Nahmanides does not accept this dictum; Grossman, however, argues that Nahmanides does not attempt to clarify the biblical text in any systematic fashion. Rather, he argues, Ramban selects individual verses that interest him and interprets them as independent units. Avraham Grossman, "Biblical Interpretation in Sepharad from the Thirteenth through the Fifteenth Centuries" (Hebrew) in *Moreshet Sepharad: The Sephardic Legacy*, ed. Ha'im Beinart (Jerusalem: Magnes Press, Hebrew University, 1992), 111–113. While Grossman is correct in pointing out Nahmanides' tendency towards reading in exhaustive detail verses that are of particular interest to him, Elman's suggestion that Nahmanides' exegesis is essentially systematic is in the end more convincing. Nahmanides' attempt to maintain a stream of biblical narrative by filling in and accounting for inconsistencies or gaps illustrates quite clearly the methodical quality of his interpretation.

34. For example, Nahmanides rehearsed the formula "there is no before and after in the Torah" in response to a sequential lapse in Genesis 32:23–25 ("And he rose up that night, and took his two wives, and his two handmaids, and his eleven children, and passed over the ford of the Jabbok. And he took them, and sent them over the stream, and sent over that which he had. And Jacob was left alone; and there wrestled a man with him until the breaking of the day"). However, rather than using this as an explanation, Nahmanides extrapolated a chain of events in which Jacob saw fit to ferry his family over then return to the other side of the river (Chavel, *Perush Ha-Ramban*, 1:185).

35. Elman borrows the term "omni-significance" from James Kugel, *The Idea of Biblical Poetry: Parallelism and Its History* (New Haven, CT: Yale University Press, 1981), 103–104.

36. Elman, "'It Was No Empty Thing,'" 52–53.

37. Chavel, *Perush Ha-Ramban*, 1:27.

38. Though making a different point than I make here, Amos Funkenstein calls attention to the duality of meaning in Nahmanides' understanding of the *peshat*: "Nachmanides seems to be the first biblical interpreter to include within the plain sense of scriptures (*peshat*) the full scope of philosophical allegoresis. 'In the beginning God created the Heavens and the Earth' means literally, he claims, that at the beginning of cosmic time God created out of nothingness the prime matter of celestial bodies and the prime matter of the realm of generation and corruption. On the one hand, then, Nachmanides disagrees with ibn Ezra about the scope of philosophic allegoresis: his is a maximalist attitude . . . ; there is no limit to the natural science to be found in the Scriptures. On the other hand, though, he does not regard the philosophical allegoresis as a hidden meaning (as Maimonides did). It is the plain meaning of the Scriptures" (Funkenstein, *Perceptions of Jewish History*, 105). Elliot Wolfson also takes up this issue: "What is crucial for Nahmanides . . . is that this notion of *peshat* is itself contained in a broader conception of a scriptural text that comprises all meanings including the mystical" (Elliot R. Wolfson, "Beautiful Maiden without Eyes: *Peshat* and *Sod* in Zoharic Hermeneutics," in *The Midrashic Imagination: Jewish Exegesis, Thought, and History*, ed. Michael Fishbane [Albany: SUNY Press, 1993], 159–161).

39. Marc Saperstein, "Jewish Typological Exegesis after Nahmanides," *Jewish Studies Quarterly* 1, no. 1 (1993–94), 158–170; Pedaya, *Ha-Ramban*, 412–414 on the Zohar, and through 433 on his legacy among later generations of kabbalists.

40. Chavel, *Perush Ha-Ramban*, 1:1–2.

41. Michael Signer points to the tendency among these exegetes to debate even the authorship of the Bible. While Nahmanides does not go so far as to raise the question in explicit terms, the desire to prove Moses' authority seems to lay at the base of this discussion. See Signer, "*Peshat, Sensus Litteralis*, and Sequential Narrative: Jewish Exegesis and the School of St. Victor in the Twelfth Century," 203–216.

42. David Damrosch, *The Narrative Covenant: Transformations of Genre in the Growth of Biblical Literature* (San Francisco: Harper & Row, 1987). I use this term, coined by Damrosch in his work of biblical criticism, because it provides a vivid literary allusion. However, it would not be appropriate to enter in this context into the academic discussion of which Damrosch's work is a part over biblical criticism and the origins and development of a biblical narrative style.

43. Jerusalem Talmud *Shekalim* 25b; *Suta* 37a; and *Midrash Tanhuma* 1. Also *Bereshit Rabbah* argues that the Torah predates creation by two thousand years (*Bereshit Rabbah* 8, 2, in Hanokh Albeck and Yehuda Theodor, eds., *Midrash Bereshit Rabbah*, 3 vols. [Jerusalem: Wahrmann Books, 1965], 3:57).

44. For a discussion of the tradition known as *merkavah* mysticism, see David Halperin, *Faces of the Chariot: Early Jewish Responses to Ezekiel's Vision*

(Tübingen: Mohr/Siebeck, 1988); Moshe Idel, *Kabbalah: New Perspectives* (New Haven, CT and London: Yale University Press, 1988), 78–96; Rebecca Lesses, *Ritual Practices to Gain Power: Angels, Incantations, and Revelation in Early Jewish Mysticism* (Harrisburg, PA: Trinity Press, 1998), 254–260; Peter Schäfer, *The Hidden and Manifest God: Some Major Trends in Early Jewish Mysticism* (Albany: SUNY Press, 1992); Gershom Scholem, *Major Trends in Jewish Mysticism* (New York: Schocken Books, 1961), 40–79.

45. Chavel, *Perush Ha-Ramban*, 1:2–3; Newman, *The Commentary of Nahmanides*, 23.

46. As Elliot R. Wolfson has pointed out, "many ideas expressed in the kabbalistic texts, such as speculation on the divine attributes of mercy and judgment and the divine names to which they are correlated, developed organically out of aggadic passages on similar themes" (Wolfson, "'By Way of Truth'," 156). Such a transformation is evident also in Nahmanides' uses of prooftexts in this context.

47. Jerusalem Talmud *Shekalim* 25b; *Suta* 37a; and *Midrash Tanhuma* 1. Abraham ibn Ezra includes a polemical argument against precisely this *aggadah* in his biblical commentary, labeling it an inadmissible and mistaken belief with no basis in rational thought, which should be laid to rest (Abraham ibn Ezra, *Perush al ha-Torah*, introduction).

48. "The present (like an Aristotelian place) is of any size, or many sizes, from a duration much shorter than consciousness can capture to one that spans centuries. In the writing of a book or the birth of a volcano, the event is a whole but not because of any imagined discreteness from other events, but because of the organic connectedness of its parts, the conditioning of what comes later by what went before, and the dependence on the outcome as a whole on what happens now" (Lenn E. Goodman, "Time, Creation, and the Mirror of Narcissus," *Philosophy East and West* 42, no. 1 [1992]: 73). See also Paul Ricoeur, *Time and Narrative*, trans. Kathleen McLaughlin and David Pellauer, 3 vols. (Chicago: University of Chicago Press, 1984–1988), especially 1:5–30 and 1:52–87.

49. Particularly helpful for the following discussion are Ricoeur, *Time and Narrative*; Hans Meyerhoff, *Time in Literature* (Berkeley: University of California Press, 1960), 23–63. See also Norbert Elias, *Time: An Essay*, trans. Edmund Jephcott (Oxford and Cambridge, MA: Blackwell, 1992).

50. I would like to thank David Biale for drawing my attention to this connection.

51. The significance assigned to the earlier stages of creation varied, as we saw above, from one exegete to the next. According to Abraham ibn Ezra, for example, Genesis tells the story of how God formed primordial matter into an organized natural universe governed by predictable laws and rules. Rashi, however, understands the creation story as a shorthand rendering of events which are naturally beyond human comprehension.

52. A good deal of scholarship has been devoted to classifying and analyzing Nahmanides' system of symbolic referents. Gershom Scholem points to the symbolic as one of several elements characterizing Nahmanides' thought; see Gershom Scholem, *Origins of the Kabbalah,* trans. Allan Arkush (Princeton, NJ: Jewish Publication Society and Princeton University Press, 1987), 386. Elliot R. Wolfson provides the most complete examination of Nahmanides' symbolism in a very thorough and challenging essay. See Wolfson, "'By Way of Truth'," 129–153. Moshe Idel examines the limits Nahmanides placed on kabbalistic interpretation in his writing, and compares Nahmanides' approach to the more open strategy of the younger kabbalists of Girona; see Idel, "'We Have No Kabbalistic Tradition on This'," 51–73, especially 63–67.

53. David Novak has argued that the corpus of Nahmanides' biblical commentary presents a systematic theology. I agree with Novak on a number of points. He argues that Nahmanides' greatest contribution to Jewish thought was the articulation of a practical or reality-based understanding of revelation that has everyday implications in the real world. Novak also sees the drive to discover the roots of Kabbalah in Nahmanides' exegesis as having distracted attention from the content of this work: "Many students of his commentary have failed to see that system[atic theology] because they have looked *wholly* for kabbalistic systematic theology" (David Novak, "Nahmanides' Commentary on the Torah," *The Solomon Goldman Lectures* 5 [1990]: 100). In a later adaptation of these ideas, Novak traces several themes through the body of Nahmanides' writings. His methodology is to identify the dominant themes in Nahmanides' thought, then synthesize these views into a systematic theology. But whereas Novak frames his argument in terms of *halakhah* and Nahmanides' view of the requirements for living a Jewish life, I am more interested in the way these ideas fit in Nahmanides' view of time, history, and creation. This process illuminates the interconnectedness of divergent aspects of Nahmanides' thought. However, Novak's final product has an artificial feel to it. Nahmanides' theology, as presented by Novak is seamless, almost modern in the ease and consistency with which ideas flow through a vast body of writings on numerous topics. Indeed, in his effort to find consistency in Nahmanides' theology, Novak threatens to erase the integrity of Nahmanides' works as individual compositions containing unique and independent arguments. See David Novak, *The Theology of Nahmanides Systematically Presented* (Atlanta: Scholars Press, 1992).

54. "*And God called the firmament heavens*: On the second day He called the heavens by this name when they adorned the form of the firmament because on the first day the heavens were still being created, but the name did not hold on them until they took on this form.... It is as if He said that they [the heavens] are waters stretched and drawn like a tent between the waters on high and the waters below. It is known that the name heavens contain a secret of their formation. In the *Gemora* in tractate *Hagiga* (12:1) 'what is *shamayim* but "there is water" (*sham mayim*).' If this is the case, the absence of one *mem* joins two equivalent letters...."

Or it might mean "the name of water" (*shem mayim*), in other words, the name by which God called water when it wore another form. This is the simple meaning of the verse according to the interpretation of Rashi, and it is also the opinion of Rav whom we mentioned above. There was a name for the heavens and the earth in the first verse to call them by in the future, for it is not possible to know [those names] just from this language. A more correct reading of the simple meaning of the verse is that the heavens mentioned in the first verse are the upper heavens, which are not of the spheres but are above the divine chariot, for example, 'and over the heads of the living creatures there was the likeness of a firmament, like the color of the terrible ice, stretched out over their heads above' (Ezekiel 1:23). On account of them, the Holy One, blessed is He, is called 'the one who rides on the heavens.' There is no story in the scripture about their creation, just as there is no mention of the angels and the life of the chariot, or anything distinguished by the fact that it is bodiless, it just mentions that the heavens were created, that is to say, they were brought forth from nothingness" (Chavel, *Perush Ha-Ramban*, 1:19; Newman, *The Commentary of Nahmanides*, 42).

55. According to Gershom Scholem, this nascent model of divine emanations developed among the kabbalists of Girona in the mid-thirteenth century. Scholem argues that while *Sefer Yetzirah*, a treatise on the process of divine emanation, did not play a formative role in the development of Kabbalah in general, it was an important influence on the way certain circles of kabbalists understood their tradition. This influence appears most clearly in the symbolic interpretation of creation in terms of emanations which is now associated with the Girona school. See Scholem, *Origins of the Kabbalah*, 422–430 and 445–454.

56. This identification of *hokhmah* as the first emanation, as well as the prooftexts he cites for it comprised an already well-established formula by the time Nahmanides used it in his commentary. It appears first in a letter, written, according to Scholem, between 1230 and 1240, concerning the validity of Maimonides' writings from a certain Samuel ben Mordechai to Yequtiel ha-Cohen (ibid., 224–225).

57. Chavel, *Perush Ha-Ramban*, 1:10–11.

58. Funkenstein, *Perceptions of Jewish History*, 110.

59. Ibid., 107–111. For further discussion of the Christian and other influence on Nahmanides' interpretation, see Wolfson, "'By Way of Truth'," 109–112; Gershom Scholem, *On the Kabbalah and Its Symbolism*, trans. Ralph Manheim (New York: Schocken Books, 1996), 38–40. In addition see Berger, "Miracles," 107–128, especially 112; Septimus, "'Open Rebuke and Concealed Love'," 17–21. It is important to note that Nahmanides' performance in the disputation before King James of Aragon in the synagogue of Barcelona demonstrates that he was both linguistically and culturally confident in intellectual encounters with Christians. Based on the extensive evidence of this debate, it is not unreasonable to surmise that his interest in and knowledge of Christian interpretive practices both predated and

exceeded the limits of the public disputation itself. See *Vikuah ha-Ramban*, in Chavel, *Kitvei Rabbenu Moshe ben Nahman*, 1:299–320. Also see Robert Chazan, "In the Wake of the Barcelona Disputation," *Hebrew Union College Annual* 61 (1990): 185–201; Robert Chazan, "The Messianic Calculations of Nahmanides," in *Rashi 1040–1990, Hommage á Ephraïm E. Urbach*, ed. Gabrielle Sed-Rajna (Paris: Les Éditions du Cerf, 1993), 631–637. Finally, there is evidence that suggests that Nahmanides was also proficient in Arabic. See Raphael Yoshpe, "Ha-Ramban ve-ha-Aravit," (Hebrew), *Tarbitz* 57, no. 1 (1988): 67–93.

60. Funkenstein, *Perceptions of Jewish History*, 118.

61. Ibid., 119–120. Havivah Pedaya draws a clear distinction between Nahmanides' use of historical typologies that occur on a linear temporal plane and those that recur on a cyclical basis—such as the sabbatical year. She argues that there is a link in his thought between the *sepherot* and the cyclical nature of cosmic time. See Pedaya, *Ha-Ramban*, 27–36.

62. Chavel, *Perush Ha-Ramban*, 1:30.

63. He offers an alternative, though related, suggestion that the verb "to make" is attached to "from all his works." He supports this argument with a string of prooftexts meant to demonstrate that the scripture frequently uses a similar grammatical construction in other cases that indicate cessation of an ongoing activity—i.e., a word meaning "stop," "rest," or "finish," followed by a verb indicating the activity in the infinitive case (ibid.).

64. "Now hear the proper interpretation of this verse according to its plain and clear meaning: The Lord, on him may there be a blessing, created all of creation from an indefinable nothing. There is no word in the holy language that [expresses] bringing something out of nothing except the word *bara*. And there is nothing that was made (*asah*) under the sun, or above it, that derives its existence from the original nothing. But from nothing the Lord brought the undefined, very subtle essential material that has no extension, though He provided it with potential, ready to receive form, and to bring actuality from potentiality. This is the first substance, which the Greeks called 'hyuli' (or primeval matter). After the primeval matter, He did not create (*bara*) a thing, but He formed and worked (*yetzer ve-asah*) [the matter] because from this He brought everything, and dressed the forms, and fixed them. Know that the skies and all that is in them are derived from a single matter, and the earth and all that is in it is a single matter. The Lord, on Him may there be a blessing, created both of them from nothing, and only these two were created, and everything was made from them" (ibid., 12; Newman, *The Commentary of Nahmanides*, 33). Nahmanides' interpretation of the triple use of *bara* in Genesis 1:27 is brief and does not address how this verse should be understood in relation to his understanding of the language of creation presented above. "And it says in the second verse *in His image God created him*, to distinguish the miracle that was performed for him from the other things that were created. This is the simple meaning of the verse as discovered by Josef Kimhi" (Chavel, *Perush Ha-Ramban*, 1:27; Newman, *The Commentary of Nahmanides*, 55).

65. David Novak takes the opposite stand: "The task of history is not to incorporate the events of the past into perennial patterns discernible in the present and projected into the future but to see the processes of the present as marks and symbols of the great events of the past" (Novak, *The Theology of Nahmanides*, 7).

66. Chavel, *Perush Ha-Ramban*, 1:30–31; Newman, *The Commentary of Nahmanides*, 61.

67. Norbert Elias has noted that time is typically represented with quite different levels of abstraction depending on the context in which it arises. As a concept in the context of philosophy or physics, it is expressed in highly abstract terms; but as an element of the social or cultural order, time is taken for granted as an extremely effective organizing and regulatory device. See Elias, *Time: An Essay*, 23–45.

68. Chavel, *Perush Ha-Ramban*, 1:31; Newman, *The Commentary of Nahmanides*, 62.

69. St. Augustine of Hippo formulated what was arguably the most famous and influential rendering of human history according to the 'world week' model. See Augustine, *City of God*, trans. Henry Bettenson (Middlesex: Penguin Books, 1984), 431–438.

70. Nahmanides based an entire argument in his account of the disputation on precisely this use of the word *yom* (day). Correcting the friar's literal interpretation of *yom* in a reference to messianic intervention Nahmanides draws attention to the frequent use of the word *yom* to mean years. Though his argument stopped short of a broad generalization, he might also have argued that the temporally specific terms are interchangeable particularly in the context of messianic speculation.

71. Babylonian Talmud *Sanhedrin* 97a–b. This same quote appears in the Babylonian Talmud *Avodah Zarah* 9a.

72. For example, the rabbis of the Talmud coined a formula by which any presumption of Jewish sovereignty in the diaspora was nullified in Jewish legal practice. *Dina de-malkhuta dina*, or "the law of the land (of exile) is the law," was a key feature of organized Jewish communities in diaspora. This legal construct was fundamental to the preservation of legal and practical autonomy of any particular Jewish community. During the thirteenth century, the legal basis for the independence of Jewish communities in the diaspora was long since beyond question. See Jacob Katz, *Exclusiveness and Tolerance: Studies in Jewish-Gentile Relations in Medieval and Modern Times* (Oxford: Oxford University Press, 1961), 48–59; Shmuel Shilo, *Dina de-malkhuta Dina* (Jerusalem: Hotsaat Defus Akademi bi-Yerushelayim, 1975).

73. Chavel, *Perush Ha-Ramban*, 1:31; Newman, *The Commentary of Nahmanides*, 62–63.

74. "The thickness of the sky is one tenth of a day" (Babylonian Talmud *Pesahim* 94a).

75. Nahmanides included extended commentaries on this verse in *Sefer ha-Geulah* and his account of the Barcelona disputation. In both cases, he read this verse as the only verse in Daniel which contained prophecy that had yet to be fulfilled. See Chavel, *Kitvei Rabbenu Moshe ben Nahman*, 1:261 and 1:302–320, respectively.

76. Chavel, *Perush Ha-Ramban*, 1:31–32; Newman, *The Commentary of Nahmanides*, 63.

77. Shlomo Buber, ed., *Midrash Tanhuma al Hamushah Humshe Torah* (Vilna: ha-Almanah veha-Ahim Rom, 1885), *Bereshit 12, Lekh lekhah*.

78. Chavel, *Perush Ha-Ramban*, 1:77.

79. Ibid., 1:180. On Nahmanides' commentary on the four kingdoms of the book of Daniel, see Pedaya, *Ha-Ramban*, 30–31.

80. For a full discussion on the development of this symbolism, see Gerson Cohen, "Esau as Symbol in Early Medieval Thought," in *Jewish Medieval and Renaissance Studies*, ed. Alexander Altmann (Cambridge, MA: Harvard University Press, 1967), 19–48. Joshua Levinson demonstrates that the rabbinic exegetical narrative of the meeting between Jacob and Esau, as well as the dominance of Jacob in this exchange, mobilizes a political and cultural fantasy of Jewish political success during a period of Roman subjection. See Joshua Levinson, "Dialogical Reading in the Rabbinic Exegetical Narrative," *Poetics Today* 25, no. 3 (2004): 497–528. I thank my colleague Gwynn Kessler for stressing the point that while rabbinic interpretations of Jacob and Esau present them as paradigmatic enemies, they also maintain a highly complex relationship precisely because they are brothers. It is precisely their familial proximity that is unsettling for the rabbis, not their difference. See the first chapter of her forthcoming book, *Conceiving Israel: Famous Fetuses in Rabbinic Narratives*.

81. For a survey of medieval approaches to this issue, see Talmage, "Keep Your Sons from Scripture."

82. Maimonides, *Sefer Moreh ha-Nevuhim*, trans. Shmuel bar Yehuda ibn Tibbon (Jerusalem: Mosad ha-Rav Kook, 1987), Section 2, chapter 47, 372–375. In this section, Maimonides addressed the use of *figurae* and hyperbole and examined examples that support the dictum "Torah speaks in exaggerated language." "However, about what is written in the Torah concerning the life-span of certain people, I say this: that nobody lived that long except the person who is mentioned himself, and as for the other human beings, they lived the natural and ordinary number of years. This abnormality of the person under discussion may be due to a number of causes: his diet or the way he conducted himself, or a miracle and the rules that direct miracles. It is not possible to say of this another thing" (p. 373).

83. Chavel, *Perush Ha-Ramban*, 1:47–48. Nahmanides provided a natural explanation for this change in human life: the flood polluted the air men breathed, causing the duration of life to be significantly shortened.

84. The following list includes a broad selection of biblical verses (the list of corresponding pages in Chavel's edition will appear at the end of this note) in which Nahmanides addressed the order of birth or the duration of life or events: Genesis 7:1, 8:4–5, 16:3 (in which he contemplates whether the period of Sarah's infertility should be counted from the time of her union with Abraham or from the day the couple entered the Holy Land), 23:1, 25:19 (in which he explains that the Torah brings the genealogies of Ishmael and Isaac to establish primogeniture in the case of the former, and righteousness in the case of the latter), 35:28, and 46:15 (where he provides a schematic summary of the average life-span for each generation) (1:57–60, 1:97, 1:128, 1:143–144, and 1:253–255). Maurizio Bettini provides a fascinating study of the linguistic constructions used in classical Roman literature to represent the relationship between individuals and time as it passes. See Maurizio Bettini, *Anthropology and Roman Culture: Kinship, Time, Images of the Soul,* trans. John Van Sickle (Baltimore: Johns Hopkins University Press, 1991), 121–132.

85. In his translation of *tesaper ha-yetzerah be-hidush ha-olam* Funkenstein omits the word *be-hidush* and replaces it with the bracketed clause "out of nothing." This interpretation conflates the two levels of creation Nahmanides clearly articulates in his exegesis of Genesis 1:1: the first step being creation of a prime matter, or *hyuli,* followed by the second, the formation of that matter into discrete objects and elements. Thus, I read *be-hidush* as a crucial part of this summary. See Funkenstein, *Perceptions of Jewish History,* 112.

86. Funkenstein's interpretation of the phrase *tziurei devarim* as *figurae* cannot be contested. In addition, his claim that Nahmanides was ultimately influenced by Augustine, either through firsthand knowledge of his writings or—more likely—by means of a Jewish formulation of his notion of prefiguration, such as Avraham bar Hiyya's *Megilat ha-megaleh,* becomes that much stronger when we consider Nahmanides' suggestion that the patriarchs' seed was imprinted with the pattern for specific historical and social manifestations. On Avraham bar Hiyya's sense of time, see Abraham bar Hiyya, *Sefer Megilat ha-megaleh* (Jerusalem: 1968), 18–42. Also Meir Wachsmann, "Ha-Mahshavah Ha-Philosophit ve-ha-Datit shel Avraham bar Chiyya," in *Sefer ha-Yovel likhvod Tsvi Wolfson li-melot lo shivim ve-hamesh shannah* (Jerusalem: American Academy for Jewish Research, 1965), 143–168.

87. Introduction to Exodus, Chavel, *Perush Ha-Ramban,* 1:279.

88. Although Funkenstein downplays the linguistic aspect, it is operative—albeit less frequently—in Nahmanides' exegesis; see Funkenstein, *Perceptions of Jewish History,* 114–115.

89. The view of biblical text and the temporal conception represented in Nahmanides' typological exegesis, as Mark Saperstein has demonstrated, became influential in shaping the sense of time and history disseminated to Jewish communities through weekly sermons beginning in the fourteenth century. Saperstein

argues that typology became a common method of discourse in sermons and preaching manuals, and he makes the case that Nahmanides' biblical commentary provided a model for these later preachers. In this treatment, Saperstein successfully refutes Funkenstein's claim that Nahmanides was the only Jewish exegete who used typological exegesis; however, he makes no attempt to challenge Funkenstein's suggestion that the Ramban's systematic application of typological hermeneutics was path-breaking. See Saperstein, "Jewish Typological Exegesis," 161–167.

90. "The second Ashkenazic literary manifestation of any overt interest in messianism is Rashi's commentaries to the Book of Daniel and the Talmud, in which he indicated that the Messiah was to be expected in 1352 or in 1478. However, Rashi's conclusions, far from betraying an avid expectation of the messianic redemption, actually lend support to our contention. Rashi's dates were nothing more than an exegetes' elucidation of texts, which he interpreted with no greater emphasis than he had the rest of the vast corpus of Scripture and Talmud. He could not very well have skipped over these particular passages in Daniel and the Talmud. But there is a far more revealing point about Rashi's interpretations, which excludes them from the genre of genuine messianic speculation. If there is one characteristic that underlies two thousand years of messianic literature from the Book of Daniel in the second century B.C.E. to the commentary of Meir Leibush Malbim in the nineteenth century C.E., it is the relative imminence of the messianic denouement. . . . Far from being messianically oriented, Rashi's commentary, by postponing the end some three or four centuries, was the very antithesis of millenarist excitation" (Gerson D. Cohen, "Messianic Postures of Ashkenazim and Sephardim [Prior to Sabbathai Zevi]," in *Studies of the Leo Baeck Institute*, ed. Max Kreutzberger [New York: Frederick Unger, 1967], 126–127). In a paper delivered at Touro College, Elisheva Carlebach called for a reevaluation of Cohen's thesis. She argues that Cohen was predisposed to view the Ashkenazic authorities as naturally more hesitant than their Sephardic equivalents about predicting the time of messianic redemption. She suggests that Cohen's interpretation was shaped by the assumption that Sephardic culture was more vibrant and creative than Ashekenazic culture. "Cohen's study was informed by the Jewish historiographical tradition to which he was heir and its biases which were deeply embedded. In this tradition, medieval Ashkenaz became a metaphor for the 'rabbinic elite' which was identified with fundamentalism and intolerance. . . . The real deficiency of Ashkenaz, then, resided not in its messianic posture, but in its deficient alignment with the temper of the historian" (Elisheva Carlebach, "Between History and Hope: Jewish Messianism in Ashkenaz and Sepharad," paper presented at the Third Annual Lecture of the Victor J. Selmenowitz Chair of Jewish History, Graduate School of Jewish Studies, Touro College, 1998, 16). Carlebach calls attention to continuities between Ashkenazic and Sephardic messianic views which Cohen overlooks, but she does not find fault with his representation of Rashi's neutrality to the issue of messianic deliverance.

91. Abraham bar Hiyya lived and wrote for a time in Barcelona. For bibliographic data, see Norman Roth, ed., *Medieval Jewish Civilization: An Encyclopedia* (New York: Routledge, 2003), 3–5.
92. Hiyya, *Sefer Megilat ha-megaleh*, 14–47.
93. Ibid., 72–85.
94. Alan L. Mintz, *Hurban: Responses to Catastrophe in Hebrew Literature* (New York: Columbia University Press, 1984), 1–105; David G. Roskies, *Against the Apocalypse: Responses to Catastrophe in Modern Jewish Culture* (Cambridge, MA: Harvard University Press, 1984), 1–53; Yerushalmi, *Zakhor*, 31–52.

Chapter 3   The Barcelona Disputation

1. Friar Paul is known in the literature by a variety of names depending upon the language of composition: Friar Pau, Pau Cristià, Crestià Pablo Christiano (or Pablo Christiá), and Paul Christian. Nahmanides' Hebrew transcript refers to him as Frai Pol (or Fray Paul); similarly, the Latin disputation account refers to him simply as frater Paulus. In this study, I will use Friar Paul Christiani.

2. Some examples of this literature include: David Berger, ed., *The Jewish-Christian Debate in the High Middle Ages: A Critical Edition of the Nizzahon Vetus* (Philadelphia: Jewish Publication Society of America, 1979); Bernhard Blumenkranz, ed., *Disputatio Iudei et Christiani et anonymi auctoris: disputationis Iudei et Christiani continuatio ad fidem codicum recensuit prolegomenis notisque instruxit* (Utrecht: In Aedibus Spectrum, 1956); Gemma Escribà and Raquel Ibáñez-Sperber, *The Tortosa Disputation: Regesta of Documents from the Archivo de la Corona de Aragón, Fernando I, 1412–1416* (Jerusalem: Ginzci Am Olam The Central Archives for the History of the Jewish People: Hispania Judaica Dinur Institute, Hebrew University of Jerusalem, 1998); Ora Limor, *Vikua'h Mayorkah, 1286: mahadurah bi-kortit u-mavo* (Jerusalem: Hebrew University, 1985); Reuben Margaliot, *Vikuah rabenu Yehiel me-Paris* (Lwów: R. Margulies, 1928); Frank Talmage, ed., *Sefer ha-berit ve-vikueh RaDaK em ha-Natzrut* (Jerusalem: Hotza'at Mosad Bialik, 1974); J. C. M. van Winden, *An Early Christian Philosopher: Justin Martyr's Dialogue with Trypho* (Leiden: Brill, 1971).

The secondary literature in the field is sizable. A partial list includes the following: David Berger, "Gilbert Crispin, Alan of Lille, and Jacob ben Reuben: A Study of the Transmission of Medieval Polemic," *Speculum* 49, no. 1 (1974): 34–47; David Berger, "Mission to the Jews and Jewish-Christian Contacts in the Polemical Literature of the High Middle Ages," *The American Historical Review* 91, no. 3 (1986): 576–591; Jeremy Cohen, "Medieval Jews on Christianity: Polemical Strategies and Theological Defense," in *Interwoven Destinies: Jews and Christians through the Ages*, ed. Eugene J. Fisher (New York: Paulist Press, 1993), 77–89; Amos

Funkenstein, "Changes in Religious Polemics between Jews and Christians in the Twelfth-Century," (Hebrew) *Tziyon* 33, no. 3–4 (1968): 125–144; Gavin Langmuir, "Doubt in Christendom," in *Toward a Definition of Antisemitism* (Berkeley: University of California Press, 1990), 100–133; Richard Lim, *Public Disputation: Power and Social Order in Late Antiquity* (Berkeley: University of California Press, 1995), 2–24; Marcel Simon, *Verus Israel: étude sur les relations entre chrétiens et juifs dans l'empire romain (135–425)*, 2nd ed. (Paris: E. de Boccard, 1964); Oskar Skarsaune, *The Proof from Prophecy: A Study in Justin Martyr's Proof-text Tradition, Text-Type, Provenance, Theological Profile* (Leiden: E. J. Brill, 1987); Hanne Trautner-Kromann, "Jewish Polemics against Christianity in Medieval France and Spain: Can the Intensity of Argumentation Be Measured?" in *Rashi 1040–1990, Hommage á Ephraïm E. Urbach*, ed. Gabrielle Sed-Rajna (Paris: Les Éditions du Cerf, 1993), 639–644; Hanne Trautner-Kromann, *Shield and Sword: Jewish Polemics against Christianity and the Christians in France and Spain from 1100–1500*, trans. James Manley (Tübingen: Mohr, 1993).

3. For a discussion of the Friar Paul's polemical innovations, see Lena Roos, "Paul Christian—A Jewish Dominican Preaching for the Jews," *Studia Theologica* 57, no. 1 (2003): 49–60.

4. Recent scholarship by Jaume Riera i Sans has cast doubt on Nahmanides' authorship of this document. A full discussion of Riera i Sans follows below.

5. Several editions of this work have been published. For consistency I use Chavel's edition: Haim Dov Chavel, *Kitvei Rabbenu Moshe ben Nahman*, 2 vols. (Jerusalem: Mosad Ha-Rav Kook, 1964), 1:302–326. Also Rueven Margulies, ed., *Vikuah ha-Ramban* (Lwów: Lemberg, 1929). For translations into English, see Charles Ber Chavel, ed., *The Disputation at Barcelona* (New York: Shilo, 1983); Hyam Maccoby, *Judaism on Trial: Jewish-Christian Disputations in the Middle Ages* (London: Associated University Presses, 1982), 39–75. In Catalan see Eduard Feliu, ed., *Disputa de Barcelona de 1263 entre mestre Mossé de Girona i Fra Pau Cristià* (Barcelona: Columna Edicions, 1985). In Italian, Moshe Idel and Mauro Perani, *Nahmanide, esegeta e cabbalista: Studi e testi* (Florence: Giuntina, 1998), 387–409. And in French, see Nahmanides, *La dispute de Barcelone: suivi du Commentaire sur Esaïe 52–53*, trans. Eric Smilévitch and Luc Ferrier (France: Verdier, 1984).

6. Yitzhak Baer, "The Disputations of Rabbi Yechiel of Paris and of Nahmanides," (Hebrew), *Tarbitz* 2, no. 2 (1931): 185–187; Don Pére Heinrich Denifle, "Quellen zur Disputation Pablos Christiani mit Mose Nachmani su Barcelona 1263," *Historisches Jahrbuch* 8 (1887): 231–234; Charles de Tourtoulon, ed., *Jacme I, le conquérant, roi d'après les chroniques et les documents inédits*, 2 vols. (Montpellier: Imprimerie typographique de Gras, 1863–1867), 2:594.

7. Many historians have assumed that this account is the official record of the disputation. According to Jaume Riera i Sans, however, it is very unlikely that a royal clerk would have submitted an official record without affixing his signature.

It is more likely, he argues, that the extant Latin report was written by Friar Paul, who remained anonymous in an effort to make his biased account appear official and objective. See Jaume Riera i Sans, "Les Fontes Històriques de la Disputa de Barcelona," in *Disputa de Barcelona de 1263 entre mestre Mossé de Girona i Fra Pau Cristià*, ed. Eduard Feliu (Barcelona: Columna Edicions, 1985), xii–xiii.

8. An account written and circulated by Nahmanides became the center of controversy two years following the disputation when the rabbi was charged with propagating blasphemy. He was later expelled from the Crown of Aragon by order of the pope. In some respects, the hostility with which Nahmanides' account was received by Christian authorities has overshadowed the form and content of the document itself.

9. Jacob ben Elijah, "Iggeret," in *Jeschurun*, ed. Joseph Kobak (1868): 1–13.

10. Jeremy Cohen, "The Mentality of the Medieval Jewish Apostate: Peter Alfonsi, Hermann of Cologne, and Pablo Christiani," in *Jewish Apostasy in the Modern World*, ed. Todd Endelman (New York: Holmes and Meier, 1987), 36–40.

11. Elijah, "Iggeret," 1–13; Robert Chazan, "The Letter of R. Jacob ben Elijah to Friar Paul," *Jewish History* 6, no. 1–2 (1992): 51–63; J. Cohen, "The Mentality," 39–40.

12. The exact duration of this event is unclear. The anonymous Latin document claims that the disputation ended abruptly after the first day. Nahmanides' longer, more detailed Hebrew document, however, claims that the disputation concluded after four full days.

13. Nahmanides refers explicitly to a sum of 300 *dineri* in his disputation account. See Chavel, *Kitvei Rabbenu Moshe ben Nahman*, 1:320. (According to Yitzhak Baer, the sum was 600 *dineri*. See Baer, "The Disputations," 181.) On its face, this story smacks of dramatic hyperbole, however Yom Tov Assis has discovered archival evidence confirming that the king took a loan in the same amount from a Jewish money lender during the summer of 1263. For a detailed discussion of King James I's policy towards Jewish money lenders, see Yom Tov Assis, *Jewish Economy in the Medieval Crown of Aragon, 1213–1327: Money and Power* (Leiden: E. J. Brill, 1997), 15–25. According to Assis, James was extremely fair and savvy in his regulation of money lending. Loans were recorded in the royal registry. With the aid of these records, the king was able to collect revenue from those members of Christian society (whether corporate bodies or individuals, such as monasteries and the clergy), who were exempted from paying taxes, while at the same time regulating the money lenders' income as a possible source of emergency revenue. Assis has noted that this is an interesting and striking coincidence that was made possible by the king's efforts to improve record keeping. James's concessions to the friars took the form of compulsory sermons, which entire Jewish communities were expected to attend, preached by friars, often in synagogues. The Jews of Barcelona were compelled to attend one such sermon immediately following the disputation. See Chavel, *Kitvei Rabbenu Moshe ben Nahman*, 1:319–320.

14. These documents were reproduced in Denifle, "Quellen zur Disputation Pablos Christiani mit Mose Nachmani su Barcelona 1263," 238–244.

15. Robert Chazan and others have argued convincingly that Nahmanides' account of the disputation was the document in question here. See Baer, "The Disputations," 181–184; Robert Chazan, *Barcelona and Beyond: The Disputation of 1263 and Its Aftermath* (Berkeley and Los Angeles: University of California Press, 1992), 92–98; Martin A. Cohen, "Reflections on the Text and Context of the Disputation of Barcelona," *Hebrew Union College Annual* 35 (1964): 187–189; Cecil Roth, "The Disputation at Barcelona (1263)," *Harvard Theological Review* 43, no. 2 (1950): 141–143.

16. Denifle, "Quellen zur Disputation Pablos Christiani mit Mose Nachmani su Barcelona 1263," doc. #8, 239; J. Cohen, "The Mentality," 39–40.

17. Nahmanides never returned to Girona. He set off for Palestine in 1267 and died there in 1270. In keeping with the historical and messianic thrust of his exegesis, Nahmanides believed that repossession of the Holy Land was an objective in the history of the Jewish people. For a survey of Nahmanides' opinions concerning Israel, see Aryeh Newman, "The Centrality of Eretz Yisrael in Nachmanides," *Tradition* 10, no. 1 (1968): 21–30. In response to the friars' appeal, Pope Clement IV issued a bull in which he praised Friar Paul for his knowledge of Jewish texts and condemned the Jews for their obstinacy. See Thomas Ripoll, ed., *Bullarium Ordinis Fratrum Praedicatorum*, 8 vols. (Rome: Typographia Hieronymi Mainardi, 1729), 1:488.

18. Randolph Starn, "Truths in the Archives," *Common Knowledge* 8, no. 2 (2002): 401.

19. Carlo Ginzburg, *Myths, Emblems, Clues*, trans. John and Anne C. Tedeschi (London: Huchinson Radius, 1990), 102.

20. Ibid., 106–121. Here Ginzburg argues that the evidentiary paradigm described above is echoed in art history, anthropology, medicine, and psychiatry. This argument, especially in its application to historical writing, is quite compelling.

21. This view is evident most recently in Robert Chazan's collected works on Jewish-Christian relations, which includes works on the Crusades, the Barcelona disputation, and the legacy of medieval antisemitism in the modern world. Chazan's analysis is certainly based in archival and solid historical research, but his narrative is shaped to a large degree by the inevitability of legal persecution, violent attack, and expulsion.

22. I will address the trends in modern scholarship on the disputation at length below.

23. Chazan, *Barcelona and Beyond*, 4–16. Within these pages Chazan includes a detailed description of the methodology applied in his book.

24. A detailed review of the many contributions to this century-long debate is beyond the scope of this chapter, though I will touch on portions of that discussion as they become relevant. The central works include Baer, "The Disputa-

tions," 172–187; Yitzhak Baer, *A History of the Jews in Christian Spain: From the Reconquest to the Fourteenth Century*, trans. Louis Schoffman, 2 vols. (Philadelphia: Jewish Publication Society of America, 1961), 1:152–157; Haim Hillel Ben-Sasson, "Rabbi Moshe ben Nahman, the Man in the Context of His Time" (Hebrew), *Molad* 1 (1967): 360–366; Robert I. Burns, "The Barcelona 'Disputation' of 1263: Conversionism and Talmud in Jewish-Christian Relations," *The Catholic Historical Review* 79, no. 3 (1993): 488–495. In his review of Chazan's *Barcelona and Beyond*, Burns raises a number of issues of great import for the contextualization of the Barcelona disputation in the history of Jews in Catalonia and the Crown of Aragon. See also Robert Chazan, "The Barcelona 'Disputation' of 1263: Christian Missionizing and Jewish Response," *Speculum* 52, no. 4 (1977): 824–842; Robert Chazan, "From Friar Paul to Friar Raymond: The Development of Innovative Missionizing Argumentation," *Harvard Theological Review* 76, no. 3 (1983): 289–306; Robert Chazan, *Daggers of Faith: Thirteenth-Century Christian Missionizing and Jewish Response* (Berkeley: University of California Press, 1989), 183–201; Robert Chazan, "In the Wake of the Barcelona Disputation," *Hebrew Union College Annual* 61 (1990): 185–201; Chazan, *Barcelona and Beyond*; Jeremy Cohen, *The Friars and the Jews: The Evolution of Medieval Anti-Judaism* (Ithaca, NY: Cornell University Press, 1982), 108–128; M. A. Cohen, "Reflections," 157–192; Marvin Fox, "Nahmanides on the Status of Aggadot: Perspectives on the Disputation at Barcelona, 1263," *Journal of Jewish Studies* 40, no. 1 (1989): 95–109; Heinrich Graetz, "Die Disputation des Bonastruc mit Frai Pablo in Barcelona," *Monatsschrift für Geschichte und Wissenschaft des Judentums* 14 (1865): 428–433; Isidore Loeb, "La Controverse de 1263 à Barcelone entre Paulus Christiani et Moise ben Nahman," *Revue des Études juives* 15 (1887): 1–18; Roth, "The Disputation at Barcelona (1263)," 117–144; Solomon Schechter, "Nachmanides," *The Jewish Quarterly Review* o.s. 5 (1893): 78–121. Solomon Schechter noted with irony that scholarly interest in polemics and disputation literature was misguided and unbalanced, but nevertheless went on to discuss Nahmanides' contribution to this literature as well as the scholarly dispute that generated around it.

25. Graetz, "Die Disputation," 428–433. On the social, political, and cultural influences on the early development of critical Jewish scholarship in the nineteenth century, see Michael Meyer, "The Emergence of Modern Jewish Historiography: Motives and Motifs," *History and Theory* 27, no. 4 (1988): 160–175. See also Michael Meyer, "Jewish Religious Reform and Wissenschaft des Judentums: The Positions of Zunz, Geiger, and Frankel," *Leo Baeck Institute Year Book* 16 (1971): 19–41. Susannah Heschel has argued that the early school of critical Jewish scholarship represents a radical rereading, or counterhistory, of the dominant narrative of the Christian West. The history of the western tradition as presented by Graetz, Geiger, and others was a history of violent persecution in which Christianity rose to a dominant role in the west by treading heavily on the backs of Jews. According to Heschel, the lachrymose view of the Jewish past, which trains attention on the victimization and persecution of Jews, served a very important cultural and

political role in transforming the mythology of the middle ages. See Susannah Heschel, "Jewish Studies as Counterhistory," in *Insider/Outsider: American Jews and Multiculturalism*, ed. David Biale, Michael Galchinsky, and Susannah Heschel (Berkeley: University of California Press, 1998), 101–115, especially 108–111.

26. Graetz, "Die Disputation," 428–433.

27. Baer, "The Disputations," 172–187; Baer, *A History of the Jews in Christian Spain*, 1:152–157; Loeb, "La Controverse de 1263," 1–18.

28. In particular, see Chazan, *Barcelona and Beyond*, 142–147; M. A. Cohen, "Reflections," 169–170; Maccoby, *Judaism on Trial*, 94–95.

29. Gil Anidjar, "Jewish Mysticism Alterable and Unalterable: On Orienting Kabbalah Studies and the 'Zohar of Christian Spain'," *Jewish Social Studies: History, Culture, and Society* 3, no. 1 (1996): 89–157. See Arthur Green's introduction to Daniel Matt's Zohar translation, Daniel C. Matt, ed., *The Zohar: Pritzker Edition*, 3 vols. (Stanford, CA: Stanford University Press, 2004–2005), 1:liv–lxviii; Daniel C. Matt, "'New-Ancient Words': The Aura of Secrecy in the Zohar," in *Gershom Scholem's Major Trends in Jewish Mysticism 50 Years After: Proceedings of the Sixth International Conference on the History of Jewish Mysticism*, ed. Peter Schäfer and Joseph Dan (Tübingen: J. C. B. Mohr [Paul Siebeck], 1993); Gershom Scholem, *Major Trends in Jewish Mysticism* (New York: Schocken Books, 1961), 156–204.

30. Daniel Abrams, "Orality in the Kabbalistic School of Nahmanides: Preserving and Interpreting Esoteric Traditions and Texts," *Jewish Studies Quarterly* 3, no. 1 (1996): 85–102. Moshe Idel, "Rabbi Moshe ben Nahman: Kabbalah, Halakhah and Spiritual Leadership" (Hebrew), *Tarbiz* 64, no. 4 (1995): 535–580; Moshe Idel, "The Vicissitudes of Kabbalah in Catalonia," in *The Jews of Spain and the Expulsion of 1492*, ed. Moshe Lazar and Stephem Haliczer (Lancaster, CA: Labyrinthos, 1997): 25–49; Haviva Pedaya, *Ha-Ramban: Hitalut—Zeman Mahzori ve-Tekst Kadosh* (Tel Aviv: Am Oved, 2003).

31. Martin Cohen refers in particular to Nahmanides' claim that *aggadah* is not binding in "Reflections," 168–171. Cohen's assessment is based on Scholem's argument that Nahmanides was a student of the Girona circle of kabbalists. He does not, however, bring independent examples from Nahmanides' writings to demonstrate this point. Marc Saperstein, on the other hand, faults Robert Chazan for failing to take seriously how important and painful it must have been for Nahmanides to articulate this argument. See Marc Saperstein, "Review of Robert Chazan, *Barcelona and Beyond: The Disputation of 1263 and Its Aftermath*," *The Journal of Religion* 74, no. 1 (1994): 121–123. For Chazan's discussion of this line of argument in Nahmanides' disputation account, see Chazan, *Barcelona and Beyond*, 142–153. Most recently, Shalem Yahalom suggested that when Nahmanides made this argument in the disputation it applied explicity to the issue of faith, not to the status of *aggadah* in the canon. See Shalem Yahalom, "The Barcelona Disputation and the Status of the Aggadah in Nahmanides' Teachings" (Hebrew), *Tziyon* 69, no. 1 (2004): 25–43.

32. See Nahmanides' commentary on Genesis 12:11–13, for example. As is his frequent practice throughout, he quotes Rashi quoting *Midrash Rabba*, followed by his own reading. Rashi himself employed the same strategy. See Haim Dov Chavel, *Perush ha-Ramban al ha-Torah*, 2 vols. (Jerusalem: Mosad Ha-Rav Kook, 1959), 1:80. Bernard Septimus addresses Nahmanides' evaluation of traditional sources in kabbalistic terms: Bernard Septimus, "'Open Rebuke and Concealed Love': Nahmanides and the Andalusian Tradition," in *Rabbi Moses Nahmanides (Ramban): Explorations in His Religious and Literary Virtuosity*, ed. Isadore Twersky (Cambridge, MA: Harvard University Press, 1983), 16–21.

33. Fox, "Nahmanides on the Status of Aggadot," 96. Like M. A. Cohen, Kenneth Stow argues that Nahmanides was unwillingly forced into this position by his adversary. Astonishingly, the only secondary source he brings to support this argument is Marvin Fox, who clearly does not hold the same view. See Kenneth Stow, *Alienated Minority: The Jews of Medieval Latin Europe* (Cambridge, MA: Harvard University Press, 1992), 253.

34. Avraham Saltman applied a similar strategy of analysis in his reading of the conversion narrative of Hermannus Quodam Judaeus. Hermannus' *Opusculum de Conversione Sua* maps the chain of events that ultimately led to his conversion as a young adult—including a childhood encounter and meal with the king, some symbolic dreams, his attempt to kidnap and convert a younger brother, and finally, a religious debate in which he claims to have engaged with Rupert of Deutz just prior to his conversion. The thrust of Saltman's argument is that the details provided by the author of this narrative do not ring true as Jewish. The methodological problems in Saltman's reasoning run quite deep. For example, his claim that Hermannus' dream sequences lack Jewish symbolism seems to demand that an essentialist Jewishness radiate from this text. See Avraham Saltman, "Hermann's *Opusculum de Conversione sua*: Truth and Fiction," *Revue des Études juives* 147, no. 1–2 (1988): 31–56.

35. For a discussion of the motivations for and development of this new, dangerous missionizing strategy, see Chazan, *Barcelona and Beyond*, 18–27. An assessment of Nahmanides' perception of and response to this new approach to missionizing occupies much of Chazan's book. In conclusion, he summarizes his argument that Nahmanides rebuffed this effort with the composition of three works (the narrative of the disputation, his *Sefer Ha-Geulah*, and a full-length commentary on the suffering servant of Isaiah 53): "Rabbi Moses ben Nahman attempted rebuttal of the new missionizing thrusts through formats with which he was intimately familiar—commentary and the topical treatise—and through a format he tried his hand at for the first time—the narrative account—with astonishingly successful results. In these three differing literary treatments, Nahmanides addressed a broad spectrum of issues, affording wide-ranging guidance and reassurance to his beleaguered brethren. From the comprehensive response of the rabbi of Girona to the innovative missionizing, we have emerged with a firm sense

of the seriousness of the new challenge and its impact on a variety of facets of late thirteenth-century Jewish creativity" (Chazan, *Barcelona and Beyond*, 194).

36. "I have for some time now argued that the Christian report is the accurate one, in its emphasis on the proving of Christian truth from Jewish sources. The question that must be raised is the reason for Nahmanides' distortion. The answer, I believe, lies in the rabbi's determination to make his narrative the occasion for a broad refutation of Christianity and affirmation of Judaism. His skewed presentation of the agenda suggests to the Jewish reader from the outset that the underlying issue is ultimate religious truth, whether it resides in the Christian vision or in the Jewish vision. While this was surely not the issue in the carefully manipulated encounter in Barcelona, the rabbi of Girona made his report on that encounter the occasion for raising the broader issues that Friar Paul and the Dominicans had gone to such pains to eliminate" (Chazan, *Barcelona and Beyond*, 123–124).

37. For example, see M. A. Cohen, "Reflections," 157–192. See also Norman Roth, "The Jews in Spain at the Time of Maimonides," in *Moses Maimonides and His Time*, ed. Eric L. Ormsby (Washington, DC: Catholic University of America Press, 1989), 1–20.

38. "Nahmanides ... went to great length to reassure his fellow-Jews throughout his narrative that the lengthy exile was meaningful in its own terms and that Jewish hopes for future redemption were firmly grounded, reasonable, and correct" (Chazan, *Barcelona and Beyond*, 130).

39. Salo Baron coined the term "lachrymose conception of Jewish history" in the diaspora in an early article criticizing the tendency among historians to represent Jewish history as consisting of never-ending cycles of tolerance to persecution. See Salo W. Baron, "Ghetto and Emancipation," *Menorah Journal* 14 (1928): 515–528. After receiving harsh criticism for this view from Yitzhak Baer, Baron reiterated his distaste for this narrative mode in an address to the American Academy for Jewish Research (1941). See Salo W. Baron, "The Jewish Factor in Medieval Civilization," in *Ancient and Medieval Jewish History: Essays by Salo Wittmayer Baron*, ed. Leon Feldman (New Brunswick, NJ: Rutgers University Press, 1972), 239–267, see note 54 (513–514) in particular. In this article, Baron emphasizes that the Jews of medieval Europe enjoyed relative safety and security, which accounts for their cultural achievements.

40. I am fully aware that this observation applies equally to my own treatment of these documents as well.

41. Baer balances the examples of rise and decline of tolerance for Jews in *A History of the Jews in Christian Spain*, however, it is striking that he viewed the success of Jewish communities and culture in medieval Christianity as ultimately destructive. The Zionist thrust of Baer's argument, or the sense that Judaism and Jews are only safe in a state of cultural, religious, even geographic isolation, certainly shapes his interpretation of the particular Jewish culture that developed in

Spain. For a discussion of the so-called Jerusalem school of Jewish historiography, see David N. Myers, *Re-inventing the Jewish Past: European Jewish Intellectuals and the Zionist Return to History* (New York: Oxford University Press, 1995). On Baer's historiography and reception, also see Pinchas Rosenblüth, "Yitzchak Baer: A Reappraisal of Jewish History," *Leo Baeck Institute Yearbook* 22 (1977): 115–135; Israel Yuval, "Yitzhak Baer and the Search for Authentic Judaism," in *The Jewish Past Revisited: Reflections on Modern Judaism*, ed. David N. Myers and David B. Ruderman (New Haven, CT: Yale University Press, 1998), 77–87.

42. J. Cohen, *The Friars and the Jews*, 108–128.

43. Riera i Sans, "Les Fontes Històriques," ix–xv.

44. According to Robert Burns, Norman Roth is engaged in a study in which he develops a similar argument. To my knowledge he has not yet published the results of his research. See Burns, "The Barcelona 'Disputation' of 1263," 491.

45. For an excellent representation of the unique tension between acculturation and Jewish peculiarity that characterized Jewish life in Renaissance Italy, see Robert Bonfil, *Rabbis and Jewish Communities in Renaissance Italy*, trans. Jonathan Chipman (Oxford: Oxford University Press, 1990).

46. It is worth noting that the vast majority of them would be deemed similarly problematic were scholars to place the same demands on Nahmanides' works universally. On the question of forgery during the middle ages, see Giles Constable, "Forgery and Plagiarism in the Middle Ages," *Archiv für Diplomatik, Schriftgeschichte Siege, und Wappenkunde* 29 (1983): 1–41; Giles Constable, "Forged Letters in the Middle Ages," in *Fälschungen im Mittelalter* (Hannover: Hahnsche Buchhandlung, 1988), 11–37.

47. "The historical imagination is limited to plausibly filling gaps in the record, and 'throwing new light' on a phenomenon requires the discovery of hitherto unknown information. . . . Indeed all sources tend to be treated in narrowly documentary terms, that is, in terms of factual or referential propositions that may be derived from them to provide information about specific times and places. There is, moreover, an explicit or implicit hierarchy among sources whereby a preferential position is accorded to seemingly direct informational documents such as bureaucratic reports, wills, registers, diaries, eye-witness accounts and so forth." He goes on to argue that intellectual history has been marginalized precisely because such a documentary approach is at most ancillary to its practice. See Dominick LaCapra, *History and Criticism* (Ithaca, NY: Cornell University Press, 1985), 18.

48. Ibid., 21.

49. Solomon Schechter, "Nachmanides," in *Studies in Judaism* (Philadelphia: Jewish Publication Society, 1938), 104. In addition to Schechter's essay there are several biographical studies of Nahmanides; many of them, however, verge on hagiography: Charles B. Chavel, *Ramban: His Life and Teachings* (New York: Philipp Feldheim, 1960); Yaacov Even-Chen, *Ha-Ramban. Rabenu Mosheh ben Nahman*

(Hebrew) (Jerusalem: Hotsaat Ginzakh Rishonim le-Tziyon, 1976); Chayim Henoch, *Ramban ke-hoker vke-mekubal: Haguto ha-toranit me-tokh parshanuto le-mitzvot* (Jerusalem: Hotza'at Torah le'am, 1978). (Henoch's biography is now in English as well: Chayim Henoch, *Ramban: Philosopher and Kabbalist, on the Basis of His Exegesis to the Mitzvot* [Northvale, NJ: Aronson, 1998].) For a more balanced and critical analysis of Nahmanides' writings, see Ephraim Kanarfogel, "On the Assessment of R. Moses ben Nahman (Nahmanides) and His Literary Oeuvre," *Jewish Book Annual* 51 (1993–94): 158–172; David Novak, *The Theology of Nahmanides Systematically Presented* (Atlanta: Scholars Press, 1992).

50. On the conventions of representing Jewish-Christian debates, see Funkenstein, "Changes in Religious Polemics," 125–144.

51. Baer, "The Disputations," 172–187; Chazan, *Barcelona and Beyond*, 123–124; M. A. Cohen, "Reflections," 159.

52. Chavel, *Kitvei Rabbenu Moshe ben Nahman*, 1:302.

53. Ibid.

54. Maccoby, *Judaism on Trial*, 97–99.

55. Maccoby has suggested that the Hebrew account was likely a translation of the text Nahmanides composed in the vernacular for the bishop of Girona: "[T]here is some likelihood that the Hebrew version was written some years after the disputation, and was a translation by someone other than Nahmanides. There are some indications in the Hebrew text that it may have been written by someone who, at times, did not fully understand Nahmanides' argument" (ibid., 99). Maccoby does not indicate which passages strike him as problematic.

56. To date there is no systematic study of the individual psychological motivations for and collective or institutional responses to apostasy in Iberian Jewish society prior to the late fourteenth century. Joseph Shatzmiller deals with some of the social and family concerns that made apostasy an appealing option in southern France and northern Spain during the high to late middle ages. See Joseph Shatzmiller, "Converts and Judaizers in the Early Fourteenth Century," *Harvard Theological Review* 74, no. 1 (1981): 63–77; Joseph Shatzmiller, "Jewish Converts to Christianity in Medieval Europe, 1200–1500," in *Cross Cultural Convergences in the Crusader Period: Essays Presented to Aryeh Grabois on His Sixty-Fifth Birthday*, ed. Michael Goodich, Sophia Menache, and Sylvia Schein (New York: Peter Lang, 1995), 295–318. For a discussion of these issues in the medieval Ashkenazic context, see Edward Fram, "Repentant Apostates in Medieval Ashkenaz and Premodern Poland," *AJS Review* 21, no. 2 (1996): 299–339; Alfred Haverkamp, "Baptised Jews in German Lands during the Twelfth Century," in *Jews and Christians in Twelfth-Century Europe*, ed. Michael Signer and John Van Engen (Notre Dame, IN: University of Notre Dame Press, 2001), 255–310; William Chester Jordan, "Adolescence and Conversion in the Middle Ages: A Research Agenda," in *Jews and Christians in Twelfth-Century Europe*, ed. Michael Signer and John Van Engen (Notre Dame, IN: University of Notre Dame Press, 2001), 77–93. For a discussion

of apostasy in Britain, see Robert C. Stacey, "The Conversion of the Jews to Christianity in Thirteenth-Century England," *Speculum* 67, no. 2 (1992): 263–283. Jacob Katz groups apostates and proselytes together. He is concerned with the ritual and cultural methods used by Jews to integrate or segregate individuals whose status was unclear vis-á-vis the Jewish community. See Jacob Katz, *Exclusiveness and Tolerance: Studies in Jewish-Gentile Relations in Medieval and Modern Times* (Oxford: Oxford University Press, 1961), 67–81. For a discussion of the proselytizing techniques used by the Church, and by the mendicant friars in particular, see J. Cohen, *The Friars and the Jews*, especially 86–88 and 163–169; on Friar Paul, see Cohen, "The Mentality," 20–47. On the early modern period see Elisheva Carlebach's recent study of apostasy among medieval and early modern German Jews: Elisheva Carlebach, *Divided Souls: Converts from Judaism in Germany, 1500–1750* (New Haven, CT: Yale University Press, 2001).

57. I do not intend to suggest that Nahmanides' account is, or is not, an accurate representation of the event; only that he specifically makes a point to claim it was (Chavel, *Kitvei Rabbenu Moshe ben Nahman*, 1:302).

58. Ibid., 1:302–303.

59. Nahmanides used this instructive session on the basic Jewish texts to great rhetorical effect. It rendered the king a highly sympathetic character whose understanding of and commitment to Christianity and the Church did not preclude a genuine interest in beliefs and practices of Judaism. At the same time, it allowed Nahmanides to present himself as an expert, willing to make Jewish tradition and texts accessible and interesting to his audience. Friar Paul, in contrast, is presented as a charlatan lacking either the subtlety or the talent to accurately instruct an audience of Jews or Christians in the complexity of Jewish texts.

60. Chavel, *Kitvei Rabbenu Moshe ben Nahman*, 1:304–305.

61. James C. Scott, *Domination and the Arts of Resistance: Hidden Transcripts* (New Haven, CT: Yale University Press, 1990), 136–182. Leo Strauss advanced a similar argument concerning the production of potentially controversial philosophical works by Jews, like Maimonides, who lived as minorities under fundamentalist regimes. See Leo Strauss, *Persecution and the Art of Writing* (Chicago: University of Chicago Press, 1988), especially 22–94.

62. Babylonian Talmud, *Sanhedrin* 43b.

63. "If your brother, your own mother's son, or your son or daughter, or the wife of your bosom, or your closest friend entices you in secret saying come let us worship other gods—whom neither you nor your fathers have experienced—(13:8) from among the gods of the peoples around you, either near to you or distant, anywhere from one end of the earth to the other: (13:9) do not assent or give heed to him, show him no pity or compassion and do not shield him; (13:10) but take his life, let your hand be the first against him to put him to death, and the hand of the rest of the people thereafter. (13:11) Stone him to death, for he sought to make you stray from the Lord your God who brought you out of the Land of

Egypt, out of the house of bondage" (translation slightly amended. *JPS Hebrew-English Tanakh* [Philadelphia, 2000]).

64. Babylonian Talmud, *Avodah Zarah* 1:1–3.

65. See Schmuel Trigano, "The Conventionalization of Social Boundaries and the Strategies of Jewish Society in the Thirteenth Century," in *New Horizons in Sephardic Studies*, ed. Yedida K. Stillman and George K. Zucker (Albany: SUNY Press, 1993), 45–66. He argues that social and demographic changes within Jewish society along the Pyrenees, combined with the import of philosophical and mystical movements to this region, resulted in an intensified effort to formalize interpretive methodology to preserve cohesion. Apostates represented a radical and dangerous form of transformation.

66. Fram, "Repentant Apostates," 299–339; Haverkamp, "Baptised Jews," 255–310; Jordan, "Adolescence and Conversion," 77–93; Shatzmiller, "Jewish Converts," 295–318; Stacey, "The Conversion of the Jews," 263–283.

67. "The apostate is like a non-Jew in all halakhic respects" (Jerusalem Talmud *Eruvin* 6:2; Babylonian Talmud *Yevamot* 47b).

68. "[T]ractate *Avodah Zarah* goes well beyond the claim that idolatry is no longer a Jewish problem. It constitutes a statement that *avodah zarah* is intrinsically non-Jewish; indeed, that everything non-Jewish, *even if not idolatrous*, pertains to *avodah zarah*. *Avodah Zarah* is no longer a cult which both Jews and non-Jews may be tempted to follow; it has become, in the Mishnah, an inherent, *ethnic* characteristic of all non-Jewish peoples, and it is to some extent co-terminus with the non-Jewish world" (Sacha Stern, "The Death of Idolatry?" *Le'ela* April, no. 35 [1993]: 27).

69. For a discussion of the symbolic link between the mourning ritual *shivah*, which calls for mourners to separate themselves from the normal business of society for a week, and the halakhic treatment of idolaters, see Reena Zeidman's analysis of intertextual conversations about the boundaries of Jewish society and culture within rabbinic literature. Zeidman argues that the requirement that Jews abstain from business or social relations with idolaters three days before and three days after idolatrous rituals functions is a parody of *shivah*. "[T]he idolaters are, in a sense, dead themselves, and the Israelites are obligated to engage in mourning rites for them.... In this way, the activity [of avoiding contact with them] assumes a derisive tone because the Jews are applying a sacred ritual to an anti-halakhic group of people. Moreover, the pagan clearly is *unaware* of the mockery.... The ruling, therefore, expresses a statement about the God of the Jews: their God is living while the pagan god, by applying these mourning rites to their holidays, is dead, and so are its adherents" (Reena Zeidman, "A Time to Mourn: Methods of Reading Intertextuality in the Laws of Idolatry," *Approaches to Ancient Judaism*, n.s. 10, no. 42 [1997]: 135). For a more conceptual discussion of the various analogies used in the Talmud to compare idolatry with loss or betrayal, including

marital infidelity, see Moshe Halbertal and Avishai Margalit, *Idolatry*, trans. Naomi Goldblum (Cambridge, MA: Harvard University Press, 1992), 7–36 and 108–123. Also Carlebach, *Divided Souls*, 26–32.

70. Carlebach, *Divided Souls*, 24–26; Haverkamp, "Baptised Jews," 262–263; S. Stern, "The Death of Idolatry," 26–28.

71. "This is the matter of the debates in their entirety. To my knowledge, I did not change a word in them. Afterwards, and on the same day [that the proceedings ended] I stood before the king, our lord, and he said 'let the disputation be adjourned, for I have never seen a man argue a fallacious case as well as you have done'" (Chavel, *Kitvei Rabbenu Moshe ben Nahman*, 1:319). Nahmanides reiterated the king's approval of his performance at the very end of his account: Chavel, *Kitvei Rabbenu Moshe ben Nahman*, 1:320.

72. Jean Régné, *History of the Jews in Aragon: Regesta and Documents, 1213–1327*, ed. Yom Tov Assis and Adam Gruzman (Jerusalem: Magnes Press, Hebrew University, 1978), doc. #84, 16, doc. #137, 26, doc. #319, 57–58. For an interpretation of these documents, see Chazan, *Barcelona and Beyond*, 199–200.

73. Denifle, "Quellen zur Disputation Pablos Christiani mit Mose Nachmani su Barcelona 1263," 239.

74. Chavel, *Kitvei Rabbenu Moshe ben Nahman*, 1:310–311.

75. *Tosaphot*, Babylonian Talmud *Avodah Zarah* 2a.

76. Berger, "Gilbert Crispin," 34–47; Berger, ed., *The Jewish-Christian Debate*.

77. This is true even in the case of the Paris disputation of 1240, in which representatives for Jewish communities in France were compelled to answer accusations that the Talmud contained mistakes, blasphemy, and heresy. Like the Barcelona disputation, two accounts of the Paris disputation are extant, the first was written in Hebrew describing the arguments made by Rabbi Yehiel ben Joseph, and the second in Latin by Nicholas Donin, a convert from Judaism who petitioned the pope to investigate the grave mistakes contained in Jewish literature. Both accounts agree that Donin's most persuasive argument was the revelation that Jews organized their ritual and legal institutions around laws defined in the Talmud, not biblical law. Clearly the historical significance of Jewish ritual, at least in the eyes of the Christian authorities, is linked here with the Christian interpretation of history and change. In the traditional Christian view, Jews are historically important only in so far as they can attest to the temporal change brought to earth by Christ. See J. Cohen, *The Friars and the Jews*, 60–76.

78. The Latin account lays out the agenda in essentially this order. Since Nahmanides' account was formulated as a progressive, eyewitness report, a summary of the friars' mission would have compromised its literary structure. For the friars' mission statement, see Baer, "The Disputations," 185. On the friars' goals, see Chazan, *Barcelona and Beyond*, 40–45; J. Cohen, *The Friars and the Jews*, 60–128, especially 108–128.

79. According to Nahmanides' account, the rabbi requested that the disputation sponsors guarantee that he be permitted to speak openly and freely during the proceedings. After some discussion, the sponsors of the event agreed, provided that Nahmanides promised to refrain from speaking derisively about Christian dogma or Jesus and the holy family. "The King, our lord, ordered me to debate in his palace before him and his council in Barcelona with Friar Paul. I answered: 'I will do as you commanded me my lord, the King, if you give me permission to speak as I wish. And I request [this] permission be granted by the King and by Friar Raymon de Peñaforte and his entourage with him here.' Friar Ramon de Peñaforte answered: 'Only if he does not speak blasphemous words.' I said to them: 'I do not want to break your law on this matter. But I must be able to say what I wish during the debate, just as you say whatever you wish. As for me, I understand I must speak according to the guidelines, but it must be as I wish.' And they all granted me permission to speak freely" (Chavel, *Kitvei Rabbenu Moshe ben Nahman*, 1:302–303). This concession to Nahmanides' request for free speech has provided the basis for much discussion concerning the veracity of the debate. See Chazan, *Barcelona and Beyond*, 94–97.

80. Chavel, *Kitvei Rabbenu Moshe ben Nahman*, 1:304.

81. *Eikha Rabbatai* 1:51 and Babylonian Talmud *Sanhedrin* 98a.

82. That the king did not rescind Jewish self-government and the freedom of Jews to interpret their traditions demonstrates that this line of argument did not convince him. King James did, however, give the friars free reign to conduct compulsory sermons in Jewish quarters throughout the Crown. See Régné, *History of the Jews in Aragon*, doc. #386, 68. According to Yitzhak Baer, "[t]he king reaffirmed his previous order that Jews were not to be compelled to attend missionary sermons delivered outside the Jewish quarter. . . . The Jews were not required to reply to the allegations that the Talmud contained hostile references to Christians, unless specific blasphemies of Jesus, Mary and the saints were pointed out. The Jewish apologists had apparently won their point that the Talmudic laws concerning idolatry (*Abodah Zara; Abotat Kokhabim*) and the references to Gentiles (*Nokhrim; Goyim*) did not deal with Christianity and Christians at all. Further privileges permitted Jews to purchase foodstuffs from Christians and to sell them ritually slaughtered meat. The king confirmed full ownership of rights of the *aljamas* to their synagogues and cemeteries. He excused the Jews from wearing the badge, and required them to wear only the round cape. The Jewish courtiers and officials were permitted to dispense with the cape as well" (Baer, *A History of the Jews in Christian Spain*, 1:159–160). Also see J. Cohen, *The Friars and the Jews*, 80–85 and 108–128.

83. Samuel Krauss, *The Jewish-Christian Controversy, from the Earliest Times to 1789*, trans., ed., and revised by William Horbury (Tübingen: J. C. B. Mohr [Paul Siebeck], 1995).

84. At least two encyclopedic polemical guides circulated through medieval Jewish communities: Judah Rosenthal, ed., *Sefer Yosef ha-Mekane* (Jerusalem: Mekitse Nidarim, 1970) and *Sefer Nitzahon Yashan*. The latter, for example, presents a catalogue of Christian polemical arguments and convincing Jewish rebuttals, systematically organized in the order of the biblical books. The response to a christological interpretation of Genesis 49:10 focuses on the issue of political power: "A certain apostate argued that the Hebrew verse, 'Until Shilo comes and to him . . .' (*ad ki yavo Shilo ve-lo* [Gen. 49:10] constitutes an acrostic for Jesus (*Yeshu*). The answer to this is in the very same verse, for the Hebrew verse, 'The scepter shall not depart from Judah, nor the ruler's staff from between his feet, until Shilo comes and to him' is an acrostic for the Hebrew phrase, 'There is no blemish as evil as Jesus.' Furthermore, the phrase 'Shilo comes and the homage of peoples shall be his' yields the acrostic, 'Jesus will lead them astray.'

". . . The heretics, however, say that the verse [Gen. 49:10] means 'until the messenger,' i.e., Jesus, 'comes'; then the kingdom of Judah will cease. And so, indeed, it came to pass that when Jesus came the kingdom of Judah ceased. Moreover, it is written, 'And the homage of peoples shall be his'; i.e., the nations shall congregate before him and turn to him. Furthermore, 'he tethers his ass to a vine' [Gen. 49:11] refers to Jesus, who entered Jerusalem on a donkey.

"The answer is that they are refuted by their own words, for how can one maintain that the kingdom of Judah did not cease until Jesus? There was, after all, no king in Israel from the time of Zedekiah, for even in the days of the second Temple there was no king in Israel but only governors subordinate to the kings of Media, Persia, or Rome. Now, a long time passed between Zedekiah and the birth of Jesus, and so how can the verse say that the kingdom would not depart from Judah until Jesus comes? Furthermore, what relationship is there between 'Shiloh' and Jesus' name?

"Moreover, the inference that there would be a king in Israel until the advent of Shiloh, i.e., Jesus, but afterwards the kingdom would cease and no king would arise again is refuted by the following prophecy of Jeremiah: 'And I will gather the remnant of my flock [out of all the countries] whither I have driven them, and will bring them again to their folds; and they shall be fruitful and increase' [Jer. 23:3–6]. . . ." (Berger, ed., *The Jewish-Christian Debate*, 60–61).

85. In particular, he argued that the Jews of his time had no claim to the title rabbi because no institution existed that had the authority to ordain rabbis. See Chavel, *Kitvei Rabbenu Moshe ben Nahman*, 1:304–305. The Latin account confirms this thrust in the debate. See Baer, "The Disputations," 186.

86. Chavel, *Kitvei Rabbenu Moshe ben Nahman*, 1:304.

87. Ibid.

88. The traditional rabbinic spelling begins with an *aleph*. However Nahmanides spells *aggadah* with a *heh*. Unless I am quoting Nahmanides' account, I will use the traditional spelling.

89. Chavel, *Kitvei Rabbenu Moshe ben Nahman*, 1:306. It is interesting that Nahmanides chose to summarize this argument, rather than present it as a direct quote from Friar Paul's mouth. On the other hand, rather than paraphrase the *Midrash*, he cites it in its entirety.

90. *Midrash Lamentations* is a relatively early rabbinic midrash dating—roughly—from the fifth century. Though the biblical book of Lamentations reflects on the destruction of the First Temple, the *Midrash* focuses on the destruction of the Second Temple and the tensions that preceded and followed this traumatic event. See Galit Hasan-Rokem, *Web of Life: Folklore and Midrash in Rabbinic Literature*, trans. Batya Stein (Stanford, CA: Stanford University Press, 2000); Alan L. Mintz, *Hurban: Responses to Catastrophe in Hebrew Literature* (New York: Columbia University Press, 1984), 49–83.

91. Chavel, *Kitvei Rabbenu Moshe ben Nahman*, 1:306. Nahmanides' refusal to attribute equal authority to all rabbinic sources has been an issue of considerable interest in the scholarly literature. Cecil Roth and Martin Cohen, among others, took this denial as an indication that Nahmanides argued not from conviction, but instead, from necessity. According to this argument, Nahmanides saw the Christian argument as a real threat and thus used the extreme measure of advancing an argument that Roth and M. A. Cohen thought must have been violently at odds with his personal beliefs. See Cohen, "Reflections," 157–192; Roth, "The Disputation at Barcelona (1263)," 117–144. More recently, Jeremy Cohen has suggested that Friar Paul's explicit goal in this debate was to back Nahmanides into a corner, from which his only recourse would be the denial of his own sacred texts. "Pablo knew very well that, were the rabbi discredited publicly, the Jewish community would lose much of its ability to withstand Christian missionary efforts. By summoning the rabbi to the disputation in Barcelona, Pablo forced him to serve as the defender of the faith of Spanish Jewry, as the symbol of contemporary Judaism. And by placing Nahmanides in the position of having to deny classical rabbinic texts which supposedly proclaimed the advent of the messiah, those texts authoritative among Jews, Pablo endeavored to emphasize that Nahmanides and contemporary Jewry had broken with the faith of their ancient ancestors" (J. Cohen, *The Friars and the Jews*, 114). The problem with this argument is that it assumes that the vast majority of medieval Jews were wavering on the verge of conversion, and the intellectual elite recognized this. Robert Chazan, Marvin Fox, Hyam Maccoby, and Bernard Septimus, on the other hand, have shown, with great success, I think, that Nahmanides' use of *aggadot* throughout his writings reflects a critical and measured method of evaluating these sources. See Chazan, *Barcelona and Beyond*, 142–153; Fox, "Nahmanides on the Status of Aggadot," 95–109; Maccoby, *Judaism on Trial*, 46–48; Septimus, "'Open Rebuke and Concealed Love'," 20–22.

92. In fact, Nahmanides went so far as to insert into the narrative the temporal boundary of a break in the debate and the lapse of a day between the two parts of this argument. "They stood then, and the king gave a time [for us] to return and

debate the following Monday. On that day the king went to the Cloisters that are in the city and there gathered all the people of the city, Gentiles and Jews" (Chavel, *Kitvei Rabbenu Moshe ben Nahman*, 1:308–309). Also see Baer, "The Disputations," 187. According to his narrative of the debate, the continuation of this topic opens the discussion on the second day. The author of the Latin transcript claimed that Nahmanides was driven by desperation to deny the truth of this *aggadah* and that the disputation came to an abrupt end at the close of the first day of proceedings.

93. "Know that we have three genres of literature (*minim sefarim*). The first is the Bible (*ha-bibliya*), and all of us believe it in its entirety. The second is called *Talmud*, and it explains the *mitzvot* (commandments) contained in the Torah, for the Torah has 613 *mitzvot*, and not one of them is not explained in the Talmud. All of us accept the interpretations of the *mitzvot*. Also, we have a third book [i.e., body of literature] called *Midrash*, which is to say, *Sermones*. It is as if a bishop stood and gave a sermon, and a member of the audience thought it was good, and wrote it down. It is this literature [about which I said] if one believes it, all the better, but if one doesn't believe it, there is no damage" (Chavel, *Kitvei Rabbenu Moshe ben Nahman*, 1:308).

94. In particular, see Chazan, *Barcelona and Beyond*, 1:80–99. His central thesis suggests that the Christians' effort to build a failsafe method of proselytizing Jews provides the key to understanding Nahmanides' arguments, as well as his behavior in the years following the disputation.

95. See Schmuel Trigano's comments on the impact of such vocal apostates on internal Jewish community relations in "The Conventionalization of Social Boundaries," 56–57. Also see Fram, "Repentant Apostates," 299–339; Simha Goldin, "Juifs et Juifs convertis au moyen age 'Es-tu encore mon frère?'," *Annales: Histoire, Sciences Sociales* no. 4 (July–August 1999): 851–874; Jordan, "Adolescence and Conversion," 77–93. Haverkamp, "Baptised Jews," 255–310; Shatzmiller, "Converts and Judaizers in the Early Fourteenth Century," 63–77; Shatzmiller, "Jewish Converts," 295–318; Stacey, "The Conversion of the Jews," 263–283; Zeidman, "A Time to Mourn," 125–145.

96. Daniel Boyarin would likely insist that this statement be reformulated to show that Paul's ultimate goal was to convert Judaism itself. "The issue is not whether ethnic Jews have been displaced from significance within the Christian community but whether a community of faith (= grace) has replaced a community of flesh (= genealogy and circumcision) as Israel. Precisely *because* the signifier Israel is and remains central for Paul, it has been transformed in its signification into another meaning, an allegory for which the referent is the new community of the faithful Christians, including both those faithful Jews (as a privileged part) and the faithful gentiles but excluding Jews who do not accept Christ" (Daniel Boyarin, *A Radical Jew: Paul and the Politics of Identity* [Berkeley: University of California Press, 1994], 202).

97. For example, Petrus Alfonsi, who wrote a dialogue between his converted Christian self and his former Jewish self, and Hermannus Quodam Judeaus, who wrote a conversion testimonial, are two such cases. See John V. Tolan, *Petrus Alfonsi and His Medieval Readers* (Gainesville: University of Florida Press, 1993); Gerlinde Niemeyer, ed., *Hermannus Quondam Judaeus, Opusculam de Conversione Sua* (Weimar: H. Bohlaus Nachfolger, 1963); or Karl F. Morrison, *Conversion and Text: The Cases of Augustine of Hippo, Herman-Judah, and Constantine Tsatsos* (Charlottesville: University Press of Virginia, 1992). Also see Saltman, "Hermann's *Opusculum*," 31–56. For a general analysis of this genre see Amos Funkenstein, *Perceptions of Jewish History* (Berkeley: University of California Press, 1993), 169–208; and more recently, Carlebach, *Divided Souls*.

98. Not accidentally, the rise in the number of converts who were willing to subject their abandoned faith and its constituents to intense and hostile scrutiny coincided with an increased interest in examining the beliefs and traditions central to contemporary Judaism on the part of powerful men within the Christian power structure, in particular, mendicant friars. This, of course, is a well-studied theme in medieval Jewish history. Jeremy Cohen, for example, has examined the role played by mendicant friars in the transformation of western European Christendom from a culture and society in which Jews were permitted to live and practice Judaism as a "humiliated people" into a society which viewed Judaism and its adherents as a malignant threat. He argues that the friars were central to this process in part due to the very nature of the mendicant orders. They were able to collect information about new or unconventional views and broadcast warnings with relative speed because they were not bound to specific geographic locations and, most importantly, their mission—to establish and administer an ideal of orthodoxy throughout Christendom—provided them with unique access to Jews and apostates. See Cohen, *The Friars and the Jews*, 52–60.

99. Both accounts point to the interpretation of rabbinic texts that hint that the messiah was born some 1,200 years before as the central issue of the debate. See Baer, "The Disputations," 185–187 for the text of the Latin transcript. Also, for a longer discussion of the content of this text, see Chazan, *Barcelona and Beyond*, 40–44.

100. Scholars typically date this text to the seventh century. See Joseph Dan, *Ha-sipur ha-ivri bi-yeme ha-benayim: iyunim ba-taldotav* (Jerusalem: Keter, 1974), 122–132. Amos Funkenstein groups this document in the larger category of counterhistories, "a specific genre of history written since antiquity.... Their function is polemical. Their method consists of the systematic exploitation of the adversary's most trusted sources against their grain.... Their aim is the distortion of the adversary's self-image, of his identity, through the deconstruction of his memory" (37). In Funkenstein's words, *Sefer Toldot Yeshu* "employed the sources of the adversary—in this case, the Gospels—in order to turn Christian memory on its head. Jesus, it tells us, was the son of an illicit affair. He became a magician, having

acquired by ruse possession of the explicit divine names (*shem hameforash*), and thus he turned into a powerful seducer of the unlearned multitude (*mesit umediach*). The Jewish legal establishment (the Sanhedrin), at the end of its wits, knew no better remedy than to have one of its own ranks volunteer to infiltrate the heretical movement in disguise and destroy it. The name of this hero was Judas Iscariot. The Gospel's heroes turn into villains, its villains into heroes" (Funkenstein, *Perceptions of Jewish History*, 39). Nahmanides' use of this historical timeline in his arguments against Friar Paul suggests the undercurrent of a subversive discourse criticizing Christianity that is veiled by the conventions of pleasantry and the promise not to blaspheme Christianity.

101. Elliot Wolfson has shown that Nahmanides uses the formula *be-derekh ha-emet* in his biblical exegesis to signal a kabbalist or mystical interpretation. In some sense, Nahmanides is using this phrase in the same manner here: it seems to indicate what he believes to be the clear meaning of the text, which would be obvious to all knowledgeable Jewish readers. See Elliot R. Wolfson, "'By Way of Truth': Aspects of Nahmanides' Kabbalistic Hermeneutic," *AJS Review* 14 (1989): 103–178.

102. Chavel, *Kitvei Rabbenu Moshe ben Nahman*, 1:306.

103. Chazan argues that Nahmanides employed these dramatic narrative techniques in order to communicate a twofold message to his Jewish audience. On the one hand, Chazan argues, Nahmanides intended his account as a road map that others who may have been confronted with this missionizing approach could follow; on the other hand, he intended it as an edifying narrative, meant to strengthen the faith of Jews in the diaspora. See Chazan, *Barcelona and Beyond*, 100–141.

Chapter 4   At the Threshold of Redemption

1. Rashi counted 1,335 years from 62 c.e., when the regular sacrificial offering at the Second Temple came to a halt, not from the date of the destruction, as Nahmanides did. For a discussion of the mechanism by which Rashi arrived at this date, see Robert Chazan, "Rashi's Commentary on the Book of *Daniel*: Messianic Speculation and Polemical Argumentation," in *Rashi et la culture juive en France du Nord au moyen âge*, ed. Gilbert Dahan, Gérard Nahon, and Elie Nicolas (Paris-Louvain: E. Peeters, 1997): 114–115.

2. Jeremy Cohen, *The Friars and the Jews: The Evolution of Medieval Anti-Judaism* (Ithaca, NY: Cornell University Press, 1982); Jeremy Cohen, *Living Letters of the Law: Ideas of the Jew in Medieval Christianity* (Berkeley: University of California Press, 1999); Moshe Idel, *Messianic Mystics* (New Haven, CT: Yale University Press, 1998); Moshe Idel, "Rabbi Moshe ben Nahman: Kabbalah, Halakhah

and Spiritual Leadership" (Hebrew), *Tarbiz* 64, no. 4 (1995): 535–580; Moshe Idel, "Some Concepts of Time and History in Kabbalah," in *Jewish History and Jewish Memory: Essays in Honor of Yosef Hayim Yerushalmi*, ed. Elisheva Carlebach, John Efron, and David Myers (Hanover, NH and London: Brandeis University Press, 1998), 153–188; Robert E. Lerner, "Ecstatic Dissent," *Speculum* 67, no. 1 (1992): 33–57; Robert Lerner, "The Medieval Return to the Thousand Year Sabbath," in *The Apocalypse in the Middle Ages*, ed. Richard K. Emmerson and Bernard McGinn (Ithaca, NY: Cornell University Press, 1992), 51–71; Harvey J. Hames, "From Calabria Cometh the Law, and the Word of the Lord from Sicily: The Holy Land in the Thought of Joachim of Fiore and Abraham Abulafia," *Mediterranean Historical Review* 20, no. 2 (2005): 187–199.

3. Abraham Abulafia, who lived during the second half of the thirteenth century, had a rather remarkable and tumultuous career as a teacher and interpreter of philosophy and mysticism, and as a self-proclaimed messianic figure. Following a mystical experience in Sicily Abulafia fashioned himself as the Jewish messiah. He later attempted to convey this message to the pope in a personal audience. There have recently been several articles published on Abulafia's thought and career. Most interesting for the purposes of this work are a handful of studies that place Abulafia in the context of thirteenth-century apocalyptic thought in the Mediterranean. See Clifford R. Backman, "Arnau de Vilanova and the Franciscan Spirituals in Sicily," *Franciscan Studies* 50 (1990): 7; Hames, "From Calabria Cometh the Law," 187–199; Mariuccia Bevilacqua Krasner, "Abraham ben Shmuel Abulafia e Arnaldo de Vilanova: due experienze religiose in Sicilia," in *Ebrei e Sicilia*, ed. Nicolò Bucaria, Michele Luzzati, and Angela Tarantino (Palermo: Regione Siciliana Assessorato dei Beni Culturali e Ambientali e della Pubblica Instruzione, 2002), 193–200.

4. Moshe Idel, "The Land of Israel in Medieval Kabbalah," in *The Land of Israel: Jewish Perspectives*, ed. Lawrence A. Hoffman (Notre Dame, IN: University of Notre Dame Press, 1986), 176–178; Michael Nahorai, "The Land of Israel in the Teaching of the Rambam and the Ramban" (Hebrew), in *The Land of Israel in Medieval Jewish Thought*, ed. Moshe Hallamish and Aviezer Ravitzky (Jerusalem: Yad Yitzhak Ben-Tzvi, 1991), 123–137; Aryeh Newman, "The Centrality of Eretz Yisrael in Nachmanides," *Tradition* 10, no. 1 (1968): 21–30; Haviva Pedaya, "The Spiritual vs. The Concrete Land of Israel in the Geronese School of Kabbalah" (Hebrew) in *The Land of Israel in Medieval Jewish Thought*, ed. Moshe Hallamish and Aviezer Ravitzky (Jerusalem: Yad Izhak Ben-Zvi, 1991), 264–289; Michael A. Signer, "The Land of Israel in Medieval Jewish Exegetical and Polemical Literature," in *The Land of Israel: Jewish Perspectives*, ed. Lawrence A. Hoffman (Notre Dame, IN: University of Notre Dame Press, 1986), 200–233; Geulah Bat-Yehudah, "Torat aretz Yisra'el shel ha-Ramban b'mahshevet ha-tehiyah," *Sinai*, no. 61 (1967): 226–239.

5. For an extended discussion of rabbinic denials of the possibility of messianic redemption in the middle ages and early modern periods, see Eric Lawee,

"'Israel Has No Messiah' in Late Medieval Spain," *The Journal of Jewish Thought and Philosophy* 5 no. 2 (1996): 245–279. Also see Gerson D. Cohen, "Messianic Postures of Ashkenazim and Sephardim (Prior to Sabbathai Zevi)," in *Studies of the Leo Baeck Institute*, ed. Max Kreutzberger (New York: Frederick Unger, 1967), 117–156; Joseph Sarachek, *The Doctrine of the Messiah in Medieval Jewish Literature*, 2nd ed. (New York: Hermon Press, 1968); Gershom Scholem, *The Messianic Idea in Judaism* (New York: Schocken, 1971); Dov Schwartz, *Ha-raayon ha-meshihi be-hagut ha-yehudit be-yameh ha-benayim* (Ramat-Gan: Bar Ilan University, 1997); Abba Hillel Silver, *A History of Messianic Speculation in Israel from the First through the Seventeenth Centuries* (New York: Macmillan, 1927).

6. Babylonian Talmud *Sanhedrin*, 97b. For a comparison between Jewish and early Christian approaches to apocalyptic discourse, see Christopher Rowland, *The Open Heaven: A Study of Apocalyptic in Judaism and Early Christianity* (New York: Crossroad, 1982), 61–75. Rowland argues that the most significant difference between Jewish and Christian apocalyptic cycles is the tendency among Jewish writers to use pseudonyms or remain anonymous from fear that false predictions would crack the foundation of tradition. Also see John J. Collins, *The Apocalyptic Imagination: An Introduction to Jewish Apocalyptic Literature*, 2nd ed. (Grand Rapids, MI: William B. Eerdmans, 1989 and 1998); John J. Collins, *Seers, Sybils, and Sages in Hellenistic-Roman Judaism* (Leiden: E. J. Brill, 1997).

7. Abraham Halkin and David Hartman, eds., *Crisis and Leadership: Epistles of Maimonides* (Philadelphia: Jewish Publication Society, 1985), 114–115. Maimonides composed the body of this letter in Judeo-Arabic; for a Hebrew translation, see Abraham Halkin, ed., *Igeret Teman le'rabbenu Moshe ben Maimon* (New York: American Academy of Jewish Research, 1952), 40. In his discussion of the dangers posed by calculating the time of redemption, Maimonides used examples from the book of Daniel to support his claim that any information about the precise time messianic redemption would begin had been and would continue to be sealed and hidden for eternity. In contrast, Nahmanides claimed that information concerning the time of redemption had been hidden from previous generations of authorities, but had been made available to his own age.

8. In a paper entitled "Some Thoughts on *Sefer Hasidim*" presented at the December 2000 meeting of the Association of Jewish Studies in Boston, Hayim Soloveichik suggested that the *Hasidei Ashkenaz* were not inclined to indulge in the active hope for messianic redemption for all of *Am Yisra'el*. Instead, they concerned themselves with the salvation of individuals or small groups.

9. Reuven Margoliot, ed., *Sefer Hasidim* (Jerusalem: Mosad ha-Rav Kook, 1957), 195, #206.

10. "Nahmanides, one of the most famous Jewish thinkers in the Middle Ages, composed an eschatological book named *Sefer ha-Ge'ulah*. In it he calculated the precise time of the arrival of the Messiah in 1358, thereby subscribing to a linear type of time. At the same time, he exposed a theory of cyclical macrochronos, known in Kabbalah as cosmic *shemittah* and *yovelim*, regarding them as

pulses of the divine organism, similar to the rhythm of inspiration and expiration. Moreover, he supported the microchronic cycle related to ritual. All these coexisted without creating tensions within his system" (Idel, "Some Concepts of Time," 160).

11. Robert Chazan, "The Messianic Calculations of Nahmanides," in *Rashi 1040–1990, Hommage á Ephraïm E. Urbach*, ed. Gabrielle Sed-Rajna (Paris: Les Éditions du Cerf, 1993), 631–637; Robert Chazan, "In the Wake of the Barcelona Disputation," *Hebrew Union College Annual* 61 (1990): 185–201; Robert Chazan, *Barcelona and Beyond: The Disputation of 1263 and Its Aftermath* (Berkeley and Los Angeles: University of California Press, 1992), 130–135 and 176–179.

12. Haim Dov Chavel, *Perush ha-Ramban al ha-Torah*, 2 vols. (Jerusalem: Mosad Ha-Rav Kook, 1959), 1:1–39. See my analysis of Nahmanides' biblical commentary in chapter two.

13. Haviva Pedaya, *Ha-Ramban: Hitalut—Zeman Mahzori ve-Tekst Kadosh* (Tel Aviv: Am Oved, 2003), 213–273.

14. Haim Dov Chavel, *Kitvei Rabbenu Moshe ben Nahman*, 2 vols. (Jerusalem: Mosad Ha-Rav Kook, 1964), 1:312. It is interesting that the Latin account of the debate touches on the interpretation of this verse with only a fleeting reference. This could be, as Chazan has suggested, because Nahmanides expanded and dramatized this discussion specifically for the purpose of his representation of the disputation to the Jewish communities. See Chazan, *Barcelona and Beyond*, 134–137.

15. Joseph Dan, *Ha-sipur ha-ivri bi-yeme ha-benayim: iyunim ba-taldotav* (Jerusalem: Keter, 1974), 122–132.

16. Nahmanides developed this discussion at length in his *Sefer ha-Geulah*. See Chavel, *Kitvei Rabbenu Moshe ben Nahman*, 1:291–297.

17. In particular, see the introduction to his biblical exegesis: Chavel, *Perush Ha-Ramban*, 1:1–8.

18. For a discussion of Nahmanides' engagement with exegetical tradition, see Bernard Septimus, "'Open Rebuke and Concealed Love': Nahmanides and the Andalusian Tradition," in *Rabbi Moses Nahmanides (Ramban): Explorations in His Religious and Literary Virtuosity*, ed. Isadore Twersky (Cambridge, MA: Harvard University Press, 1983), 11–34.

19. Chavel, *Kitvei Rabbenu Moshe ben Nahman*, 1:313.

20. Chazan develops a similar argument in a close reading of medieval Jewish approaches to this source. Focusing on Saadya Gaon and Nahmanides, he argues that Jewish exegesis of Daniel 9:24–27 was influenced by and directly responded to the use of this text by Christian exegetes as a prophetic and historical demonstration that Jesus was the promised messiah. However, Chazan is primarily interested in how Saadya and Nahmanides developed interpretations of Daniel 9:24–27 that were at once satisfactory Jewish commentaries and refutations of the Christian reading. See Robert Chazan, "Daniel 9:24–27: Exegesis and Polemics," in *Con-

tra Iudaeos: Ancient and Medieval Polemics between Christians and Jews, ed. Ora Limor and Guy G. Stroumsa (Tübingen: J. C. B. Mohr, 1996), 143–159.

21. In addition to *Sefer Toldot Yeshu*, he used *Seder Olam Zuta* to inform his historical chronology. This work chronicles the period from the time of creation until the destruction of the Second Temple. See Moshe Weinstock, ed., *Seder Olam Zuta Ha-Shalem* (Jerusalem: Batei ve-Rosheh Goldrey, 1957).

22. See chapter two above.

23. "And I say, before our lord the king, and all of the peoples, that there is no mention of the time of the coming of the messiah in this verse (Daniel 9:24–27), or in all of the words of Daniel except at the end of the book. For it is explained in the Scriptures in regard to what was told to him in that chapter and in other chapters, that he was always praying to know the time of the end, and in the end they told him the time of the end in the verse that said: *and from the time that the regular offering is abolished, and an appalling abomination is set up, it will be one thousand two hundred and ninety days* (Daniel 12:11). And now I will explain before the people the meaning of this verse, although it may be difficult for the Jews who are here. He says that from the time that the regular offering ceases until the 'appalling abomination' that removed it—that is the people of Rome, who destroyed the Temple—it will be one thousand, two hundred and ninety years, since the 'days' (*yamim*) referred to here are 'years,' as in 'the redemption period will be a year' (Leviticus 25:29). . . . And afterwards, Daniel said 'happy is he who waits and arrives at one thousand, three hundred and thirty-five days' (Dan. 12:12). He added forty-five years. And the meaning is that in the first [period of] time, the messiah will come, and he will eliminate the appalling abomination that worships that which is not God and obliterate it from the world. And afterwards, he will gather the banished [people] of Israel into the *wilderness of the peoples* (Ezekiel 30:35), as it is said, *and I will bring her into the wilderness, and speak tenderly to her* (Hosea 2:16), and Israel will come into her land. [This will be like what] Moshe Rabbenu (on him may there be peace) accomplished during the first redemption, and it will be forty-five years. And after that, Israel will settle on the land and *will rejoice with the Lord, their God and with David, their king* (Jeremiah 30:9). Happy is he who waits and reaches these happy days. Right now, there are one thousand, one hundred and ninety-five years since the time of the destruction. Thus, we are ninety-five years short of the number that Daniel gave. And we are hoping that the redeemer will come at that time, for this explanation is correct and fitting and it is reasonable to believe in it" (Chavel, *Kitvei Rabbenu Moshe ben Nahman*, 1:313–314).

24. Ibid., 1:314.

25. This portion of Nahmanides' disputation narrative takes a very interesting dramatic turn. To discredit Nahmanides' symbolic interpretation of *yom*, Friar Paul pulled a Jewish passerby off the street and asked him simply to translate the word *yom* into the vernacular. "He cried out to the king and they brought in the

first Jew they found, and asked him 'What does *yom* mean in your language?' He said, '*dia*'" (ibid.). See chapter five for a complete discussion of this passage and its role in Nahmanides' literary construction of the disputation.

26. Ibid., 1:251–285.

27. See, for example, ibid., 1:254.

28. He continued with a brief description of the distinction between Moses' brand of prophecy, which is mainly legal in tone, and the prophecy that provides instruction about the future: "For Moses our teacher (on him may there be peace) alone was the prophet of the Commandments; they came on account of him and were told to us. Since that time no prophet has been permitted to issue new laws. . . . Thus, most of his [Moses'] words do not enlighten us as to the future, they just tell of the future troubles to come by way of warning, and of good things and comforts by way of encouragement [depending on the degree to which we follow the commandments]. All this demonstrates the principle: life and good come with our devotion, death and evil accompany our treachery" (ibid., 1:261). Nahmanides refers here to Moses' effort to explain to the people of Israel the benefits of keeping the covenant: "See, I have set before you this day life and good and death and evil; in that I command you this day to love the Lord your God, to walk in his ways, and to keep his commandments and his statutes and his judgments" (Deut. 30:15–17).

29. See his discussion of the settlement of Judah and Benjamin in Israel at the time of Ezra in ibid., 1:271–272.

30. Ibid., 1:267.

31. Nahmanides was certainly not the first to comment on the connection between Ezra, Nehemiah, and I Chronicles. The rabbis of the Talmud also took note of the substantive, stylistic, and thematic similarities between these three books. See Babylonian Talmud *Babba Batra* 15a.

32. Chavel, *Kitvei Rabbenu Moshe ben Nahman*, 1:312–314.

33. According to the canonical Bible used today, this verse reads "they are written in the book of the Kings of Israel and Judah (*ketuvim al sefer malkhai Yisra'el ve-Yehudah*)."

34. Chavel, *Kitvei Rabbenu Moshe ben Nahman*, 1:272.

35. This is a reference to *Seder Olam Rabbah*, which states that the refugees "rose as one man" to return to Jerusalem. See Weinstock, ed., *Seder Olam Zuta Ha-Shalem*, 3:445.

36. Chavel, *Kitvei Rabbenu Moshe ben Nahman*, 1:273.

37. See Chavel, *Perush ha-Ramban*, 1:31; Jacob Newman, *The Commentary of Nahmanides on Genesis* (Leiden: E. J. Brill, 1960), 62. Also see chapter two of the present work.

38. Chavel, *Kitvei Rabbenu Moshe ben Nahman*, 1:273–274. *Seder 'Olam* also calls attention to the demography of the first return. However, it makes no attempt

to read this return as the promised redemption; by the same token, neither does it have any need to defend the primacy of Judaism as *Verus Israel*. See Weinstock, ed., *Seder Olam Zuta Ha-Shalem*, 3:444–445.

39. This interpretation fits neatly with Nahmanides' understanding of legal interpretation and tradition as a progressive process which improved and became increasingly sophisticated over time. See Moshe Halbertal, "The *Minhag* and the History of Halakhah in the Teaching of Nahmanides" (Hebrew), *Tziyon* 67, no. 1 (2002): 25–56; Moshe Halbertal, "The History of Halakhah, Views from Within: Three Medieval Approaches to Tradition and Controversy" (paper presented at the Harvard Law School Gruss Lectures, Harvard University Law School, Cambridge, MA, 1994, http://www.law.harvard.edu/programs/Gruss/halbert.html).

40. Nahmanides slightly altered the language of the text, replacing the word *etzman*, or "their bones," with *ruhan*, "their spirit." Nahmanides most likely knew this text in the same version available to us today because he cites it in that version elsewhere. It is possible that he did not have the source at hand as he composed this portion of his text, and thus cited the passage from memory. Alternatively, it is possible that Nahmanides intentionally shifted the meaning to stress a more spiritual interpretation of the world to come (*olam ha-ba*). On Nahmanides' redemption in spiritual terms, rather than political and national, see Moshe Halbertal, "Nahmanides' Conception of Death, Sin, and Redemption" (Hebrew), *Tarbitz* 71, no. 1–2 (2001–2002): 133–162.

41. Chavel, *Kitvei Rabbenu Moshe ben Nahman*, 1:290.

42. Ibid.

43. Indeed, in the same paragraph, Nahmanides brings a source from the Talmud (*Sanhedrin* 97b) which voices this problem directly. The rabbis were concerned that a false prediction would irreparably damage the community's faith that the promise of redemption would be fulfilled: "In the words of the sages the logic of their utterances swelled the power of those who ruminate about the end—they said: 'since the end approached and didn't come, don't say again that it didn't come, rather wait for it, as it says, "if it tarries, hope for it, for what is expected will come" (Sanhedrin 97).' The intention in this is that because they know from people of their generation who would divide the endtime in close proximity to that time, and would [thus] multiply in it the obstacles between that which is close and that which is far, it will be misleading for those without learning (*amei ha-aretz*), thus it is necessary to conceal it from the eye of man, and to be expectant of this matter. But now we speak and we do no harm . . ." (ibid.).

44. Ibid., 1:289–291.

45. Even if Nahmanides was severely limited in what he was able to say during the disputation itself, as much of the scholarship suggests, these issues were addressed directly at the textual level in the controversy that arose over Nahmanides' disputation account. See Chazan, *Barcelona and Beyond*, 42–77.

46. Idel, *Messianic Mystics*, 58–100.

47. E. Randolph Daniel, "A Re-Examination of the Origins of Franciscan Joachitism," *Speculum* 43, no. 4 (1968): 671–676; E. Randolph Daniel, "The Double Procession of the Holy Spirit in Joachim of Fiore's Understanding of History," *Speculum* 55, no. 3 (1980): 469–483; E. Randolph Daniel, "Joachim of Fiore: Patterns of History in the Apocalypse," in *The Apocalypse in the Middle Ages*, ed. Richard K. Emmerson and Bernard McGinn (Ithaca, NY: Cornell University Press, 1992), 72–88; E. Randolph Daniel, "Abbot Joachim of Fiore and the Conversion of the Jews," in *Friars and Jews in the Middle Ages and Renaissance*, ed. Steven J. McMichael and Susan E. Myers (Leiden: Brill, 2004), 1–21; Harold Lee, "*Scrutamini Scripturas*: Joachimist Themes and *Figurae* in the Early Religious Writing of Arnold of Vilanova," *Journal of the Warburg and Courtauld Institutes* 37 (1974): 33–56; Harold Lee, Marjorie Reeves, and Giulio Silano, eds., *Western Mediterranean Prophecy: The School of Joachim of Fiore and the Fourteenth-Century Breviloquium* (Toronto: Pontifical Institute of Mediaeval Studies, 1989); Lerner, "Ecstatic Dissent," 33–57; Robert E. Lerner, *The Feast of Saint Abraham: Medieval Millenarians and the Jews* (Philadelphia: University of Pennsylvania Press, 2001); Elías Olmos, "Inventario de los documentos escritos en pergamino del Archivo de la Catedral de Valencia," *Boletin de la Academia de la Historia* 103 (1933): 141–293 and 543–616; Marjorie Reeves, "Pattern and Purpose in History in the Later Medieval and Renaissance Periods," in *Apocalypse Theory and the Ends of the World*, ed. Malcolm Bull (Oxford: Blackwell, 1995): 90–111; Marjorie Reeves, *The Influence of Prophecy in the Later Middle Ages: A Study in Joachimism* (Oxford: Clarendon Press, 1969); Marjorie Reeves, "The Abbot Joachim's Disciples and the Cistercian Order," *Sophia* 19 (1951): 355–371; Marjorie Reeves and Morton W. Bloomfield, "The Penetration of Joachism into Northern Europe," *Speculum* 29, no. 4 (1954): 772–793; Marjorie Reeves and B. Hirsch-Reich, "The *Figurae of Joachim of Fiore*: Genuine and Spurious Collections," *Mediaeval and Renaissance Studies* 3 (1954): 170–199; Marjorie Reeves and B. Hirsch-Reich, "The Seven Seals in the Writings of Joachim of Fiore," *Recherches de Théologie Ancienne et Médiévale* 21 (1954): 211–247; Hames, "From Calabria Cometh the Law," 187–199.

48. Daniel, "Joachim of Fiore: Patterns of History in the Apocalypse," 72–88.

49. Joachim made this point most strongly in his *Concordia veteris ac novi testamenti*, in which he utilized a method of drawing concordance or continuity between the Old and New Testaments. This approach established a unity of purpose and meaning between the two canonical works whereby one book of scripture informed and elucidated the other. See Daniel, "The Double Procession of the Holy Spirit," especially 175–199.

50. Joaquín Carreras y Artau, "Arnau de Vilanova y las culturas orientales," in *Homenaje a Millàs Vallicrosa* (Barcelona: Consejo Superior de Investigaciones Científicas, 1954), 309–321; Joaquín Carreras y Artau, "La 'Allocutio super Tetragrammatron' de Arnaldo de Vilanova," *Sefarad* 9 (1949): 75–105; Clifford R. Backman, "The Reception of Arnau of Vilanova's Religious Ideas," in *Christendom and*

Its Discontents: Exclusion, Persecution, and Rebellion, ed. Scott L Waugh and Peter D. Diehl (Cambridge: Cambridge University Press, 1996), 112–131; Miguel Batllori, "Les versions italianes medievales d'obres religiouses de mestre Arnau de Vilanova," *Archivio italiano per la storia della pietà* 1 (1951): 397–462; Miguel Batllori, "Orientaciones bibliográficas para el estudio de Arnau de Villanova," *Pensamiento* 10 (1954): 311–324; John August Bollweg, "Sense of a Mission: Arnau of Vilanova on the Conversion of Muslims and Jews," in *Iberia and the Mediterranean World of the Middle Ages: Studies in Honor of Robert I. Burns*, ed. Larry J. Simon (Leiden: E. J. Brill, 1995), 50–74; E. Randolph Daniel, *The Franciscan Concept of Mission in the Middle Ages* (Lexington: University of Kentucky Press, 1975); Lee, "*Scrutamini Scripturas*," 33–56; Robert E. Lerner, "The Pope and the Doctor," *Yale Review* 78 (1988–89): 33–57; Josep Perarnau i Espelt, "El text primitiu del *De mysterio cymbalorum ecclesiae* d'Arnau de Vilanova," *Arxiu de textos catalans antics* 7–8 (1988–89): especially 1–52.

51. This rhetorical imbalance is clearly the product of a parallel power imbalance between Christian polemicists and their Jewish audience: Jews had little recourse when compelled by Christian authorities, whether clerical or secular, to submit to forced sermons or debates. Nevertheless, the difficulty of fashioning a scholarly approach that captures the vulnerability of the minority community as well as self-determined actions, beliefs, or practices on the part of its members is apparent even in the revisionist scholarship. Robert Lerner's recent study of Christian apocalyptic thinkers and their understanding of the role played by Jews and Judaism in the redemptive process, for example, seems to fashion the Jewish contribution to this discourse as passive and unwitting. Jeremy Cohen's important and innovative study of the rhetorical construction of Jews and Judaism in Christian theology similarly positions Jews only on the margin of this rhetoric. The same argument could be advanced concerning the Christian view of and approach to Islam. John Tolan's *Saracens*, which presents an original reading of the Christian imagination of Islam, casts Christian missionaries and theologians as actively engaged and the Muslims are rendered as disengaged, at times even disinterested observers, even while he shows that the Christian encounter with Islam necessarily transformed deeply held assumptions. Although none of these works sets out to reformulate the typical strategies employed to examine interfaith relations and conversations, it is significant that they accept the Christian predominance in these exchanges without question. See Daniel, *The Franciscan Concept*; Lerner, *The Feast of Saint Abraham*; Cohen, *Living Letters of the Law*, 313–363; John V. Tolan, *Saracens: Islam in the Medieval European Imagination* (New York: Columbia University Press, 2002), 214–274.

52. Nahmanides wrote and distributed his first person account of the Barcelona disputation two years following the event. This text was written first as a present for the bishop of Girona, presumably in the Catalan vernacular. Nahmanides came under attack after the document fell into the hands of the friars. He was

censured by the pope, and later expelled from the Crown of Aragon by the king. A summary of the complaint against Nahmanides can be found in a document from the royal archive dated 12 April, 1265, which is reproduced in Don Pére Heinrich Denifle, "Quellen zur Disputation Pablos Christiani mit Mose Nachmani su Barcelona 1263," *Historisches Jahrbuch* 8 (1887): 239–240. The document refers to him as Bonstrugo de Porta—for a demonstration that Bonastrugo was, in fact, identical to Nahmanides, see Chazan, *Barcelona and Beyond,* 199–203. Also see J. Cohen, *The Friars and the Jews,* 17–38; Martin A. Cohen, "Reflections on the Text and Context of the Disputation of Barcelona," *Hebrew Union College Annual* 35 (1964): 182–188; Cecil Roth, "The Disputation at Barcelona (1263)," *Harvard Theological Review* 43, no. 2 (1950): 122–128.

53. A thorough survey along these lines is beyond the scope of the present study, however this is a theme I hope to pursue in future research.

54. For a sketch of Arnau's life, see Lerner, "The Pope and the Doctor."

55. Perarnau í Espelt, "El text primitiu," 134–69. There is some disagreement among scholars about when this text was completed. Harold Lee has argued that it was composed in 1288–89, whereas Perarnau í Espelt suggests a composition date of 1297. Lee's argument is compelling because it accounts for Arnau's intellectual and spiritual development. See Lee, "*Scrutamini Scripturas,*" 33; Backman, "The Reception," 115–116; Bollweg, "Sense of a Mission," 53.

56. Carreras y Artau, "La 'Allocutio super Tetragrammatron,'" 80; Joaquín Carreras y Artau, "Arnaldo de Vilanova, apologista antijudaico," *Sefarad* 7, no. 1 (1947): 50–51. On the other hand, Clifford Backman has argued that Arnau knew only "a smattering of Hebrew." See Clifford Backman, "Arnau de Vilanova and the Body at the End of the World," in *Last Things: Death and the Apocalypse in the Middle Ages,* ed. Carolyn Walker Bynum and Paul Freedman (Philadelphia: University of Pennsylvania Press, 2000), 143. In either case, it is clear that Arnau was exposed to a wide variety of works by Jewish authors on medicine as well as biblical interpretation.

57. Ramón Martí used his gift for languages to study and refute Jewish and Muslim theology on their own terms. *Pugio fidei adversus Mauros et Iudaeous* is a massive and exhaustive compendium of Hebrew sources and arguments on the central points of Christian faith, including the time of the messianic age, the character of the messiah, and the trinity. Rabbinic sources are quoted first in Hebrew, followed by a Latin translation. Martí demonstrated his knowledge of medieval Judaism by citing medieval exegetical and halakhic authorities throughout. This text is remarkable for its scope as well as for the prooftexts Martí's team was able to assemble. Part two of this extensive work is committed to demonstrating that the Jewish messiah had arrived already in the form of Jesus. See Raymundi Martini, *Pugio Fidei adversus Mauros et Judaeous* (Leipzig: Bibliothecae Paulinae Academiae Lipsiensis, 1687); Robert Chazan, *Daggers of Faith: Thirteenth-Century Christian Missionizing and Jewish Response* (Berkeley: University of California

Press, 1989), 115–136; J. Cohen, *The Friars and the Jews,* 126–156. On the view of Judaism represented in *Pugio Fidei,* see Reuven Bonfil, "The Nature of Judaism in Raymundus Martini's *Pugio Fidei*" (Hebrew), *Tarbitz* 40 (1971): 360–375.

58. On the conflict between the Dominicans and Arnau, see Joaquín Carreras y Artau, "La polémica gerundense sobre el Anticristo entre Arnau de Vilanova y los dominicos," *Anales del Instituto de Estudios Gerundenses* 5 (1950): 1–58.

59. Although it is impossible to determine the degree to which he understood Hebrew, his library contained a handful of Hebrew books. More significant for this discussion, he referred to and apparently owned portions of Ramón Martí's *Pugio Fidei.* See Joaquín Carreras y Artau, "La llibreria d'Arnau de Vilanova," *Analecta sacra Tarraconensia* 11 (1935): 63–86.

60. Lee, Reeves, and Silano, eds., *Western Mediterranean Prophecy*; Reeves and Bloomfield, "The Penetration of Joachism, 772–793"; Reeves and Hirsch-Reich, "The *Figurae of Joachim of Fiore*," 170–199; Reeves and Hirsch-Reich, "The Seven Seals," 211–224.

61. Perarnau i Espelt, "El text primitiu," 89.

62. "[S]ince sacred words pronouncing all of these events have been provided by God to the church for their direction, it is credible that an understanding of these words would be released to them before they [the events] would approach" (ibid., 96). See Bollweg, "Sense of a Mission," 50–74; Lee, "*Scrutamini Scripturas,*" 33–56; Lerner, "Ecstatic Dissent"; Lerner, "The Pope and the Doctor," 62–79.

63. For example, Daniel 9 refers to the "seventy weeks" of desolation which will be replaced with a period of redemption.

64. "These verses clearly lead us towards Daniel and two things concerning these verses beg to be noted: the first is that faith is holding that very word at a distance. The second is that Daniel, with the word *abmoniationis,* is speaking about that maker of great tribulations, whom God described, namely the Antichrist" (Perarnau i Espelt, "El text primitiu," 147).

65. Arnau was accused of judaizing by Henry of Harclay for this very interpretation. For discussion of this controversy, see Bollweg, "Sense of a Mission," 64–66; Perarnau i Espelt, "El text primitiu," 37–38.

66. Perarnau i Espelt, "El text primitiu," 147. Arnau explored the same question in *Tractatus de mysterio cymbalorum ecclesiae,* see Perarnau i Espelt, "El text primitiu," 91–92.

67. Arnau also weighed the validity of the solar versus the lunar calendrical system when counting pre-Christian history. See Perarnau i Espelt, "El text primitiu," 150–152.

68. Chavel, *Kitvei Rabbenu Moshe ben Nahman,* 313–314.

69. Arnau's interpretation of Augustine's admonition appears in Perarnau i Espelt, "El text primitiu," 157–159.

70. Robert Chazan has noted that this text is especially susceptible to such interpretations. See Chazan, "Daniel 9:24–27," 141–159; Chazan, "Rashi's Commentary on the Book of *Daniel*," 111–121.

71. There is evidence that Arnau had some familiarity with Jewish medical writings. See Lola Ferre, "Los regímenes de salud de Maimónides y Arnau de Vilanova en sus versiones Hebreas," in *La ciencia en la España medieval: musulmanes, judíos y cristianos*, ed. Lola Ferre, José Ramon Ayaso, and Maria José Cano (Granada: Universidad de Granada, Instituto de Ciencias de la España, 1992), 117–126.

72. Larry Simon makes a similar argument in a recent article on Jewish-Christian relations in Catalan through a focus on public disputes and legal struggles which involved Catalonian Jews and mendicants. See Larry J. Simon, "Intimate Enemies: Mendicant-Jewish Interaction in Thirteenth-Century Mediterranean Spain," in *Friars and Jews in the Middle Ages and Renaissance*, ed. Steven J. McMichael and Susan E. Myers (Leiden: Brill, 2004), 53–80, especially 61–74. Also see Harvey J. Hames' masterful and complex study of interchange between kabbalists in late thirteenth- and early fourteenth-century Catalonia, *The Art of Conversion: Christianity and Kabbalah in the Thirteenth Century* (Leiden: Brill, 2000), especially 190–283.

73. Lerner, *The Feast of Saint Abraham*; Bollweg, "Sense of a Mission," 54–55; Daniel, "Abbot Joachim," 1–22.

74. This effort to regulate the terms of contact between Christians and religious outsiders was not limited to Jews. Similar though more explicitly coercive measures were extended to Muslims and Christian heretics during the same period. See R. I. Moore, *The Formation of a Persecuting Society: Power and Deviance in Western Europe, 950–1250* (Oxford: Blackwell, 1987).

Chapter 5   Language and Literature

1. Haim Dov Chavel, *Kitvei Rabbenu Moshe ben Nahman*, 2 vols. (Jerusalem: Mosad Ha-Rav Kook, 1964), 1:314.

2. Jacques Derrida, *Monolingualism of the Other; or, The Prosthesis of Origin*, trans. Patrick Mensah (Stanford, CA: Stanford University Press, 1998), 25.

3. Anne Norton, *95 Theses on Politics, Culture, and Method* (New Haven, CT: Yale University Press, 2004), 16.

4. Catalan was the standard language of exchange in the court of Aragon and was actively imposed upon recently conquered territories during the thirteenth century. By the beginning of the fourteenth century, Catalan was a lingua franca of international business and diplomacy. See Anthony Bonner, ed., *Selected Works of Ramón Llull (1232–1316)*, 2 vols. (Princeton, NJ: Princeton University Press, 1985), 1:8–9. Also J. N. Hillgarth, *The Spanish Kingdoms, 1250–1516*, 2 vols. (Oxford: Clarendon Press, 1976), 1:146–147.

5. Nahmanides also used Catalan words in his explanation of the different genres contained in the Jewish canon, however in this case, the Catalan words are imbedded in an extended speech rendered in Hebrew. Again, the vernacular serves to clarify his point. See Chavel, *Kitvei Rabbenu Moshe ben Nahman*, 1:308.

6. "In the same way as there is a holy land (theirs but not appropriable, only allotted, lent by God, the only legitimate proprietor of the land), the holy language, similarly, is theirs only to the extent that they do not 'speak' it, and to the extent that it is employed in prayer (for 'they only can pray' in it) only for testifying: 'attestation' (Zeugnis) that 'their linguistic life always feels (dis)located in an alien land, and that their personal linguistic fatherland [seine eigentliche Sprachheimat] is known to be elsewhere, in the sphere of the holy language, inaccessible to everyday speech.'" This quotation is excerpted from Derrida's meditation on Franz Rosenzweig's understanding of the nature of Jewish ethnic, national, cultural, and linguistic identity. See Derrida, *Monolingualism of the Other; or, The Prosthesis of Origin*, 80.

7. Medieval Jewish biblical commentary (including Nahmanides' commentary) is not strictly monovocal, since commentators frequently frame their interpretations as discussions with or counterpoints to other authoritative commentaries. Unlike the disputation account, however, which professes to replicate opposing views, the contrary voice in the commentary is the product of the author's distillation of entire works for the purpose of rhetorically bolstering arguments.

8. Throughout this book, I have presumed a sharp distinction between the textual evidence of the disputation that survives and the event itself. Such a distinction is all the more important in this chapter as I intend to approach Nahmanides' account as a work of literature that was intended to be read as such, rather than a chronicle intended merely to inform the reader about what happened and when.

9. Gil Anidjar has thematized the issue of language and place in his study of Maimonides. Anidjar has shown that Maimonides' language is dislocated, simultaneously rooted in a lost and mourned location and culture, and disembodied. See Gil Anidjar, *"Our Place in al-Andalus": Kabbalah, Philosophy, Literature in Arab Jewish Letters* (Stanford, CA: Stanford University Press, 2002), 10–57.

10. Gilles Deleuze and Félix Guattari, *Kafka: Toward a Minor Literature*, trans. Dana Polan (Minneapolis: University of Minnesota Press, 1986), 16–27.

11. Ibid., 18. Rene Potok has applied these criteria in her analysis of Anton Shamas. See Rene N. Potok, "Borders, Exiles, Minor Literatures: The Case of Palestinian-Israeli Writing," in *Borders, Exiles, Diasporas*, ed. Elazar Barkan and Marie-Denise Shelton (Stanford, CA: Stanford University Press, 1998), 291–310.

12. As has been noted, neither account is very generous about crediting the opposing side with intelligence or rhetorical acuity. If we assume that the disputants' interpretive and verbal ability lay somewhere between the complete Christian failure described in the Hebrew account and the miserable humiliation of

the rabbi described in the Latin account, it is reasonable to expect that both men succeeded in making their arguments in clear and precise terms.

13. There are a handful of models for this form in the Jewish canon. Yehudah ha-Levi's *Ha-Kuzari* is the most polished and stylized, a fictional discussion between the king of the Khazars and representatives of the central worldviews: philosophy, Christianity, Islam, and Judaism. The account of the Paris disputation also takes the form of a dialogue, but it is more a raw reaction to the humiliating event of 1240 and the subsequent destruction of hundreds of volumes of Talmud than a stylized work of literature. It is highly likely that Nahmanides knew both works, though.

14. It is thus not surprising that this text remained popular and controversial beginning in the later medieval and early modern periods. The popularity of this text and interest in the event have remained strong in the modern period as well. The BBC produced and aired a dramatization of the disputation based on Nahmanides' account which is available in many university libraries. See Hyam Maccoby and Geoffrey Sax, director, *The Disputation: A Theological Debate between Christians and Jews* (London: BBC, 1986). Even more surprisingly, live productions played to sold-out audiences in London, New York, Los Angeles, and Miami in the spring of 1999.

15. Robert Chazan's analysis of the literary qualities of this document shows that the dynamic dramatic setting of a disputation was an expertly employed literary device in Nahmanides' representation of the disputation. Chazan suggests that the drama drives the force of Nahmanides' polemical and edifying message. This characterization of Nahmanides' account as a work which consciously utilizes the genre or narrative style of realistic fiction to communicate a single, honed message represents an important contribution to the disputation scholarship. See Robert Chazan, *Barcelona and Beyond: The Disputation of 1263 and Its Aftermath* (Berkeley and Los Angeles: University of California Press, 1992), 100–112.

16. James Clifford, "Diasporas," *Cultural Anthropology* 9, no. 3 (1994): 307.

17. On the development of Jewish dialects, such as Judeo-Catalan, Judeo-Latin, and Judeo-Castilian and the relationship between speech and texts, see Paul Wexler, *Three Heirs to a Judeo-Latin Legacy: Judeo-Ibero Romance, Yiddish and Rotwelsch* (Wiesbaden: Otto Harrassowitz, 1988), 1–79. Also see Elaine R. Miller, "Linguistic Identity in the Middle Ages: The Case of the Spanish Jews," in *Crossing Boundaries: Issues of Cultural and Individual Identity in the Middle Ages and the Renaissance*, ed. Sally McKee (Turnhout: Brepols, 1999), 57–77.

18. See, for example, Marcus Salzman, *The Chronicle of Ahimaaz* (New York: Columbia University Press, 1924). Also Gerson Cohen, *A Critical Edition with a Translation and Notes of the Book of Tradition (Sefer ha-Qabbalah) by Abraham Ibn Daud* (Philadelphia: Jewish Publication Society of America, 1967). And Yosef Hayim Yerushalmi, *Zakhor: Jewish History and Jewish Memory* (New York: Schocken Books, 1989), 37–38. For the narratives of the Crusades, see A. M.

Habermann, *Sefer Gezerot Ashkenaz ve-Tzarefat: Divrei zikhronot me-benei ha-dorot she-bi-tekufot mase ha-tzalav ve-mivhar piyuteyhem* (Jerusalem: Totzaat sifrei tarshish, 1945), especially 24–50, the account of R. Solomon ben Simon.

19. Yerushalmi, *Zakhor*, 34–38.

20. Many such letters were preserved in the Cairo Geniza. A large selection have been published in Solomon D. Goitein, *A Mediterranean Society: The Jewish Communities of the Arab World as Portrayed in the Documents of the Cairo Geniza*, 6 vols. (Berkeley: University of California Press, 1967–1988). Also see Adolf Neubauer, *Mediaeval Jewish Chronicles and Chronological Notes, Edited from Printed Books and Manuscripts [Seder ha-hakhamim ve-korot ha-yamim]* (Oxford: Clarendon Press, 1895). For discussions of various aspects of the theme of inter-community communication, see Aryeh Graboïs, "The Use of Letters as a Communication Medium among Medieval European Jewish Communities," in *Communication in the Jewish Diaspora: The Pre-Modern World*, ed. Sophia Menache (Leiden: E. J. Brill, 1996), 93–105; Avraham Grossman, "Communication among Jewish Centers during the Tenth to the Twelfth Centuries," in *Communication in the Jewish Diaspora: The Pre-Modern World*, ed. Sophia Menache (Leiden: E. J. Brill, 1996), 107–125.

21. The account was written by Joseph ben Natan Official, a student of Rabbi Yehiel. The Latin and Hebrew records of this encounter indicate that Rabbi Yehiel was the only one of the four who actually testified. See Reuven Margoliot, *Vikuah rabenu Yehiel me-Paris mebaale ha-tosefot* (Lwów: R. Margulies, 1928).

22. Martin Cohen, for example, laments that "despite Nahmanides' insistence of having written an account of all the discussions, . . . his text gainsays such completeness. It is too brief to be a full record of four days' proceedings, too detailed at times to be a summary, too desultory to reflect a sense of continuity, too discursive to reveal a logical sequence, too partisan to be accepted uncritically" (Martin A. Cohen, "Reflections on the Text and Context of the Disputation of Barcelona," *Hebrew Union College Annual* 35 [1964]: 159).

23. In particular, see ibid., 157–192.

24. For a discussion of the friars' accusation that Nahmanides wrote a blasphemous account for the bishop of Giron, see chapter four. The documents pertaining to this conflict, produced in the royal court, have been published in Don Pére Heinrich Denifle, "Quellen zur Disputation Pablos Christiani mit Mose Nachmani su Barcelona 1263," *Historisches Jahrbuch* 8 (1887): 238–244.

25. Chazan, *Barcelona and Beyond*, 97–98 (the emphasis is mine). Yom Tov Assis also accepts the report that Nahmanides undertook to record his arguments in the disputation only after the bishop requested he provide an account, but he does not pursue the question of how the bishop's patronage may have contributed to or influenced Nahmanides' representation of the events. See Yom Tov Assis, *The Golden Age of Aragonese Jewry: Community and Society in the Crown of Aragon, 1213–1327* (London: Littman Library of Jewish Civilization, 1997), 50.

26. Chavel, *Kitvei Rabbenu Moshe ben Nahman*, 1:302–303.

27. Robert I. Burns, *Muslims, Christians, and Jews in the Crusader Kingdom of Valencia: Societies in Symbiosis* (Cambridge: Cambridge University Press, 1984), 161–171; Jonathan Ray, *The Sephardic Frontier: The Reconquista and the Jewish Community of Medieval Iberia* (Ithaca, NY: Cornell University Press, 2006), 75–79 and 113–119. James I used a similar strategy in organizing the local nobility, as well, see Perez-Bustamante, "El Gobierno y la Adminstracion de los territorios de la Corona de Aragon bajo Jaime I el Conquistador y su comparacion con el regimen de Castilla y Navarra," *1 y 2 Congreso de Historia de la Corona d'Aragon* X (1979): 515–536; Donald J. Kagay, "Structures of Baronial Dissent and Revolt under Jaime I of Aragon-Catalonia (1213–1276)," *Mediaevistik* 1 (1988): 61–85; Donald J. Kagay, "Royal Power in an Urban Setting: James I and the Towns of Aragon," *Mediaevistik* 8 (1995): 161–170.

28. Assis, *The Golden Age*, 19–34; Yom Tov Assis, *Jewish Economy in the Medieval Crown of Aragon, 1213–1327: Money and Power* (Leiden: E. J. Brill, 1997); J. Lee Shneidman, "Protection of Aragon Jewry in the Thirteenth Century," *Revue des Études juives* 121 (1962): 48–59; Thomas N. Bisson, *The Medieval Crown of Aragon, A Short History* (Oxford: Clarendon Press, 1986), 74–75; Elka Klein, *Jews, Christian Society, and Royal Power in Medieval Barcelona* (Ann Arbor: University of Michigan Press, 2006); Jean Régné, *History of the Jews in Aragon: Regesta and Documents, 1213–1327*, ed. Yom Tov Assis and Adam Gruzman (Jerusalem: Magnes Press, Hebrew University, 1978), 1–117.

29. Elka Klein, "Splitting Heirs: Patterns of Inheritance among Barcelona's Jews," *Jewish History* 16, no. 1 (2002): 49–71; Rebecca Winer, "Family, Community, and Motherhood: Caring for Fatherless Children in the Jewish Community of Thirteenth-Century Perpignan," *Jewish History* 16, no. 1 (2002): 15–48. Also see Yom Tov Assis, "Jews in Gentile Courts in the Thirteenth and Fourteenth Centuries" (Hebrew), in *Tarbut ve-Hevrah ba-Toldot Yisrael be-Yame ha-Benayim*, ed. Menahem Ben-Sasson et al. (Jerusalem: Merkaz Zalmon Shazar la-Toldot Yisrael, 1989), 399–430.

30. Assis, *The Golden Age*.

31. Ibid., 28; J. Lee Shneidman, *The Rise of the Aragonese-Catalan Empire, 1200–1350*, 2 vols. (New York: New York University Press, 1970), 2:422–428.

32. For literature on the application and consequences of the Fourth Lateran Council, see Jeremy Cohen, *The Friars and the Jews: The Evolution of Medieval Anti-Judaism* (Ithaca, NY: Cornell University Press, 1982), 249–264; R. I. Moore, *The Formation of a Persecuting Society: Power and Deviance in Western Europe, 950–1250* (Oxford: Blackwell, 1987).

33. Diverse works on a wide array of topics have influenced my thinking about the ritual and practice of power. On the promulgation and consciousness of power inequity within social groups, see Pierre Bourdieu, "Delegation and Political Fetishism," in *Language and Symbolic Power*, ed. John B. Thompson (Oxford: Polity Press, 1991), 203–219. Also, for a demonstration that marginalization

and even demonization had the unintended result of empowering communities bearing such unfortunate distinctions, see Carlo Ginzburg, *Ecstasies: Deciphering the Witches' Sabbath,* trans. Raymond Rosenthal (New York: Penguin, 1991); Geoffrey Koziol, *Begging Pardon and Favor: Ritual and Political Order in Early Medieval France* (Ithaca, NY: Cornell University Press, 1992); David Nirenberg, *Communities of Violence: Persecution of Minorities in the Middle Ages* (Princeton, NJ: Princeton University Press, 1996).

34. These conflicts and tensions have garnered significant attention in the scholarship on the Barcelona disputation. See M. A. Cohen, "Reflections," 180–182; J. Cohen, *The Friars and the Jews,* 17–38; Cecil Roth, "The Disputation at Barcelona (1263)," *Harvard Theological Review* 43, no. 2 (1950): 122–128.

35. Jill Webster has demonstrated that the struggle among the two mendicant orders and the lay clergy was a difficult and protracted one. "In a constant attempt to preserve their own rights and privileges and the extent of their influence the Franciscans demanded both privacy and publicity" (Jill R. Webster, "Unlocking Lost Archives: Medieval Catalan Franciscan Communities," *The Catholic Historical Review* 66, no. 4 [1980]: 538). Webster goes on to argue that the Franciscans feuded with local clergy and Dominicans for the support of the king. During much of King James I's reign, she argues, the Franciscans prevailed; however, she also shows that their victory was not so complete that they were able to withdraw from the struggle.

36. See Marcel Mauss, *The Gift: The Form and Reason for Exchange in Archaic Societies,* trans. W. D. Halls (New York: W. W. Norton, 1990). Alex Weingrod has argued that the study of patron-client relations should be attentive to the power roles of clients, patrons, allies, friends, brokers, etc., as well as the legal or political system within which they all work. Rules of conduct apply in the patron-client relationship only as long as the patron is willing to follow them and the clients gain from their definition. The benefit of calling attention to the vulnerability and possible instability of power relations, he argues, is that this focus highlights the ritual or ceremonial aspect of patronage negotiations. See Alex Weingrod, "Patronage and Power," in *Patrons and Clients in Mediterranean Society,* ed. Ernest Gellner (London: Gerald Duckworth, 1977), 41–51, especially 49–50. In his important work on the rise of court culture, Norbert Elias explains that "[c]ompetitive struggle for prestige and status can be observed in many social formations; it may be that they are to be found in all societies. What is observed in court society has in this sense a paradigmatic value. It points to a social figuration that draws the individuals forming it into an especially intense and specialized competition for the power associated with status and prestige" (Norbert Elias, *The Court Society,* trans. Edmund Jephcott [New York: Pantheon, 1983], 93). Also see Mario Biagioli, *Galileo Courtier: The Practice of Science in the Culture of Absolutism* (Chicago: University of Chicago Press, 1993). Biagioli traces Galileo's navigation and mastery of the rituals of court society, demonstrating that he publicized and legitimized his inventions and discoveries by transforming them into commodities with market

value in the court. In addition to his significant contribution to the specific field of Galileo studies, Biagioli has also demonstrated that the examination and explication of the relationship between literary, artistic, or scientific works and the power structure within which their authors struggle can provide a means for assessing how such works are produced and valued in any given social structure. Biagioli argues that obligations incurred by both parties in a patron-client relationship through such gift exchange could be used to maneuver and manipulate the rules of court for their own benefit, especially when the former exerts uncompromised power on the latter in every aspect of public life.

37. "And the King, our lord, stood, and descended from the platform and went to them. Later, I stood before our lord the king and he said to me: 'Return to your city and live in peace.' And he gave me 300 dinars" (Chavel, *Kitvei Rabbenu Moshe ben Nahman*, 1:320).

38. Much of the debate over the verisimilitude of this account revolves around the question of whether Nahmanides would have been permitted to articulate the inflammatory arguments drawn out in this text. Many of these scholars enter the discussion via a consideration of the degree of "truth" represented respectively in the Hebrew and Latin texts. Answers to this question largely fell along partisan lines: Christian scholars noting the accuracy of the description contained in the Latin version, and Jewish scholars doing the same in their reading of the Hebrew account. See the discussion in chapter three above for a detailed review of this literature.

39. On the Jews' obligations to the king of Aragon during the middle ages, see Assis, *The Golden Age*, 19–63; Burns, *Muslims, Christians, and Jews*, 126–141; Klein, *Jews, Christian Society, and Royal Power*, 142–161.

40. "The records show that payments of the king's debts from the *aljama's* taxes to his Jewish creditors, both men and women, were quite frequent, and the reasons for the debts, not always mentioned, were varied. In one of these records, for instance, Jaime I acknowledged a debt of 300 sb and a previous loan of 300 sb to Isaac, a Jew of Barcelona. Both sums were to be paid from the tax of the Jews of Barcelona. One of the loans was for a payment that was made on the king's behalf to Bonstruc de Porta, a rabbi from Gerona, who is identified by some scholars as R. Moses ben Nahman (Nahmanides)" (Assis, *Jewish Economy*, 158).

41. On the curriculum in medieval universities and cathedral schools, see Frederick Copleston, *A History of Philosophy*, 9 vols. (New York: Image Books, 1962), 2, part I, 240–245; George Makdisi, "The Scholastic Method in Medieval Education: An Inquiry into Its Origins in Law and Theology," *Speculum* 49, no. 4 (1974): 640–661; David L. Wagner, ed., *The Seven Liberal Arts in the Middle Ages* (Bloomington: Indiana University Press, 1986). On the early history of disputation in forming Christian doctrine, see Ignacio Angelilli, "The Techniques of Disputation in the History of Logic," *The Journal of Philosophy* 67, no. 20 (1970): 800–815; Richard Lim, *Public Disputation: Power and Social Order in Late Antiquity* (Berkeley: University of California, 1995). On the role of disputation and

dialectic in thirteenth-century Spanish education, see Thomas S. Hibbs, *Dialectic and Narrative in Aquinas: An Interpretation of the Summa Contra Gentiles* (Notre Dame, IN: University of Notre Dame Press, 1995), 1-34.

42. On the mendicant friars as inquisitors, see Cohen, *The Friars and the Jews*, 33-99; Edward Peters, *Inquisition*, 2nd ed. (Berkeley: University of California Press, 1989), 53-74. For more general discussions of the central position of rhetoric, disputations, and dialectic in the training of mendicant friars, see C. H. Lawrence, *The Friars: The Impact of the Early Mendicant Movement on Western Society* (London: Longman, 1994), 127-151, especially 149-150; John Moorman, *A History of the Franciscan Order from Its Origin to the Year 1517* (Oxford: Oxford University Press, 1968), 123-128; Larry J. Simon, "Intimate Enemies: Mendicant-Jewish Interaction in Thirteenth-Century Mediterranean Spain," in *Friars and Jews in the Middle Ages and Renaissance*, ed. Steven J. McMichael and Susan E. Myers (Leiden: Brill, 2004), 53-62.

43. Gabrielle M. Spiegel, *Romancing the Past: The Rise of Vernacular Prose Historiography in Thirteenth-Century France* (Berkeley: University of California Press, 1993), especially 99-118.

44. Colbert I. Nepaulsingh, *Towards a History of Literary Composition in Medieval Spain* (Toronto: University of Toronto Press, 1986), 5-63. Alfonso X was also a direct patron of literature in his support of new works and in his organization of a regulated cottage industry of book production. See George Greenia, "University Book Production and Courtly Patronage in Thirteenth Century France and Spain," in *Medieval Iberia: Essays on the History and Literature of Medieval Spain*, ed. Donald J. Kagay and Joseph T. Snow (New York: Peter Lang, 1997), 103-128.

45. Robert I. Burns, "Castle of Intellect, Castle of Force," in Robert I. Burns, ed., *The Worlds of Alfonso the Learned and James the Conqueror: Intellect and Force in the Middle Ages* (Princeton, NJ: Princeton University Press, 1985), 3-22, especially 12-17.

46. Jill R. Webster, "Patronage and Piety: Catalan Letters from Llull to March," in *The Worlds of Alfonso the Learned and James the Conqueror: Intellect and Force in the Middle Ages*, ed. Robert I. Burns (Princeton, NJ: Princeton University Press, 1985), 68-94.

47. There are several editions of this text. An early manuscript of King James I's memoir has been published in facsimile. See James I, King of Aragon, *Libre dels feyts del rey En Jacme*, trans. with an introduction by Martin de Riquer (Barcelona: Universidad del Barcelona, 1972); Ferran Soldevila, ed., *Jaume I, Crònica o Llibre dels Feits* (Barcelona: Edicions 62, 1982). There also is a recent critical translation in English: Damien Smith and Helena Buffery, eds., *The Book of Deeds of James I of Aragon: A Translation of the Medieval Catalan Llibre dels Fets* (Aldershot: Ashgate, 2003).

48. David J. Viera, *Medieval Catalan Literature: Prose and Drama* (Boston: Twayne, 1988).

49. See Martí de Riquer, *Història de la Literatura Catalana: Part Antiga*, 4 vols. (Barcelona: Editorial Ariel, S.A., 1964), 1:123-136 on James I's patronage of

literature, and 373–428 on James I's *Llibre dels Feyts*. David Viera, on the other hand, argues that the *Llibre dels Feyts* sacrifices proper realism in the effort to promote and glorify James and his successes: Viera, *Medieval Catalan Literature*.

50. Antoni M. Badia i Margarit, "La 'substitución lingüística' en la *Crónica o Libre dels Feyts del Rey en Jacme*," in *Philologica hispaniensia: in honorem Manuel Alvar* (Madrid: Gredos, 1985): 45–53. Many portions of the text appear to have been imported from folk culture or other textual sources, including moralizing or ethical tales illustrating the king's good judgment and worldly wisdom. While some of these anecdotes appear to be shaped by traditions contained in earlier Iberian literature, Samuel G. Armistead has noted an apparent link in one particular case with a much older Arabic tradition that was recorded in a thirteenth-century geographic dictionary. The anecdote concerns a bird's nest placed at the top of one of James' tents. In his desire not to disturb the inhabitants, the king ordered that the tent remain standing until such time as all of the birds were able to fly away. See Samuel G. Armistead, "An Anecdote of King Jaume I and Its Arabic Congener," in *Cultures in Contact in Medieval Spain: Historical and Literary Essays Presented to L. P. Harvey*, ed. David Hook and Barry Taylor (London: King's College, 1990), 1–8.

51. There are numerous examples throughout the book, but one should suffice here: "Then we replied to Don Rodrigo Lizana and to the others: 'We will tell you how we will do it. We will go and pitch camp near the tower, and when the next day comes, in the early morning, we will attack the town. And they will defend it. And in defending, as they struggle to hold the stockades, our men will break them. And once they enter they can cause great harm to the Moors, because those who have remained at the tower and the *albacar* will be worthless. Then we will proceed according to how we see the battle going. Thus, if you and we believe that we can take it, we will go to Borriana, with only fifteen knights, as it is a good idea not to break up the company. And on the third day we will return here with the *almajahah* and with rations for eight days." In this passage, King James described a military strategy appropriate for a specific battle. Both Arabic words used in this passage appear repeatedly in the course of the *Llibre*. *Albacar* refers to a particular type of defensive tower in Muslim towns; *almajahah*, however, is the Arabized name for a military implement which is used interchangeably with the Catalan term, *fenèvol*. See Smith and Buffery, eds., *The Book of Deeds*, 183 [chapter 200]; Soldevila, ed., *Jaume I, Crònica o Llibre dels Feits*, 209 [chapter 200].

52. According to Smith and Buffery, *bovatge* is a form of taxation that was used by the king to finance military campaigns.

53. Smith and Buffery, eds., *The Book of Deeds*, 293 [chapter 392]; Soldevila, ed., *Jaume I, Crònica o Llibre dels Feits*, 328–329 [chapter 392].

54. One might well argue that Nahmanides was not successful in this effort in the case of the Catalan version, since the accusations of blasphemy brought against him by the friars reference his inaccurate account of the disputation as the cause for their charges.

Bibliography

Abraham bar Hiyya. *Sefer Megilat ha-megaleh*. Sifriyah le-mahshevet Yisra'el, edited by Ze'ev Poznanski and Julius Guttmann. Jerusalem, 1968.
Abrams, Daniel. "Orality in the Kabbalistic School of Nahmanides: Preserving and Interpreting Esoteric Traditions and Texts." *Jewish Studies Quarterly* 3, no. 1 (1996): 85–102.
Abulafia, David. *A Mediterranean Emporium: The Catalan Kingdom of Majorca*. Cambridge: Cambridge University Press, 1994.
Albeck, Hanokh, and Yehuda Theodor, eds. *Midrash Bereshit Rabbah*. 3 vols. Jerusalem: Wahrmann Books, 1965.
Albert, Bat-Sheva. "L'image du chrétien dans les sources juives du Languedoc (XIIe–XIV siècles)." In *Les Juifs à Montpellier et dans le Languedoc à travers l'histoire du moyen age à nos jours*, edited by Carol Iancu, 113–128. Montpellier: Centre de recherches et d'études Juives et Hébraïques, 1988.
Alliez, Éric. *Capital Times: Tales from the Conquest of Time*. Translated by George Van Den Abbeele. Theory Out of Bounds 6, edited by Michael Hardt, Sandra Buckley, and Brian Massumi. Minneapolis and London: University of Minnesota Press, 1996.
Alon, Gedaliah. *Jews, Judaism, and the Classical World: Studies in Jewish History in the Times of the Second Temple and Talmud*. Translated by Israel Abrahams. Jerusalem: Magnes Press, 1977.
Alter, Robert. *The Art of Biblical Narrative*. New York: Basic Books, 1981.
Altman, Alexander. "A Note on the Rabbinic Doctrine of Creation." *Journal of Jewish Studies* 7, no. 3–4 (1956): 195–206.
Anderson, Benedict. *Imagined Communities: Reflections on the Origin and Spread of Nationalism*. London: Verso, 1983.
Angelilli, Ignacio. "The Techniques of Disputation in the History of Logic." *The Journal of Philosophy* 67, no. 20 (1970): 800–815.

Anidjar, Gil. "Jewish Mysticism Alterable and Unalterable: On *Orienting* Kabbalah Studies and the 'Zohar of Christian Spain'." *Jewish Social Studies* 3, no. 1 (1996): 89–157.

———. *"Our Place in al-Andalus": Kabbalah, Philosophy, Literature in Arab Jewish Letters.* Cultural Memory in the Present, edited by Mieke Bal and Hent de Vries. Stanford, CA: Stanford University Press, 2002.

Armistead, Samuel G. "An Anecdote of King Jaume I and Its Arabic Congener." In *Cultures in Contact in Medieval Spain: Historical and Literary Essays Presented to L. P. Harvey*, edited by David Hook and Barry Taylor, 1–8. London: King's College, 1990.

Armour, Rollin. "Review of Robert Chazan, *Barcelona and Beyond: The Disputation of 1263 and Its Aftermath*." *Church History* 64, no. 4 (1995): 652–654.

Arnau de Vilanova. *Obres Catalanes*, vol. 1: *Escrits religiosos*. Edited by Miguel Batillori. 2 vols. Els nostres classics: obres completes dels escriptors catalans medievals 53–54. Barcelona: Editorial Barcino, 1947.

Arnold, John H. *Inquisition and Power: Catharism and the Confessing Subject in Medieval Languedoc*. The Middle Ages Series, edited by Ruth Mazo Karras. Philadelphia: University of Pennsylvania Press, 2001.

Ashkenazi, Shlomo. "Printed Editions of Ramban's *Torat ha'Adam*." (Hebrew) *Koroth* 8, no. 7–8 (1983): 219–221.

Assis, Yom Tov. "Catalan Jewry before 1391: Archival and Hebrew Sources." *Materia giudaica* 6, no. 2 (2001): 133–138.

———. *The Golden Age of Aragonese Jewry: Community and Society in the Crown of Aragon, 1213–1327*. The Littman Library of Jewish Civilization, edited by Connie Webber. London: Littman Library of Jewish Civilization, 1997.

———. *Jewish Economy in the Medieval Crown of Aragon, 1213–1327: Money and Power*. Brill's Series in Jewish Studies 18, edited by David S. Katz. Leiden: E. J. Brill, 1997.

———. "Jews in Gentile Courts in the Thirteenth and Fourteenth Centuries." (Hebrew) In *Tarbut ve-Hevrah ba-Toldot Yisrael be-Yameh ha-Benayim*, edited by Menahem Ben-Sasson et al., 399–430. Jerusalem: Merkaz Zalmon Shazar la-Toldot Yisrael, 1989.

———. "Nahmánides y su concepción del judaísmo." In *Mossé ben Nahman i el seu temps: simposi commemoratiu del vuitè centenari del seu naixement, 1194–1994*, 77–90. Girona: Ajuntament Girona, 1994.

Astren, Fred. "History or Philosophy? The Construction of the Past in Medieval Karaite Judaism." *Medieval Encounters* 1, no. 1 (1995): 114–143.

Atlan, Henri. "Rationalisme et théologie: Maïmonide et Nahmanide." *Les nouveaux cahiers* 118 (1994): 5–14.

Auerbach, Erich. *Mimesis: The Representation of Reality in Western Literature*. Translated by Willard R. Trask. Princeton, NJ: Princeton University Press, 1974.

Augustine. *City of God*. Translated by Henry Bettenson. Penguin Classics. Middlesex: Penguin Books, 1984.

———. *St. Augustine on Genesis: Two Books on Genesis, Against the Manichees and On the Literal Meaning of Genesis (an unfinished book)*. The Fathers of the Church, edited by Thomas P. Halton. Washington, DC: Catholic University of America Press, 1982.

Aveni, Anthony F. *Empires of Time: Calendars, Clocks, and Cultures*. New York: Basic Books, 1989.

Ayoun, Richard. "Review of Robert Chazan, *Barcelona and Beyond: The Disputation of 1263 and Its Aftermath*." *Revue des Études Juives* 154, no. 3-4 (1993): 500-502.

Backman, Clifford R. "Arnau de Vilanova and the Body at the End of the World." In *Last Things: Death and the Apocalypse in the Middle Ages*, edited by Carolyn Walker Bynum and Paul Freedman, 140-155. Philadelphia: University of Pennsylvania Press, 2000.

———. "Arnau de Vilanova and the Franciscan Spirituals in Sicily." *Franciscan Studies* 50 (1990): 3-29.

———. "The Reception of Arnau of Vilanova's Religious Ideas." In *Christendom and Its Discontents: Exclusion, Persecution, and Rebellion*, edited by Scott L. Waugh and Peter D. Diehl, 112-131. Cambridge: Cambridge University Press, 1996.

Badia i Margarit, Antoni M. "La 'substitución lingüística' en la *Crónica o Libre dels Feyts del Rey en Jacme*." In *Philologica hispaniensia: in honorem Manuel Alvar*, 45-53. Madrid: Gredos, 1985.

Baer, Yitzhak. "The Disputations of Rabbi Yechiel of Paris and of Nahmanides." (Hebrew) *Tarbitz* 2, no. 2 (1931): 172-187.

———. *Galut*. Translated by Robert Warshow. New York: Schocken Books, 1947.

———. *A History of the Jews in Christian Spain: From the Reconquest to the Fourteenth Century*. Translated by Louis Schoffman. 2 vols. Philadelphia: Jewish Publication Society of America, 1961.

———. "The Origins of the Organisation of the Jewish Community of the Middle Ages." (Hebrew) *Tziyon* 15 (1950): 1-41.

Bann, Stephen. *The Inventions of History: Essays on the Representation of the Past*. Manchester: Manchester University Press, 1990.

Bar-Tikva, Benjamin. "Reciprocity between the Provençal School of *Piyyutim* and the Schools of Catalonia and Ashkenazi France." In *Rashi: 1040-1990, Hommage à Ephraïm E. Urbach*, edited by Gabrielle Sed-Rajna, 376-383. Paris: Les Éditions du Cerf, 1993.

Barcelona, Martí de. "Regesta de documents arnaldians coneguts." *Estudis franciscans* 47 (1935): 261-300.

Baron, Salo W. "Ghetto and Emancipation." *Menorah Journal* 14 (1928): 515-528.

———. "The Jewish Factor in Medieval Civilization." In *Ancient and Medieval Jewish History: Essays by Salo Wittmayer Baron*, edited by Leon Feldman, 239–267. New Brunswick, NJ: Rutgers University Press, 1972.

———. *A Social and Religious History of the Jews*. Vol. 9. New York: Columbia University Press, 1965.

Bartlett, Robert. *The Making of Europe: Conquest, Colonization, and Cultural Change, 950–1350*. Princeton, NJ: Princeton University Press, 1993.

Bat-Yehudah, Geulah. "Torat aretz Yisra'el shel ha-Ramban b'mahshevet ha-tehiyah." *Sinai*, no. 61 (1967): 226–239.

Batillori, Miguel. "Nuevos datos biográficos sobre Arnaldo de Vilanova." *Archivo Iberoamerico de historia de la medicina y de antropología médica* 8 (1956): 235–237.

———. "Orientaciones bibligráficas para el estudio de Arnau de Villanova." *Pensamiento* 10 (1954): 311–324.

———. "Les versions italianes medievales d'obres religiouses de mestre Arnau de Vilanova." *Archivio italiano per la storia della pietà* 1 (1951): 397–462.

Bazell, Dianne M. "De Esu Carnium: Arnald of Villanova's Defence of Carthusian Abstinence." In *Actes de la I Trobada Internacional d'Estidis sobre Arnau de Vilanova*, 1994.

Beattie, Pamela Drost. "'*Pro Exaltatione Sanctae Fidei Catholicae*': Mission and Crusade in the Writings of Ramon Llull." In *Iberia and the Mediterranean World of the Middle Ages: Studies in Honor of Robert I. Burns S.J.*, edited by Larry J. Simon, 113–129. Leiden: E. J. Brill, 1995.

Beinart, Ha'im, ed. *Moreshet Sepharad: The Sephardic Legacy*. 2 vols. Vol 1. Jerusalem: Magnes Press, Hebrew University, 1992

———."Order of the Expulsion from Spain: Antecedents, Causes, and Textual Analysis." In *Crisis and Creativity in the Sephardic World, 1391–1648*, edited by Benjamin Gampel, 79–94. New York: Columbia University Press, 1997.

Beitia, Angel Cortabarría. "Los 'Studia Linguarum' del los Dominicos en los Siglos XIII y XIV." In *La controversia judeocristiana en España (desde los orígenes hasta el siglo XIII): Homenaje a Domingo Muñoz León*, edited by Carlos de Valle Rodríguez, 253–276. Madrid: Consejo Superior de Investigaciones Cientificas, 1998.

Bejczy, István. "*Tolerantia*: A Medieval Concept." *Journal of the History of Ideas* 58, no. 3 (1997): 365–384.

Ben-Sasson, Haim Hillel. "The Maimonidean Controversy." In *Encyclopedia Judaica*, 11:749. Jerusalem and New York: Macmillan, 1971–72.

———. "Rabbi Moshe ben Nahman, the Man in the Context of His Time." (Hebrew) *Molad* 1 (1967): 360–366.

Ben-Shahar, Zeev. *Yesodot ha'luah ha-Iveri: be'tseruf nispahim al ha-luah ha-notsri veha-muslemi*. Jerusalem: Keren Or, 1987.

Ben-Shalom, Ram. "The Ban Placed by the Community of Barcelona on the Study of Philosophy and Allegorical Preaching—A New Study." *Revue des Études Juives* 159, no. 3–4 (2000): 387–404.

———. "Communication and Propaganda between Provence and Spain: The Controversy over Extreme Allegorization (1303–1306)." In *Communication in the Jewish Diaspora: The Pre-Modern World*, edited by Sophia Menache, 171–224. Leiden: E. J. Brill, 1996.

Benbassa, Esther, and Aron Rodrigue. *Sephardi Jewry: A History of the Judeo-Spanish Community, 14th–20th Centuries*. Jewish Communities in the Modern World, edited by David Sorkin. Berkeley: University of California Press, 2000.

Bender, John B., and David E. Wellbery, eds. *Chronotypes: The Construction of Time*. Palo Alto, CA: Stanford University Press, 1991.

Benin, Stephen D. "Jews and Christian Heresy: Hugh of St. Victor, Anselm of Havelburg and William of Auvergne." In *From Witness to Witchcraft: Jews and Judaism in Medieval Christian Thought*, edited by Jeremy Cohen, 203–219. Wiesbaden: Harrassowitz Verlag, 1996.

———. "The Search for Truth in Sacred Scripture: Jews, Christians, and the Authority to Interpret." In *With Reverence for the Word: Medieval Scriptural Exegesis in Judaism, Christianity, and Islam*, edited by Jane Dammen McAuliffe, Barry D. Walfish, and Joseph W. Goering, 13–32. Oxford: Oxford University Press, 2003.

Benjamin, A. Cornelius. "Ideas of Time in the History of Philosophy." In *The Voices of Time: A Cooperative Survey of Man's Views of Time as Expressed by the Sciences and by the Humanities*, edited by J. T. Fraser, 3–30. Amherst: University of Massachusetts Press, 1981.

Bennett, Andrew. "On Posterity." *The Yale Journal of Criticism* 12, no. 1 (1999): 131–144.

Bensch, Stephen P. *Barcelona and Its Rulers, 1096–1291*. Cambridge Studies in Medieval Life and Thought, 4th series, vol. 26, edited by D. E. Luscombe. Cambridge: Cambridge University Press, 1995.

Berger, David. "From Crusades to Blood Libels to Expulsions: Some New Approaches to Medieval Antisemitism." Paper presented at the Second Annual Lecture of the Victor J. Selmanowitz Chair of Jewish History, Touro College, Graduate School of Jewish Studies 1997.

———. "Gilbert Crispin, Alan of Lille, and Jacob ben Reuben: A Study of the Transmission of Medieval Polemic." *Speculum* 49, no. 1 (1974): 34–47.

———. "The Great Struggle: Provence and Northern Spain from the Late Twelfth to the Early Fourteenth Century." In *Judaism's Encounter with Other Cultures: Rejection or Integration?* edited by Jacob J. Schacter, 85–108. Northvale, NJ: Jason Aronson, 1997.

———. "How Did Nahmanides Propose to Resolve the Maimonidean Controversy?" In *Me'ah She'arim: Studies in Medieval Jewish Spiritual Life in Memory of Isadore Twersky*, edited by Ezra Fleischer, Gerald Bildstein, Carmi Horowitz, and Bernard Septimus, 135–146. Jerusalem: Hebrew University, Magnes Press, 2001.

———, ed. *The Jewish-Christian Debate in the High Middle Ages: A Critical Edition of the Nizzahon Vetus*. Judaica: Texts and Translations 4. Philadelphia: Jewish Publication Society of America, 1979.

———. "Miracles and the Natural Order in Nahmanides." In *Rabbi Moses Nahmanides (Ramban): Explorations in His Religious and Literary Virtuosity*, edited by Isadore Twersky, 107–128. Cambridge, MA: Harvard University Press, 1983.

———. "Mission to the Jews and Jewish-Christian Contacts in the Polemical Literature of the High Middle Ages." *The American Historical Review* 91, no. 3 (1986): 576–591.

———. "Review of Robert Chazan: *Barcelona and Beyond: The Disputation of 1263 and Its Aftermath*." *AJS Review* 22, no. 2 (1995): 379–388.

———. "Three Typological Themes in Early Jewish Messianism: Messiah Son of Joseph, Rabbinic Calculations, and the Figure of Amilus." *AJS Review* 10, no. 2 (1985): 141–164.

Berner, Leila. "On the Western Shores: The Jews of Barcelona during the Reign of Jaume I, 'el Conqueridor,' 1213–1276." PhD dissertation, University of California, Los Angeles, 1986.

Bettini, Maurizio. *Anthropology and Roman Culture: Kinship, Time, Images of the Soul*. Translated by John Van Sickle. Baltimore: Johns Hopkins University Press, 1991.

Bhabha, Homi K. *The Location of Culture*. London: Routledge, 1994.

Biagioli, Mario. *Galileo Courtier: The Practice of Science in the Culture of Absolutism*. Science and Its Conceptual Foundations, edited by David Hull. Chicago: University of Chicago Press, 1993.

Biale, David. "Exegesis and Philosophy in the Writings of Abraham Ibn Ezra." *Comitatus* 5 (1974): 42–62.

———. *Gershom Scholem: Kabbalah and Counter-History*. 2nd ed. Cambridge, MA: Harvard University Press, 1982.

———. *Power and Powerlessness in Jewish History*. New York: Schocken Books, 1986.

Bianchi, Luca. *Censure et Liberté Intellectuelle à l'Université de Paris (XIIIe–XIVe siècles)*. Ane d'or 9. Paris: Les Belles Lettres, 1999.

Bickerman, Elias J. *Chronology of the Ancient World*. Aspects of Greek and Roman Life, edited by H. H. Scullard. London: Thames and Hudson, 1968.

———. *From Ezra to the Last of the Maccabees: Foundations of Postbiblical Judaism*. New York: Schocken Books, 1962.

Bisson, Thomas N. *The Medieval Crown of Aragon, A Short History*. Oxford: Clarendon Press, 1986.

———. *Medieval France and Her Pyrenean Neighbours: Studies in Early Institutional History*. Studies Presented to the International Commission for the History of Representative and Parliamentary Institutions 70. London: Hambledon Press, 1989.

———. *Tormented Voices: Power, Crisis, and Humanity in Rural Catalonia, 1140–1200*. Cambridge, MA: Harvard University Press, 1998.

———. "Unheroed Pasts: History and Commemoration in South Frankland before the Albigensian Crusades." *Speculum* 65, no. 2 (1990): 281–308.

Blacker, Jean. *The Faces of Time: Portrayal of the Past in Old French and Latin Historical Narrative of the Anglo-Norman Regnum*. Austin: University of Texas Press, 1994.

Bland, Kalman P. "Medieval Jewish Aesthetics: Maimonides, Body, and Scripture in Profiat Duran." *Journal of the History of Ideas* 54, no. 4 (October 1993): 533–559.

Blidstein, Gerald J. "Individual and Community in the Middle Ages: Halakhic Theory." In *Kinship and Consent: The Jewish Political Tradition and Its Contemporary Uses*, edited by Daniel J. Elazar, 327–369. Washington, DC: University Press of America, 1997.

Blumenkranz, Bernhard. "Anti-Jewish Polemics and Legislation in the Middle Ages: Literary Fiction or Reality?" *Journal of Jewish Studies* 15 (1964): 125–140.

———, ed. *Disputatio Iudei et Christiani et anonymi auctoris: disputationis Iudei et Christiani continuatio ad fidem codicum recensuit prolegomenis notisque instruxit*. Stromata patristica et mediaevalia 3. Utrecht: In Aedibus Spectrum, 1956.

———. "Les Juifs en Franche-Comté médiévale." In *Juifs en France: Écrits dispersés*, edited by Bernhard Blumenkranz, 62–88. Paris: Franco-Judaïca, 1989.

Bodian, Miriam. *Hebrews of the Portuguese Nation: Conversos and Community in Early Modern Amsterdam*. The Modern Jewish Experience, edited by Paula Hyman and Deborah Dash Moore. Bloomington: Indiana University Press, 1997.

Bollweg, John August. "Sense of a Mission: Arnau of Vilanova on the Conversion of Muslims and Jews." In *Iberia and the Mediterranean World of the Middle Ages: Studies in Honor of Robert I. Burns*, edited by Larry J. Simon, 50–74. Leiden: E. J. Brill, 1995.

Bonfil, Robert (Reuven). "Can Medieval Storytelling Help Understanding Midrash? The Story of Paltiel: A Preliminary Study on History and Midrash." In *The Midrashic Imagination: Jewish Exegesis, Thought, and History*, edited by Michael Fishbane, 228–254. Albany: SUNY Press, 1993.

———. "The Nature of Judaism in Raymundus Martini's *Pugio Fidei*." (Hebrew) *Tarbitz* 40 (1971): 360–375.

———. *Rabbis and Jewish Communities in Renaissance Italy*. Translated by Jonathan Chipman. The Littman Library. Oxford: Oxford University Press, 1990.

Bonner, Anthony, ed. *Selected Works of Ramón Llull (1232–1316)*. 2 vols. Vol. 1. Princeton, NJ: Princeton University Press, 1985.

Borst, Arno. *The Ordering of Time: From the Ancient Computus to the Modern Computer*. Translated by Andres Winnard. Chicago: University of Chicago Press, 1993.

Bourdieu, Pierre. "Delegation and Political Fetishism." In *Language and Symbolic Power*, edited by John B. Thompson, 203–219. Oxford: Polity Press, 1991.

———. *Outline of a Theory of Practice*. Translated by Richard Nice. Cambridge Studies in Social Anthropology 16, edited by Jack Goody. Cambridge: Cambridge University Press, 1977.

———. "The Work of Time." In *The Gift: An Interdisciplinary Perspective*, edited by Aafke E. Komter, 135–147. Amsterdam: Amsterdam University Press, 1996.

Boyarin, Daniel. *Carnal Israel: Reading Sex in Talmudic Culture*. The New Historicism: Readings in Cultural Poetics 25, edited by Stephan Greenblatt. Berkeley: University of California Press, 1993.

———. "Darkham be-kodesh al shitat limud ha-talmud be-kerev megorshi sefarad." *Peamim* 3 (1979): 73–82.

———. *Intertextuality and the Reading of Midrash*. Indiana Studies in Biblical Literature, edited by Herbert Marks and Robert Polzin. Bloomington: Indiana University Press, 1990.

———. *A Radical Jew: Paul and the Politics of Identity*. Contraversions: Critical Studies in Jewish Literature, Culture, and Society, edited by Daniel Boyarin and Chana Kronfeld. Berkeley: University of California Press, 1994.

Brann, Ross. *Power in the Portrayal: Representations of Jews and Muslims in Eleventh- and Twelfth-Century Islamic Spain*. Jews, Christians, and Muslims: From the Ancient to the Modern World, edited by R. Stephen Humphreys et al. Princeton, NJ: Princeton University Press, 2002.

Bregman, Marc. "Midrash Rabbah and the Medieval Collector Mentality." *Prooftexts* 17, no. 1 (1997): 63–76.

Brenneman, James E. *Canons in Conflict: Negotiating Texts in True and False Prophecy*. New York and Oxford: Oxford University Press, 1997.

Brody, Robert. *The Geonim of Babylonia and the Shaping of Medieval Jewish Culture*. New Haven, CT: Yale University Press, 1998.

Brueggemann, Walter. *The Prophetic Imagination*. 2nd ed. Minneapolis: Fortress Press, 2001.

Brumberg, A. Y. "Ha-Ramban k-pharshan ve-hashkaphat olamo." *Sinai* 61, no. 5–6 (1967): 249–258.

Buber, Shlomo, ed. *Midrash Tanhuma al Hamushah Humshe Torah.* Vilna: ha-Almanah veha-Ahim Rom, 1885.
Budick, Sanford, and Geoffrey H. Hartman, eds. *Midrash and Literature.* New Haven and London: Yale University Press, 1986.
Bull, Malcolm. *Seeing Things Hidden: Apocalypse, Vision, and Totality.* London: Verso, 1999.
Burko-Falcman, Berthe. "Du temps des Juifs au temps juif." *Temps Modernes* 50, no. 584 (1995): 90–97.
Burns, Robert I. "The Barcelona 'Disputation' of 1263: Conversionism and Talmud in Jewish-Christian Relations." *The Catholic Historical Review* 79, no. 3 (1993): 488–495.
———. "Castle of Intellect, Castle of Force: The Worlds of Alfonso the Learned and James the Conqueror." In *The Worlds of Alfonso the Learned and James the Conqueror: Intellect and Force in the Middle Ages,* edited by Robert I. Burns, 3–22. Princeton, NJ: Princeton University Press, 1985.
———. *Diplomatarium of the Crusader Kingdom of Valencia, the Registered Charters of Its Conqueror Jaume I, 1257–1276.* 2 vols. Vol. 1. Princeton, NJ: Princeton University Press, 1985.
———. "The *Guidaticum* Safe-Conduct in Medieval Aragon-Catalonia: A Mini-Institution for Muslims, Christians, and Jews." *Medieval Encounters* 1, no. 1 (1995): 51–113.
———. "Jaume I and the Jews of the Kingdom of Valencia." In *X Congreso de Historia de la Corona de Aragón: Jaime I y su época,* 245–322. Zaragoza: Institución Fernando el Catalico, 1979.
———. *Jews in the Notarial Culture: Latinate Wills in Mediterranean Spain, 1250–1350.* Berkeley: University of California Press, 1996.
———. *Muslims, Christians, and Jews in the Crusader Kingdom of Valencia: Societies in Symbiosis.* Cambridge Iberian and Latin American Studies, edited by P. E. Russell. Cambridge: Cambridge University Press, 1984.
———. "The Spiritual Life of James the Conqueror, King of Arago-Catalonia, 1208–1276: Portrait and Self-Portrait." *The Catholic Historical Review* 62, no. 1 (1976): 1–35.
———, ed. *The Worlds of Alfonso the Learned and James the Conqueror: Intellect and Force in the Middle Ages.* Princeton, NJ: Princeton University Press, 1985.
Butler, Thomas, ed. *Memory: History, Culture, and the Mind.* Wolfson College Lectures [1988]. New York and Oxford: B. Blackwell, 1989.
Cabré, Miriam. "Italian and Catalan Troubadours." In *The Troubadours: An Introduction,* edited by Simon Gaunt and Sarah Kay, 127–140. Cambridge: Cambridge University Press, 1999.
Caputo, Nina. "'*In the beginning*'. Typology, History, and the Unfolding Meaning of Creation in Nahmanides' Exegesis." *Jewish Social Studies* 6, no. 1 (1999): 54–82.

———. "'To kill the thorns in the vineyard': A Medieval Rabbi's Argument for Diversity within Unity." In *Orthodoxie, Christianisme, Histoire*, edited by Susanna Elm, Éric Rebillard, and Antonella Romano, 35–55. Rome: École Française de Rome, 2000.

Carlebach, Elisheva. "Between History and Hope: Jewish Messianism in Ashkenaz and Sepharad." Paper presented at the Third Annual Lecture of the Victor J. Selmenowitz Chair of Jewish History, Graduate School of Jewish Studies, Touro College 1998.

———. *Divided Souls: Converts from Judaism in Germany, 1500–1750*. New Haven, CT: Yale University Press, 2001.

Carmilly-Weinberger, Moshe. *Censorship and Freedom of Expression in Jewish History*. New York: Sepher Harmon, 1977.

Carr, David. *Time, Narrative, and History*. Bloomington: University of Indiana Press, 1986.

Carreras y Artau, Joaquín. "La 'Allocutio super Tetragrammatron' de Arnaldo de Vilanova." *Sefarad* 9 (1949): 75–105.

———. "Arnaldo de Vilanova, apologista antijudaico." *Sefarad* 7, no. 1 (1947): 49–61.

———. "Arnau de Vilanova y las culturas orientales." In *Homenaje a Millàs Vallicrosa*, 309–321. Barcelona: Consejo Superior de Investigaciones Científicas, 1954.

———. "L'espistolari d'Arnau de Vilanova." *Institut d'Estudis Catalans* 10 (1950): 7–27.

———. "Del epistolario espiritual de Arnaldo de Vilanova." *Estudios franciscanos* 49 (1948): 79–94, 301–406.

———. "La llibreria d'Arnau de Vilanova." *Analecta sacra Tarraconensia* 11 (1935): 63–86.

———. "La patria y la familia de A. de V. A propósito de un libro reciente." *Analecta sacra Tarraconensia* 20 (1947): 5–75.

———. "La polémica gerundense sobre el Anticristo entre Arnau de Vilanova y los dominicos." *Anales del Instituto de Estudios Gerundenses* 5 (1950): 1–58.

Carroll, Robert P. *When Prophecy Failed: Reactions and Responses to Failure in the Old Testament Prophetic Traditions*. London: SCM Press, 1979.

Castoriadis, Cornelius. "Time and Creation." In *Chronotypes: The Construction of Time*, edited by John Bender and David Wellbery, 38–64. Palo Alto, CA: Stanford University Press, 1991.

Chavel, Haim Dov (Charles Ber), ed. *The Disputation at Barcelona*. New York: Shilo, 1983.

———. *Kitvei Rabbenu Moshe ben Nahman*. 2 vols. Jerusalem: Mosad Ha-Rav Kook, 1964.

———. *Perush ha-Ramban al ha-Torah*. 2 vols. Jerusalem: Mosad Ha-Rav Kook, 1959.

———. *Ramban: His Life and Teachings*. New York: Philipp Feldheim, 1960.
Chazan, Robert. *Barcelona and Beyond: The Disputation of 1263 and Its Aftermath*. Berkeley and Los Angeles: University of California Press, 1992.
———. "The Barcelona 'Disputation' of 1263: Christian Missionizing and Jewish Response." *Speculum* 52, no. 4 (1977): 824–842.
———. "Confrontation in the Synagogue of Narbonne: A Christian Sermon and a Jewish Reply." *Harvard Theological Review* 67 (1974): 437–457.
———. *Daggers of Faith: Thirteenth-Century Christian Missionizing and Jewish Response*. Berkeley: University of California Press, 1989.
———. "Daniel 9:24–27: Exegesis and Polemics." In *Contra Iudaeos: Ancient and Medieval Polemics between Christians and Jews*, edited by Ora Limor and Guy G. Stroumsa, 143–159. Tübingen: J. C. B. Mohr, 1996.
———. *European Jewry and the First Crusade*. Berkeley: University of California Press, 1987.
———. *Fashioning Jewish Identity in Medieval Western Christendom*. Cambridge: Cambridge University Press, 2004.
———. "From Friar Paul to Friar Raymond: The Development of Innovative Missionizing Argumentation." *Harvard Theological Review* 76, no. 3 (1983): 289–306.
———. "In the Wake of the Barcelona Disputation." *Hebrew Union College Annual* 61 (1990): 185–201.
———. "The Letter of R. Jacob ben Elijiah to Friar Paul." *Jewish History* 6, no. 1–2 (1992): 51–63.
———. *Medieval Jewry in Northern France: A Political and Social History*. Johns Hopkins University Studies in Historical and Political Science, 91st series, 2. Baltimore: Johns Hopkins University Press, 1973.
———. "The Messianic Calculations of Nahmanides." In *Rashi 1040–1990, Hommage à Ephraïm E. Urbach*, edited by Gabrielle Sed-Rajna, 631–637. Paris: Les Éditions du Cerf, 1993.
———. "Rashi's Commentary on the Book of *Daniel*: Messianic Speculation and Polemical Argumentation." In *Rashi et la culture juive en France du Nord au moyen âge*, edited by Gilbert Dahan, Gérard Nahon, and Elie Nicolas, 111–121. Paris-Louvain: E. Peeters, 1997.
———. "The Timebound and the Timeless: Medieval Jewish Narration of Events." *History and Memory* 6, no. 1 (1994): 5–34.
———. "Undermining the Jewish Sense of Future: Alfonso of Valladolid and the New Christian Missionizing." In *Christians, Muslims, and Jews in Medieval and Early Modern Spain: Interaction and Cultural Change*, edited by Mark D. Meyerson and Edward D. English, 179–194. Notre Dame, IN: University of Notre Dame Press, 1999.
Clifford, James. "Diasporas." *Cultural Anthropology* 9, no. 3 (1994): 302–338.

Cohen, Gerson D. *A Critical Edition with a Translation and Notes of the Book of Tradition (Sefer ha-Qabbalah) by Abraham Ibn Daud*. Philadelphia: Jewish Publication Society of America, 1967.

———. "Esau as Symbol in Early Medieval Thought." In *Jewish Medieval and Renaissance Studies*, edited by Alexander Altmann, 19–48. Cambridge, MA: Harvard University Press, 1967.

———. "Messianic Postures of Ashkenazim and Sephardim (Prior to Sabbathai Zevi)." In *Studies of the Leo Baeck Institute*, edited by Max Kreutzberger, 117–156. New York: Frederick Unger, 1967.

Cohen, Jeremy. *The Friars and the Jews: The Evolution of Medieval Anti-Judaism*. Ithaca, NY: Cornell University Press, 1982.

———. *Living Letters of the Law: Ideas of the Jew in Medieval Christianity*. Berkeley: University of California Press, 1999.

———. "Medieval Jews on Christianity: Polemical Strategies and Theological Defense." In *Interwoven Destinies: Jews and Christians through the Ages*, edited by Eugene J. Fisher, 77–89. New York: Paulist Press, 1993.

———. "The Mentality of the Medieval Jewish Apostate: Peter Alfonsi, Hermann of Cologne, and Pablo Christiani." In *Jewish Apostasy in the Modern World*, edited by Todd M. Endelman, 20–47. New York: Holmes and Meier, 1987.

———. "The Muslim Connection: On the Changing Role of the Jew in High Medieval Theology." In *From Witness to Witchcraft: Jews and Judaism in Medieval Christian Thought*, edited by Jeremy Cohen, 141–162. Wiesbaden: Harrassowitz, 1996.

———. "Review of Robert Chazan, *Barcelona and Beyond: The Disputation of 1263 and Its Aftermath*." *American Historical Review* 98, no. 4 (1993): 1227–1228.

———. "Scholarship and Intolerance in the Medieval Academy: The Study and Evaluation of Judaism in European Christendom." *American Historical Review* 91, no. 3 (1986): 592–613.

Cohen, Mark R. *Jewish Self-Government in Medieval Egypt: The Origins of the Office of Head of the Jews, ca. 1065–1126*. Princeton Studies in the Near East. Princeton, NJ: Princeton University Press, 1980.

———. "Persecution, Response, and Collective Memory: The Jews of Islam in the Classical Period." In *The Jews of Medieval Islam: Community, Society, and Identity*, edited by Daniel Frank, 145–164. Leiden: E. J. Brill, 1995.

———. *Under Crescent and Cross: The Jews in the Middle Ages*. Princeton, NJ: Princeton University Press, 1994.

Cohen, Martin A. "Reflections on the Text and Context of the Disputation of Barcelona." *Hebrew Union College Annual* 35 (1964): 157–192.

Cohen, Menachem, ed. *Mikra'ot gedolot 'ha-keter': Bereshit, 1*. Ramat-Gan: Bar-Ilan University, 1997.

Cohn, Norman. *The Pursuit of the Millennium*. Fairlawn, NJ: Essential Books, 1957.

Collins, John J. *The Apocalyptic Imagination: An Introduction to Jewish Apocalyptic Literature*. Edited by Astrid B. Beck et al. 2nd ed. The Biblical Resource Series. Grand Rapids, MI: William B. Eerdmans, 1989 and 1998.

———. *The Apocalyptic Vision of the Book of Daniel*. Harvard Semitic Museum, Harvard Semitic Monographs 16, edited by Frank Moore Cross, Jr. Missoula, MT: Scholars Press, 1977.

———. *Seers, Sybils, and Sages in Hellenistic-Roman Judaism*. Supplements to the Journal for the Study of Judaism 54, edited by John J. Collins. Leiden: E. J. Brill, 1997.

Constable, Giles. "Forged Letters in the Middle Ages." In *Fälschungen im Mittelalter*, 11–37. Hannover: Hahnsche Buchhandlung, 1988.

———. "Forgery and Plagiarism in the Middle Ages." *Archiv für Diplomatik, Schriftgeschichte Siegel und Wappenkunde* 29 (1983): 1–41.

Cooper, Alan M. "Imagining Prophecy." In *Poetry and Prophecy: The Beginnings of a Literary Tradition*, edited by James L. Kugel, 26–44. Ithaca, NY: Cornell University Press, 1990.

———. "On the Social Role of Biblical Interpretation: The Case of Proverbs 22:6." In *With Reverence for the Word: Medieval Scriptural Exegesis in Judaism, Christianity, and Islam*, edited by Jane Dammen McAuliffe, Barry D. Walfish, and Joseph W. Goering, 180–193. Oxford: Oxford University Press, 2003.

Copleston, Frederick. *A History of Philosophy*. 9 vols. Vol. 2, part 1. New York: Image Books, 1962.

Coulet, Noël. "La communauté des juifs de Provence à la fin du XIVe siècle: Nouveaux doucments sur la *tallia judeorum*." *Revue des Études juives* 155, no. 1–2 (1996): 55–73.

———. "Les juristes dans les villes de la Provence médiévale." In *Les sociétés urbaines en France Méridionale et en Péninsule Ibérique au moyen âge*, edited by Départment de Recherches 'Pyrenaica' Université de Pau et des Pays de l'Adour, 311–327. Paris: Centre National de la Recherche Scientifique, 1991.

Dahan, Gilbert. *The Christian Polemic against the Jews in the Middle Ages*. Translated by Jody Gladding. Notre Dame, IN: University of Notre Dame Press, 1998.

———. "La connaissance de l'Hébreu dans les correctoires de la Bible du XIIIe siècle." In *Rashi: 1040–1990, Hommage à Ephraïm E. Urbach*, edited by Gabrielle Sed-Rajna, 567–578. Paris: Les Éditions du Cerf, 1993.

———. "Un Miracle de Notre Dame: La Juive de Narbonne Convertie, Etude et Edition." In *Medieval Studies in Honour of Avrom Saltman*, edited by Bat-Sheva Albert, Yvonne Friedman, and Simon Schwartzfuchs. Ramat Gan: Bar-Ilan University, 1995.

Dales, Richard. "Time and Eternity in the Thirteenth Century." *Journal of the History of Ideas* 49, no. 1 (1988): 27–45.

Damrosch, David. *The Narrative Covenant: Transformations of Genre in the Growth of Biblical Literature*. San Francisco: Harper & Row, 1987.
Dan, Joseph. "Ashkenazi Hasidim and the Maimonidean Controversy." *Maimonidean Studies* 3 (1992–1993): 29–77.
———. *Ha-sipur ha-ivri bi-yeme ha-benayim: iyunim ba-taldotav*. Jerusalem: Keter, 1974.
———. "Prayer as Text and Prayer as Mystical Experience." In *Torah and Wisdom: Studies in Jewish Philosophy, Kabbalah, and Halacha: Essays in Honor of Arthur Hyman*, edited by Ruth Link-Salinger. New York: Shengold, 1992.
Daniel, E. Randolph. "Abbot Joachim of Fiore and the Conversion of the Jews." In *Friars and Jews in the Middle Ages and Renaissance*, edited by Steven J. McMichael and Susan E. Myers, 1–21. Leiden: Brill, 2004.
———. "The Double Procession of the Holy Spirit in Joachim of Fiore's Understanding of History." *Speculum* 55, no. 3 (1980): 469–483.
———. *The Franciscan Concept of Mission in the Middle Ages*. Lexington: University of Kentucky Press, 1975.
———. "Joachim of Fiore: Patterns of History in the Apocalypse." In *The Apocalypse in the Middle Ages*, edited by Richard K. Emmerson and Bernard McGinn, 72–88. Ithaca, NY: Cornell University Press, 1992.
———. "A Re-Examination of the Origins of Franciscan Joachitism." *Speculum* 43, no. 4 (1968): 671–676.
de Ridder-Symoens, Hilde, ed. *Universities in the Middle Ages, A History of the University in Europe*. Cambridge: Cambridge University Press, 1992.
Deleuze, Gilles, and Félix Guattari. *Kafka: Toward a Minor Literature*. Translated by Dana Polan. Theory and History of Literature 30. Minneapolis: University of Minnesota Press, 1986.
Denifle, Don Pére Heinrich. "Quellen zur Disputation Pablos Christiani mit Mose Nachmani su Barcelona 1263." *Historisches Jahrbuch* 8 (1887): 225–244.
Derrida, Jacques. *Given Time: I. Counterfeit Money*. Translated by Peggy Kamuf. Chicago: University of Chicago Press, 1992.
———. *Monolingualism of the Other; or, The Prosthesis of Origin*. Translated by Patrick Mensah. Cultural Memory in the Present, edited by Mieke Bal and Hent de Vrie. Stanford, CA: Stanford University Press, 1998.
Deyermond, A. D. *The Middle Ages: A Literary History of Spain*. London: Ernest Benn, 1971.
Dicky, Constance Lee. "Time, Narrative and Identity in Medieval French and Occitan Literature." PhD dissertation, University of California, Berkeley, 1991.
Diesendruck, Z. "Saadya's Formulation of the Time Argument for Creation." In *Jewish Studies in Memory of George A. Kohut, 1874–1933*, edited by Salo W. Baron and Alexander Marks, 145–158. New York: Alexander Kohut Memorial Foundation, 1935.

Dobbs-Weinstein, Idit. "The Maimonidean Controversy." In *History of Jewish Philosophy*, edited by Daniel H. Frank and Oliver Leaman, 331–349. London: Routledge, 1997.
Duhamel-Amado, Claudie. "Les Juifs a Béziers avant 1209: Entre la tolérance et la persécution." In *Les Juifs à Montpellier et dans le Languedoc à travers l'histoire du moyen age à nos jours*, edited by Carol Iancu, 144–156. Montpellier: Centre de recherches et d'études Juives et Hébraïques, 1988.
Duhem, Pierre Maurice Marie. *Medieval Cosmology: Theories of Infinity, Place, Time, Void, and the Plurality of Worlds*. Translated by Roger Ariew. Chicago: University of Chicago Press, 1985.
Dunphy, William. "Maimonides' Not-So-Secret Position on Creation." In *Moses Maimonides and His Time*, edited by Eric L. Ormsby, 151–172. Washington, DC: Catholic University of America Press, 1989.
Einbinder, Susan L. *Beautiful Death: Jewish Poetry and Martyrdom in Medieval France*. Jews, Christians, and Muslims from the Ancient to the Modern World, edited by R. Stephen Humphreys, William Chester Jordan, and Peter Schäfer. Princeton, NJ: Princeton University Press, 2002.
Elazar, Daniel J. "The Kehillah." In *Kinship and Consent: The Jewish Political Tradition and Its Contemporary Uses*, 2nd rev. ed., edited by Daniel J. Elazar, 233–276. New Brunswick, NJ: Transaction, 1997.
Eliade, Mircea. *The Myth of Eternal Return or, Cosmos and History*. Translated by Willard R. Trask. Bollingen Series 46. Princeton, NJ: Princeton University Press, 1965, © 1954.
———. *The Sacred and the Profane: The Nature of Religion*. Translated by Willard R. Trask. San Diego: Harcourt, Brace, 1959.
Elias, Norbert. *The Court Society*. Translated by Edmund Jephcott. New York: Pantheon, 1983.
———. *Time: An Essay*. Translated by Edmund Jephcott. Oxford and Cambridge, MA: Blackwell, 1992.
Elijah, Jacob ben. "Iggeret." In *Jeschurun*, edited by Joseph Kobak, 1–13. 1868.
Elior, Rachel. "Not *All* is in the Hands of Heaven: Eschatology and Kabbalah." In *Eschatology in the Bible and in Jewish and Christian Tradition*, edited by Henning Graf Reventlow, 49–61. Sheffield, UK: Sheffield Academic Press, 1997.
Elman, Yaakov. "'It Was No Empty Thing': Nahmanides and the Search for Omnisignificance." *The Torah U-Madda Journal* 4 (1993): 1–83.
———. "Moses ben Nahman/Nahmanides (Ramban)." In *Hebrew Bible / Old Testament: The History of Its Interpretation*, edited by Magne Sæbo, 416–432. Göttingen: Vandenhoeck & Ruprecht, 2000.
Elukin, Jonathan M. "The Discovery of the Self: Jews and Conversion in the Twelfth Century." In *Jews and Christians in Twelfth-Century Europe*, edited by Michael Signer and John Van Engen, 63–76. Notre Dame, IN: University of Notre Dame Press, 2001.

Escribà i Bonastre, Gemma, and Maria Pilar Frago i Pérez. "Introduction." In *Documents dels Jueus de Girona (1124–1595): Arxiu Històric de la Ciutat, Arxiu Diocesà de Girona*, edited by Gemma Escribà i Bonastre and Maria Pilar Frago i Pérez, 43–51. Girona: Ajuntament de Girona, 1992.

Escribà, Gemma, and Raquel Ibáñez-Sperber. *The Tortosa Disputation: Regesta of Documents from the Archivo de la Corona de Aragón, Fernando I, 1412–1416.* Sources for the History of the Jews in Spain 6. Jerusalem: Ginzei Am Olam, The Central Archives for the History of the Jewish People, Hispania Judaica Dinur Institute, Hebrew University of Jerusalem, 1998.

Even-Chen, Yaacov. *Ha-Ramban. Rabenu Mosheh ben Nahman.* (Hebrew) Jerusalem: Hotsaat Ginzakh Rishonim le-Tziyon, 1976.

Even-Shmuel, Yehuda. *Midrashei Geulah: Perakei ha-Apocalypsah ha-Yehudit mehamimah ha-Talmud ha-Bavil ve-ad Reshit ha-eleph ha-shishi.* Jerusalem and Tel Aviv: Mosad Bialek, 1954.

Fabian, Johannes. *Time and the Other: How Anthropology Makes Its Object.* New York: Columbia University Press, 1983.

Faur, José. "Anti-Maimonidean Demons." *Review of Rabbinic Judaism* 6, no. 1 (2003): 3–52.

———. *Golden Doves with Silver Dots: Semiotics and Textuality in Rabbinic Tradition.* Bloomington: Indiana University Press, 1986.

Feldman, Seymour. "The End of the Universe: A Medieval Debate." In *Creation and the End of Days: Judaism and Scientific Cosmology; Proceedings of the 1984 Meeting of the Academy for Jewish Philosophy*, edited by David Novak and Norbert Samuelson, 215–244. Lanham, MD: University Press of America, 1986.

———. "The End of the Universe in Medieval Jewish Philosophy." *AJS Review* 11, no. 1 (1986): 53–77.

Feliu i Mabres, Eduard, ed. *Disputa de Barcelona de 1263 entre mestre Mossé de Girona i Fra Pau Cristià*. Barcelona: Columna Edicions, 1985.

———. *El Llibre de la Redempció i Altres Escrites de Mossé Ben Nahman de Girona*. Translated by Eduard Feliu i Mabres. Biblioteca Judaico-Catalana 1, edited by Dr. Josep Ribera-Florit. Barcelona: Universitat de Barcelona, 1993.

Fenton, Paul B. "Abraham Maimonides (1187–1237): Founding a Mystical Dynasty." In *Jewish Mystical Leaders and Leadership in the 13th Century*, edited by Moshe Idel and Mortimer Ostow, 127–154. Northvale, NJ: Jason Aronson, 1998.

Fernandez, Emilio Mitre. *La muerte vencida: imágenes e historia en el Occidente medieval (1200–1348)*. Libros de bolsillo 47. Madrid: Encuentro Ediciones, 1988.

Ferre, Lola. "Los regímenes de salud de Maimónides y Arnau de Vilanova en sus versiones Hebreas." In *La ciencia en la España medieval: musulmanes, judíos y cristianos*, edited by Lola Ferre, José Ramon Ayaso, and Maria José Cano,

117–126. Granada: Universidad de Granada, Instituto de Ciencias de la España, 1992.

Finkelstein, Louis. *Jewish Self-Government in the Middle Ages*. New York: Jewish Theological Seminary of America, 1924.

Fisch, Menachem. *Rational Rabbis: Science and Talmudic Culture*. Jewish Literature and Culture, edited by Alvin H. Rosenfeld. Bloomington: Indiana University Press, 1997.

Fishbane, Michael A. *Biblical Interpretation in Ancient Israel*. Oxford: Clarendon Press, 1985.

———. *The Exegetical Imagination: On Jewish Thought and Theology*. Cambridge, MA: Harvard University Press, 1998.

———. *The Garments of Torah: Essays in Biblical Hermeneutics*. Indiana Studies in Biblical Literature. Bloomington: Indiana University Press, 1989.

Fishman, Talya. "The Penitential System of Hasidei Ashkenaz and the Problem of Cultural Boundaries." *The Journal of Jewish Thought and Philosophy* 8, no. 2 (1999): 201–229.

Fleischer, Ezra. "The 'Gerona School' of Hebrew Poetry." In *Rabbi Moses Nahmanides (Ramban): Explorations in His Religious and Literary Virtuosity*, edited by Isadore Twersky, 35–49. Cambridge, MA: Harvard University Press, 1983.

Fletcher, Angus. *Allegory: The Theory of a Symbolic Mode*. Ithaca, NY: Cornell University Press, 1964.

Forman, Frieda Johles, and Caoran Sowton, eds. *Taking Our Time: Feminist Perspectives on Temporality*. The ATHENE Series, edited by Gloria Bowles, Renate Klein, and Janice Raymond. Oxford: Pergamon Press, 1989.

Foucault, Michel. *The Archeology of Knowledge and the Discourse on Language*. Translated by A. M. Sheridan Smith. New York: Pantheon Books, 1972.

Fox, Marvin. *Interpreting Maimonides: Studies in Methodology, Metaphysics, and Moral Philosophy*. Chicago Studies in the History of Judaism, edited by William Scott Green and Calvin Goldscheider. Chicago: University of Chicago Press, 1990.

———. "Nahmanides on the Status of Aggadot: Perspectives on the Disputation at Barcelona, 1263." *Journal of Jewish Studies* 40, no. 1 (1989): 95–109.

Fram, Edward. "Repentant Apostates in Medieval Ashkenaz and Premodern Poland." *AJS Review* 21, no. 2 (1996): 299–339.

Frank, Daniel H. "David Novak, *The Theology of Nahmanides Systematically Presented*." *AJS Review* 20, no. 2 (1995): 417–419.

Frank, Edgar. *Shabbath—The Time of Its Beginning and Termination: A Halachic Investigation*. New York: Philipp Feldheim, 1964.

———. *Talmudic and Rabbinical Chronology: The Systems of Counting Years in Jewish Literature*. New York: Philipp Feldheim, 1956.

Freedman, Paul. *The Origins of Peasant Servitude in Medieval Catalonia*. Cambridge Iberian and Latin American Studies, edited by P. E. Russell. Cambridge: Cambridge University Press, 1991.

Funkenstein, Amos. "Changes in Religious Polemics between Jews and Christians in the Twelfth-Century." (Hebrew) *Tziyon* 33, no. 3–4 (1968): 125–144.
——. "Gershom Scholem: Charisma, *Kairos*, and the Messianic Dialectic." *History and Memory* 4, no. 1 (1992): 123–140.
——. "Nahmanides' Symbolic Reading of History." In *Studies in Jewish Mysticism, Proceedings of Regional Conferences Held at the University of California, Los Angeles and McGill University in April 1978*, edited by Joseph Dan and Frank Talmage, 129–150. Cambridge, MA: Association of Jewish Studies, 1982.
——. "Nahmanides' Typological Reading of History." (Hebrew) *Tziyon* 45, no. 1 (1980): 35–49.
——. *Perceptions of Jewish History*. Berkeley: University of California Press, 1993.
——. *Theology and the Scientific Imagination from the Middle Ages to the Seventeenth Century*. Princeton, NJ: Princeton University Press, 1986.
Gallego, María Angeles. "The Languages of Medieval Iberia and Their Religious Dimension." *Medieval Encounters* 9, no. 1 (2003): 107–139.
Geertz, Clifford. *The Interpretation of Cultures*. New York: Basic Books, 1973.
Geiger, Abraham. *Judaism and Its History*. Translated by Marice Mayer. New York: Thalmessinger, 1865.
Gelles, B. J. *Peshat and Derash in the Exegesis of Rashi*. Leiden: Brill, 1981.
Gellner, Ernest. "Patrons and Clients." In *Patrons and Clients in Mediterranean Society*, edited by Ernest Gellner and John Waterbury, 1–6. London: Duckworth, 1977.
Gellrich, Jesse M. *The Idea of the Book in the Middle Ages: Language Theory, Mythology, and Fiction*. Ithaca, NY: Cornell University Press, 1985.
Gerber, Jane. *The Jews of Spain: A History of the Sephardic Experience*. New York: The Free Press, 1992.
Gines, Juan Vernet. "El mundo cultural en la Corona de Aragón con Jaime I." In *X Congreso de Historia de la Corona de Aragón: Jaume I y su Época*. Zaragoza: Institución 'Fernando el Católico', 1979.
Ginsburg, Elliot K. "The *Havdalah* Ceremony in Zoharic Kabbalah." *Jerusalem Studies in Jewish Thought* 8 (1989): 183–216.
——. "Kabbalistic Rituals of Sabbath Preparation." In *Essential Papers on Kabbalah*, edited by Lawrence Fine, 400–437. New York: New York University, 1995.
——. *The Sabbath in the Classical Kabbalah*. Albany: SUNY Press, 1989.
——. *Sod ha-Shabbat: The Mystery of the Sabbath*. Albany: SUNY Press, 1989.
Ginzburg, Carlo. "Checking the Evidence: The Judge and the Historian." In *Questions of Evidence: Proof, Practice, and Persuasion across the Disciplines*, edited by James Chandler, Arnold I. Davidson, and Harry Harootunian, 290–303. Chicago: University of Chicago Press, 1991.

———. *Clues, Myths, and the Historical Method.* Translated by John and Anne Tedeschi. Baltimore: Johns Hopkins University Press, 1989.

———. *Ecstasies: Deciphering the Witches' Sabbath.* Translated by Raymond Rosenthal. New York: Penguin, 1991.

———. *Myths, Emblems, Clues.* Translated by John and Anne C. Tedeschi. London: Huchinson Radius, 1990.

Giralt, Sebastià. "Entorn de la tradició textual de la *Practica summaria* d'Arnau de Vilanova." *Dynamis* 24 (2004): 269–280.

Girbal, Enrique Claudio. *Los Judíos en Gerona: Colección de noticias históricas referentes a los de esta localidad, hasta la época de su espulsión de los dominios Españoles.* Gerona: Imp. de Gerardo Cumané, 1870.

Given, James B. *Inquisition and Medieval Society: Power, Discipline, and Resistance in Languedoc.* Ithaca, NY: Cornell University Press, 1997.

———. *State and Society in Medieval Europe: Gwynedd and Languedoc under Outside Rule.* The Wilder House Series in Politics, History, and Culture, edited by David Laitin. Ithaca, NY: Cornell University Press, 1990.

Glick, Thomas F. "*Convivencia:* An Introductory Note." In *Convivencia: Jews, Muslims, and Christians in Medieval Spain,* edited by Vivian Mann, Thomas F. Glick, and Jerrilynn D. Dodd, 1–9. New York: George Braziller, 1992.

———. *Islamic and Christian Spain in the Early Middle Ages.* 2nd rev. ed. The Medieval and Early Modern Iberian World 27, edited by Larry J. Simon et al. Leiden: Brill, 2005.

Goitein, Solomon D. *A Mediterranean Society: The Jewish Communities of the Arab World as Portrayed in the Documents of the Cairo Geniza.* 6 vols. Vol. 1. Berkeley: University of California Press, 1967–1988.

Goldberg, Sylvie Anne. *La Clepsydre: Essai sur la pluralité des temps dans le judaïsme.* Idées. Paris: Bibliothèque Albin Michel, 2000.

———. "Questions of Times: Conflicting Time Scales in Historical Perspective." *Jewish History* 14, no. 3 (2000): 267–286.

Goldin, Simha. "'Companies of Disciples' and 'Companies of Colleagues': Communication in Jewish Intellectual Circles." In *Communication in the Jewish Diaspora: The Pre-Modern World,* edited by Sophia Menache, 127–138. Leiden: E. J. Brill, 1996.

———. *Ha-Yihud ve-ha-Yihad: Hidat hashradotan shel ha-kevutzot ha-yehudiyot be-yamei ha-benayim (Uniqueness and Togetherness: The Enigma of the Survival of the Jews in the Middle Ages).* Tel Aviv: Tel Aviv University, 1997.

———. "Juifs et Juifs convertis au moyen age 'Es-tu encore mon frère?'" *Annales: Histoire, Sciences Sociales,* no. 4 (July–August 1999): 851–874.

———. "The Role of Ceremonies in the Socialization Process: The Case of Jewish Communities of Northern France and Germany in the Middle Ages." *Archives de Sciences Sociales des Religions* 95 (July–September 1996): 163–178.

———. "Tafqidei 'ha-herem' ve-ha-taqanot ba-kehillah ha-yehudit ha-Ashkenazit be-yamei ha-beniyim." *International Congress of Jewish Studies* 11, no. 1 (1994): 105–112.

González-Casonvas, Roberto J. *The Apostalic Hero and Community in Ramon Llull's Blanquerna: A Literary Study of a Medieval Utopia*. Catalan Studies: Translations and Criticism 3, edited by Josep M. Solà-Solé. New York: Peter Lang, 1995.

Goodman, Lenn E. "Time, Creation, and the Mirror of Narcissus." *Philosophy East and West* 42, no. 1 (1992): 69–112.

Goodman, Micha. "On the Connection with the Nations of the World in the Thought of Nahmanides." (Hebrew) *Tarbitz* 73, no. 3 (2004): 459–478.

Gotlieb, Ephraim. "Ha-Ramban Ka-Mekubal." In *Research in the Literature of Kabbalah*, edited by Yosef Haker, 88–95. Tel Aviv: Tel Aviv University Press, 1976.

———. "Ha-Yehes she-bein Sefer ha-Amunah ve-ha-Betiahon le-vein Sefer Meshiv Devarim Nekohim." In *Jacob ben Sheshet: Meshiv Devarim Nekohim*, edited by Gedalyahu Vadya, 18–20. Jerusalem: Ha-Akademyah ha-le'umit ha-Yisraelit le-mada'im, 1968.

———. "The Meaning and Sense of 'Interpretations of the Creation' in Early Kabbalah." In *Research in the Literature of Kabbalah,* edited by Yosef Haker, 59–87. Tel Aviv: Tel Aviv University Press, 1976.

———. "Review of *Kitvei Rabbenu Moshe ben Nahman,* ed. Chavel." *Kiriyat Sefer* 40, no. 1 (1965): 1–9.

Gow, Andrew Colin. *The Red Jews: Antisemitism in an Apocalyptic Age, 1200–1600*. Studies in Medieval and Reformation Thought 55, edited by Heiko A. Oberman. Leiden: E. J. Brill, 1995.

Graboïs, Aryeh. "Les écoles de Narbonne au XIIIe siècle." In *Juifs et judaïsme de Languedoc,* edited by Édouard Privat, 141–156. Toulouse: Les Cahiers de Fanjeaux, 1977.

———. "L'exégèse rabbinique." In *Le moyen âge et la Bible,* edited by Pierre Riché and G. Lobrichon, 233–260. Paris: Beauchesne, 1984.

———. "Le Non-conformisme Intellectuel au XIIe Siècle: Pierre Abélard et Abraham Ibn Ezra." In *Modernité et Non-conformisme en France à Travers Les Âges,* edited by Myriam Yardeni, 3–13. Leiden: E. J. Brill, 1983.

———. *Les sources hebraiques medievales*. Typologie des sources du Moyen Age Occidental 50. Turnhout: Brepols, 1987–1993.

———. "The Use of Letters as a Communication Medium among Medieval European Jewish Communities." In *Communication in the Jewish Diaspora: The Pre-Modern World,* edited by Sophia Menache, 93–105. Leiden: E. J. Brill, 1996.

Graetz, Heinrich. "Die Disputation des Bonastruc mit Frai Pablo in Barcelona." *Monatsschrift für Geschichte und Wissenschaft des Judentums* 14 (1865): 428–433.

———. *History of the Jews*. Vol. 3. Philadelphia: Jewish Publication Society of America, 1946.

Grafton, Anthony. *Defenders of the Text: The Traditions of Scholarship in an Age of Science, 1450–1800*. Cambridge, MA: Harvard University Press, 1991.

———. *Forgers and Critics: Creativity and Duplicity in Western Scholarship*. Princeton, NJ: Princeton University Press, 1990.

Grayzel, Solomon. *The Church and the Jews in the XIIIth Century: A Study of Their Relations during the Years 1158–1254*. 2nd rev. ed. New York: Hermon Press, 1966.

———. "The Talmud and the Medieval Papacy." In *Essays in Honor of Solomon B. Freehof*, edited by Frederick C. Schwartz, Walter Jacob, and Vidgor W. Kavaler, 220–245. Pittsburgh: Rodef Shalom Congregation, 1964.

Green, Arthur. "Kabbalistic Re-Vision: A Review Article of Elliot Wolfson's *Through a Speculum that Shines*." *History of Religions* 36, no. 3 (1997): 265–274.

———. "The Zohar: Jewish Mysticism in Medieval Spain." In *Essential Papers on Kabbalah*, edited by Lawrence Fine, 27–66. New York: New York University Press, 1995.

Greenberg, Moshe. "The Relationship between the Commentary of Rashi and Rashbam and the Pentateuch." In *Sefer Yovel Isaac Leo Seeligman*, edited by A. Rofe and Y. Zakovitch, 559–567. Jerusalem: E. Rubinstein, 1983.

Greenia, George. "University Book Production and Courtly Patronage in Thirteenth Century France and Spain." In *Medieval Iberia: Essays on the History and Literature of Medieval Spain*, edited by Donald J. Kagay and Joseph T. Snow, 103–128. New York: Peter Lang, 1997.

Gross, Abraham. "Gerona: A Sephardic Cradle of Jewish Learning and Religiosity." *Materia giudaica* 6, no. 2 (2001): 161–166.

Grossman, Avraham. "Between Spain and France." (Hebrew) In *Galut Ahar Golah [Haim Beinart Festschrift]*, edited by Aaron Mirsky et al., 75–101. Jerusalem: yad Ben Tsevi ve-ha-universitah ha-ivrit bi-yerushalayim, 1988.

———. "Biblical Interpretation in Sepharad from the Thirteenth through the Fifteenth Centuries." (Hebrew) In *Moreshet Sepharad: The Sephardic Legacy*, edited by Ha'im Beinart, 110–117. Jerusalem: Magnes Press, Hebrew University, 1992.

———. "Communication among Jewish Centers during the Tenth to the Twelfth Centuries." In *Communication in the Jewish Diaspora: The Pre-Modern World*, edited by Sophia Menache, 107–125. Leiden: E. J. Brill, 1996.

———. *Hakhmei Ashkenaz ha'Rishonim*. Jerusalem: Judah Magnes Press, Hebrew University, 1981.

———. "The Jewish-Christian Polemic and Jewish Biblical Exegesis in Twelfth-Century France." (Hebrew) *Tziyon* 51, no. 1 (1985): 29–60.

Gruenwald, Ithamar. *Apocalyptic and Merkavah Mysticism*. Institutum Judaicum, Tübingen Arbeiten zur Geschicte des Antiken Judentums und des Urchrstentums 14. Leiden: E. J. Brill, 1980.

———. "Reflections on the Nature and Origins of Jewish Mysticism." In *Gershom Scholem's Major Trends in Jewish Mysticism 50 Years After: Proceedings of the Sixth International Conference on the History of Jewish Mysticism*, edited by Peter Schäfer and Joseph Dan, 25–48. Tübingen: J. C. B. Mohr (Paul Siebeck), 1993.

Guilleré, Christian, ed. *Girona al Segle XIV*. Publicacions de l'Abadia de Montserrat 1 and 2. Girona: Ajuntament de Girona, 1993.

Gutenmacher, Daniel. "The Legal Concept of Political Obligation in Medieval Spanish Jewish Law." *Diné Israel, An Annual of Jewish Law* 15 (1989–90): 63–95.

Gutmann, Julius. *Philosophies of Judaism: The History of Jewish Philosophy from Biblical Times to Franz Rosenzweig*. Translated by David Silverman. New York: Holt, Rinehart, and Winston, 1964.

Gutwein, Daniel. "Traditional and Modern Communications: The Jewish Context." In *Communication in the Jewish Diaspora: The Pre-Modern World*, edited by Sophia Menache, 409–426. Leiden: E. J. Brill, 1996.

Gutwirth, Eleazar. "Gender, History and the Judeo-Christian Polemic." In *Contra Iudaeos: Ancient and Medieval Polemics between Christians and Jews*, edited by Ora Limor and Guy Straumsa, 257–278. Tübingen: J. C. B. Mohr (Paul Seibeck), 1996.

———. "A Song and Dance: Transcultural Practices of Daily Life in Medieval Spain." In *Jews, Muslims, and Christians in and around the Crown of Aragon: Essays in Honor of Elena Lourie*, edited by Harvey J. Hames, 207–227. Leiden: Brill, 2004.

———. "Widows, Artisans, and the *Issues of Life*: Hispano-Jewish Bourgeois Ideology." In *In Iberia and Beyond: Hispanic Jews between Cultures, Proceedings of a Symposium to Mark the 500th Anniversary of the Expulsion of Spanish Jewry*, edited by Bernard Dov Cooperman, 143–173. Newark: University of Delaware Press, 1998.

Habermann, A. M. *Sefer Gezerot Ashkenaz ve-Tzarefat: Divrei zikhronot me-benei ha-dorot she-bi-tekufot mase ha-tzalav ve-mivhar piyuteyhem*. Jerusalem: Totzaat sifrei tarshish, 1945.

Hailperin, Herman. *Rashi and the Christian Scholars*. Pittsburgh: University of Pittsburgh Press, 1963.

Halbertal, Moshe. "The Hidden Torah." (Hebrew) *Kabbalah: Journal for the Study of Jewish Mystical Texts* 7 (2002): 257–280.

———. "The History of Halakhah, Views from Within: Three Medieval Approaches to Tradition and Controversy." Paper presented at the Harvard Law School Gruss Lectures, Harvard University Law School, Cambridge, MA, 1994. http://www.law.harvard.edu/programs/Gruss/halbert.html.

———. "The *Minhag* and the History of Halakhah in the Teaching of Nahmanides." (Hebrew) *Tziyon* 67, no. 1 (2002): 25–56.

———. "Nahmanides' Conception of Death, Sin, and Redemption." (Hebrew) *Tarbitz* 71, no. 1–2 (2001–2002): 133–162.

Halbertal, Moshe, and Avishai Margalit. *Idolatry*. Translated by Naomi Goldblum. Cambridge, MA: Harvard University Press, 1992.

Halivni, David Weiss. *Peshat and Derash: Plain and Applied Meaning in Rabbinic Exegesis*. Oxford: Oxford University Press, 1991.

Halkin, Abraham S., ed. *Igeret Teman le'rabbenu Moshe ben Maimon*. New York: American Academy of Jewish Research, 1952.

Halkin, Abraham S., and David Hartman, eds. *Crisis and Leadership: Epistles of Maimonides*. Philadelphia: Jewish Publication Society, 1985.

Halperin, David. *Faces of the Chariot: Early Jewish Responses to Ezekiel's Vision*. Tübingen: Mohr/Siebeck, 1988.

Hames, Harvey J. *The Art of Conversion: Christianity and Kabbalah in the Thirteenth Century*. The Medieval Mediterranean: Peoples, Economies, and Cultures, 400–1453, edited by Hugh Kennedy. Leiden: Brill, 2000.

———. "From Calabria Cometh the Law, and the Word of the Lord from Sicily: The Holy Land in the Thought of Joachim of Fiore and Abraham Abulafia." *Mediterranean Historical Review* 20, no. 2 (2005): 187–199.

Harvey, L. P. *Islamic Spain 1250 to 1500*. Chicago: University of Chicago Press, 1990.

Hasan-Rokem, Galit. *Web of Life: Folklore and Midrash in Rabbinic Literature*. Translated by Batya Stein. Contraversions: Jews and Other Differences, edited by Daniel Boyarin, Chana Kronfeld, and Naomi Seidman. Stanford, CA: Stanford University Press, 2000.

Hasidah, Y. "Sholosh slihot hadashot le-ha-Ramban." *Sinai* 61, no. 5–6 (1967): 240–248.

Haverkamp, Alfred. "Baptised Jews in German Lands during the Twelfth Century." In *Jews and Christians in Twelfth-Century Europe*, edited by Michael Signer and John Van Engen, 255–310. Notre Dame, IN: University of Notre Dame Press, 2001.

Heinemann, Isaak. *Darkhe ha-agadah*. Mahad. 3. ed. Yerushalayim: Hotsa'at sefarim 'al shem Y. L. Magnes ha-Universitah ha-'Ivrit, 1970.

———. *Ta'ame ha-mitsvot be-sifrut Yisra'el*. Mahad. 3., metukenet be-tosefet mekorot. ed. Yerushalayim: ha-Mador ha-Dati be-Ma'hlakah le-Inyane ha-Noar vehe-Haluts shel Hanhalat ha-Histadrut ha-Tsiyonit, 1953.

Heinemann, Joseph, and Dov Noy. *Studies in Aggadah and Folk-literature*. Scripta Hierosolymitana 22. Jerusalem: Magnes Press, 1971.

Heinemann, Joseph, and Samuel Werses. *Studies in Hebrew Narrative Art throughout the Ages*. Scripta Hierosolymitana 27. Jerusalem: Magnes Press, Hebrew University, 1978.

Henoch, Chayim. *Ramban ke-hoker vke-mekubal: Haguto ha-toranit me-tokh parshanuto le-mitzvot*. Jerusalem: Hotza'at Torah le'am, 1978.

———. *Ramban: Philosopher and Kabbalist, on the Basis of His Exegesis to the Mitzvot*. Northvale, NJ: Aronson, 1998.

Heschel, Susannah. "Jewish Studies as Counterhistory." In *Insider/Outsider: American Jews and Multiculturalism*, edited by David Biale, Michael Galchinsky, and Susannah Heschel, 101–115. Berkeley: University of California Press, 1998.

Hibbs, Thomas S. *Dialectic and Narrative in Aquinas: An Interpretation of the Summa Contra Gentiles*. Revisions, edited by Stanley Hauerwas and Alasdair MacIntyre. Notre Dame, IN: University of Notre Dame Press, 1995.

Higgins, Anne. "Medieval Notions of the Structure of Time." *Journal of Medieval and Renaissance Studies* 19, no. 2 (1989): 227–250.

Hildesheimer, Ezriel, ed. *Sefer Halakhot Gedolot*. 2 vols. Jerusalem, 1971–1980.

Hillgarth, J. N. *The Spanish Kingdoms, 1250–1516*. 2 vols. Vol. 1. Oxford: Clarendon Press, 1976.

Himmelfarb, Lea. "The Exegetical Role of the *Pasaq*." *Sefarad* 58, no. 2 (1998): 243–260.

Hirsch, S. A. "Public Disputations in Spain." In *The Cabbalists and Other Essays*, edited by S. A. Hirsch, 167–198. London: William Heinemann, 1922.

Honah, Hayim. "Sod ha-devekut etzel ha-Ramban." *Sinai* 11, no. 1–3 (1942–43): 86–98.

Horowitz, Elliott. "'And It Was Reversed': Jews and Their Enemies in the Festivities of Purim." (Hebrew) *Tziyon* 59, no. 2–3 (1994): 129–168.

———. "Coffee, Coffee Houses, and the Nocturnal Rituals of Early Modern Jewry." *Association for Jewish Studies Review* 14, no. 1 (1989): 17–46.

———. "The Eve of Circumcision: A Chapter in the History of Jewish Nightlife." *Journal of Social History* 23, no. 1 (1989): 45–70.

———. "The Rite To Be Reckless: On the Perpetration and Interpretation of Purim Violence." *Poetics Today* 15, no. 1 (1994): 9–54.

———. "The Way We Were: Jewish Life in the Middle Ages." *Jewish History* 1, no. 1 (1986): 75–90.

Hughes, Diane Owen, and Thomas R. Trautmann, eds. *Time: Histories and Ethnologies*. The Comparative Studies in Society and History Book Series, edited by Raymond Grew. Ann Arbor: University of Michigan Press, 1995.

Idel, Moshe. "Abraham Abulafia and *Unio Mystica*." In *Studies in Medieval Jewish History and Literature*, edited by Isadore Twersky and Jay M. Harris, 147–178. Cambridge, MA: Harvard University Press, 2000.

———. *Kabbalah: New Perspectives*. New Haven, CT: Yale University Press, 1988.

———. "The Land of Israel in Medieval Kabbalah." In *The Land of Israel: Jewish Perspectives*, edited by Lawrence A. Hoffman, 170–187. Notre Dame, IN: University of Notre Dame Press, 1986.

———. *Messianic Mystics*. New Haven, CT: Yale University Press, 1998.
———. *Messianism and Mysticism*. (Hebrew) Jerusalem: Gali Tsahal, Misrad ha-Bitahon, 1992.
———. "Orienting, Orientalizing, or Disorienting the Study of Kabbalah: 'An Almost Absolutely Unique' Case of Occidentalism." *Kabbalah: Journal for the Study of Jewish Mystical Texts* 2 (1997): 13–47.
———. "Rabbi Moshe ben Nahman: Kabbalah, Halakhah, and Spiritual Leadership." (Hebrew) *Tarbiz* 64, no. 4 (1995): 535–580.
———. "Some Concepts of Time and History in Kabbalah." In *Jewish History and Jewish Memory: Essays in Honor of Yosef Hayim Yerushalmi*, edited by Elisheva Carlebach, John Efron, and David Myers, 153–188. Hanover, NH and London: Brandeis University Press, 1998.
———. "An Unknown Commentary on Ramban's Doctrine of Secrets." *Da'at* 2–3 (1980–1981): 121–126.
———. "The Vicissitudes of Kabbalah in Catalonia." In *The Jews of Spain and the Expulsion of 1492*, edited by Moshe Lazar and Stephem Haliczer, 25–49. Lancaster, CA: Labyrinthos, 1997.
———. "'We Have No Kabbalistic Tradition on This'." In *Rabbi Moses Nahmanides (Ramban): Explorations in His Religious and Literary Virtuosity*, edited by Isadore Twersky, 51–73. Cambridge, MA: Harvard University Press, 1983.
Idel, Moshe, and Mortimer Ostow, eds. *Jewish Mystical Leaders and Leadership in the 13th Century*. Northvale, NJ: Jason Aronson, 1998.
Idel, Moshe, and Mauro Perani. *Nahmanide, esegeta e cabbalista: Studi e testi*. Florence: Giuntina, 1998.
Irsigler, Hurbert. "Speech Acts and Intention in the 'Song of the Vineyard' Isaiah 5:1–7." *Old Testament Essays* 10, no. 1 (1997): 39–68.
Ivry, Alfred L. "Maimonides on Creation." In *Creation and the End of Days: Judaism and Scientific Cosmology; Proceedings of the 1984 Meeting of the Academy for Jewish Philosophy*, edited by David Novak and Norbert Samuelson, 185–213. Lanham, MD: University Press of America, 1986.
James I, King of Aragon. *Libre dels feyts del rey En Jacme*. Translated with an introduction by Martin de Riquer. Barcelona: Universidad del Barcelona, 1972.
Janowitz, Naomi. "Rabbis and Their Opponents: The Construction of the 'Min' in Rabbinic Anecdotes." *Journal of Early Christian Studies* 6, no. 3 (1998): 449–462.
Japhet, Sara, ed. *The Bible in the Light of Its Interpreters: Sarah Kamin Memorial Volume*. Jerusalem: Magnes Press, 1994.
———. "The Tension between Rabbinic Legal Midrash and the 'Plain Meaning' (*Peshat*) of the Biblical Text—An Unresolved Problem? In the Wake of Rashbam's Commentary on the Pentateuch." In *Sefer Moshe: The Moshe Weinfeld Jubilee Volume, Studies in the Bible and the Ancient Near East, Quran,*

and Post-Biblical Judaism, edited by Chaim Cohen, Avi Hurvitz, and Paul M. Shalom, 403–425. Winona Lake, IN: Eisenbraus, 2004.

Japhet, Sara, and R. B. Salters. *The Commentary of R. Samuel Ben Meir (Rashbam) on Qoheleth.* Jerusalem and Leiden, 1985.

Johnston, Mark D. "Ramon Llull and the Compulsory Evangelization of Jews and Muslims." In *Iberia and the Mediterranean World of the Middle Ages: Studies in Honor of Robert I. Burns S.J.,* edited by Larry J. Simon, 3–37. Leiden: E. J. Brill, 1995.

Jordan, William Chester. "Adolescence and Conversion in the Middle Ages: A Research Agenda." In *Jews and Christians in Twelfth-Century Europe,* edited by Michael Signer and John Van Engen, 77–93. Notre Dame, IN: University of Notre Dame Press, 2001.

———. *The French Monarchy and the Jews: From Phillip Augustus to the Last Capetians.* Middle Ages Series, edited by Edward Peters. Philadelphia: University of Pennsylvania Press, 1989.

Jospe, Raphael. "Faith and Reason: The Controversy over Philosophy." In *Great Schisms in Jewish History,* edited by Raphael Jospe and Stanley M. Wagner, 73–117. Denver: University of Denver, Center for Jewish Studies, and Ktav Publishing, 1981.

Kagay, Donald J. "The Line between Memoir and History: James I of Aragon and the *Llibre del Feyts*." *Mediterranean Historical Review* 11 (1996): 165–176.

———. "Royal Power in an Urban Setting: James I and the Towns of Aragon." *Mediaevistik* 8 (1995): 161–170.

———. "Structures of Baronial Dissent and Revolt under Jaime I of Aragon-Catalonia (1213–1276)." *Mediaevistik* 1 (1988): 61–85.

Kamelhar, Moshe, ed. *Perushe rabbi David Kimhi (Radak) al ha-Torah.* Jerusalem: Mosad ha-Rav Kook, 1970.

Kamin, Sarah. "Affinities between Jewish and Christian Exegesis in Twelfth Century Northern France." In *Jews and Christians Interpret the Bible,* edited by Sarah Kamin, 12–26 (English section). Jerusalem: Magnes Press, Hebrew University, 1991.

———. "Rashbam's Conception of the Creation in Light of the Intellectual Currents of His Time." *Scripta Hierosolymitana* 31 (1986): 99–132.

———. *Rashi, His Exegetical Categorization in Respect to Peshat and Derash.* (Hebrew) Jerusalem: Magnes Press, 1986.

Kanarfogel, Ephraim. "Nedrim ve-Nidrei Issur be-Mishnatam shel ha-Rambam ve-ha-Ramban." *ha-Darom* 50 (1990): 79–84.

———. "On the Assessment of R. Moses ben Nahman (Nahmanides) and His Literary Oeuvre." *Jewish Book Annual* 51 (1993–94): 158–172.

———. "Rabbinic Attitudes toward Nonobservance in the Medieval Period." In *Jewish Tradition and the Non-traditional Jew,* edited by J. J. Schacter, 3–35. Northvale, NJ: J. Aronson, 1992.

Katz, Jacob. *Exclusiveness and Tolerance: Studies in Jewish-Gentile Relations in Medieval and Modern Times*. Scripta Judaica 3. Oxford: Oxford University Press, 1961.
Katz, Steven T. "Mysticism and Ethics in Western Mystical Traditions." *Religious Studies* 28, no. 3 (1988): 407–423.
Kedar, Benjamin Z. *Crusade and Mission: European Approaches toward the Muslims*. Princeton, NJ: Princeton University Press, 1988.
Kellner, Menachem. *Dogma in Medieval Jewish Thought from Maimonides to Abravanel*. The Littman Library of Jewish Civilization. Oxford: Oxford University Press, 1986.
———. "Heresy and the Nature of Faith in Medieval Jewish Philosophy." *Jewish Quarterly Review* 77, no. 4 (1987): 299–318.
———. *Maimonides on the "Decline of the Generations" and the Nature of Rabbinic Authority*. SUNY Series in Jewish Philosophy, edited by Kenneth Seeskin. Albany: SUNY Press, 1996.
Kermode, Frank. *The Sense of an Ending: Studies in the Theory of Fiction*. The Mary Flexner Lectures. Oxford: Oxford University Press, 1967.
Kiener, Ronald. "From *Ba'al ha-Zohar* to Prophet to Ecstatic: The Vicissitudes of Abulafia in Contemporary Scholarship." In *Gershom Scholem's Major Trends in Jewish Mysticism 50 Years After: Proceedings of the Sixth International Conference on the History of Jewish Mysticism*, edited by Peter Schäfer and Joseph Dan, 145–159. Tübingen: J. C. B. Mohr (Paul Siebeck), 1993.
Kienzle, Beverly Mayne. *Cistercians, Heresy, and Crusade in Occitania, 1145–1229: Preaching in the Lord's Vineyard*. Rochester, NY: York Medieval Press, 2001.
Kirshenblatt-Gimblett, B. "The Cut That Binds: The Western Ashkenazic Torah Binder as Nexus between Circumcision and Torah." In *Celebration: Studies in Festivity and Ritual*, edited by Victor Turner, 136–146. Washington, DC: Georgetown University Press, 1982.
Klausner, Joseph. *The Messianic Idea in Israel from Its Beginning to the Completion of the Mishnah*. Translated by W. F. Stinespring. New York: Macmillan, 1955.
Klein, Elka. *Jews, Christian Society, and Royal Power in Medieval Barcelona*. History, Language, and Cultures of the Spanish and Portuguese Worlds, edited by Sabine MacCormack. Ann Arbor: University of Michigan Press, 2006.
———. "Power and Patrimony: The Jewish Community of Barcelona, 1050–1250." PhD dissertation, Harvard University, 1996.
———. "Splitting Heirs: Patterns of Inheritance among Barcelona's Jews." *Jewish History* 16, no. 1 (2002): 49–71.
———. "The Widow's Portion: Law, Custom, and Marital Property among Medieval Catalan Jews." *Viator* 31 (2000): 147–163.
Kogman-Appel, Katrin. "Jewish Art and Non-Jewish Culture: The Dynamics of Artistic Borrowing in Medieval Hebrew Manuscript Illumination." *Jewish History* 15, no. 3 (2001): 187–234.

Korpel, Marjo C. A. "The Literary Genre of the Song of the Vineyard (Isa. 5:1–7)." In *The Structural Analysis of Biblical and Canaanite Poetry*, edited by Willem van der Meer and Johannes C. de Moor, 116–155. Sheffield, UK: Sheffield Academic Press, 1988.

Koziol, Geoffrey. *Begging Pardon and Favor: Ritual and Political Order in Early Medieval France*. Ithaca, NY: Cornell University Press, 1992.

Kramer, Joel. "Maimonides on Aristotle and Scientific Method." In *Moses Maimonides and His Time*, edited by Eric L. Ormsby, 53–88. Washington, DC: Catholic University of America Press, 1989.

Krasner, Mariuccia Bevilacqua. "Abraham ben Shmuel Abulafia e Arnaldo de Vilanova: due experienze religiose in Sicilia." In *Ebrei e Sicilia*, edited by Nicolò Bucaria, Michele Luzzati, and Angela Tarantino, 193–200. Palermo: Regione Siciliana Assessorato dei Beni Culturali e Ambientali e della Pubblica Instruzione, 2002.

Krauss, Samuel. *The Jewish-Christian Controversy, from the Earliest Times to 1789*. Translated, edited, and revised by William Horbury. Texte und Studien zum Antiken Judentum 56, edited by Martin Hengel and Peter Schäfer. Tübingen: J. C. B. Mohr (Paul Siebeck), 1995.

Kreisel, Howard. *Prophecy: The History of an Idea in Medieval Jewish Philosophy*. Amsterdam Studies in Jewish Thought 8. Dordrecht: Kluwer Academic Publishers, 2001.

Kristeva, Julia. "Women's Time." In *The Kristeva Reader*, edited by T. Moi. New York: Columbia University Press, 1986.

Kruger, Steven F. "Medieval Christian (Dis)identifications: Muslims and Jews in Guibert of Nogent." *New Literary History* 28, no. 2 (1997): 185–203.

———. *The Spectral Jew: Conversion and Embodiment in Medieval Europe*. Medieval Cultures 40. Minneapolis: University of Minnesota Press. 2006.

Kugel, James L. *The Idea of Biblical Poetry: Parallelism and Its History*. New Haven, CT: Yale University Press, 1981.

———, ed. *Poetry and Prophecy: The Beginnings of a Literary Tradition*. Myth and Poetics. Ithaca, NY: Cornell University Press, 1990.

———. "Poets and Prophets: An Overview." In *Poetry and Prophecy: The Beginning of a Literary Tradition*, edited by James L. Kugel, 1–25. Ithaca, NY: Cornell University Press, 1990.

LaCapra, Dominick. *History and Criticism*. Ithaca, NY: Cornell University Press, 1985.

Ladner, Gerhart B. "Medieval and Modern Understanding of Symbolism: A Comparison." *Speculum* 54, no. 2 (1979): 223–256.

Ladurie, Emmanuel Le Roy. *Montaillou: The Promised Land of Error*. Translated by Barbara Bray. New York: George Braziller, 1978.

Lancaster, Irene. "Abraham Ibn Ezra's Definitions of Creation." In *Abraham Ibn Ezra y su Tiempo*, edited by Fernando Díaz Estaban, 175–180. Madrid: Asociación Española de Orientalistas, 1990.

Landes, David. *Revolution in Time: Clocks and the Making of the Modern World*. Cambridge, MA: Harvard University Press, 1983.
Landes, Richard. "Lest the Millennium Be Fulfilled: Apocalyptic Expectations and the Pattern of Western Chronography 100–800 CE." In *The Use and Abuse of Eschatology in the Middle Ages*, edited by Werner Verbeke et al., 137–211. Leuven: Leuven University Press, 1988.
Langermann, Y. Tzvi. "Acceptance and Devaluation: Nahmanides' Attitude towards Science." *Jewish Thought and Philosophy* 1 (1992): 223–245.
Langmuir, Gavin I. "Doubt in Christendom." In *Toward a Definition of Antisemitism*, 100–133. Berkeley: University of California Press, 1990.
———. "Majority History and Postbiblical Jews." In *Toward a Definition of Antisemitism*, 21–41. Berkeley: University of California Press, 1990.
———. *Toward a Definition of Antisemitism*. Berkeley: University of California Press, 1990.
Lasker, Daniel J. "Popular Polemics and Philosophical Truth in the Medieval Jewish Critiques of Christianity." *The Journal of Jewish Thought and Philosophy* 8, no. 2 (1999): 243–259.
Lawee, Eric. "'Israel Has No Messiah' in Late Medieval Spain." *The Journal of Jewish Thought and Philosophy* 5, no. 2 (1996): 245–279.
Lawrence, C. H. *The Friars: The Impact of the Early Mendicant Movement on Western Society*. The Medieval World, edited by David Bates. London: Longman, 1994.
Le Goff, Jacques. *History and Memory*. European Perspectives, translated by Steven Rendall and Elizabeth Claman. New York: Columbia University Press, 1992.
———. *The Medieval Imagination*. Translated by Arthur Goldhammer. Chicago: University of Chicago Press, 1988.
———. *Time, Work, and Culture in the Middle Ages*. Translated by Arthur Goldhammer. Chicago: University of Chicago Press, 1980.
———. *Your Money or Your Life: Economy and Religion in the Middle Ages*. Translated by Patricia Ranum. New York: Zone Books, 1988.
Leach, Edmund. "Two Essays Concerning the Symbolic Representation of Time." In *Rethinking Anthropology*, edited by Edmund Leach. London: Athlone, 1961.
Leaman, Oliver. *Evil and Suffering in Jewish Philosophy*. Cambridge Studies in Religious Traditions 6, edited by John Clayton et al. Cambridge: Cambridge University Press, 1995.
Lee, Harold. "*Scrutamini Scripturas*: Joachimist Themes and *Figurae* in the Early Religious Writing of Arnold of Vilanova." *Journal of the Warburg and Courtauld Institutes* 37 (1974): 33–56.
Lee, Harold, Marjorie Reeves, and Giulio Silano, eds. *Western Mediterranean Prophecy: The School of Joachim of Fiore and the Fourteenth-Century Breviloquium*. Studies and Texts 88. Toronto: Pontifical Institute of Mediaeval Studies, 1989.

Leff, Gordon. *Paris and Oxford Universities in the Thirteenth and Fourteenth Centuries: An Institutional and Intellectual History*. New Dimensions in History: Essays in Comparative History. New York: Wiley, 1968.

Lehman, James H. "Polemic and Satire in the Poetry of the Maimonidean Controversy." *Prooftexts* 1, no. 2 (1981): 133–151.

Leibowitz, Joshua. "The Book *Torat ha'Adam* of Rabbi Moses ben Nahman (1194–1270)." *Koroth* 8, no. 7–8 (1983): 257–262 (English), 209–212 (Hebrew).

Lemke, Werner E. "Life in the Present and Hope for the Future." *Interpretation* 38, no. 2 (1984): 165–180.

Lerner, Robert E. "Ecstatic Dissent." *Speculum* 67, no. 1 (1992): 33–57.

———. *The Feast of Saint Abraham: Medieval Millenarians and the Jews*. The Middle Ages Series, edited by Ruth Mazo Karras. Philadelphia: University of Pennsylvania Press, 2001.

———. "The Medieval Return to the Thousand Year Sabbath." In *The Apocalypse in the Middle Ages*, edited by Richard K. Emmerson and Bernard McGinn, 51–71. Ithaca, NY: Cornell University Press, 1992.

———. "The Pope and the Doctor." *Yale Review* 78 (1988–89): 62–79.

Leroy, Béatrice. *The Jews of Navarre in the Late Middle Ages*. Translated by Jeffrey Green. Hispania Judaica 4, edited by Haim Beinart. Jerusalem: Magnes Press, Hebrew University, 1985.

———. "Les relations entre les Juifs du Languedoc-Provence et les Juifs navarro-aragonais. Quelques exemples aux XIIIe-XIVe siécles." In *Les Juifs à Montpellier et dans le Languedoc à travers l'histoire du moyen age à nos jours*, edited by Carol Iancu, 167–176. Montpellier: Centre de recherches et d'études Juives et Hébraïques, 1988.

Lesses, Rebecca. *Ritual Practices to Gain Power: Angels, Incantations, and Revelation in Early Jewish Mysticism*. Harvard Theological Studies 44. Harrisburg, PA: Trinity Press, 1998.

Levi, Leo. *Jewish Chrononomy: The Calendar and Times of Day in Jewish Law (together with extensive tables)*. Brooklyn: Gur Aryeh Institute of Advanced Jewish Scholarship, 1967.

Levine, Michelle J. "The Inner World of Biblical Character Explored in Nahmanides' Commentary on Genesis." *Journal of Jewish Studies* 56, no. 2 (2005): 306–334.

———. "Nahmanides' Literary Approach to Biblical Narrative: Varied Repetition in the Joseph Story." *Torah u-Madda Journal* 13 (2005): 88–147.

Levinson, Joshua. "Dialogical Reading in the Rabbinic Exegetical Narrative." *Poetics Today* 25, no. 3 (2004): 497–528.

Lewittes, Mendel. "Vagaries of a Jewish Leap-Year: An Examination of Talmudic and Other Scriptural and Literary Sources Concerning the Fixing of the Jewish Calendar Year and the Observance of Various Holidays and Rituals in Eretz Israel." *Judaism* 42, no. 3 (1993): 344–348.

Libson, Gideon. "Halakhah and Reality in the Gaonic Period: Taqqanah, Minhag, Tradition, and Consensus—Some Observations." In *The Jews of Medieval Islam: Community, Society, and Identity*, edited by Daniel Frank, 67–99. Leiden: E. J. Brill, 1995.

Licht, Y. "Tanakh Parshanut: Ramban." In *Entzyclopidea Mekra'it*, 683–689. Jerusalem: Hotza'at mosad Bialik, 1982.

Lichtenberg, A. L., ed. *Kovetz Teshuvot ha-Rambam ve-Egerotav*. Leipzig, 1859.

Liebes, Yehuda. "Myth vs. Symbol in the Zohar and in Lurianic Kabbalah." In *Essential Papers on Kabbalah*, edited by Lawrence Fine, 212–242. New York: New York University Press, 1995.

Lifshitz, Avraham. "Le-Torat ha-Beri'ah shel Rabbi Moshe ben Nahman." *Sinai* 100 (1987): 525–541.

Lifshitz, Felice. "The Politics of Historiography: The Memory of Bishops in Eleventh-Century Rouen." *History and Memory* 10, no. 2 (1998): 118–137.

Lim, Richard. *Public Disputation: Power and Social Order in Late Antiquity*. The Transformation of Classical Heritage 23, edited by Peter Brown. Berkeley: University of California Press, 1995.

Limor, Ora. "Beyond Barcelona. Review of Robert Chazan, *Barcelona and Beyond: The Disputation of 1263 and Its Aftermath*." *Jewish History* 9, no. 1 (1995): 107–112.

———. *Vikuah Mayorkah, 1286: mahadurah bi-kortit u-mavo, Pirsume ha-Midrashah le-limudim mitkadmim*. Jerusalem: Hebrew University, 1985.

Limor, Ora, and Guy G. Stroumsa, eds. *Contra Iudaeos: Ancient and Medieval Polemics between Christians and Jews*. Texts and Studies in Medieval and Early Modern Judaism 10, edited by Maurice R. Hayoun. Tübingen: J. C. B. Mohr (Paul Siebeck), 1996.

Linehan, Peter. *History and Historians of Medieval Spain*. Oxford: Clarendon Press, 1993.

———. "Religion, Nationalism, and National Identity in Medieval Spain." In *Religion and National Identity*, edited by Stuart Mews. Oxford: Basil Blackwell, 1982.

———. "Review of Robert Chazan, *Barcelona and Beyond: The Disputation of 1263 and Its Aftermath*." *The English Historical Review* 110, no. 438 (1995): 980–981.

Linville, James R. "Rethinking the Nature of Prophetic Literature: Stirring a Neglected Stew (A Response to David Petersen)." In *Prophecy and Prophets: The Diversity of Contemporary Issues in Scholarship*, edited by Yehoshua Gitay, 23–40. Atlanta: Scholars Press, 1997.

Lock, Richard. *Aspects of Time in Medieval Literature*. Garland Publications Comparative Literature. New York: Garland, 1985.

Lockshin, Martin. "Rashbam as a 'Literary' Exegete." In *With Reverence to the Word: Medieval Scriptural Exegesis in Judaism, Christianity, and Islam*, edited by Jane Dammen McAuliffe, Barry Walfish, and Joseph W. Goering, 83–91. Oxford: Oxford University Press, 2003.

Loeb, Isidore. "La Controverse de 1263 à Barcelone entre Paulus Christiani et Moise ben Nahman." *Revue des Études juives* 15 (1887): 1–18.

Loew, R. "The Plain Meaning of Scriptures in Early Jewish Exegesis." *Papers of the Institute for Jewish Studies London* 1 (1964): 140–185.

Lomax, Derek W. *The Reconquest of Spain*. London: Longman, 1978.

Lorberbaum, Menachem. *Politics and the Limits of the Law: Secularizing the Political in Medieval Jewish Thought*. Contraversions: Jews and Other Differences, edited by Daniel Boyarin, Chana Kronfeld, and Naomi Seidman. Stanford, CA: Stanford University Press, 2001.

Lorberbaum, Menachem, Michael Walzer, and Noam J. Zohar, eds. *The Jewish Political Tradition*. Vol. 1. New Haven, CT: Yale University Press, 2000.

Luckmann, Thomas. "The Constitution of Human Line in Time." In *Chronotypes: The Construction of Time*, edited by John Bender and David Wellbery, 151–166. Palo Alto, CA: Stanford University Press, 1991.

Luzzatto, Samuel David. *Vikuah al hokhmat ha-Kabbalah ve-al kadmut sefer ha-Zohar ve-kadmut ha-nekudot ve-hataamim*. Gorice: J. B. Seitz, 1852.

Lynch, Kevin. *What Time Is This Place*. Cambridge, MA: MIT Press, 1993.

Maccoby, Hyam. *Judaism on Trial: Jewish-Christian Disputations in the Middle Ages*. The Littman Library of Jewish Literature. London: Associated University Presses, 1982.

Maccoby, Hyam, and Geoffrey Sax, director. *The Disputation: A Theological Debate between Christians and Jews*. London: BBC, 1986.

MacCormack, Sabine. "History, Memory, and Time in Golden Age Spain." *History and Memory* 4, no. 2 (1992): 38–68.

Madaule, Jacques. *The Albigensian Crusade: An Historical Essay*. Translated by Barbara Wall. London: Burns & Oates, 1967.

Maimonides. *The Guide of the Perplexed*. Translated by Shlomo Pines. 2 vols. Chicago: University of Chicago Press, 1963.

———. *Sefer Moreh ha-Nevuhim*. Translated by Shmuel bar Yehuda ibn Tibbon. Edited by Yehudah ibn Shmuel. Jerusalem: Mosad ha-Rav Kook, 1987.

Makdisi, George. "The Scholastic Method in Medieval Education: An Inquiry into Its Origins in Law and Theology." *Speculum* 49, no. 4 (1974): 640–661.

Marcus, Ivan G. "History, Story, and Collective Memory: Narrativity in Early Ashkinazic Culture." *Prooftexts* 10, no. 3 (1990): 365–388.

———. *Piety and Society: The Jewish Pietists of Medieval Germany*. Leiden: E. J. Brill, 1981.

———. *Rituals of Childhood: Jewish Acculturation in Medieval Europe*. New Haven, CT: Yale University Press, 1996.

Margoliot, Reuven, ed. *Sefer Hasidim*. Jerusalem: Mosad ha-Rav Kook, 1957.

———, ed. *Vikuah ha-Ramban*. Lwów: Lemberg, 1929.

———. *Vikuah rabenu Yehiel me-Paris mebaale ha-tosefot*. Lwów: R. Margulies, 1928.
Martini, Raymundi. *Pugio Fidei adversus Mauros et Judaeous*. Leipzig: Bibliothecae Paulinae Academiae Lipsiensis, 1687.
Matt, Daniel C. "The Mystic and the *Mitzwot*." In *Jewish Spirituality: From the Bible through the Middle Ages*, edited by Arthur Green, 367–404. New York: Crossroad, 1986.
———. "'New-Ancient Words': The Aura of Secrecy in the Zohar." In *Gershom Scholem's Major Trends in Jewish Mysticism 50 Years After: Proceedings of the Sixth International Conference on the History of Jewish Mysticism*, edited by Peter Schäfer and Joseph Dan, 181–207. Tübingen: J. C. B. Mohr (Paul Siebeck), 1993.
———, ed. *The Zohar: Pritzker Edition*. 3 vols. Vol. 1. Stanford, CA: Stanford University Press, 2004–2005.
Mauss, Marcel. *The Gift: The Form and Reason for Exchange in Archaic Societies*. Translated by W. D. Halls. New York: W. W. Norton, 1990.
May, Henry Farnham. *Coming to Terms: A Study in Memory and History*. Berkeley: University of California Press, 1987.
McGinn, Bernard. "The End of the World and the Beginning of Christendom." In *Apocalypse Theory and the Ends of the World*, edited by Malcolm Bull, 58–79. Oxford: Blackwell, 1995.
———. "John's Apocalypse and the Apocalyptic Mentality." In *The Apocalypse in the Middle Ages*, edited by Richard K. Emmerson and Bernard McGinn, 3–19. Ithaca, NY: Cornell University Press, 1992.
———. *Visions of the End: Apocalyptic Traditions in the Middle Ages*. Records of Civilization: Sources and Studies 96, edited by W. T. H. Jackson. New York: Columbia University Press, 1979.
McGrath, Joseph Edward, and Janice R. Kelly. *Time and Human Interaction: Towards a Social Psychology of Time*. New York: Guilford Press, 1986.
McKinney, Ronald. "The Origins of Modern Dialectics." *Journal of the History of Ideas* 44, no. 2 (1983): 179–190.
Melechen, Nina. "Calling Names: The Identification of Jews in Christian Documents from Medieval Toledo." In *On the Social Origins of Medieval Institutions: Essays in Honor of Joseph F. O'Callaghan*, edited by Donald J. Kagay and Theresa M. Vann, 21–34. Leiden: Brill, 1998.
———. "The Jews of Medieval Toledo: Their Economic and Social Contacts with Christians from 1150 to 1391." PhD dissertation, Fordham University, 1999.
———. "Loans, Land, and Jewish-Christian Relations in Archdiocese of Toledo." In *Iberia and the Mediterranean World of the Middle Ages: Studies in Honor of Robert I. Burns*, edited by Larry J. Simon, 185–215. Leiden: E. J. Brill, 1995.
Menache, Sophia. "Communication in the Jewish Diaspora: A Survey." In *Communication in the Jewish Diaspora: The Pre-Modern World*, edited by Sophia Menache, 15–56. Leiden: E. J. Brill, 1996.

———, ed. *Communication in the Jewish Diaspora: The Pre-Modern World*. Brill's Series in Jewish Studies 16, edited by David S. Katz. Leiden: E. J. Brill, 1996.

Menocal, María Rosa. *The Ornament of the World: How Muslims, Jews, and Christians Created a Culture of Tolerance in Medieval Spain*. Boston: Little, Brown, 2002.

Merchavia, H. *Ha-Talmud bi-Rei ha-Natzrut, 500–1248*. Jerusalem: Mosad Bialik, 1970.

Merkur, Dan. "The Visionary Practices of Jewish Apocalyptists." *Psychoanalytic Study of Society* 14 (1989): 119–148.

Meyer, Michael. "The Emergence of Modern Jewish Historiography: Motives and Motifs." *History and Theory* 27, no. 4 (1988): 160–175.

———. "Jewish Religious Reform and Wissenschaft des Judentums: The Positions of Zunz, Geiger, and Frankel." *Leo Baeck Institute Year Book* 16 (1971): 19–41.

Meyerhoff, Hans. *Time in Literature*. Berkeley: University of California Press, 1960.

Meyerson, Mark D. *A Jewish Renaissance in Fifteenth-Century Spain*. Jews, Christians, and Muslims from the Ancient to the Modern World, edited by S. Stephen Humphreys, William Chester Jordan, and Peter Schäfer. Princeton, NJ: Princeton University Press, 2004.

———. *Jews in an Iberian Frontier Kingdom: Society, Economy, and Politics in Morvedre, 1248–1391*. Medieval and Early Modern Iberian World 20. Leiden: Brill, 2004.

———. "Review of Robert Chazan, *Barcelona and Beyond: The Disputation of 1263 and Its Aftermath*." *Speculum* 69, no. 3 (1994): 758–759.

Millás Vallicrosa, José Mariá. "The Beginning of Science among the Jews of Spain." In *Jewish Intellectual History in the Middle Ages*, edited by Joseph Dan, 35–46. Westport, CT and London: Praeger, 1994.

Miller, Elaine R. *Jewish Multiglossia: Hebrew, Arabic, and Castilian in Medieval Spain*. Juan de la Cuesta Hispanic Monographs, edited by Tom Lathrop. Newark, DE: Juan de Cuesta, 2000.

———. "Linguistic Identity in the Middle Ages: The Case of the Spanish Jews." In *Crossing Boundaries: Issues of Cultural and Individual Identity in the Middle Ages and the Renaissance*, edited by Sally McKee, 57–77. Turnhout: Brepols, 1999.

Minnis, A. J. *Medieval Theory of Authorship*. 2nd ed. The Middle Ages Series. Philadelphia: University of Pennsylvania Press, 1988.

Minty, Mary. "*Kiddush ha-Shem* in the Eyes of the Christians of Germany in the Middle Ages." (Hebrew) *Tziyon* 59, no. 2 (1994): 206–266.

Mintz, Alan L. *Hurban: Responses to Catastrophe in Hebrew Literature*. New York: Columbia University Press, 1984.

Mittleman, Alan. *The Scepter Shall Not Depart from Judah: Perspectives on the Persistence of the Political in Judaism*. Religion, Politics, and Society in the New

Millennium, edited by Michael Novak. Lanham, MD: Lexington Books, 2000.
Momigliano, Arnaldo. "Time in Ancient History." In *Essays in Ancient and Modern Historiography*, 179–204. Middletown, CT: Wesleyan University Press, 1987.
Moore, R. I. *The Birth of Popular Heresy*. Documents of Medieval History, edited by G. W. S. Barrow and Edward Miller. New York: St. Martin's Press, 1976.
———. *The Formation of a Persecuting Society: Power and Deviance in Western Europe, 950–1250*. Oxford: Blackwell, 1987.
Moore, Wilbert E. *Man, Time, and Society*. New York: John Wiley, 1963.
Moore-Ede, Martin C., Frank M. Sulzman, and Charles A. Fuller, ed. *The Clocks That Time Us: Physiology of the Circadian Timing System*. Cambridge, MA: Harvard University Press, 1982.
Moorman, John. *A History of the Franciscan Order from Its Origin to the Year 1517*. Oxford: Oxford University Press, 1968.
Mopsik, Charles. *Lettre sur La Sainteté: Le secret de la relation entre l'homme et la femme dans la cabale, Les Dix Paroles*. Lagrasse: Éditions Verdier, 1986.
———. "Pensée, voix, et parole dans le Zohar." *Revue de l'Histoire des Religions* 213, no. 4 (1996): 385–414.
Morell, Samuel. "The Constitutional Limits of Communal Government in Rabbinic Law." *Jewish Social Studies* 33, no. 2–3 (1971): 87–119.
Moreshet, Menahem. "Ha-Ramban ka-balshan al-pei pirusho la-Torah." *Sinai* 50, no. 5–6 (1967): 193–210.
Morgan, M. L. "Overcoming the Remoteness of the Past, Memory and Historiography in Modern Jewish Thought." *Judaism* 38, no. 2 (1989): 160–173.
Morrison, Karl F. *Conversion and Text: The Cases of Augustine of Hippo, Herman-Judah, and Constantine Tsatsos*. Charlottesville: University Press of Virginia, 1992.
———. "The Exercise of Thoughtful Minds: The Apocalypse in Some German Historical Writings." In *The Apocalypse in the Middle Ages*, edited by Richard K. Emmerson and Bernard McGinn, 352–373. Ithaca, NY: Cornell University Press, 1992.
———. *Understanding Conversion, The Page-Barbour Lecture for 1990*. Charlottesville: University of Virginia Press, 1992.
Mossé ben Nahman i el seu temps: simposi commemoratiu del vuitè centenari del seu naixement, 1194–1994. Col·lectió Història de Girona 23. Girona: Ajuntament Girona, 1994.
Myers, David N. *Re-inventing the Jewish Past: European Jewish Intellectuals and the Zionist Return to History*. Studies in Jewish History. New York: Oxford University Press, 1995.
———. "Was There a 'Jerusalem School?' An Inquiry into the First Generation of Historical Researchers at the Hebrew University." *Studies in Contemporary Jewry* 10 (1994): 66–92.

Nahmanides. *La dispute de Barcelone: suivi du Commentaire sur Esaïe 52–53*. Translated by Eric Smilévitch and Luc Ferrier. France: Verdier, 1984.

Nahon, Gérard. "Condition fiscale et économique des Juifs." In *Juifs et judaïsme de Languedoc*, edited by Édouard Privat, 51–84. Toulouse: Les Cahiers de Fanjeaux, 1977.

Nahorai, Michael. "The Land of Israel in the Teaching of the Rambam and the Ramban." (Hebrew) In *The Land of Israel in Medieval Jewish Thought*, edited by Moshe Hallamish and Aviezer Ravitzky, 123–137. Jerusalem: Yad Yitzhak Ben-Tzvi, 1991.

———. "Torat ha-nes ve-ha-teva etzel ha-Ramban ve-zikatah le'rav Yehuda ha-Levi." *Da'at* 17 (Summer 1986): 23–31.

Neher, André. "The View of Time and History in Jewish Culture." In *Cultures and Time*, edited by L. Gardet et al., 149–167. Paris: UNESCO Press, 1976.

Nepaulsingh, Colbert I. *Apples of Gold in Filigrees of Silver*. New Perspectives: Jewish Life and Thought, edited by Berel Lang. New York: Holmes & Meier, 1995.

———. *Towards a History of Literary Composition in Medieval Spain*. University of Toronto Romance Series 54. Toronto: University of Toronto Press, 1986.

Netanyahu, Benzion. *The Marranos of Spain, from the Late 14th to the 16th Century, According to Hebrew Sources*. 3rd ed. Ithaca, NY: Cornell University Press, 1999.

Neubauer, Adolf. *Mediaeval Jewish Chronicles and Chronological Notes, Edited from Printed Books and Manuscripts [Seder ha-hakhamim ve-korot ha-yamim]* 2 vols. Vol. 2. Anecdota Oxoniensia Semitic Series. Oxford: Clarendon Press, 1895.

Neusner, Jacob. *Messiah in Context: Israel's History and Destiny in Formative Judaism*. The Foundations of Judaism: Method, Teleology, Doctrine. Philadelphia: Fortress Press, 1984.

Newman, Aryeh. "The Centrality of Eretz Yisrael in Nachmanides." *Tradition* 10, no. 1 (1968): 21–30.

Newman, Jacob. *The Commentary of Nahmanides on Genesis*. Pretoria Oriental Series 4, edited by A. Van Selms. Leiden: E. J. Brill, 1960.

Niemeyer, Gerlinde, ed. *Hermannus Quondam Judaeus, Opusculam de Conversione Sua*. Monumenta Germaniae Historica: die deutschen Geschichtsquellen des Mittelalters 500–1500. Quellen zur Geistesgeschichte des Mittelalters 4. Weimar: H. Bohlaus Nachfolger, 1963.

Nirenberg, David. *Communities of Violence: Persecution of Minorities in the Middle Ages*. Princeton, NJ: Princeton University Press, 1996.

———. "Conversion, Sex, and Segregation: Jews and Christians in Medieval Spain." *American Historical Review* 107, no. 4 (2002): 1065–1093.

———. "A Female Rabbi in Fourteenth-Century Zaragoza?" *Sefarad* 51, no. 1 (1991): 179–182.

———. "Les juifs, la violence, et le sacré." *Annales: Histoire, Sciences Sociales* 50, no. 1 (1995): 109–131.

Nora, Pierre. "Between Memory and History: *Les Lieux de Mémoire.*" *Representations* 26 (Spring 1989): 7–24.

Norton, Anne. *95 Theses on Politics, Culture, and Method*. New Haven, CT: Yale University Press, 2004.

Novak, David. *Covenantal Rights: A Study in Jewish Political Theory*. New Forum Books, edited by Robert P. George. Princeton, NJ: Princeton University Press, 2000.

———. *The Election of Israel: The Idea of the Chosen People*. Cambridge: Cambridge University Press, 1995.

———. "Nahmanides' Commentary on the Torah." *The Solomon Goldman Lectures* 5 (1990): 87–104.

———. *The Theology of Nahmanides Systematically Presented*. Brown Judaic Studies 271, Studies in Medieval Judaism 2, edited by Shaye J. D. Cohen et al. Atlanta: Scholars Press, 1992.

Novikoff, Alex. "Between Tolerance and Intolerance in Medieval Spain: An Historiographic Enigma." *Medieval Encounters* 11, no. 1–2 (2005): 7–36.

O'Callaghan, Joseph F. *A History of Medieval Spain*. Ithaca, NY: Cornell University Press, 1975.

———. *Reconquest and Crusade in Medieval Spain*. The Middle Ages Series, edited by Ruth Mazo Karras and Edward Peters. Philadelphia: University of Pennsylvania Press, 2003.

O'Leary, Stephen D. *Arguing the Apocalypse: A Theory of Millennial Rhetoric*. Oxford: Oxford University Press, 1994.

O'Neil, W. M. *Time and the Calendars*. Sydney: Sydney University Press, 1975.

Olmos, Elías. "Inventario de los documentos escritos en pergamino del Archivo del la Catedral de Valencia." *Boletin de la Academia de la Historia* 103 (1933): 141–293, 543–616.

Ong, Walter J. "From Allegory to Diagram in the Renaissance Mind: A Study in the Significance of the Allegorical Tableau." *The Journal of Aesthetics and Art Criticism* 17, no. 4 (1959): 423–440.

Orfali, Moisés. "Review of Robert Chazan, *Barcelona and Beyond: The Disputation of 1263 and Its Aftermath.*" *Sefarad* 54, no. 1 (1994): 196–198.

Ormsby, Eric L., ed. *Moses Maimonides and His Time*. Studies in Philosophy and the History of Philosophy 19, edited by Jude P. Dougherty. Washington, DC: Catholic University of America Press, 1989.

Oron, Michael. "Kavvim le-Torat ha-Nefesh ve-ha-Gilgul be-Kabbalah be-Me'ah ha-Yod-Gimmel." In *Mehkrim be-Hagut Yehudit*, edited by Sarah O. Heller-Willensky and Moshe Idel, 277–289. Jerusalem: Hebrew University, Yehuda Magnes Press, 1989.

Osborne, Peter. *The Politics of Time: Modernity and the Avant Garde*. London: Verso, 1995.

Östör, Akos. *Vessels of Time: An Essay on Temporal Change and Social Transformation*. Delhi: Oxford University Press, 1993.
Pagis, Dan. *Ha-shir davur al ofanav: Mehkarim ve-masot ba-shirah ha-Ivrit shel yemei ha-benayim*. Jerusalem: Magnes Press, Hebrew University, 1993.
———. *Hebrew Poetry of the Middle Ages and the Renaissance*. The Taubman Lectures in Jewish Studies. Berkeley: University of California Press, 1991.
———. "Poet as Prophet in Medieval Hebrew." In *Poetry and Prophecy: The Beginning of a Literary Tradition*, edited by James L. Kugel, 140–150. Ithaca, NY: Cornell University Press, 1990.
Pastor, Jordi Pardo. "Anticristo y teología en Arnau de Vilanova: Una interpretacion a raíz de la *Lliço de Narbona*." *La corónica* 32, no. 2 (2004): 85–90.
Patai, Raphael. *The Messiah Texts*. Detroit: Wayne State University Press, 1979.
Pattaro, German. "The Christian Conception of Time." In *Cultures and Time*, edited by Louis Gardet et al. Paris: UNESCO Press, 1976.
Pedaya, Haviva. *Ha-Ramban: Hitalut—Zeman Mahzori ve-Tekst Kadosh*. Aron Sefarim Yehudi. Tel Aviv: Am Oved, 2003.
———. "The Spiritual vs. the Concrete Land of Israel in the Geronese School of Kabbalah." (Hebrew) In *The Land of Israel in Medieval Jewish Thought*, edited by Moshe Hallamish and Aviezer Ravitzky, 233–289. Jerusalem: Yad Izhak Ben-Zvi, 1991.
Pegg, Marc Gregory. *The Corruption of Angels: The Great Inquisition of 1245–1246*. Princeton, NJ: Princeton University Press, 2001.
Perani, Mauro. "Esegesi biblica e storia nel *Sefer ha-ge'ullah*." In *Nahmanide, esegeta e cabbalista: Studi e testi*, edited by Moshe Idel and Mauro Perani, 97–106. Florence: Giuntina, 1998.
———. "Mistica e filosofia: la mediazione di Nahmanide nella polemica sugli scritti di Maimonide." In *Nahmanide, esegeta e cabbalista: Studi e testi*, edited by Moshe Idel and Mauro Perani, 107–127. Florence: Giuntina, 1998.
———. "Senso letterale e senso Cabalistico nel commento di Mosheh b. Nahman al 'episodio del vitello d'oro." *Henoch* 8, no. 1 (1986): 39–46.
———. "Storia e prefigurazione tipologica nell'esegesi biblica." In *Nahmanide, esegeta e cabbalista: Studi e testi*, edited by Moshe Idel and Mauro Perani, 87–95. Florence: Giuntina, 1998.
Perarnau i Espelt, Josep. "Arnau de Vilanova, Polemista antijueu a Lleida el 1303?" *Revista catalana de teologia* 19 (1994): 109–118.
———. "El text primitiu del *De mysterio cymbalorum ecclesiae* d'Arnau de Vilanova." *Arxiu de textos catalans antics* 7–8 (1988–89): 7–169.
Perez-Bustamante. "El Gobierno y la Adminstracion de los territorios de la Corona de Aragon bajo Jaime I el Conquistador y su comparacion con el regimen de Castilla y Navarra." *1 y 2 Congreso de Historia de la Corona d'Aragon* X (1979): 515–536.

Perles, Joseph. "Nachträge über R. Moses ben Nachman." *Monatsschrift für Geschichte und Wissenschaft des Judentums* 9 (1860): 184-195.
Peters, Edward. *Inquisition*. 2nd ed. Berkeley: University of California Press, 1989.
Pines, Shlomo. "Nahmanides on Adam in the Garden of Eden in the Context of Other Interpretations of Genesis, 2 and 3." (Hebrew) In *Galut ahar golah: Mehkarim be-toldot Am Yisrael mugashim le-Professor Hayim Bainart li-melot lo shivin shanah*, edited by Avraham Grossman, Aharon Mirsky, and Yosef Kaplan, 159-164. Jerusalem: Yad Ben Zvi and Hebrew University of Jerusalem, 1988.
Piterberg, Gabriel. "Domestic Orientalism: The Representation of 'Oriental' Jews in Zionist/Israeli Historiography." *British Journal of Middle Eastern Studies* 23, no. 2 (1996): 125-145.
Plato. "Timaeus." In *Timaeus and Critias*. Translated by Desmond Lee. London: Penguin Books, 1977.
Polak, Joseph A. "Interpreting Catastrophe: Insights from the Halakhic Literature on the Prague Fire of 1689." In *Celebrating Elie Wiesel: Stories, Essays, Reflections*, edited by Alan Rosen, 93-111. Notre Dame, IN: University of Notre Dame Press, 1998.
Poole, Reginald L. "The Beginning of the Year in the Middle Ages." In *Studies in Chronology and History*, edited by Austin Lane Poole, 1-27. Oxford: Clarendon Press, 1934.
——. "The Earliest Use of the Easter Cycle of Dionysius." In *Studies in Chronology and History*, edited by Austin Lane Poole, 28-37. Oxford: Clarendon Press, 1934.
Potok, Rene N. "Borders, Exiles, Minor Literatures: The Case of Palestinian-Israeli Writing." In *Borders, Exiles, Diasporas*, edited by Elazar Barkan and Marie-Denise Shelton, 291-310. Stanford, CA: Stanford University Press, 1998.
Prawer, Joshua. *The History of the Jews in the Latin Kingdom of Jerusalem*. 2nd ed. Oxford: Clarendon Press, 1996.
Privat, Édouard, ed. *Juifs et judaïsme de Languedoc*. Collection d'Histoire religieuse du Languedoc au XIIIe et au début du XIV e siécles 12. Toulouse: Les Cahiers de Fanjeaux, 1977.
Pryor, John H. *Geography, Technology, and War: Studies in the Maritime History of the Mediterranean 649-1571*. Cambridge: Cambridge University Press, 1988.
Rabinowitz, P. "Wreckage upon Wreckage: History, Documentary, and the Ruins of Memory." *History and Theory* 32, no. 2 (1993): 119-137.
Rambam. *The Book of Seasons*. Translated by Solomon Gandz and Hyman Klein. New Haven, CT: Yale University Press, 1961.
Rapaport-Hartstein, Meir Eliezer. *Toldot ha-Ramban: Kol korot haye rabbenu Moshe ben Nahman, zal, ve-korot sifrav ha-yekarim*. Cracow: Verlag des Verfassers, 1898.

Rappaport, Roy A. "Ritual, Time, and Eternity." *Zygon* 27, no. 1 (1992): 5–30.
Rashdall, Hastings. *The Universities of Europe in the Middle Ages*. Vol. 1. Oxford: Oxford University Press, 1936.
Ravitzky, Aviezer. *Messianism, Zionism, and Jewish Religious Radicalism*. Chicago Studies in the History of Judaism, edited by William Scott Green. Chicago: University of Chicago Press, 1991.
Ray, Jonathan. "Beyond Tolerance and Persecution: Reassessing Our Approach to Medieval *Convivencia*." *Jewish Social Studies* 11, no. 2 (2005): 1–18.
———. *The Sephardic Frontier: The Reconquista and the Jewish Community of Medieval Iberia*. Conjunctions in Religion and Power in the Medieval Past, edited by Barbara Rosenwein. Ithaca, NY: Cornell University Press, 2006.
Reeves, Marjorie. "The Abbot Joachim's Disciples and the Cistercian Order." *Sophia* 19 (1951): 355–371.
———. *The Influence of Prophecy in the Later Middle Ages: A Study in Joachimism*. Oxford: Clarendon Press, 1969.
———. "Pattern and Purpose in History in the Later Medieval and Renaissance Periods." In *Apocalypse Theory and the Ends of the World*, edited by Malcolm Bull, 90–111. Oxford: Blackwell, 1995.
Reeves, Marjorie, and Morton W. Bloomfield. "The Penetration of Joachism into Northern Europe." *Speculum* 29, no. 4 (1954): 772–793.
Reeves, Marjorie, and B. Hirsch-Reich. "The *Figurae of Joachim of Fiore*: Genuine and Spurious Collections." *Mediaeval and Renaissance Studies* 3 (1954): 170–199.
———. "The Seven Seals in the Writings of Joachim of Fiore." *Recherches de Théologie Ancienne et Médiévale* 21 (1954): 211–247.
Régné, Jean. *History of the Jews in Aragon: Regesta and Documents, 1213–1327*. Edited by Yom Tov Assis and Adam Gruzman. Hispania Judaica 1. Jerusalem: Magnes Press, Hebrew University, 1978.
Reiche, Harald A. T. "The Archaic Heritage: Myths of Decline and End in Antiquity." In *Visions of Apocalypse: End or Rebirth*, edited by Saul Friedländer, 21–43. New York: Holmes & Meier, 1985.
Ribémont, Bernard, ed. *Le Temps, sa mesure et sa perception au Moyen Age, Actes du colloque Orléans 12–13 avril, 1991*. Caen: Paradigme, 1992.
Ribera Florit, Josep. "La Comunidad Judia de Provenza en el S.XII y Abraham Ibn Ezra." In *Abraham Ibn Ezra y su Tiempo*, edited by Fernando Diáz Estaban, 251–257. Madrid: Asociación Española de Orientalistas, 1990.
Richler, Benjamin. "Manuscripts of Moses ben Nahman's *Torat ha'Adam*." *Koroth* 8, no. 7–8 (1983): 265–267 (English), 217–218 (Hebrew).
Ricoeur, Paul. "The History of Religion and the Phenomenology of Time Consciousness." In *The History of Religions, Retrospect and Prospect*, edited by Joseph M. Kitagawa, 13–30. New York: Macmillan, 1985–1988.

———. *Time and Narrative.* Translated by Kathleen McLaughlin and David Pellauer. 3 vols. Chicago: University of Chicago Press, 1984.
Riera i Sans, Jaume. "Les Fontes Històriques de la Disputa de Barcelona." In *Disputa de Barcelona de 1263 entre mestre Mossé de Girona i Fra Pau Cristià*, edited by Eduard Feliu, ix–xv. Barcelona: Columna Edicions, 1985.
Rioux, J. P. "Entering the Era of the Lieux-de-Memoire: History, Anniversaries, and Memory." *Histoire* 165 (April 1993): 80–82.
Ripoll, Thomas, ed. *Bullarium Ordinis Fratrum Praedicatorum*. 8 vols. Vol. 1. Rome: Typographia Hieronymi Mainardi, 1729.
Riquer, Martí de. *Història de la Literatura Catalana: Part Antiga*. 4 vols. Vol. 1. Barcelona: Editorial Ariel, S.A., 1964.
Robbins, Ellen. "Time-Telling in Ritual and Myth." *The Journal of Jewish Thought and Philosophy* 6 (1997): 71–88.
Rojtman, Betty. *Black Fire on White Fire: An Essay on Jewish Hermeneutics from Midrash to Kabbalah*. Translated by Steven Rendall. Contraversions: Critical Studies in Jewish Literature, Culture, and Society 10, edited by Daniel Boyarin and Chana Kronfeld. Berkeley: University of California Press, 1998.
———. "Sacred Language and Open Text." In *Midrash and Literature*, edited by Geoffrey H. Hartman and Sanford Budick, 159–175. New Haven and London: Yale University Press, 1986.
Roos, Lena. "Paul Christian—A Jewish Dominican Preaching for the Jews." *Studia Theologica* 57, no. 1 (2003): 49–60.
Rosenberg, Shalom. "Hashivah le-gan edan: ha-erot la-toldot ra'ayon ha-geulah ha-restorativit ba-philosophiyah be-yamai ha-benayim." In *Ha-ra'ayon ha-mishihi b-Yisra'el: yom eyon leragel mele'et sh'monim shanah le'Gershom Sholem*, 37–86. Jerusalem: ha-Akademiyah ha-leumit ha-Yisra'elit le'me'adim, 1982.
Rosenberg, Yehuda Yodel, ed. *Sefer Zohar Torah*. Vol. 1. Jerusalem: Ha-Dorah Hadasha, 1966.
Rosenblüth, Pinchas. "Yitzchak Baer: A Reappraisal of Jewish History." *Leo Baeck Institute Yearbook* 22 (1977): 175–188.
Rosenthal, E. I. J. "Anti-Christian Polemic in Medieval Bible Commentaries." *The Journal of Jewish Studies* 11, no. 3–4 (1960): 115–135.
Rosenthal, Judah M. "Bekoret Yehudit shel ha-brit he-hadashah min ha-meah ha-yod-gimmel." In *Studies in Jewish Bibliography: History and Literature in Honor of I. Edward Kiev*, edited by Charles Berlin, 123–139. New York: Ktav, 1971
———. "Ha-Vikuah ha-anti-maimoni be-Espeklaria she ha-dorot." In *Mehkarim ve-Makorot*, 126–202. Jerusalem: Rueven Mass, 1967.
———, ed. *Sefer Yosef ha-Mekane*. Jerusalem: Mekitse Nidarim, 1970.
———. "The Talmud on Trial." *Jewish Quarterly Review* n.s. 47 (1956): 58–76, 145–169.

Rosenwein, Barbara H. *Rhinoceros Bound: Cluny in the Tenth Century*. The Middle Ages Series. Philadelphia: University of Pennsylvania Press, 1982.

Roskies, David G. *Against the Apocalypse: Responses to Catastrophe in Modern Jewish Culture*. Cambridge, MA: Harvard University Press, 1984.

Roth, Cecil. "The Disputation at Barcelona (1263)." *Harvard Theological Review* 43, no. 2 (1950): 117–144.

———. "The Medieaval Conception of the Jew: A New Interpretation." In *Essays and Studies in Memory of Linda R. Miller*, edited by Israel Davidson, 171–190. New York: Jewish Theological Seminary of America, 1938.

Roth, Norman. "The Civic Status of the Jew in Medieval Spain." In *Iberia and the Mediterranean World of the Middle Ages: Essays in Honor of Robert I. Burns S.J.*, vol. 2, edited by P. E. Chevedden, D. J. Kagay, and P. G. Padilla, 139–161. Leiden: E. J. Brill, 1996.

———. "The Jews in Spain at the Time of Maimonides." In *Moses Maimonides and His Time*, edited by Eric L. Ormsby, 1–20. Washington, DC: Catholic University of America Press, 1989.

———, ed. *Medieval Jewish Civilization: An Encyclopedia*. Routledge Encyclopedias of the Middle Ages 7. New York: Routledge, 2003.

Rowland, Christopher. *The Open Heaven: A Study of Apocalyptic in Judaism and Early Christianity*. New York: Crossroad, 1982.

———. "'Upon Whom the End of the Ages Have Come': Apocalyptic and the Interpretation of the New Testament." In *Apocalypse Theory and the End of the World*, edited by Malcolm Bull, 38–57. Oxford: Blackwell, 1995.

Rubenstein, Jeffrey L. "Mythic Time and the Festival Cycle." *The Journal of Jewish Thought and Philosophy* 6, no. 1 (1997): 157–183.

Rudavsky, Tamar M. *Time Matters: Time, Creation, and Cosmology in Medieval Jewish Philosophy*. Albany: SUNY Press, 2000.

Russell, J. L. "Time in Christian Thought." In *The Voices of Time: A Cooperative Survey of Man's Views of Time as Expressed by the Sciences and by the Humanities*, edited by J. T. Fraser, 59–76. Amherst: University of Massachusetts Press, 1981.

Russell, Jeffrey Burton. *The Devil: Perceptions of Evil from Antiquity to Primitive Christianity*. Ithaca, NY: Cornell University Press, 1977.

———. *Dissent and Order in the Middle Ages: The Search for Legitimate Authority*. Twayne's Studies in Intellectual and Cultural History, edited by Michael Roth. New York: Twayne, 1992.

Safran, Bezalel. "Rabbi Azriel and Nahmanides' Two Views of the Fall of Man." In *Rabbi Moses Nahmanides (Ramban): Explorations in His Religious and Literary Virtuosity*, edited by Isadore Twersky, 75–106. Cambridge, MA: Harvard University Press, 1983.

Sagiv-Feldman, Yael. "Living in Deferment: Maimonides vs. Nahmanides on the Messiah, Redemption, and the World to Come." *Hebrew Studies* 20–21 (1979–80): 107–116.

Said, Edward W. *Beginnings: Intentions and Method.* New York: Columbia University Press, 1985.
———. "Reflections on Exile." *Granta* 13, no. 1 (1984): 159–172.
Sala-Molins, Louis. "Le 'Libre del gentil e los tres savis': Le dialogue au temps du Mépris." In *Juifs et source juive en Occitanie,* 41–52. Enèrgas: Vent Terral, 1988.
Saltman, Avraham. "Hermann's *Opusculum de Conversione sua:* Truth and Fiction." *Revue des Études juives* 147, no. 1–2 (1988): 31–56.
Salzman, Marcus. *The Chronicle of Ahimaaz.* Columbia University Oriental Studies 18. New York: Columbia University Press, 1924.
Salzman, Michell Renee. *On Roman Time: The Codex-Calendar of 354 and the Rhythms of Urban Life in Late Antiquity.* Berkeley: University of California Press, 1990.
Samuelson, Norbert M. *Judaism and the Doctrine of Creation.* Cambridge: Cambridge University Press, 1994.
Santonja, Pedro. "La influencia del pensamiento judío en la obra de Arnau de Vilanova, médico y escritor espiritual." *Helmantica* 157 (2001): 101–129.
Saperstein, Marc. "The Conflict over the Rashba's Herem on Philosophical Study: A Political Perspective." *Jewish History* 1, no. 2 (1986): 27–38.
———. *Decoding the Rabbis: A Thirteenth-Century Commentary on the Aggadah.* Harvard Judaic Monographs 3. Cambridge, MA: Harvard University Press, 1980.
———. "Introduction." In *Essential Papers on Messianic Movements and Personalities in Jewish History,* edited by Marc Saperstein, 1–31. New York: New York University Press, 1992.
———. "Jewish Typological Exegesis after Nahmanides." *Jewish Studies Quarterly* 1, no. 1 (1993–94): 158–170.
———. "Review of Robert Chazan, *Barcelona and Beyond: The Disputation of 1263 and Its Aftermath*." *The Journal of Religion* 74, no. 1 (1994): 121–123.
Sarachek, Joseph. *The Doctrine of the Messiah in Medieval Jewish Literature.* 2nd ed. New York: Hermon Press, 1968.
———. *Faith and Reason: The Conflict over the Rationalism of Maimonides.* New York: Hermon Press, 1935.
Sarna, Nahum M. *Studies in Biblical Interpretation.* JPS Scholar of Distinction Series. Philadelphia: Jewish Publication Society, 2000.
Schäfer, Peter. *The Hidden and Manifest God: Some Major Trends in Early Jewish Mysticism.* Albany: SUNY Press, 1992.
Schechter, Solomon. "Nachmanides." In *Studies in Judaism.* Philadelphia: Jewish Publication Society, 1938.
———. "Nachmanides." *The Jewish Quarterly Review,* o.s. 5 (1893): 78–121.
Schniedewind, William M. *The Word of God in Transition: From Prophet to Exegete in the Second Temple Period.* Journal for the Study of the Old Testament,

Supplement Series 197, edited by David J. A. Clines, Sheffield, UK: Sheffield Academic Press, 1995.

Scholem, Gershom. "Chapters in the History of Literature of the Kabbalah." *Keriyat Sefer* 6, no. 3 (1929): 385–419.

———. *Major Trends in Jewish Mysticism*. New York: Schocken Books, 1961.

———. *The Messianic Idea in Judaism*. New York: Schocken, 1971.

———. *On the Kabbalah and Its Symbolism*. Translated by Ralph Manheim. New York: Schocken Books, 1996.

———. *Origins of the Kabbalah*. Translated by Allan Arkush. Edited by R. J. Zwi Werblowsky. Princeton, NJ: Jewish Publication Society and Princeton University Press, 1987.

Schorsch, Ismar. "The Emergence of Historical Consciousness in Modern Judaism." *Leo Baeck Institute Year Book* 28 (1983): 413–437.

———. "History as Consolation." *Leo Baeck Institute Year Book* 37 (1992): 33–43.

———. "The Myth of Sephardi Supremacy." *Leo Baeck Institute Year Book* 34 (1989): 47–66.

Schwartz, Dov. "Changing Fronts in the Controversies over Philosophy in Medieval Spain and Provence." *The Journal of Jewish Thought and Philosophy* 7, no. 1 (1997): 61–82.

———. *Ha-raayon ha-meshihi be-hagut ha-yehudit be-yameh ha-benayim*. Ramat-Gan: Bar Ilan University, 1997.

Schwarzfuchs, Simon. "La communauté juive de Montpellier au XIIIe et au début du XIVe siècle dans les sources hébraïques." In *Les juifs à Montpellier et dans Languedoc à travers l'histoire du moyen age à nos jours*, edited by Carol Iancu, 99–112. Montpellier: Centre de recherches et d'études Juives et Hébraïques, 1988.

———. "Religion populaire et polémique savante: Le tourant de la polémique Judéo-Chrétienne au 12ᵉ siècle." In *Medieval Studies in Honour of Avrom Saltman*, edited by Bat Sheva Albert, Yvonne Friedman, and Simon Schwarzfuchs, 189–207. Ramat Gan: Bar-Ilan University Press, 1995.

Schweid, Eliezer. *The Jewish Experience of Time: Philosophical Dimensions of the Jewish Holy Days*. Translated by Amnon Hadary. Northdale, NJ: Jason Aronson, 2000.

Scott, James C. *Domination and the Arts of Resistance: Hidden Transcripts*. New Haven, CT: Yale University Press, 1990.

Septimus, Bernard. *Hispano-Jewish Culture in Transition: The Career and Controversies of Ramah*. Harvard Judaic Monographs 4, edited by Isadore Twersky. Cambridge, MA: Harvard University Press, 1982.

———. "Kings, Coinage, and Constitutionalism: Notes on a *Responsum* of Nahmanides." *The Jewish Law Annual* 14 (2003): 295–313.

———. "'Open Rebuke and Concealed Love': Nahmanides and the Andalusian Tradition." In *Rabbi Moses Nahmanides (Ramban): Explorations in His Reli-*

gious and Literary Virtuosity, edited by Isadore Twersky, 11–34. Cambridge, MA: Harvard University Press, 1983.

———. "Piety and Power in Thirteenth-Century Catalonia." In *Studies in Medieval Jewish History and Literature,* edited by Isadore Twersky, 197–230. Cambridge, MA: Harvard University Press, 1979.

———. "A Struggle for Leadership of the Community in Barcelona during the Controversy over the Books of Maimonides." (Hebrew) *Tarbitz* 42 (1973): 389–400.

Shahar, Shulamith. *Childhood in the Middle Ages.* London: Routledge, 1990.

———. "Écrits Cathares et commentaires d'Abraham Abulafia sur le 'Livre de la création': images et idées communes." In *Juifs et judaïsme de Languedoc,* edited by Édouard Privat, 345–362. Toulouse: Les Cahiers de Fanjeaux, 1977.

Shatzmiller, Joseph. "Converts and Judaizers in the Early Fourteenth Century." *Harvard Theological Review* 74, no. 1 (1981): 63–77.

———. "Encore la *Tallia Jueorum.*" In *Rashi: 1040–1990, Hommage à Ephraïm E. Urbach,* edited by Gabrielle Sed-Rajna, 589–597. Paris: Les Éditions du Cerf, 1993.

———. "Jewish Converts to Christianity in Medieval Europe, 1200–1500." In *Cross Cultural Convergences in the Crusader Period: Essays Presented to Aryeh Grabois on His Sixty-Fifth Birthday,* edited by Michael Goodich, Sophia Menache, and Sylvia Schein, 295–318. New York: Peter Lang, 1995.

———. "Towards a Picture of the First Controversy over Maimonides' Writings." (Hebrew) *Tziyon* 34, no. 3–4 (1969): 126–144.

Shideler, John C. *A Medieval Catalan Noble Family: The Montcadas, 1000–1230.* Publications of the UCLA Center for Medieval and Renaissance Studies 20. Berkeley: University of California Press, 1983.

Shilo, Shmuel. *Dina de-malkhuta Dina.* Jerusalem: Hotsaat Defus Akademi bi-Yerushelayim, 1975.

Shneidman, J. Lee. "Protection of Aragon Jewry in the Thirteenth Century." *Revue des Études juives* 121 (1962): 48–59.

———. *The Rise of the Aragonese-Catalan Empire, 1200–1350.* 2 vols. New York: New York University Press, 1970.

Shohat, Azariel. "Concerning the First Controversy over the Writings of Maimonides." (Hebrew) *Tziyon* 36, no. 1–2 (1971): 25–60.

Shohet, David. *The Jewish Court in the Middle Ages: Studies in Jewish Jurisprudence According to the Talmud, Geonic and Medieval German Responsa.* New York: Commanday-Roth, 1931.

Shrock, Abe Tobie. *Rabbi Jonah ben Abraham of Gerona: His Life and Ethical Works.* London: Edward Goldstein, 1948.

Shulman, Yaacov Dovid. *The Ramban: The Story of Rabbi Moshe ben Nahman.* New York: CIS, 1993.

Sigal, Pierre-André. "L'église et les juifs en bas-Languedoc aux XIIIe et XIVe siecles d'apres les statuts synadaux." In *Les Juifs à Montpellier et dans le Languedoc à travers l'histoire du moyen age à nos jours*, edited by Carol Iancu, 128–143. Montpellier: Centre de recherches et d'études Juives et Hébraïques, 1988.

Signer, Michael A. "The Land of Israel in Medieval Jewish Exegetical and Polemical Literature." In *The Land of Israel: Jewish Perspectives*, edited by Lawrence A. Hoffman, 200–233. Notre Dame, IN: University of Notre Dame Press, 1986.

———. "*Peshat, Sensus Litteralis*, and Sequential Narrative: Jewish Exegesis and the School of St. Victor in the Twelfth Century." In *The Frank Talmage Memorial Volume*, edited by Barry Walfish, 203–216. Haifa: University of Haifa Press, 1993.

———. "Restoring the Narrative: Jewish and Christian Exegesis in the Twelfth Century." In *With Reverence for the Word: Medieval Scriptural Exegesis in Judaism, Christianity, and Islam*, edited by Jane Dammen McAuliffe, Barry Walfish, and Joseph W. Goering, 70–82. Oxford: Oxford University Press, 2003.

Signer, Michael, and John Van Engen, eds. *Jews and Christians in Twelfth-Century Europe*. Notre Dame Conferences in Medieval Studies 10. Notre Dame, IN: University of Notre Dame Press, 2001.

Silver, Abba Hillel. *A History of Messianic Speculation in Israel from the First through the Seventeenth Centuries*. New York: Macmillan, 1927.

Silver, Daniel Jeremy. *Maimonidean Criticism and the Maimonidean Controversy, 1180–1240*. Leiden: E. J. Brill, 1965.

———. "Who Denounced the *Moreh*?" In *The Seventy-Fifth Anniversary Volume of The Jewish Quarterly Review*, edited by Abraham A. Neuman and Solomon Zeitlan, 498–514. Philadephia: Jewish Publication Society, 1967.

Simon, Larry J. "Intimate Enemies: Mendicant-Jewish Interaction in Thirteenth-Century Mediterranean Spain." In *Friars and Jews in the Middle Ages and Renaissance*, edited by Steven J. McMichael and Susan E. Myers, 53–80. Leiden: Brill, 2004.

Simon, Marcel. *Verus Israel: étude sur les relations entre chrétiens et juifs dans l'empire romain (135–425)*. 2nd ed. Paris: E. de Boccard, 1964.

Simon, Uriel. "The Exegetical Method of Abraham ibn Ezra as Revealed in Three Interpretations of a Biblical Passage." *Bar Ilan* 3 (1965): 92–138.

Simonson, Solomon. "The Idea of Interpretation in Hebrew Thought." *Journal of the History of Ideas* 8, no. 4 (1947): 467–474.

Skarsaune, Oskar. *The Proof from Prophecy: A Study in Justin Martyr's Proof-text Tradition, Text-Type, Provenance, Theological Profile*. Supplements to Novum Testamentum 56. Leiden: E. J. Brill, 1987.

Smalley, Beryl. *The Study of the Bible in the Middle Ages*. Notre Dame, IN: University of Notre Dame Press, 1964.

Smith, Damien, and Helena Buffery, eds. *The Book of Deeds of James I of Aragon: A Translation of the Medieval Catalan Llibre dels Fets*. Crusades Texts in Translation 10. Aldershot: Ashgate, 2003.
Smith, Jonathan Z. "A Slip in Time Saves Nine: Prestigious Origins Again." In *Chronotypes: The Construction of Time*, edited by John Bender and David Wellbery, 67–76. Palo Alto, CA: Stanford University Press, 1991.
Smith, P. Christopher. *The Hermeneutics of Original Argument: Demonstration, Dialectic, Rhetoric*. Northwestern University Studies in Phenomenology and Existential Philosophy, edited by John McCumber and David Michael Levin. Evanston, IL: Northwestern University Press, 1998.
Soldevila, Ferran, ed. *Jaume I, Crònica o Llibre dels Feits*. Les millors obres de la literatura Catalana 86, edited by Joaquim Molas and Carme Arnau. Barcelona: Edicions 62, 1982.
Sommer, Doris. "Be-Longing and Bi-Lingual States." *Diacritics* 29, no. 4 (Winter 1999): 84–115.
Sorabji, Richard. *Time, Creation, and the Continuum: Theories in Antiquity and the Early Middle Ages*. Ithaca, NY: Cornell University Press, 1983.
Spiegel, Gabrielle M. *The Chronicle Tradition of Saint-Denis: A Survey*. Medieval Classics: Texts and Studies 10, edited by Joseph Szövérffy and Joseph M.-F. Marque. Brookline, MA: Classical Folia Editions, 1978.
———. *Romancing the Past: The Rise of Vernacular Prose Historiography in Thirteenth-Century France*. New Historicism 23. Berkeley: University of California Press, 1993.
Spivak, Gayatri Chakrovorly. "Time and Timing: Law and History." In *Chronotypes: The Construction of Time*, edited by John Bender and David Wellbery, 99–117. Palo Alto, CA: Stanford University Press, 1991.
Stacey, Robert C. "The Conversion of the Jews to Christianity in Thirteenth-Century England." *Speculum* 67, no. 2 (1992): 263–283.
Starn, Randolph. "Truths in the Archives." *Common Knowledge* 8, no. 2 (2002): 387–401.
Staub, Jacob J. "Gersonides and Contemporary Theories on the Beginning of the Universe." In *Creation and the End of Days: Judaism and Scientific Cosmology; Proceedings of the 1984 Meeting of the Academy for Jewish Philosophy*, edited by David Novak and Norbert Samuelson, 245–259. Lanham, MD: University Press of America, 1986.
Stemberger, Günter. "Elements of Biblical Interpretation in Medieval Jewish-Christian Disputation." In *Hebrew Bible / Old Testament: The History of Its Interpretation*, vol. 1, edited by Magne Sæbo, 578–590. Göttingen: Vandenboeck & Ruprecht, 2000.
Stern, David M. *Parables in Midrash: Narrative and Exegesis in Rabbinic Literature*. Cambridge, MA: Harvard University Press, 1991.

Stern, Gregg. "Philosophy in Southern France: Controversy over Philosophic Study and the Influence of Averroes upon Jewish Thought." In *The Cambridge Companion to Medieval Jewish Philosophy*, edited by Daniel H. Frank and Oliver Leaman, 281–303. Cambridge: Cambridge University Press, 2003.

Stern, Josef. "The Fall and Rise of Myth in Ritual: Maimonides versus Nahmanides on the *Huqqim*, Astrology, and the War against Idolatry." *The Journal of Jewish Thought and Philosophy* 6 (1997): 185–263.

———. "Nachmanides's Conceptions of *Ta'amei Mitzvot*." In *Commandment and Community: New Essays in Jewish Legal and Political Philosophy*, edited by Daniel Frank, 141–171. Albany: SUNY Press, 1995.

———. *Problems and Parables of Law: Maimonides and Nahmanides on Reasons for the Commandments (Ta'amei ha–Mitzvot)*. SUNY Series in Judaica. Albany: SUNY Press, 1998.

Stern, Sacha. "The Death of Idolatry?" *Le'ela*, no. 35 (April 1993): 26–28.

———. *Jewish Identity in Early Rabbinic Writings*. Arbeiten zur Geschichte des Antiken Judentums und des Urchristentums 23, edited by Martin Hengel et al. Leiden: E. J. Brill, 1994.

Stock, Brian. *The Implications of Literacy: Written Language and Models of Interpretation in the Eleventh and Twelfth Centuries*. Princeton, NJ: Princeton University Press, 1983.

Stow, Kenneth. *Alienated Minority: The Jews of Medieval Latin Europe*. Cambridge, MA: Harvard University Press, 1992.

Strauss, Leo. *Persecution and the Art of Writing*. Chicago: University of Chicago Press, 1988.

Strayer, Joseph R. *The Albigensian Crusades*. Ann Arbor: University of Michigan Press, 1992.

Surtz, Ronald E. "Spain: Catalan and Castilian Drama." In *The Theatre of Medieval Europe: New Research in Early Drama*, edited by Eckehard Simon, 189–206. Cambridge: Cambridge University Press, 1991.

Ta-Shma, Israel M., ed. *Ha-Ramban vi-Yetsirato*. Jerusalem: Misrad ha-hinukh ve-ha-tarbut, 1967.

———. *Minhag Ashkenaz ha'Kadmon*. Jerusalem: Magnes Press, Hebrew University, 1992.

———. "Rabbi Yonah Girondi: Spirituality and Leadership." In *Jewish Mystical Leaders and Leadership in the 13th Century*, edited by Moshe Idel and Mortimer Ostow, 155–177. Northvale, NJ: Jason Aronson, 1998.

Taithe, Bertrand, and Tim Thornton. "The Language of History: Past and Future in Prophecy." In *Prophecy: The Power of Inspired Language in History, 1300–2000*, edited by Bertrand Taithe and Tim Thornton, 1–14. Gloucestershire: Sutton Press, 1997.

Talmage, Frank Ephraim. "Apples of Gold: The Inner Meaning of Sacred Texts in Medieval Judaism." In *Jewish Spirituality from the Bible through the Middle Ages*, edited by A. Green, 313–355. New York, 1986.

———. *David Kimhi: The Man and the Commentaries.* Cambridge, MA: Harvard University Press, 1975.

———. "Keep Your Sons from Scripture: The Bible in Medieval Jewish Scholarship and Spirituality." In *Understanding Scripture: Explorations of Jewish and Christian Traditions of Interpretation,* edited by Clemens Thoma and Michael Wyschogrod, 81–101. New York: Paulist Press, 1987.

———, ed. *Sefer ha-berit ve-vikueh RaDaK em ha-Natzrut.* Jerusalem: Hotza'at Mosad Bialik, 1974.

———. "So Teach Us to Number Our Days: A Theology of Longevity in Jewish Exegetical Literature." In *Aging and the Aged in Medieval Europe,* edited by Michael M. Sheehan, 49–62. Toronto: Pontifical Institute of Mediaeval Studies, 1990.

Talmon, Shemaryahu. "The Presentation of Synchroneity and Simultaneity in Biblical Narrative." *Scripta Hierosolymitana* 27 (1978): 9–26.

Tanenbaum, Adena. *The Contemplative Soul: Hebrew Poetry and Philosophical Theory in Medieval Spain.* Etudes sur le judaïsme médiéval 25. Leiden: Brill, 2002.

Taubes, Jacob. "The Price of Messianism." *Journal of Jewish Studies* 33, no. 1–2 (1982): 595–600.

Teicher, J. L. "The Latin-Hebrew School of Translators in Spain in the Twelfth Century." In *Homenaje a Millàs-Vallicrosa,* 401–444. Barcelona: Consejo Superior de Investigaciones Cientificas, 1954.

Terdiman, Richard. "Deconstructing Memory: On Representing the Past and Theorizing Culture in France since the Revolution." *Diacritics* 15, no. 4 (Winter 1985): 13–36.

Tolan, John V. *Petrus Alfonsi and His Medieval Readers.* Gainesville: University of Florida Press, 1993.

———. *Saracens: Islam in the Medieval European Imagination.* New York: Columbia University Press, 2002.

Touati, Charles. "Les Deux Conflits autour de Maïmonide et des Études Philosophiques." In *Juifs et judaïsme de Languedoc,* edited by Bernard Blumenkranz and Marie-Humbert Vicaire, 173–184. Toulouse: Cahiers de Fanjeaux, 1977.

Tourtoulon, Charles de, ed. *Jacme I, le conquérant, roi d'après les chroniques et les documents inédits.* 2 vols. Études sur la maison de Barcelone 2. Montpellier: Imprimerie typographique de Gras, 1863–1867.

Townend, Matthew. *Language and History in Viking Age England: Linguistic Relations between Speakers of Old Norse and Old English.* Studies in the Early Middle Ages 6, edited by Elizabeth M. Tyler, Julian D. Richards, and Ross Balzaretti. Turnhout: Brepols, 2002.

Trabal, Josep Fernández i, ed. *Una Família Catalana Medieval. Els Bell-lloc de Girona, 1267–1533.* Publicacions de l'Abadia de Montserrat. Girona: Ajuntament de Girona, 1995.

Trautner-Kromann, Hanne. "Jewish Polemics against Christianity in Medieval France and Spain: Can the Intensity of Argumentation Be Measured?" In *Rashi 1040–1990, Hommage à Ephraïm E. Urbach*, edited by Gabrielle Sed-Rajna, 639–644. Paris: Les Éditions du Cerf, 1993.

———. *Shield and Sword: Jewish Polemics against Christianity and the Christians in France and Spain from 1100–1500.* Translated by James Manley. Texts and Studies in Medieval and Early Modern Judaism 8. Tübingen: Mohr, 1993.

Trigano, Schmuel. "The Conventionalization of Social Boundaries and the Strategies of Jewish Society in the Thirteenth Century." In *New Horizons in Sephardic Studies*, edited by Yedida K. Stillman and George K. Zucker, 45–66. Albany: SUNY Press, 1993.

Turner, Victor W. *The Anthropology of Performance.* New York: PAJ Publications, 1986.

———. *The Ritual Process: Structure and Anti-Structure.* Chicago: Aldine, 1969.

Twersky, Isadore. "Aspects of the Social and Cultural History of Provençal Jewry." *Cahiers d'histoire mondiale* 11 (1968): 185–207.

———. *Introduction to the Code of Maimonides (Mishneh Torah).* Yale Judaica Series 22, edited by Leon Nemoy. New Haven, CT: Yale University Press, 1980.

———, ed. *Rabbi Moses Nahmanides (Ramban): Explorations in His Religious and Literary Virtuosity.* Harvard University Center for Jewish Studies: Texts and Studies 1. Cambridge, MA: Harvard University Press, 1983.

Tzamalikos, P. "Origen and the Stoic View of Time." *The Journal of the History of Ideas* 52, no. 4 (1991): 535–561.

Unna, Isaac. *Rabbi Moshe ben Nahman (ha-Ramban): Hayav u-feulato.* Jerusalem: Kiryat Sefer, 1954.

Urbach, Ephraim. "The Role of French and Spanish Rabbis in the Dispute over Maimonides and His Writings." (Hebrew) *Tziyon* 12 (1947): 149–159.

Urban, Gregg. *Metaculture: How Culture Moves through the World.* Public Worlds 8, edited by Dipip Goankar and Benjamin Lee. Minneapolis: University of Minnesota Press, 2001.

Vajda, Georges, ed. *Sefer Meshiv Devarim Nekhohim le-r Yaaqov ben Sheshet.* Publications of the Israel Academy of Sciences and Humanities, Section of Humanities. Jerusalem: Israel Academy of Sciences and Humanities, 1968.

VanFraasen, Bastiaan C. "Time in Physical and Narrative Structure." In *Chronotypes: The Construction of Time*, edited by John Bender, 19–37. Palo Alto, CA: Stanford University Press, 1991.

VanLandingham, Marta. *Transforming the State: King, Court, and Political Culture in the Realm of Aragon (1213–1387).* The Medieval Mediterranean: Peoples, Economies, and Cultures 400–1500, 43, edited by Hugh Kennedy et al. Leiden: Brill, 2002.

Viera, David J. *Medieval Catalan Literature: Prose and Drama.* Twayne's World Authors Series, Spanish Literature, edited by Donald W. Bleznick and Janet Pérez. Boston: Twayne, 1988.

Viguier, Marie-Claire. "Un troubadour juif à Narbonne au XIIIe Siècle." In *Juifs et source juive en Occitanie*, 82–92. Enèrgas: Vent Terral, 1988.
Wachsmann, Meir. "Ha-Mahshavah Ha-Philosophit ve-ha-Datit shel Avraham bar Chiyya." In *Sefer ha-Yovel likhvod Tsvi Wolfson li-melot lo shivim ve-hamesh shannah*, 143–168. Jerusalem: American Academy for Jewish Research, 1965.
Wagner, David L., ed. *The Seven Liberal Arts in the Middle Ages*. Bloomington: Indiana University Press, 1986.
Wakefield, Walter L. *Heresy, Crusade, and Inquisition in Southern France, 1100–1250*. London: George Allen & Unwin, 1974.
Wasserstrom, Steven M. *Between Muslim and Jew: The Problem of Symbiosis under Early Islam*. Princeton, NJ: Princeton University Press, 1995.
———. "*Sefer Yesira* and Early Islam: A Reappraisal." *Journal of Jewish Thought and Philosophy* 3 (1993): 1–30.
Webster, Jill R. *Carmel in Medieval Calalonia*. The Medieval Mediterranean: Peoples, Economies and Cultures 400–1453, 23, edited by Michael Whitby. Leiden: Brill, 1999.
———. "Patronage and Piety: Catalan Letters from Llull to March." In *The Worlds of Alfonso the Learned and James the Conqueror: Intellect and Force in the Middle Ages*, edited by Robert I. Burns, 68–94. Princeton, NJ: Princeton University Press, 1985.
———. "Unlocking Lost Archives: Medieval Catalan Franciscan Communities." *The Catholic Historical Review* 66, no. 4 (1980): 537–550.
Weingrod, Alex. "Patronage and Power." In *Patrons and Clients in Mediterranean Society*, edited by Ernest Gellner, 41–51. London: Gerald Duckworth, 1977.
Weinstock, Moshe, ed. *Seder Olam Zuta Ha-Shalem*. Jerusalem: Batei ve-Rosheh Goldrey, 1957.
Westermann, Claus. *Basic Forms of Prophetic Speech*. Translated by Hugh Clayton White. Cambridge: Westminster/John Knox Press, 1991.
Wexler, Paul. *Three Heirs to a Judeo-Latin Legacy: Judeo-Ibero Romance, Yiddish, and Rotwelsch*. Mediterranean Language and Culture Monograph Series 3, edited by Alexander Bord, Sasson Somekh, and Paul Wexler. Wiesbaden: Otto Harrassowitz, 1988.
White, Hayden. *The Content of the Form: Narrative Discourse and Historical Representation*. Baltimore: Johns Hopkins University Press, 1987.
———. *Metahistory: The Historical Imagination in Nineteenth-Century Europe*. Baltimore: Johns Hopkins University Press, 1973.
———. "The Value of Narrativity in the Representation of Reality." *Critical Inquiry* 7 (1980): 5–27.
Whitman, Jon. *Allegory: The Dynamics of an Ancient and Medieval Technique*. Cambridge, MA: Harvard University Press, 1987.
Whitrow, G. J. *The Natural Philosophy of Time*. London and Edinburgh: Thomas Nelson and Sons, 1961.

———. *The Nature of Time*. Middlesex: Penguin Books, 1975.

———. *Time in History: The Evolution of Our General Awareness of Time and Temporal Perspective*. Oxford: Oxford University Press, 1988.

Wieck, Roger S. *Time Sanctified: The Book of Hours in Medieval Art and Life*. New York: G. Braziller in association with the Walters Art Gallery, Baltimore, 1988.

Wilcox, Donald J. *The Measure of Times Past: Pre-Newtonian Chronologies and the Rhetoric of Relative Time*. Chicago: University of Chicago Press, 1987.

Wills, Lawrence M. *The Jew in the Court of the Foreign King: Ancient Jewish Court Legends*. Harvard Dissertations in Religion 26, edited by Margaret R. Miles and Bernadette J. Brooten. Minneapolis: Fortress Press, 1990.

Wilson, Robert R. "Prophecy in Crisis: The Call of Ezekiel." *Interpretation* 38, no. 2 (1984): 117–130.

Winden, J. C. M. van. *An Early Christian Philosopher: Justin Martyr's Dialogue with Trypho*. Philosophia patrum 1. Leiden: Brill, 1971.

Winer, Rebecca Lynn. "Family, Community, and Motherhood: Caring for Fatherless Children in the Jewish Community of Thirteenth-Century Perpignan." *Jewish History* 16, no. 1 (2002): 15–48.

———. *Women, Wealth, and Community in Perpignan, 1250–1300: Christians, Jews, and Enslaved Muslims in a Medieval Mediterranean Town*. Aldershot, UK: Ashgate, 2006.

Wolfson, Elliot R. "Beautiful Maiden without Eyes: *Peshat* and *Sod* in Zoharic Hermeneutics." In *The Midrashic Imagination: Jewish Exegesis, Thought, and History*, edited by Michael Fishbane, 155–203. Albany: SUNY Press, 1993.

———. "'By Way of Truth': Aspects of Nahmanides' Kabbalistic Hermeneutic." *AJS Review* 14, no. 2 (1989): 103–178.

———. "Forms of Visionary Ascent as Ecstatic Experience in the Zoharic Literature." In *Gershom Scholem's Major Trends in Jewish Mysticism 50 Years After: Proceedings of the Sixth International Conference on the History of Jewish Mysticism*, edited by Peter Schäfer and Joseph Dan, 209–235. Tübingen: J. C. B. Mohr (Paul Siebeck), 1993.

———. "From Sealed Book to Open Text: Time, Memory, and Narrativity in Kabbalistic Hermeneutics." In *Interpreting Judaism in a Postmodern Age*, edited by S. Kepnes, 145–178. New York: New York University Press, 1996.

———. "Jewish Mysticism: A Philosophical Overview." In *History of Jewish Philosophy*, edited by Daniel H. Frank and Oliver Leaman, 450–499. London: Routledge, 1997.

———. "The Secret Garment in Nahmanides." *Da'at* 24 (1990): xxv–xlix.

———. *Through a Speculum That Shines: Vision and Imagination in Medieval Jewish Mysticism*. Princeton, NJ: Princeton University Press, 1994.

Woolf, Jeffrey R. "Some Polemical Emphases in the 'Sefer Miswot Gadol' of Rabbi Moses of Coucy." *The Jewish Quarterly Review* n.s. 89, no. 1–2 (1998): 81–100.

Wright, Lawrence. *Clockwork Man: The Story of Time, Its Origins, Its Uses, Its Tyranny*. New York: Horizon Press, 1968.
Yahalom, Shalem. "The Barcelona Disputation and the Status of the Aggadah in Nahmanides' Teachings." (Hebrew) *Tziyon* 69, no. 1 (2004): 25-43.
Yates, Frances Amelia. *The Art of Memory*. Chicago: University of Chicago Press, 1974.
Yerushalmi, M. D., ed. *Seder olam raba*. Jerusalem: Hotsa'at sefarim al yede gemilat hesed Hasde Barukh, 1970.
Yerushalmi, Yosef Hayim. "Exile and Expulsion in Jewish History." In *Crisis and Creativity in the Sephardic World, 1391-1648*, edited by Benjamin Gampel, 3-22. New York: Columbia University Press, 1997.
———. *Zakhor: Jewish History and Jewish Memory*. The Samuel and Althea Stroum Lectures in Jewish Studies. New York: Schocken Books, 1989.
Yoshpe, Raphael. "Ha-Ramban ve-ha-Aravit." (Hebrew) *Tarbitz* 57, no. 1 (1988): 67-93.
Young, Michael Dunlop. *The Metronomic Society: Natural Rhythms and Human Timetables*. Cambridge, MA: Harvard University Press, 1988.
Young, Michael, and Tom Schuller, ed. *Rhythms of Society*. Reports of the Institute of Community Studies. London: Routledge, 1988.
Yovel, Yimiyahu. "The New Otherness: Marrano Dualities in the First Generation." Paper presented at the 1999 Swig Lecture, the Swig Judaic Studies Program at the University of San Francisco, September 13, 1999.
Yuval, Israel. *Hakhamim be'Doram*. Jerusalem, 1988.
———. *Two Nations in Your Womb: Perceptions of Jews and Christians in Late Antiquity and the Middle Ages*. Translated by Barbara Harshav and Jonathan Chipman. Berkeley: University of California Press, 2006.
———. "Easter and Passover as Early Jewish-Christian Dialogue." In *Passover and Easter: Origin and History to Modern Times*, edited by Paul F. Bradshaw and Lawrence A. Hoffman, 98-124. Notre Dame, IN: University of Notre Dame Press, 1999.
———. "Yitzhak Baer and the Search for Authentic Judaism." In *The Jewish Past Revisited: Reflections on Modern Judaism*, edited by David N. Myers and David B. Ruderman, 77-87. New Haven, CT: Yale University Press, 1998.
———. "'The Lord Will Take Vengeance, Vengeance for His People'." (Hebrew) *Tziyon* 59, no. 2-3 (1994): 351-414.
———. "Vengeance and Curses, Blood and Libel." (Hebrew) *Tziyon* 58, no. 1 (1993): 33-90.
Zagorin, Perez. *How the Idea of Religious Toleration Came to the West*. Princeton, NJ: Princeton University Press, 2003.
Zakovitch, Yair. *"And You Shall Tell Your Son." The Concept of the Exodus in the Bible*. Jerusalem: Magnes Press, Hebrew University, 1991.
Zeidman, Reena. "A Time to Mourn: Methods of Reading Intertextuality in the Laws of Idolatry." *Approaches to Ancient Judaism*, n.s. 10, no. 42 (1997): 125-145.

Zerubavel, Eviatar. *Hidden Rhythms*. Chicago: University of Chicago Press, 1981.
———. *The Seven Day Circle: The History and Meaning of the Week*. New York: The Free Press, 1985.
Zfatman, Sara. *Bein Ashkenaz li-Sefarad: Le-Toldot ha-Sippur ha-Yehudi bimei ha-Beinayim*. Jerusalem: Magnes Press, Hebrew University, 1993.
Zimmels, H. J. *Ashkenazim and Sephardim: Their Relations, Differences, and Problems as Reflected in the Rabbinical Responsa*. The Library of Sephardic History and Thought, edited by Marc D. Angel. Hoboken, NJ: Ktav, 1996.
Zwiep, Irene E. "Everything you always wanted to know about grammar. Logic and Linguistics in Shem Tov Ibn Falaquera's *Sefer Ha-Mevaqqesh*." In *From Narbonne to Regensburg: Studies in Medieval Hebrew Texts*, edited by N. A. van Uchelen and I. E. Zwiep, 21–40. Amsterdam: Juda Palache Institute, 1993.

Index

Abraham bar Hiyya, *Megilat ha-Megaleh*, 88
Abraham ben Levi Abulafia, 131
Abraham ibn Ezra, 33, 56, 59, 65, 76, 137
  on creation, 61–62, 63, 79
aggadot, 65, 112
  defined as *sermones*, 124
  Friar Paul's use of, 92, 112, 123
  Nahmanides' understanding of, 98–99, 124–126, 203n74
Albigensian Crusade, 12, 22, 27–29. *See also* Catharism; Papal Inquisition
  cultural effects of, 29
aljama, 8–10, 12, 51, 171. *See also kehillah*
Allocutio super tetragrammaton (Arnau of Vilanova), 151. *See also* Arnau of Vilanova
Antichrist, 149–153, 155
Aristotelian philosophy, Christian ban of, 26, 28
Arnau of Vilanova, 16, 131, 150–156
  Allocutio super tetragrammaton, 151
  on book of Daniel, 151–152
  on Jewish learning, 151
  Tractatus de tempore adventus Antichristi, 150–151

Augustine, on the dangers of apocalyptic expectation, 155
avodah zarah, 115

Baer, Yitzhak, 97, 102
Barcelona disputation, 14–17
  Hebrew account of, 91–92, 94, 107, 111–112, 119, 124–126, 177
  —Jewish-Christian relations in, 113–118, 121–122, 157, 160–166, 168–170, 173–174, 178
  —preamble, 108–111, 113–118
  prophecy and history in, 120–126, 136–139, 154
  —realism in, 111, 161, 163, 177, 178
  Latin account of, 91–94, 119, 124–124, 164–166, 173
  modern interpretations of texts, 96–105, 221n2, 224n24
berurim, 8, 10
bet din, 9, 12, 24, 25, 46, 48, 171.
  See also aljama

Capetian kings, dominion in Provence and Languedoc, 25, 27–28
Catalonia, 6–7
  Jewish-Christian relations, 2, 148, 156–157, 160–165, 166–174

Catharism, 28
  regulation of, 22, 27, 28
Chazan, Robert, 96, 100–101, 134, 148, 167–169
Chronicle of Ahimaaz, 165. See also medieval Jewish historical writing, chronicles; *Seder Olam Rabbah*; *Sefer Toldot Yeshu*
Clifford, James, 164
Cohen, Jeremy, 92, 102, 121, 131
Cohen, Martin, 98–99, 100
convivencia, 3
cosmic time, 6, 55–56, 126. See also historic time
creation, Nahmanides' interpretation of. See Genesis and history, Nahmanides' commentary on
Crown of Aragon, Jews of, 6–11, 23, 93, 94, 112, 116, 121, 170–172
  royal notaries of, 9. See also wills, Jewish

Daniel, book of, messianic time frame, 83, 129, 135, 137–138, 140, 144–148, 150, 156–157, 160–162
  Nahmanides' reading of, 83, 129–130, 132–133, 135–140, 144–148, 154
David ben Saul, 21, 30
David Kimhi, 22, 48,
dayyanim, 8, 10
Deleuze, Gilles, 162–163. See also Guattari, Félix; Kafka, Franz
derash, Nahmanides' use of, 55, 206n7, 212n38. See also Genesis and history, Nahmanides' commentary on
Derrida, Jacques, 160
disputatio, 175
disputation literature, as genre, 91, 105–107, 125, 162–164, 165–167. See also Barcelona disputation

Dominicans, 17, 109, 134, 151, 171, 175. See also Franciscans; mendicant friars

Elman, Yaakov, 65
emanations (*sepherot*), 75–76, 206n7

Fox, Marvin, 99–100
Franciscans, 22, 175. See also Dominicans; mendicant friars
French rabbis, *herem* on Maimonidean philosophy, 21, 29, 30, 32, 35, 37, 41, 43, 44, 47, 53
Friar Paul Christiani, 15, 17, 88, 91–93, 97, 102, 103, 107, 109, 110, 111–112, 114, 116, 117, 118, 120–122, 123–127, 136, 137–138, 142, 150, 159–160, 166, 168–170. See also Nahmanides, on apostates to Christianity
  use of prooftexts, 121, 123–126, 138
Funkenstein, Amos, 5, 77–78, 87–88
  on *peshat* and *sod* in Nahmanides' commentary, 206n7, 212n38

Genesis and history, 54
  Nahmanides' commentary on, 12, 13, 54–58, 63–89, 129, 138–139, 141, 150
  sequence of, 54, 58–59, 64–65, 68–69, 80
Ginzburg, Carlo, 95
Girona
  Christian clergy of, 4, 17, 93–94, 103, 162, 165, 167–169, 173–174, 178
  Jewish community of, 6, 11, 51, 98, 116
Graetz, Heinrich, 97
Guattari, Félix, 162–163

halakhah, 4
  local interpretations, 10
  precedent, 37

Hasidai Ashkenaz. *See* messianic
  expectation, in *Sefer Hasidim*
herem. *See* Maimonidean controversy;
  Maimonides, philosophical
  writings, *herem* on
historic time, 6, 55. *See also* cosmic
  time

idolatry, 40, 110, 113–115, 116. *See
  also* Jesus, as Jewish apostate;
  Nahmanides, on apostates to
  Christianity

Jacob ben Elijah, 92
Jesus, as Jewish apostate, 108–118.
  See also idolatry; Nahmanides,
  on apostates to Christianity
Jewish customs and practices, local, 6,
  9–10, 23–24, 27–28, 29, 36–38, 42,
  43–44, 48, 164, 166
Jewish leadership, 23
Jewish self-government, 7–8, 171–172
  Christian involvement in, 25–26,
  171
Jewish-Christian polemics, 4, 5, 16, 92,
  105, 119, 120, 135, 148, 156, 164
Joachim of Fiore, 131, 149–151, 153,
Jonah Gerundi, 21, 22, 30, 46–47,
  118n4, 203n78

Kafka, Franz, 162
kehillah, 10, 12, 24, 25. *See also aljama*
King Alfonso X of Castile, 175
King James I of Aragon
  and the Barcelona disputation, 15,
  91, 93, 99, 101, 102, 103, 111, 121,
  171–174
  Catalan literature, 101, 169, 175–178
  and Jews, 7–8, 170–172
  Llibre dels Feyts, 176–178
King James II of Aragon, 150
Klein, Elka, 23, 189n7

LaCapra, Dominick, 105
Lateran Council, Fourth (1215), 172
literary patronage, 173–178, 255n36
Llibre dels Feyts (King James I),
  176–178. *See also* King James I of
  Aragon, Catalan literature

Maimonidean controversy, 4, 10–13,
  19–23, 25–31, 34, 36, 37, 39, 43, 46,
  49, 50
  Christian authorities' role in, 25–26,
  28
  modern interpretation, 31, 194n34
  Nahmanides' role in, 11, 32–50
Maimonides, 37, 50, 59, 85, 98, 132, 133,
  137
  Letter to the Jews of Yemen, 37,
  132–133
  Mishneh Torah, 20, 21, 35, 42
  philosophical writings, 12, 19, 20–23,
  27–28, 31, 34, 41, 42, 43, 44
  —burning of, 22, 31, 47
  —followers of, 21, 29, 30, 31, 32, 35,
  42, 46, 47
  —*herem* on, 10, 19–25, 27–31, 34, 37,
  44–47
  —*Moreh ha-Nevukhim*, 21, 28, 30,
  34, 35, 42, 43
  —*Sefer ha-Madda*, 21, 22, 28, 30, 34,
  43, 203n74
medieval Jewish historical writing,
  chronicles, 125–126, 165–170.
  See also Seder Olam Rabbah;
  Sefer Toldot Yeshu
medieval polemics, cultural
  significance, 105–106
Megilat ha-Megaleh (Abraham bar
  Hiyya), 88
mendicant friars, 28, 157, 172. *See also*
  Dominicans; Franciscans
  compulsory sermons for Jews, 131,
  157, 171

messianic expectation
   Jewish-Christian intersections, 107, 116, 130–131, 148, 149, 150–153, 154–157, 160–162, 178
   Maimonides on, 133
   in *Sefer Hasidim*, 133–134
   in the Talmud, 82, 86, 88, 132, 145, 146–147
Midrash Lamentations, 123, 125
Midrash Rabbah, 57, 121
Mishneh Torah (Maimonides), 20, 21, 35, 42. *See also* Maimonides, philosophical writings
Montpellier, 20, 25
   Albigensian Crusade, 27–28
   Arnau of Vilanova, 150
   Friar Paul, 92–93, 112
   Maimonidean controversy, 19–23
Moreh ha-Nevukhim (Maimonides), 21, 28, 30, 34, 35, 42, 43. *See also* Maimonides, philosophical writings
Moses, 61, 68
   Nahmanides on authorship of, 63–64, 68–73, 87, 89, 135

Nahmanides
   on apostates to Christianity, 14–16, 106–107, 110, 113–118
   application of sequential exegesis, 66, 68–72, 83–87, 137–141, 145
   charges of blasphemy against, 17, 93–94, 165, 167, 168, 169
   on chronology and history, 65, 85, 125–126, 136–138, 142
   on continuity in Jewish history, 2, 5–6, 12–14, 16, 32, 33, 39, 46, 48–50, 54–55, 61, 64, 70–74, 76, 80, 87–89, 130, 164–165, 178–179
   creation, interpretation of. *See* Genesis and history, Nahmanides on
   derekh ha-emet (way of truth), 75, 126, 206n7
   disputation account. *See* Barcelona disputation, Hebrew account of
   on ethics of Jewish community leadership, 33, 35, 43, 49, 51
   historical exegesis, 74, 78, 80–84, 86–87
   and kabbalah, 1, 32, 53, 55, 56
   on legal precedent, 38–39, 43, 44, 46
   letter to Béziers, 47
   letter to the French rabbis, 12–13, 28, 31–35, 38, 39–41, 44–46, 48–49, 51, 196n45
   on local practice, 36
   on Maimonides' philosophy, 33
   on messianic advent, 80–84, 89, 119, 130–131, 134–135, 145–147, 153, 155–156
   on narrative in Torah, 54, 57–59, 63–70, 72–74, 76–80, 85–89. *See also derash*, Nahmanides' use of; Nahmanides, application of sequential exegesis; Nahmanides, typological exegesis
   on prophecy and redemption, 80–84, 119–126, 129–131, 135, 138–147, 153
   on thousand year historical epochs, 14, 74–83, 85–88, 135
   typological exegesis, 5, 64, 76–79, 81–83, 88, 135, 144, 179
   use of prooftexts, 38–43, 48–50, 65–66, 86, 108, 113–115, 123, 124, 125–126
Nicholas Donin, 166, 233n76
Norton, Anne, 160

orthodoxy, definition and maintenance of, 22–23, 25–29, 31, 36–37, 42, 45
Papal Inquisition, 28, 167, 172. *See also* Albigensian Crusade; Catharism, regulation of

Paris disputation, 166, 167, 233n76
  Hebrew account of, 166, 167
Pedaya, Haviva, 55
peshat (plain sense of the text)
  Nahmanides' use of, 53, 55–56, 59, 66, 73, 74, 87
  Rashi's use of, 88
prophecy, interpreting units of time in, 135–140, 152–157, 160–161
Pugio Fidei (Ramón Martí), 150, 151, 155

rabbi, office of in medieval Aragon, 11, 112, 116
Ramón Martí, 150–151, 155
Rashi, 33, 54, 56, 62, 65, 76, 88, 109–110, 137
  on creation, 59–61, 63, 75, 79
  on the messianic advent, 88, 130
Raymond de Peñeforte, 93, 150, 170
Raymond Llull, 101, 169
reconquista, and Jews, 7, 170, 177
Riera i Sans, Jaume, 102–104

Saadya Gaon, 33, 56, 61,
Schechter, Solomon, 105
Scholem, Gershom, 5, 32, 184n16
Second Temple, 81, 99, 122, 125, 129, 136–137, 140, 142, 153, 155
  Arnau of Vilanova's interpretation of, 153, 155
  destruction of, 81, 99, 123, 125, 129, 140
  Friar Paul's interpretation of, 122, 123, 125, 136–137, 128
  Nahmanides' interpretation of, 81, 99, 123, 129, 142
Seder Olam Rabbah, 142. *See also* medieval Jewish historical writing, chronicles; *Sefer Toldot Yeshu*

Sefer ha-Geulah (Nahmanides), 12, 16, 86, 88, 103, 129, 130, 134, 140–147, 148, 150, 153, 154, 155
Sefer ha-Kabbalah (Abraham ibn Daud), 165. *See also* medieval Jewish historical writing, chronicles; *Seder Olam Rabbah*; *Sefer Toldot Yeshu*
Sefer ha-Madda (Maimonides), 21, 22, 28, 30, 34, 43, 203n74. *See also* Maimonides, philosophical writings
Sefer ha-Zohar, 67, 98
Sefer Toldot Yeshu, 125, 136. *See also* medieval Jewish historical writing, chronicles; *Seder Olam Rabbah*
sod (hidden sense of the text), Nahmanides' use of, 55, 59, 74
Solomon ben Abraham, 12, 19, 21–31, 35, 42, 43, 46, 47, 50, 51, 92

Tosaphot, 4, 117, 118
Tractatus de tempore adventus Antichristi (Arnau of Vilanova), 150–151

vernacular literature, 17, 175
  Catalan, 17, 101, 160–162, 164–165, 167, 168–169, 175, 176–178
  Hebrew, 161–163, 164–165, 167–169
  realism in, 177–178

wills, Jewish, 9, 171
world week
  in Christian exegesis, 81
  in rabbinic exegesis, 82

Yehiel ben Joseph of Paris, 166
Yerushalmi, Yosef Hayim, 165
yom, meaning in prophecy, 139, 154, 159–161. *See also* prophecy, interpreting units of time in

Nina Caputo

is assistant professor of history at the University of Florida.
She has published a number of articles and reviews
on medieval and Jewish history.

www.ingramcontent.com/pod-product-compliance
Lightning Source LLC
Chambersburg PA
CBHW031705230426
43668CB00006B/120